The Pricing of Progress

The Pricing of Progress

*Economic Indicators and the
Capitalization of American Life*

Eli Cook

Harvard University Press

CAMBRIDGE, MASSACHUSETTS

LONDON, ENGLAND

2017

Library of Congress Cataloging-in-Publication Data

Names: Cook, Eli, 1981– author.
Title: The pricing of progress : economic indicators and the capitalization
of American life / Eli Cook.
Description: Cambridge, Massachusetts : Harvard University Press, 2017. |
Includes bibliographical references and index.
Identifiers: LCCN 2017011999 | ISBN 9780674976283 (hardcover : alk. paper)
Subjects: LCSH: Capitalism—United States—History. | Economic indicators—United
States—History. | Valuation—United States—History. | Progress.
Classification: LCC HC110.C3 C66 2017 | DDC 339.373—dc23
LC record available at https://lccn.loc.gov/2017011999

To Tali

CONTENTS

The Pricing of Progress

INTRODUCTION

IN THE MIDST OF AN impassioned sermon on the dangers of drinking, delivered in 1832 in upstate New York, the fervent moral reformer and abolitionist Theodore Dwight Weld pulled out of his pocket a piece of paper containing a series of statistics. Reading from his back-of-the-envelope calculations, which extrapolated data from a single county onto the entire nation, he declared that of the 300,000 drunks in America, 30,000 would die every year from heavy drinking; of the 200,000 paupers, half had alcohol to blame for their problems; and of the 30,000 people committed to institutions for the insane, half had gone crazy as a result of drinking. Implementing the innovative language of statistics, a novel form of quantitative knowledge that was spreading throughout the Western world, Weld measured the social costs of alcohol consumption by examining the physical, social, and mental effects such drinking had on the American people. Similar statistics about insanity, health, and pauperism—along with those on illiteracy, crime, prostitution, education, and incarceration—appeared frequently in Jacksonian Era political debates, statistical almanacs, government documents, and moral reform reports. Using the term-of-art from Europe, where these measures first emerged, Americans referred to such figures as "moral statistics."[1]

Yet as these moral statistics were taking America by storm during the Protestant religious revival and reform movement known as the Second Great Awakening, the manner in which Americans measured the social cost of alcohol consumption was beginning to change radically. In 1830, the New York State Temperance Society, which was led not by clergymen but rather by well-to-do Albany businessmen, quantified the social damage produced by excessive drinking not by detailing the fate of the drinkers themselves but by pricing the overall cost to the city. "There cannot be a doubt," the society concluded after a series of in-depth calculations, "that the city suffers a dead yearly loss of three hundred thousand dollars" due to "time spent drinking," "drunkenness and strength diminished by it," "expenses of criminal persecutions," and "loss to the public by carelessness." Treating the consumption of alcohol as a "tax," these Albany businessmen, who had accumulated much of their wealth by investing in urban real estate, used Temperance Society figures to place a price tag on time and space. "At the present value of money," they argued, "the tax the city of Albany pays to alcohol would pay the interest on six million of dollars yearly; would build 200 houses each year costing 1500 dollars each; and rent 2000 tenements at 150 dollars rent per year."[2]

There exists a crucial distinction between these two forms of social quantification. While middle-class Americans in rapidly industrializing towns wielded moral statistics mostly as disciplinary instruments of paternalistic social control, such figures nevertheless focused squarely on the physical, social, and mental well-being of the drinkers themselves. For better or for worse, they placed people at the center of their statistical vision. On the contrary, the Albany businessmen's monetized temperance statistics focused on the effect—measured in money prices—that certain drinking habits would have on their town's moneymaking capacities. While Weld's corporeal moral statistics epitomize the rise of what Michel Foucault labeled "governmentality," the distinctly capitalist form of social accounting at work in the Albany calculations is a rather different quantitative animal, one that I refer to in this book as "investmentality."[3]

Imagining their entire town as a capitalized investment and its inhabitants as income-bearing inputs of human capital that could be plugged into output-maximizing equations of economic growth, the Albany businessmen's novel investmentality measured progress and well-being by pricing the effect certain labor and consumption patterns had on market productivity and capital accumulation. According to this profit-seeking logic, which deemed income generation the main function and goal of American life, social problems such as excessive alcohol consumption were frowned upon not necessarily because they ruined lives but rather because they negatively affected economic growth. Anticipating the rise of national economic indicators, the groundbreaking calculative mind-set of these ambitious businessmen did not stop at Albany's city limits. Estimating the cost of intemperance at "$300,000 for every 25,000 inhabitants," they went on to price the annual revenue loss from the nation's appetite for alcohol at "the enormous sum of one hundred and forty five millions of dollars yearly."[4]

Such calculations were still very much an outlier in the 1830s, an era in which moral statistics ruled the day. Yet by the early twentieth century such a pricing of everyday life would move from the margins of the American polity to the center. Once more, temperance statistics offer a useful lens into this transformation. By 1917, Irving Fisher was not only the head of a committee demanding wartime prohibition in the United States but also the most highly regarded American economist of his day, and a widely heralded Progressive reformer who rarely met a social problem he did not price. In one of his countless articles, Fisher echoed the pro-temperance sentiments of those antebellum Albany businessmen, albeit with a calculative rigor befitting an era that was not only the "Age of Reform" but also the age of scientific management. "By keeping sober one or two hundred thousand men now incapacitated by drunkenness, and by increasing the productive power of those who, while not drunk, are 'slowed down' by alcohol," Fisher declared, prohibition "would speed up production probably at least ten percent." Crunching the numbers, the first truly mathematical economist in America priced the benefits of outlawing alcohol at "$2 billions to our national dividend." Given that Fisher was also a self-proclaimed expert at forecasting the stock market, his use of the term *dividend* suggests that he was thinking of the United States as a securitized asset.[5]

Pricing prohibition was a typical Fisherian move, as he spent much of his time pricing things such as tuberculosis ($1.1 billion), national health care ($3 billion), the average American adult ($2,900), and even the average American baby ($90). In explaining how he reached these last two prices, Fisher noted that "the best method of estimating the economic value of life and its increased duration is by the capitalization of earning power." Through this asset-pricing process of capitalization, Fisher calculated the "worth of an average American life" using the same techniques he would use for any investment: by subtracting annual costs from annual revenue and then translating this future yearly cash inflow, through a process known as discounting, into the net present value of the income-bearing capital good. In this instance, the capital investment in question was a human being, so this meant discounting the individual's "future earnings" after deducting the cost of "rearing" and "maintenance."[6]

Fisher was no lone wolf. In 1897, around the time Fisher first began pricing Progressivism and capitalizing American lives, Reverend A. H. Thompson, pastor of Bennett Memorial Church in Baltimore, was condemning intemperance by pricing it at "nearly $1 million annually" in a sermon titled "The Economic Value of Righteousness." Alcohol consumption was not the only moral statistic to be monetized during the Progressive Era. As the U.S. commissioner of education warned at an Industrial League conference in 1914, "The rapid increase in adult illiteracy . . . is costing an economic loss of $500,000,000 a year." A year earlier, the secretary of the National Committee for Mental Hygiene asserted that the insane were "responsible for loss of $135,000,000 a year to the nation."[7]

These calculative practices continue today. "The cost of excessive alcohol consumption in the United States reached $223.5 billion," the Centers for Disease Control and Prevention (CDC) announced in a 2011 study, "or about $1.90 per drink." Eerily similar to the Albany temperance report written more than a century and a half before, the study argued that 72 percent of that cost resulted from a loss of "workplace productivity," 11 percent from "health care expenses," 9 percent from "criminal justice expenses," and 6 percent from "motor vehicle crash costs." At the end of the report, the CDC added a caveat: "The study did not consider a number of other costs such as those because of pain and suffering among either the excessive drinker or others that were affected by their drinking." In 2015, the director of the National Institute of Mental Health stated that the "financial cost of mental disorders was at least $467 billion." Citing a study published in the *American Journal of Psychiatry,* the director explained that the main costs of serious mental illness arose from "lost earnings." On the website of Literary Partners—a nonprofit organization whose board of directors includes "senior-level executives from prominent corporations" such as Twitter, Samsung, Citigroup, Google, Time, and Bloomberg—one learns that "every dollar invested in adult literacy yields $7.14 in return."[8]

The striking resemblance between these contemporary calculations and earlier acts of social pricing is no coincidence. After the great nineteenth-century struggles over how progress should be measured, price statistics that imagined society as a capitalized investment gained the upper hand by the early twentieth century, supplanting moral statistics and other non-pecuniary social measures as the leading benchmarks of American prosperity. As use of these investmentality metrics spread, the maximization of monetized market production and consumption became a chief statistical objective of American social policy, concurrently transforming prices into the standard unit Americans used to value not only their goods and businesses but also their future, their communities, their environment, and even their own selves.

This was an unprecedented transition in human history. Money and markets have been around for thousands of years, yet for millennia people in societies as different as ancient Greece, imperial China, and medieval Europe did not think that prices could serve as accurate measures of human prosperity or social valuation, nor did they treat their societies as income-generating investments. This book is about how such a pricing of progress came to be.

My central argument is that the pricing of progress emerged from the rise of American capitalism and, more specifically, the capitalization of everyday American life that accompanied its ascent. Historians of various ideological stripes have contended that the key element in the transition to capitalism was the expansion of market relations and commodity exchange—be it in the form of labor, land, slaves, wheat, cotton, spices, gold, iron, or wool. I, on the other hand, believe that markets, commodities, and consumer goods, while certainly necessary components, do not a capitalist society make. In moving away from this "market revolution" narrative, I shift the historical emphasis from commodification to capitalization, from consumer goods to capital goods, and from market exchange to capital investment.[9]

The extension and penetration of markets into previously uncommodified realms of life, especially labor relations, undoubtedly played a crucial role in the making of American and global capitalism. But at the heart of both the capitalist revolution and the pricing of progress in the United States (and likely elsewhere as well—the rise of economic indicators is by no means an exclusively American story) lay a significantly distinct process of capitalization. One of the key elements that distinguishes capitalism from previous forms of social and cultural organization is capital investment, the act through which basic elements of society and life—including natural resources, technological discoveries, cultural productions, urban spaces, educational institutions, human beings, and the fiscal nation-state—are transformed (or "capitalized") into income-generating assets valued and allocated in accordance with their capacity to make money and yield profitable returns.

In modern economic parlance, *capitalization* has multiple specific meanings. In the stock market, corporations are often valued by their market capitalization, which is the number of outstanding shares multiplied by share price. In financial circles, the term is used, precisely as Fisher used it a century ago, to describe the process in which future income flows are translated into a present stock of wealth. In accounting, the term has two meanings. The first refers to the amount of capital that has been invested in a company, be it in the form of stock, bonds, or retained earnings. The second, often found in the verb form *to capitalize,* is to record an expense not as an operating cost but rather as a capital expenditure.[10]

While these meanings differ, they all share a commonality that gets to the heart of my own, more general use of the term: to capitalize is to treat, conceive, handle, manage, or quantify something (or someone or somewhere) as an income-generating, moneymaking capital good or investment. Martin Grideau, who also has advocated for a broader use of the term, notes that capitalization is the "jointly social and technical process through which capital is constituted as capital." In his view, as in mine, quantification is crucial to this process, since "to capitalize is to produce capital through accounting inscriptions." Investmentality is also a prerequisite of capitalization. To treat and quantify people, places, or things as an investment, one must first imagine them as such. As sociologist Fabian Muniesa has commented, "Capitalization is about envisaging the value of things in the terms of an investment." The rise of modern economic indicators and the pricing of American progress are about the very same thing. For example, an 1856 article in *Hunt's Merchants Magazine* priced the capital gains from educating New York children at $500 million. The author did so because he had concluded that "the brain is . . . an agricultural product of great commercial investment" and that "the great problem of political economy" was "how most economically to produce the best brain and render it most profitable."[11]

In emphasizing capital investments rather than mere market exchange, this book chronicles the contested rise of price-based economic indicators from the mid-seventeenth century to the early twentieth century by following not the money but the capital. It demonstrates that the pricing of progress and the capitalization of life took root only where large amounts of income-generating capital were being produced and invested. Such capital took various forms: the enclosure of land into a rent-earning asset in early modern England; the emergence of sugar-producing, slavery-dominated Caribbean societies that functioned more as absentee investments than as settler communities; the issuance of sovereign debt bonds that capitalized the taxing powers of the American state; the spatial colonization of the midwestern urban frontier by eastern real estate investors; a highly financialized cotton boom that turned American slaves from pieces of property into pieces of capital; the railroad revolution's funneling of great swaths of American wealth into publicly traded corporations; the rise of mechanized factories that calculated the cost of feeding men and the cost of fueling machines in the same way; and a corporate merger movement that securitized American industry into a steady stream of income-yielding assets, bought and sold on the stock market.

As capital flowed into these new channels, the localized social and market relations that had sparked the need for moral statistics began to be upended by socially disembedded investors who—through loans, bonds, lots, stocks, banks, mortgages, and other financial instruments—invested in communities in which they might never even set foot. As local businesspeople and proprietary producers lost significant social and economic power to institutional investors, investment banks, railroad managers, and the large manufacturing companies that made up the Dow Jones Industrial Average, a national corporate elite came into being that cared far less about the number of prostitutes in Peoria or drunks in Detroit and far more about a town's industrial output, population growth, real estate prices, labor costs, and railway traffic.

That said, while capitalization was the main economic engine that pushed the pricing of progress forward, it was hardly the only force in play. Many other political, cultural, and social developments played crucial roles: the fiscal nation-state, bourgeois liberalism, male patriarchy, neoclassical economics, consumer culture, white racism, administrative bureaucracy, a national business press, the invention of the calorie, the Civil War, Progressive reform, the Panic of 1837, and class conflict. A history of U.S. pricing of progress, therefore, is also a history of the making of modern America.

———◆◆◆———

Today, when you turn on the car radio during your commute or tune in to the nightly news when you get home, you are far more likely to hear about the latest movements of the Dow Jones Industrial Average—a metric invented in 1889 that gauges the stock prices of leading American corporations—than you are to hear about fluctuations in rates of incarceration, illiteracy, health, inequality, discrimination, or poverty. The only thing the American media seem to follow as closely as corporate investment patterns is the weather. "How can it be," asked a concerned Pope Francis in his first papal exhortation in 2013, "that it is not a news item when an elderly homeless person dies of exposure, but it is news when the stock market loses two points?" Apparently perturbed by the pope's query and hoping to prove that he was wrong to question the progress of "market-oriented economic systems," a JPMorgan Chase economist responded with a research note that included an Excel chart tracking the ever-rising level of American gross domestic product (GDP) per capita back to 1877.[12]

While there is much irony in this economist's retort, given the pope's critique of precisely such indicators, it is hardly surprising that Wall Street turned to GDP to make their point on American prosperity. Gross domestic product, an economic indicator that measures a nation's "economic growth" by aggregating the monetary values of all market goods and services produced within its boundaries in a given year, is without a doubt the most famous (and infamous) manifestation of the pricing of progress. In the past few years, a veritable cottage industry has emerged to examine the meteoric rise and impact of GDP, which came into being in 1934 (first as gross net product) thanks to the joint efforts of Harvard economist Simon Kuznets, the U.S. government, and the National Bureau of Economic Research (an institution that may sound like a government agency but, as we shall see, most assuredly is not). While some of these works provide "a brief but affectionate history" of GDP, others have been far more critical, claiming that the indicator does not "add up" and thus has become the central cause of the "mismeasuring of our lives." Regardless of their different opinions, all agree that such economic growth metrics wield enormous and unequaled social, cultural, and political power, since they have "come to define American greatness" and have "increasingly been thought as measures of societal well-being."[13]

What is more, the impact of these GDP figures soon transcended the borders of the nation that first invented them. In separating "developing" nations from "developed" ones, determining the promotion hopes of Chinese Communist Party officials, or serving as the definitive metric for cost-benefit analyses on the environmental future of our planet, GDP is an invention that has grown—as one of the more entertaining histories of the metric has quipped—"from narrow tool to global rule."[14]

How did this happen? "The logic of buying and selling no longer applies to material goods alone," argues Michael Sandel convincingly in *What Money Can't Buy*. "Market values have come to govern our lives as never before."

Yet when Sandel, a top legal scholar and ethicist, seeks to explain this phenomenon, he notes that "we did not arrive at this condition through any deliberate choice. It is almost as if it came upon us." Nor, in their own critique of GDP, do the incisive economists Joseph Stiglitz, Amartya Sen, and Jean-Paul Fitoussi delve much into why or how that economic indicator became hegemonic. One gets the sense in reading their report that GDP emerged mostly out of a series of mistakes—the "mismeasuring of our lives" stems from a "wrong metric" with "systemic errors" and "flawed inferences."[15]

The pricing of progress and the rise of economic indicators were not mistakes or accidents, nor did they fall from the sky. They were creatures of history. In attempting to tell this history, recent historians have focused mostly on the twentieth-century economists, statisticians, organizations, and policy makers who invented, disseminated, and institutionalized such economic indicators as GDP and the Consumer Price Index (CPI). Save for the obligatory hat tip to William Petty and his founding of political arithmetic in seventeenth-century England, histories of GDP in particular and economic quantification more generally usually focus on twentieth-century developments. The gist of these arguments is that in the wake of the global economic and social devastation brought on by the Great Depression and two world wars, an assortment of macroeconomic indicators emerged as much-needed planning tools with which economic experts and nation-states could manage and steer the novel and reified construct we moderns commonly refer to as "the economy."[16]

There is no denying the veracity of these important histories. Nevertheless, they are incomplete. The meteoric rise of economic indicators has roots far deeper and broader than twentieth-century macroeconomic expertise. Long before Simon Kuznets sat down to estimate the annual income of the American nation in the 1930s, the "great transformation" that brought about modern capitalism and industrial revolution was accompanied, according to Karl Polanyi, by a "mystical readiness to accept the social consequences of economic improvement, whatever they might be," as well as an ardent belief among liberal elites "that all human problems could be resolved given an unlimited amount of material commodities." Christopher Lasch echoed these sentiments, demonstrating that the rise of American liberalism corresponded with "an elaborate ideology of progress based on the division of labor, unprecedented gains in productivity, the upgrading of tastes, and the expansion of consumer demand." The idea that one could gauge social progress and

human welfare by adding up the monetized amount of market goods produced and consumed is a foundational cornerstone of modern liberalism
and capitalism, and thus has a far longer history than GDP. It is because of
this that I treat the invention of GDP not as the opening scene of the American pricing of progress but rather as the final act of a long, contested, and
global drama that began not in the United States at all, but rather with the
enclosure of English lands and the enslavement of African bodies in the seventeenth and eighteenth centuries.[17]

This longer, "pre-GDP" history of such quantifying practices has only
begun to be told.[18] There are a number of reasons for this, but two seem most
pertinent. On one hand, historians of statistics have not placed a great deal
of emphasis on capitalism, choosing instead to focus more on issues of prob-
ability, trust, certainty, bureaucracy, and objectivity. On the other hand, since
the days of Werner Sombart and Max Weber, those who have fixated on the
bonds between capitalism and quantification have preferred to focus on business practices such as double-entry accounting. Far less attention has been
given to the rise of economic indicators and other forms of social or national
accounting that sought to measure the performance not of a company or firm
but of a community, city, region, or nation-state.[19]

The relative lack of attention paid to the history of such monetized metrics
is unfortunate, since that history poignantly demonstrates how, as Michael
Zakim and Gary Kornblith have put it, capital was transformed into an "ism" in
the nineteenth century as "the specific exigencies of doing business had acquired a general application to human affairs." Tracing the history of economic
indicators allows us to see how capitalist forms of quantification used to manage
or invest in railroad corporations, textile factories, real estate holdings, or
cotton plantations escaped the narrow confines of the nineteenth-century business world and seeped into nearly every nook and cranny of American society.
The micromanaging of labor led to macroeconomic indicators, corporate
cost-accounting figures gave way to government cost-of-living indices, and
shareholder revenue reports foreshadowed national income accounting.[20]

When I began researching this book, I assumed that I would devote significant portions to the quantification practices of all Americans, including poor
laborers, African American slaves, and immigrant women. What I discovered,

however, was that middle- to upper-class white men have dominated the realm of social measurement since its early beginnings, because it took a significant amount of cultural power, economic privilege, and political clout to develop statistical gauges of social success or failure. Historians in recent years have begun to unearth the differing forms of numeracy among women or slaves. Yet to focus on such people would have made this book not only unwieldy but also misleading. It would have suggested that national metrics and economic indicators emerged as "bottom-up" constructs shaped by grassroots movements. This was not usually the case. Women such as Leonora Barry—a poverty-stricken seamstress who climbed the ranks of the Knights of Labor to become its foremost statistician—were not common. In the rare instances when such marginalized Americans gained the social power needed to affect how their society quantified progress, I have told their story. But such instances are few and far between. The pricing of progress was many things, but democratic it was not.[21]

This, however, is not to say that the pricing of progress was not a contested process—it most certainly was. While many Americans today may view the economic indicators that bombard them on a daily (if not hourly) basis as natural, commonsense measures of societal well-being, in the nineteenth century the question of which statistics should serve as the yardsticks of American society remained wide open. Seemingly cold numbers were the subject of many a heated debate. As Alexander Hamilton and many other progress-pricing pioneers in early America learned the hard way, most Americans did not value the world as though it were a capitalized investment. Until the 1850s, moral statistics served as the dominant social metrics. Even when economic indicators did begin their ascent as the standard-bearers of social measurement, such developments were blocked, challenged, and contested at every turn. The pricing of progress—much like American capitalism in general—was never a foregone conclusion.[22]

Throughout the latter half of the nineteenth century, just as the pricing of progress gained momentum, an eclectic group of union organizers, populist farmers, muckraking journalists, middle-class reformers, "eight-hour-day" advocates, and government bureaucrats aggressively challenged the notion that capitalizing statistics could or should serve as the main barometers of American society. Still very much enamored of numbers, these statistical activists infiltrated state bureaucracies and offered up a series of alternative metrics that measured not economic growth, market productivity, cost of living, or purchasing power but rather urban poverty, gender discrimination, proprietary independence, rural tenancy, class mobility, social justice, and rent-seeking behavior. Even when utilizing market data, the metrics they developed were drastically different from those proposed by most economic elites. Rather than focus on capital gains, they focused on crushing indebtedness. Instead of measuring the increasing growth of the economic pie, they preferred to examine how it was sliced and distributed. Rather than force Americans to conform to a single "standard of living," they preferred measuring economic autonomy. In place of calculating the costs of labor, they quantified its exploitation.

Despite these challenges, by the outbreak of World War I those elites who believed in the pricing of progress—whether at the Massachusetts Bureau of Labor Statistics, the Rockefeller Foundation, the Yale economics department, or the *New York Times*—managed to use their social power and cultural clout to greatly influence how mainstream acts of social measurement would be carried out. They were able to seize the means of quantification, thus greatly effecting what data would be collected, especially by the emerging "statistical state." Alternative forms of measuring progress were pushed to the side. Economic indicators became a central part of American culture, governance, thought, politics, and everyday life. This victory followed a complex, winding, and unpredictable path that I trace in this book. There is nothing "natural" about our current obsession with economic indicators. Things could have been different.

———————

The pricing of progress had far-reaching implications for the United States and the world. Nineteenth-century investors usually did not funnel money into new business endeavors unless they could, at least roughly, imagine their future returns. It was therefore difficult to whet the appetite of global or American capital without feeding it a steady dose of market statistics. As a result, priced indicators came to have a strong influence on the allocation of capital, helping to determine whether resources would be diverted to Chicago or St. Louis, cotton plantations or textile mills, oil fields or steel factories, bank stocks or insurance bonds.

Yet beginning in the mid-nineteenth century with the central role economic indicators came to play in sectional debates over slavery, the influence of the pricing of progress expanded well beyond the business press or stock portfolio. When, for instance, South Carolina governor, planter, and enslaver James Henry Hammond sought to legitimize slavery in his famous 1858 "Cotton Is King" speech, he did so, in large part, with the same kind of productivity figures he had developed on his plantation in order to track, discipline, and value his cotton-picking slaves. "There is not a nation on the face of the earth, with any numerous population, that can compete with us in produce per capita," Hammond declared. "It amounts to $16.66 per head." When Bostonian railroad analyst Henry Varnum Poor sought to challenge such southern statistical claims of slavery's success, he did so with remarkably similar kinds of investmentality statistics he had developed in order to advise American and European capitalists. After the Civil War, monied metrics continued to be deeply implicated in the most important social, political, and cultural developments of the day including the legitimacy of wage labor, the closing of the frontier, the justness of the gold standard, the debate surrounding the tariff, the demand for public health, the rise of consumer culture, and the power of the modern corporation.[23]

By the Progressive Era, nascent cost-benefit analyses carried out by technocratic reformers strived to ensure that prices would not only allocate market resources but shape social policy as well. "This is an age of progress, intellectual, social and, above all, material," declared J. Pease Norton, editor of *American Health Magazine,* in his call for more government spending on health care. "Societies, like skillful capitalists, should strive to invest their revenues so as to yield maximum returns." After imagining society as a capital investment and people as mechanical factors of capitalist production, Norton went on to price both in order to prove his point that the government must work to extend the lives of its productive citizens. "If the average life-span of a class of the population can be increased from 40 to 45 years," he argued, "the economic gain would be $25 to $50 per head" or "$800,000,000 to $1,600,000,000 per annum." Who, exactly, would receive these "economic gains"? By focusing far more on labor productivity than on labor compensation, Progressives such as Norton often avoided that prickly question.[24]

When such accounting practices migrated from the realm of business to the realm of policy or culture, they reshaped social relations, especially between metric-wielding elites and the everyday Americans they often priced. Recently the historiography of capitalism has revolved more around abstract processes of commodification than tangible social developments such as the formation of a working class. While it is crucial that historians tackle such airy abstractions, this shift has often had the inadvertent tendency to transform capitalism, to quote Jeffrey Sklansky, into a "faceless sovereign" that "appears as a realm with no rulers." In such an apparent power vacuum, historical agents are cast as "subjects of the seemingly authorless edicts of 'the market.'" Such edicts often come in the form of monetary prices.[25]

I have tried to avoid such pitfalls by embedding the abstract nature of pecuniary indicators in the social relations and power dynamics of their time, thus making the intangible a bit more tangible and the authorless a bit more authoritarian. Behind every monied metric or growth indicator lay not the faceless sovereign of a self-regulating market but the actual faces—and interests—of such elite white men as William Petty, James Glen, Alexander Hamilton, Samuel Blodget Jr., Tench Coxe, Freeman Hunt, George Tucker, Hinton Helper, John Henry Hammond, Henry Varnum Poor, Edward Atkinson, David Wells, Nelson Aldrich, John D. Rockefeller Jr., and Irving Fisher.

If we embed economic indicators in the power relations of the nineteenth century, it becomes evident that measuring prosperity according to the Dow Jones Industrial Average, industrial productivity, or per capita wealth made a good deal of sense for America's upper classes, since they were usually the ones who possessed the stocks, owned the factories, and held the wealth. The same could not be said for those Americans who did not own property or, in the case of slaves, even their own labor. (And it says nothing of what such measures meant for the fate of American air, American natural landscapes, or American wildlife.) Even though many Gilded Age and Progressive Era laborers came to accept certain aspects of the pricing of progress in the late nineteenth century—namely, the idea of a measurable "living wage"—working-class Americans were, broadly speaking, always less enthusiastic than their bosses about the rise of investmentality. This was largely because they believed the human experience to be "priceless" (an important term that, along with "the almighty dollar," takes off around the same time progress begins to be priced) and because they rightly viewed such figures as surveillance tools that could be used to ramp up production or cut wages.

While laborers were wary about the pricing of progress, elite businessmen and policy makers embraced national wealth statistics, price indices, and aggregated output metrics since they enabled them to statistically transcend the single business enterprise, isolated factory, or lone commodity and get a glimpse of the "general price level," "overall productivity," or "business cycle" of *all* industries, sectors, markets, and trades. Economic indicators were fast becoming a crucial managerial instrument through which government bureaucracies, nonprofit organizations, middle managers, and academic economists could make legible the boom-and-bust nature of modern capitalism while rationalizing, stabilizing, and legitimizing the new corporate social order. Thanks to the homogenizing powers of monied indexation, these indicators could statistically unite coal mining, steel production, and textile manufacturing via single, easy-to-use metrics, thus allowing economic elites to overcome the narrow sectorial politics of their specific industry and view themselves as part of a consolidated corporate class with shared interests, concerns, and obstacles.

Statistics can never be objective. The very choice of what to count is always subjective. As a result, capitalizing indicators often served as quantified ideological carriers, injecting certain political views, gender roles, racial prejudices, class interests, or cultural preferences wherever they might be implemented or circulated. The more these statistics spread, the more the investmentality that shaped these statistics spread with them, reproducing the ideology that had first given them life. The more these seemingly apolitical figures were used to value American society and life, the more the capitalist values that undergirded these figures exerted social power.[26]

As monetized metrics served to remind the American people time and again, capitalism was quite good at increasing market production and consumption—a fact we should not take lightly, as it has clearly improved the material lives of most generations of Americans. Yet what these ascending, dollar-denominated graphs of glorious per capita growth could not demonstrate were the social costs or benefits that accompanied the rise of American capitalism. Economic indicators had the unique ability to diminish, if not altogether eliminate, anything that could not be measured in dollars and cents. Be it a woman's labor in the home, an African American's freedom in the South, a steelworker's control of his own bodily rhythms, or a farmer's mortgage-backed anxieties, the 1800s did not lack such unpriceable issues, nor have the 1900s and 2000s.[27]

In equating money with value—a philosophical development guided by three centuries of classical and neoclassical economists—economic indicators also reversed the linkages earlier Americans had made between economic activity and social well-being. Instead of seeking to measure the effect certain economic policies or social developments had on the physical, spiritual, mental, or social welfare of the American citizenry, price-based measures gauged the monetized effect that productive labor, human behavior, personal skills, or cultural preferences had on economic growth, capital accumulation, and market productivity. Rather than measure the extent to which economic relations were satisfying the needs of Americans, economic indicators examined whether humanity was satisfying the needs of pecuniary growth. In 1911, scientific management originator Frederick Winslow Taylor, a man who dreamed of measuring every human movement in terms of price, bluntly articulated this reversal of ends and means: "In the past the man has been first; in the future the system must be first."[28]

"The system" may be known today as "the economy," but in the end Taylor got his wish. Whether in the Keynesian 1950s or the neoliberal 1980s, since the mid-twentieth century economic indicators have painted a picture of American society as a capital investment whose main goal, like that of any investment, is ever-increasing monetary growth. Americans have surely benefited materially from the remarkable economic growth of this era, a phenomenon wholly unique to capitalist societies. Nevertheless, by making market expansion and capital accumulation synonymous with progress, and the axiomatic objective and function of American life, monetized metrics have turned human betterment into a secondary concern that has been trumped by the need for unceasing capitalist expansion. By the early twenty-first century, American society's top priority had become its bottom line, net worth was synonymous with self-worth, and a billionaire businessman who promised to run the country like a real estate investment was elected president.[29]

ONE

The Political Arithmetic of Price

It was the dramatic social upheaval in the English countryside of the sixteenth and seventeenth centuries that first provoked the pricing of progress and the capitalization of everyday life. By the turn of the sixteenth century, as global trade intensified, many English landholders—be they nobles, gentry, or yeomen—began to recognize the potential profit in "enclosing" and "engrossing" subsistence plots, fens, and open fields and turning them into commodity-producing farms or pasture. Finding it exceedingly difficult to extract significant surpluses from peasants through extra-economic means, as in earlier feudal times, English elites appropriated customary "copyhold" tenures and communal lands and consolidated them into privatized factors of market production. In a long, complex, and historically unprecedented process, most English peasants lost their direct access to the fruit of the soil.[1]

In the place of peasants, many landholders began to lease their enclosed lands to the highest-bidding tenant, transforming rent from a relation mediated by custom and coercion to one mediated by profit and gain. As recognized by Stephen Primatt, author of one of the leading "how-to" pamphlets on landed investment in the seventeenth century, leaseholders were developing a keen business sense regarding rental values; they "are very wary and cautious in making their Bargains, and will not accept of any Propositions, but such as they have some reasonable profit for their industrious labour." With an eye toward the bottom line, entrepreneurial tenants haggled with landowners over rent rates as they set out to "improve" their landlords' enclosed plots into profitable farms.[2]

As for the dispossessed peasants, many still worked the land—only now as wage laborers hired by those market-minded tenant farmers. No longer able to directly consume the fruits of their labor, laborers had little choice but to spend their wages on the bare necessities of life in commodity form—often the same commodities they were laboring to produce on the now-enclosed lands their ancestors had resided upon for generations. It has been estimated that by the end of the seventeenth century only 30 percent of England remained unenclosed. Landlords who lived mainly on rent payments leased out roughly three-quarters of all cultivable land in the country by 1700, while owner-occupied farms received only a third of the national income generated by land.[3]

The emerging competition among tenants and the deterioration of customary feudal relations led to a doubling of rents between 1590 and 1640. To maintain their livelihood in an environment of rapidly rising rents, tenant farmers had to increase their market output and, as Primatt noted, "improve the Landlords ground, so that they may honestly pay their Landlords their Rents." Since enclosed farms were frequently leased to the tenant farmer who could pay the highest rent, the money output of labor and land often determined the fate of a farm and thus grew to be a prime concern of agrarian English life, as the ubiquitous "improvement" literature of the era suggests. Driven not only by the market but also by Enlightenment beliefs that centered on human capacity for reason, agency, improvement, and progress, tenant farmers greatly increased the productivity of their hired labor and rented land through various agricultural innovations, experiments, and investments.[4]

This enclosure of the countryside revolutionized not only agricultural practices and social relations but also how English elites conceived of nature and humankind. For centuries, the profit motive had been quarantined from much of English society, emerging only in isolated pockets of activity such as long-distance commercial trade. Now, as rent-seeking enclosure and wage labor upended the daily rhythms, feudal obligations, and social customs of everyday agrarian life, nature and humanity could be reimagined as impersonal, uniform, and thus quantifiable inputs of economic production. Dispossession begat abstraction: just as enclosure ripped peasants off their lands and out of the complex tapestry of fixed duties, hierarchical positions, and feudal tenures that formed the fabric of their society, so too did it rend the idea of nature and human into two discrete economic units: land and labor. Fittingly, by the mid-sixteenth century the word *rent* had two distinct meanings (although of different origins): money paid to someone to use land, and a tear in something (such as fabric).[5]

Land, for the first time, was coming to be seen as an annual stream of cash. Such a view would have been impossible in earlier centuries because the value of land had never before been determined by its future capacity to produce a given amount of commodities for the market. In medieval times there were varying overlapping claims and obligations to most lands, and the value of land was embedded in a myriad of traditional tributes to the lord that conveyed social subordination (i.e., fees for hunting or for water access). Because so much of the surplus that feudal landlords extracted from their subjects took the form of direct services or tributes that did not require monetary exchange (payments in wheat, working demesne lands, military obligations), it made no sense to try to value a piece of land according to its annual flow of money. The complex web of extra-economic privileges and obligations that formed the foundation of feudal land tenure had no price tag.[6]

A survey taken in 1590 of monastic property reveals how feudal traditions inserted a wedge between monetary values and social life. It was discovered that a majority of monastic tenants were continuing to pay rents well below the market rate of the time because they had been granted customary leases of ninety-nine years sometime between 1491 and 1535. In a revealing sign of the times, surveyors lamented that past custom was effectively blocking the alignment of rent payments with market values, and they proposed that market forces should supplant these traditional relations by greatly limiting the length of future land leases. By the seventeenth century, the new standard for leases had been shortened to around twenty years.[7]

The engrossment and enclosure of land, the dissolution of non-monetary feudal services, the shortening of rental leases, and the transfer of customary copyholds into market leaseholds all helped to monetize the relationship between landlord and tenant. Feudal rent was slowly morphing into capitalist rent. This monetization of the feudal ladder, meanwhile, flowed not only down but up. By the mid-seventeenth century, many landlords had few obligations to their aristocratic superiors save for the quitrent, which referred to the quitting of feudal services and their replacement with annual cash payments.[8]

English people's newfound interest in land's monetary output reflected this social revolution, as many came to imagine nature as an income-bearing asset. By the early seventeenth century, the farmer Robert Loder was keeping meticulous accounts of his wheat and barley yields, obsessively comparing them to determine which brought in a greater return on capital. In 1615, he calculated his overall profit at £393 19s. 10d. by not only tracking his revenue from sales of produce and costs of labor but also discounting opportunity costs by deducting the interest on the money invested in growing the crop.[9]

While Loder's investmentality was somewhat of an outlier (he even priced the value of his sheep dung), it offered a sign of things to come. In 1641, Henry Best noted that his pasture lands used to rent for only 3 shillings an acre "but nowe, being enclosed, they will lette for thrice as much." By the 1660s, the Royal Society was conducting surveys on average wheat yields in different types of soil. When banker-turned-landed-gentleman James Bankes of Winstanley advised his son to improve one of the holdings he was to inherit by adding marl, a calcium-based soil additive, he explained to him that "if the sam tenement be well lok into and marreld, it wyll yeald yow at the lest fyfe pondes a yeare rent." In the original family records, Bankes had first written "ten pounds," only to cross it out and write "five." Clearly, the wheels of investmentality were briskly turning in the minds of some seventeenth-century elites.[10]

That the former banker used the word *yield* to describe not only cash revenue but also crop production offers further testimony that a widespread capitalization of nature was afoot. Yet another sign of the changing times can be seen in the self-fashioning of landed elites. Only when profit-maximizing behavior took hold did landowners begin to feel the need to portray themselves in the exact opposite light. Of one, his eulogy noted that "not markes and pounds but hawkes and hounds, is ever his desire"; of another, it was written that his tenants' "rents were not raised, their fines but small, and many poore tenants paid nothing at all."[11]

As a result of the enclosure revolution, by the seventeenth century previously vague and customary assessments of land were commonly being revalued in terms of a multiplier known as "years of purchase," which quickly priced the value of a property according to how much rental income it would yield in the future. According to Primatt's pamphlet, a typical agriculture plot near a major English city was said to be worth around "twenty years of purchase" in the second half of the seventeenth century. As Primatt patiently explained to his readers, this meant that if a piece of land yielded £10 of rent a year, it should be worth roughly £200 on the open market since then it would take twenty years for the initial investment to be returned.

Such a calculative technique for asset pricing—in which future income flows are mathematically translated into a stock of present wealth—is known as capitalization today, a fitting label since such calculations are wholly unique to capitalist societies.[12]

As land came to be treated as income-bearing capital, Englishmen began to see a connection between interest rates (the return on monied capital) and annual rent payments (the return on landed capital). Twenty years' purchase was simply another way of saying that one's annual return (£10) on capital (£200) would be 5 percent a year. Henry Phillips, one of Primatt's predecessors in the real estate advice business, had already associated land prices with interest rates in the 1650s, noting that "when money went at 8 for an hundred, ye Land was worth 18 years purchase. So now money is at 6 for the hundred, Land is well worth twenty years purchase." Implicit in such years-of-purchase calculations was the assumption that land was not a static piece of property, rooted in feudal traditions of the past, but rather a dynamic piece of capital whose value lay in the income flows of the future.[13]

Even Isaac Newton took part in this novel culture of capitalization. In 1685, he developed leasing tables so as to rationalize haphazard feudal customs into a uniform and standardized investment system. In one table, Newton showed that while the relatively limited social obligations inherent in freehold tenures were such that an investor needed to seek only a 5 percent return on capital, investments in more peasant-friendly copyhold tenures should garner 6 percent. Centuries of social struggle regarding the rights and obligations of lord and peasant were, in Newton's hands, being reduced to a single percentage point of interest.[14]

Along with land, the English elite's view of mankind was also changing rapidly. By the mid-seventeenth century, England was awash with pamphlets that advised profit-oriented farmers and rent-seeking landholders how best to utilize their wage laborers in order to maximize a farm's revenue. These treatises on agricultural improvement recommended collecting measures of labor productivity, or as one of them put it, "a general computation of men and cattels labours: what each may do without hurt daily." As this cult of productivity grew, pamphlets were filled with calculations such as how many acres one man could plow in a day if it was "stiffe grounds" (apparently 2.5 acres), "light ground" (4 acres), or a "rough uneven meadow" (1 acre). With a flexible labor force that could be hired and fired, agricultural improvers began to imagine their workers as mobile units of monetized labor that could be allocated in different ways. Take, for example, how a typical working day was now described:

> He plowed his 8 acres a day, he found but 3 men to the work, he went to plow with two Teems, two horses and one man to one plough, and two horses and one man together in the morning, & one man to shift them at noon, and meat and gear them, and then he brought in two Teem in the afternoon, two horses in a Teem with the same men, and so plowed, as aforesaid, his eight acres: I saw the ground thus plowed, & the poor man got his three shilling and four pence for his men and himself, that is ten pence a day a man, which is good wages in Norfolk.[15]

Acres a day and pence per man became the new language of economic life in the seventeenth century, and agricultural productivity rates greatly increased. By 1680, the transformation of labor power into a manageable, income-bearing resource led commentators such as William Petyt to capitalize men and women, as they argued that labor was "capital material . . . raw and undigested . . . committed into the hands of supreme authority, in whose prudence and disposition it is to improve, manage and fashion it to more or less advantage."[16]

The reimagining of wage-earning men, women, and children as abstract factors of market production is perhaps best understood by tracing the subtle shift that occurred in the oft-heard concept of a "balance of trade"—a leading candidate for the title of first economic indicator in Western history. Invented in the mid-sixteenth century, balance of trade first emerged as an extension to the merchant's ledger. It was an act of double-entry accounting on a national scale, intended to gauge whether England sold to other countries more than it purchased. A well-known economic tract from the 1540s—the same decade in which the first double-entry accounting manual appeared in English—expressed the mercantile logic behind the balance of trade, warning that "we must alwaies take hede that we bie no more of strangers then we sell them; for so wee sholde empouerishe owr selves and enriche theme." Rather than focus on domestic productivity—which was then seen as "sterile," thanks to a zero-sum logic that assumed wealth could only be traded not created from whole cloth—the merchants and rulers who first began using the balance-of-trade measure appear to have been mostly interested in international trade, since this was seen as the main determinant of whether one's country was bleeding silver or hoarding gold. Initial balance-of-trade statistics, in short, remained on the international periphery, aptly reflecting a society in which market relations surely existed yet the cash nexus had not yet trickled down into everyday domestic life.[17]

As happened with many a statistical indicator, however, the meaning of balance of trade subtly changed over time. While still used to measure the national specie supply, by the middle of the seventeenth century balance of trade had also morphed into a leading barometer of domestic market productivity. As England became a global export hub for manufactured commodities, merchants and manufacturers began to realize that the best way to improve one's balance of trade was to maximize domestic output for export. As Samuel Fortrey explained in a pamphlet, "To be rich, is to have plenty of that commoditie to vent." This emphasis on domestic productivity shifted the statistical focus from international trade to the everyday laborer, causing economic thinker Charles Davenant to declare that it was the English people who were "the first matter of power and wealth, by whose labor and industry the nation must be the gainers in the balance." Petyt was in agreement, noting that "sufficient stores of treasure cannot otherwise be got than by the industry of the people." Continuing, he contended that "people are, therefore, the chiefest most fundamental and precious commodity, out of which may be derived all sorts of manufactures, navigation, riches, conquests and solid dominion."[18]

Implicit in these idioms, metaphors, and arguments was the notion that only labor could generate the added value that transformed raw materials into finished goods and filled English coffers through exports. Liberals since Adam Smith have derided mercantilists for obsessing over gold, but by the late seventeenth century it had become almost a cliché among English economic thinkers that the real "treasure of the nation" lay in "the bodies of men." As a result, population growth came to be seen, for the first time, not as a burden on English society but as a boon.[19]

———————✦———————

As years-of-purchase calculations and balance-of-trade figures reveal, progress was beginning to be priced in mid-seventeenth-century England. No one played a greater role in this development than Sir William Petty and his "political arithmetic." An adamant follower of Sir Francis Bacon's emerging empiricism, from the early 1660s until his death in 1687 Petty wrote numerous economic and political treatises, intended mostly for the king (and published only posthumously in the 1690s), in which he sought to paint an accurate picture of English and Irish social and economic life through the use of empirical data. "Instead of using comparative and superlative Words, and intellectual Arguments," Petty explained in 1671 while paraphrasing Bacon, "I . . . express myself in terms of Number, Weight or Measure; to use only Arguments of Sense, and to consider only such Causes, as have visible Foundations in Nature."[20]

Petty, however, often turned to a very specific form of "Number, Weight or Measure" that priced and capitalized the productive value of land and labor into aggregated measures of national progress. In so doing, Petty laid the groundwork for national income accounting, modern economic indicators, classical economics, and the concept of human capital. Contemporary calculators of the era recognized the importance of Petty's political arithmetic well enough (as did later commentators such as Karl Marx, who saw him as the "founder of political economy"). In the 1690s, when Petty's economic calculations were all the rage, Davenant contended that the balance of trade could "no way be found out, but by political arithmetic," since "the spring and original of it, in all Nations, is the natural or artificial product of the country; that is to say, what their land, or what their labor and industry produces." No longer did English elites believe that national wealth could be measured solely by subtracting exports from imports. Rather, they came to believe that in order to measure the wealth of a society, one had to measure the aggregate income of the nation and the productive capacities of nature and human.[21]

Tracing the roots of Petty's political arithmetic reveals just how central a role the rise of capitalist tenantry, the enclosure movement, and the dispossession of peasants played in the pricing of progress. For Petty's political arithmetic was born not in a university classroom, a London salon, a merchant's brokerage house, or a king's palace but rather in the lush, green, and confiscated lands of conquered Ireland. Following Cromwell's conquest of Ireland, the English needed to pay the soldiers who had fought in the war as well as the "adventurers" who had funded it. To recompense these men, Cromwell confiscated nearly 8 million acres of land, mostly from Irish Catholics. A basic problem quickly emerged, however: how would the English divvy up the Irish countryside so that each solider and adventurer received roughly the amount of compensation he had been promised? To do so, Ireland would have to be transformed from a physical place into a pecuniary reimbursement. Enter William Petty.[22]

A walking embodiment of the bourgeois revolution under way, Petty was born to a family of middling clothiers with no aristocratic ties. He began his remarkable life journey in 1637 as a lowly fourteen-year-old cabin boy looking for adventure on the high seas. By 1651, however, he had become a fixture in London's most highly regarded intellectual institutions and academic circles. Within little more than a decade, Petty had studied under Thomas Hobbes, debated with René Descartes, become a member of the London Philosophical Society, and been hired not only as a professor of anatomy at Oxford but as a professor of music at Gresham College as well. All the while, young Petty had begun to take a great interest in Sir Francis Bacon's emphasis on empiricism, measurement, and observation. Of no blue blood, Petty supported the Parliamentarians during the English Civil War, aligning himself with Oliver Cromwell against the Royalists.[23]

In 1651, Petty put his flourishing academic career on hold in order to serve as a physician-general in Cromwell's conquest of Ireland. After the war ended, it was Petty who was tasked with the crucial job of mapping, surveying, and valuing the confiscated Irish lands intended for English soldiers and Cromwell's financial backers. The Down Survey, as it came to be called, was far more than a surveying mission. Since the confiscated lands were intended to settle debts, Cromwell's men determined to turn them into rent-yielding assets. Petty would later refer to Ireland as a scientific experiment, and in many ways it was: an experiment in capitalist social engineering, as Ireland was to be transformed into a series of moneymaking assets.[24]

Petty was a natural choice for the job. Prior to his journey to Ireland, he had been a member of the Hartlib Circle, a Bacon-inspired group dedicated to, among many other things, the rational improvement of agriculture through the pursuit of scientific, quantitative, and empirical husbandry. Some of the men Petty met in this circle, including its founder, Samuel Hartlib, were busy writing the very agricultural improvement pamphlets that had begun to quantify labor and land's productivity. Recent historians have rightly placed the Hartlib Circle—and not some irrational obsession with gold—at the heart of

THE PRICING OF PROGRESS

mercantilism, as this was the era in which the goal of maintaining the social status quo gave way to a burning desire, driven by religious, scientific, and economic change, for increased economic growth, material well-being, and market productivity. The full title of one of Hartlib's own pamphlets nicely summarizes the circle's market-minded goals: *A DISCOVERIE For Division or Setting out of Land, as to the best Form. Published by* Samuel Hartlib *Esquire, for Direction and more Advantage and Profit of the Adventurers and Planters in the* FENS *and other Waste and undisposed Places in England and Ireland. Whereunto are added some other Choice Secrets or Experiments of* Husbandry. *With a Philosophical Quere concerning the* Cause of Fruitfulness. AND An Essay to shew How all Lands may be *improved in a New Way to become the ground of the increase of Trading and Revenue to this Common-wealth.*[25]

Within a paltry ten months and with only some 1,000 men, Petty managed to create what contemporaries believed was the most accurate map of Ireland in history. Spatially classifying the Irish countryside into such categories as "arable" or "bogg," Petty's map was a most impressive display of Francis Bacon's scientific method. It also had the financial interests of Cromwell's soldiers and financiers clearly in its sights. The borders Petty drew to divide up the country were largely determined by whether the land was fit for commodity production. Many of the maps, in fact, were accompanied by a statistical chart in which Petty aggregated the number of acres in each parish under his classification of "profitable" or "unprofitable." Cromwell's army had physically removed Irish men, women, and children from the direct source of their subsistence and the material basis of their society. The Down Survey served a similar purpose in the abstract. By observing the Irish countryside solely through the investmentality binary of profitable / unprofitable, Petty disentangled Irish lands from the myriad of social obligations in which they were enmeshed. Much like England, Ireland was being rent apart.[26]

Enclosure extinguished common rights and feudal relations by turning customary tenures, common lands, and communal fields into private property—or, as Blackstone would define it a century later, "the sole and despotic dominion which one man claims and exercises over the external things of the world, in total exclusion of the right of any other individual in the universe." It was precisely this "sole and despotic dominion" brought on by the privatization of land that would allow Petty to reduce the endlessly complex relations embedded within the Irish countryside into a single, profit-minded value of land and labor that could be isolated, observed, and measured.[27]

Valuation—the quantified assessment of an object's singular worthiness through the use of a uniform and standardized unit of measure—would form the heart of Petty's political arithmetic. And it was through his work on the Down Survey that he first confronted the dogged question that would shape (and haunt) his valuation attempts more than any other: when evaluating the world in numbers, what should be the unit of measure? Or, to put the question another way: how does one measure the value of people, places, and things in such a manner that the three can be contrasted, compared, and aggregated? If Petty was to successfully transform the world into "Number, Weight or Measure," he would need to answer this riddle and thus provide a common quantitative denominator for such varying things as wheat, wool, land, and men.[28]

The founding father of GDP did not initially believe that money could serve as this common measure of value. Not long after he had finished the Down Survey, Petty referred to land prices in his personal papers as merely the "casual and circumstantial" value of land, and distinguished such fluctuating rates from land's "natural and intrinsic" value. While grappling with this question led Petty to make some ambiguous and contradictory statements—in one passage he conceded that rent rates could be used to measure land values so long as they were accompanied by hard data on bushels per seed planted—it appears that he distrusted market prices mostly because he believed that value should be eternal, concrete, and grounded in the tangible, physical world rather than in the mood swings of the ever-fluctuating market. Referring to market rent rates and money prices as "accidental," "casual," and "extrinsic" measures of value in his 1662 "Treatise of Taxes," Petty questioned their use as arbiters of value since they were determined "according to the bargains which a few men make one with another, through ignorance, haste, false suggestion, or else in their passion or drink."[29]

Yet in the same "Treatise of Taxes," Petty took a major step toward the pricing of everyday life. In what are quite possibly the two most important passages in the history of classical economic thought, Petty explained why land's annual productivity—and hence its inherent value—could in fact be measured by examining rent prices:

> Suppose a man could with his own hands plant a certain scope of Land with Corn, that is, could Digg, or Plough, Harrow, Weed, Reap, Carry home, Thresh, and Winnow so much as the Husbandry of this Land requires; and had withal Seed wherewith to sow the same. I say, that when this man hath subducted his seed out of the proceed of his Harvest, and also what himself hath both eaten and given to others in exchange for Clothes, and other Natural necessities; that the Remainder of Corn is the natural and true Rent of the Land for that year. . . .
>
> [H]ow much English money this Corn or Rent is worth? I answer, so much as the money, which another single man can save within the same time, over and above his expence, if he imployed himself wholly to produce and make it; viz., Let another man go travel into a Countrey where is Silver, there Dig it, Refine it bring it to the same place where the other man planted his Corn; Coyne it, etc., the same person, all the while of his working for Silver, gathering also food for his necessary livelihood, and procuring himself covering, etc. I say, the Silver of the one, must be esteemed of equal value with the Corn of the other. The one, being perhaps twenty Ounces and the other twenty Bushels. From whence it follows that the price of a Bushel of this Corn to be an Ounce of silver.[30]

Like most revolutionary ideas, Petty's story was simple enough to be convincing yet just far-fetched enough not to have been thought of yet. If one spent the same amount of time growing corn and mining silver, he argued, then the surpluses each activity yielded, after deducting labor costs, were equal in value and must represent nature's intrinsic contribution to the production of value. Since in the second half of Petty's comparison nature's tangible bounty conveniently consisted of the very same metallic material out of which money was made, Petty was able to happily conclude that the concrete value of an acre of farmland could, in fact, be measured in silver coins. With some inspired storytelling, Petty had made the revolutionary leap from the tangible to the abstract, as land's productive value could now be measured by the prices of the market.[31]

While Petty prided himself on his inductive methods, the foundation of his claim that market prices represented natural value was based on his own deductive—and highly creative—logic. Perhaps because of this, Petty seemed unconvinced by his own argument and remained somewhat reluctant to use monetary prices as his central unit of value measurement. Only a few pages after he equated bushel prices with silver, Petty once again reverted to his previous musings. "All things ought to be valued," he wrote, "by two natural Denominations, which is Land and Labour; that is, we ought to say, a Ship or garment is worth such a measure of Land, with such another measure of Labour."[32]

In a later work from 1672, Petty would move away from money and toward caloric energy as his measure of value, arguing that one could measure the value of "an Irish Cabbin at the number of days food, which the Maker spent in building of it." In that same essay he also suggested that the only way to truly measure the value of land and labor would be to perform a tangible experiment. A calf would be placed for one month in a field and allowed to graze. Then, on the same field, a man would be placed to work the land for one month. The increase in the calf's weight would reveal the land's true productive capacity, and the amount of wheat the man produced would reveal his. In planning this experiment, Petty seemed to be admitting that money would not do, and that the quest for an alternative unit with which to measure the value of land and labor was "the most important Consideration in Political Oeconomics."[33]

While Petty's doubts would continue to linger, the "Treatise of Taxes" nevertheless marks a turning point in Petty's approach to market prices. Unable to quantify the world using his "intrinsic" and tangible units of materialism, Petty appears to have reluctantly accepted the equation of money with value. Like every statistician, Petty was dependent on the data he had at his disposal, and the only available measure that could make the world consistently quantifiable in England's budding capitalist society was money. So despite Petty's misgivings regarding the relationship between money and value, his need for data that could be aggregated, compared, and contrasted led him to argue that prices could accurately measure the value of nature and man.

Petty's political arithmetic took off once he accepted money as his measure of value. In this regard, one work stands out above the rest: an essay titled "Verbum Sapienti ['word to the wise' in Latin] and the Value of People," which Petty apparently penned in 1665, only a few years after he had first equated money prices with value. While the title reveals the ultimate goal of the piece, the steps he took to get there became the intellectual foundation for national income accounting, the pricing of progress, and the capitalization of life.

Petty's mission to uncover the "value of people" by calculating their price was likely inspired, in part, by his mentor Thomas Hobbes. In *Leviathan,* Hobbes claimed that "the *Value,* or WORTH of man, is as of all other things, his Price; that is to say, so much as would be given for the use of his Power." In equating a man's value with how much it costs to buy his labor power, Hobbes appears to have been influenced by the emerging wage labor market that followed enclosure.[34] In his own essay on the the value of people written a generation later, Petty expands greatly on Hobbes's market metaphor, by envisioning England as a complete market society in which all objects of social value must be procured and consumed as commodities. Reducing value to something that could be attained only in commodity form, this society-as-market approach allowed Petty to assume that he could measure the entire wealth of the English nation just by observing the goings-on in local markets where laborers purchased their subsistence. The symbiotic relationship between political arithmetic and the nascent rise of English capitalism is evident: just as the rise of wage labor shaped Hobbes's concept of man's value, so too did it influence Petty's choice to measure the wealth of the nation solely through market transactions, since such an approach would have been unthinkable in a society where most people consumed only what they themselves had produced.[35]

Petty's observations of peasant consumption in the English marketplace allowed him to roughly extrapolate that English people spent around £40 million on food, housing, and other consumable goods per annum. Petty then concluded that this £40 million worth of consumption had to equal the aggregate productive output of England, since whatever commodities are consumed must first be produced. This was the invention of the basic equation between national production and consumption that still lies as the heart of GDP figures today, and it appears to have been the first time in recorded history that someone sought to measure the wealth of a society solely by aggregating the prices of all commodities produced and consumed.[36]

Petty, however, was interested not just in gauging the aggregate wealth of the nation but also in valuing the two main factors of production that generated it: labor and land. To do so, Petty once again turned to the market for his data. Thanks to his new theory of value, Petty was able to make the crucial assumption that rent rates represented land's intrinsic value. Using tax data to estimate the aggregated rent payments of all landholders at roughly

£8 million per annum, Petty announced that this figure represented nature's contribution to the total wealth of England. Subtracting this amount from the £40 million of total wealth he had calculated earlier, as well as the income received from shipping, housing, cattle, and other forms of property (which came to £7 million per annum), Petty concluded that English laborers must have produced the remaining £25 million of annual income. Not including Sundays and sick days—Petty left few stones unturned—this amounted to 7 pence a day per working man or woman.[37]

Petty had estimated the amount of income the average English laborer produced per year and even per day—but he was not done yet. Just as landholders of the era were coming to value their land as a financial asset by capitalizing (in terms of years of purchase) its income-yielding rent, Petty was interested in valuing people as financial assets by capitalizing their income-yielding labor. To do so, Petty would have to translate a laborer's future annual revenue stream into a present-day asset price that represented the market value not of their labor power but of their very body. And so, in his next step, Petty multiplied the annual income of the English laborer by 16.6 years of purchase (an interest rate of 6 percent) and concluded that "the value of the people" was £417 million in total or £138 per person. In so doing, Petty casually noted that he had used the same interest rate and years-of-purchase for humans as was used to capitalize landed property since "the Species of them is worth as many as Land." The concept of human capital was born.[38]

The ease with which Petty could quantify nature and human beings into commensurable units of income and capital stemmed from one crucial assumption that had emerged from his corn-into-silver narrative: that rent prices reflected the productive value of land. This assumption carried with it enormous political ramifications because it not only equated price with value but also conflated compensation and productivity. In both his deductive corn model and his inductive political arithmetic, Petty assumed that the amount of money a landowner received in rent was equal to the productivity of the land. If a landowner earned 5 shillings per acre, according to Petty, this was not because he had managed to monopolize the means of human subsistence, turning it into a scarce and minority-owned resource, but rather because that simply happened to be the natural fertility of the land he owned.

Absent from Petty's economic worldview, therefore, was any notion of exploitation, asymmetrical exchange, or power. Through a series of seemingly logical and empirical moves, Petty had painted an image of a society in which laborers and landholders were naturally compensated for their contributions to the production process: landholders received their rent payment, since that was the productive value of the land, and workers received their wage payment, since that was the productive value of their labor. Without royal decrees or parliamentary laws, the market had somehow managed to ensure that each received what he or she deserved. More than a century before Adam Smith would speak of the self-regulating system of "perfect liberty," Petty had naturalized (Marx would later say fetishized) capitalist social relations simply by assuming that the wage or rent prices generated by the market reflected the productivity of humans and nature.[39]

What had led Petty down this path? One motive was his desire to quantify the world around him. As opposed to his initial valuation techniques, which required a series of incredibly complex (and probably impossible) experiments, Petty's political arithmetic was easily executed precisely *because* it assumed that the market's distribution of wealth in English society mirrored the value of each factor of production. However, Petty's empiricism was hardly the only force at work here. To fully understand the motives behind Petty's pricing of progress and capitalization of life, we must turn to the politics behind political arithmetic. Here, two historical developments stand above the rest: the rise of a bourgeois fiscal state in Restoration England and Petty's own meteoric ascendance into the landholding class.

———————

Born to a middling family of clothiers, Petty would die an incredibly wealthy man, as over the course of his lifetime he managed to leverage his unique position as surveyor into an agrarian windfall of some 50,000 acres of prime, rent-yielding Irish real estate. Like many of the men in Cromwell's army, Petty was compensated for his contribution to the cause with confiscated Irish land. Unlike the other men, however, Petty's work on the Down Survey had offered him an insider's understanding of which lands were the most valuable. Following his work on the survey, Petty would go on to play a chief role in the redistribution of the confiscated lands. That Petty reaped such a reward from his strategic position in Ireland was not overlooked by his Cromwellian contemporaries, and for years he would be hounded by accusations of wrongdoing.[40]

Petty's long-lasting interest in land productivity, therefore, stemmed not only from his intellectual hunt for a commensurate measure of value but also from his economic self-interest. Having catapulted himself into the upper echelon of English society practically overnight, Petty soon found that his annual income was dependent on the market output of the land he owned and the laborers who worked it. As a result, his turn toward the pricing and capitalizing of land and labor meshed nicely with the fact that these had become the central factors of his own revenue stream, which by 1685 was estimated at about £6,700 a year. Moreover, a fairly large tax burden caused Petty's financial interests to bump up against the prickly question of land valuation, as he was often displeased with the ways in which local tax collectors assessed and valued his land. What is more, Petty's seemingly objective and rigorous approach to land valuation allowed him to deflect accusations of fraud.[41]

Yet a closer look at the assumptions that undergird Petty's pricing of land and labor reveals how his political arithmetic was shaped not only by his own narrow economic interests but also by the broader ideology of a burgeoning class of market-oriented landowners. First off, there is Petty's notion that rent rates reflected nature's contribution to the production process. By erasing any hint of exploitation, the argument that landholders earned their wealth from land, not people, conveniently legitimized the social relations among landlord, tenant, and wage-laboring peasant. What is more, Petty's argument for the usefulness of productivity figures buttressed the efforts of improvement-oriented landholders to maximize production by carefully allocating resources and appropriately disciplining the labor force. "Knowing the fertility and Capacity of our Land," Petty wrote early on, "Wee can tell whether it hath not produced its utmost through the labours of the people. Wee can see whether plenty makes them lazey, and remeddy it. In briefe wee can find the best wayes & motives to make as many hands as possible to work, and that to the best Advantage."[42]

After pricing the value of people in "Verbum Sapienti," Petty did not wait long to employ his calculations of human capital for these efficiency-maximizing purposes. In that essay he used his newfound data on the value of people to price a worker's dinnertime and figure out how to reduce that cost, suggesting that if laborers could only "fast of Fryday nights and Dine in one hour and an half, whereas they take two," the wealth of the nation would increase by £250,000 a month. Viewing public health reforms as an additional method of revenue maximization, Petty also priced the plague of 1655 at a "near £7 millions loss to the Kingdom." In his analyses of Ireland, Petty priced Irish unemployment in order to demonstrate to the king how much potential wealth was being wasted: If a human produces 7 pence a day, and "Having shew'd that 340,000 of spare hands are in Ireland," Petty explained, it follows the king was missing out on £2,380,000 a day.[43]

Petty, in short, priced the world in a manner conducive not only to his own private investments but also to those of the English economic elite as a whole. Yet he never framed his acts of social quantification in terms of private wealth or class politics, preferring instead to present his political arithmetic as a public service to both king and country. Petty's political arithmetic, therefore, is a good place to begin to explore the pricing of progress: not only did Petty equate value with price, conflate markets with society, and capitalize human beings and nature, but he universalized his own class interests by couching his calculations in the aggregated, non-distributional, and seemingly apolitical language of "true original gain of the Nation," "annual proceed," or "publick good." This focus on the aggregate or national, however, did not stem solely from Petty's desire to underplay his own class prerogatives. Centuries-long political processes were also at play, in the form of a rising bourgeois fiscal state.[44]

A main engine of modern state formation was the increase in military expenditures. While taxation had always been a crucial component of European societies, until the fifteenth century most of the English Crown's revenue came from its own royal demesne holdings and other feudal tenures and dues. Prolonged military campaigns in the fifteenth and sixteenth centuries, however, compelled English royalty to rely less on their own estates for income and more on a uniform set of customs, property, and excise taxes levied throughout the territory covered by the monarch's political sovereignty and collected by an increasingly specialized administrative bureaucracy. By the 1590s, the English language was reflecting this sweeping structural shift, as people began to refer to England not as a "country," "kingdom," or "realm" but as a "state." No longer merely a lord of lords, the Crown was dissolving feudal relations, forging new bureaucratic forms of political authority, and, in doing so, creating an unprecedented political animal: the modern nation-state.[45]

The novel virtues of market maximization were not lost on England's cash-strapped royals. In the last years of Elizabeth's reign, the English government spent about £300,000 a year. By the 1660s, when Charles II was king and William Petty's political arithmetic was born, the annual budget had quadrupled to £1.2 million. As English rulers became more and more dependent on tax receipts, they realized that an uptick in land and labor's market productivity would lead to a subsequent rise in their revenue. While the tradition-driven, status-quo-seeking paternalism of the Tudors had led earlier English rulers to try to limit enclosure, unregulated markets, and the general encroachment of capitalist relations into everyday life, by the time Charles II reclaimed the throne in 1660 the financial pressures of war had aligned the fiscal interests of the Crown with the economic goals of England's market-oriented elites. Both had come to support the ever-growing expansion of market relations and capital accumulation.[46]

Few intellectual exercises, political treatises, or cultural artifacts reflect the nascent synergy between state and capital better than William Petty's political arithmetic. The immediate political concern behind nearly all of Petty's calculations was fiscal in nature. The main purpose of his groundbreaking corn-as-silver model was to provide the king with a more accurate method of assessing and taxing landed wealth. When Petty first set out to price the value of people in "Verbum Sapienti," his main goal was to demonstrate that political arithmetic could serve as a powerful tool for setting tax rates and managing state revenues. Petty's emphasis on state matters played a crucial role in his revolutionary shift in focus from the singular household to the aggregate nation. While Hartlibian improvers and profit-oriented landholders were coming to price the productivity of land and labor in order to maximize the market produce of their own private holdings, Petty's political arithmetic was doing so on a national scale in order to maximize the public revenue of England.[47]

In Petty's opinion, political arithmetic was crucial to the modern ruler's tax-collecting goals: "Not knowing the Wealth of the people, the Prince knows not what they can bear." Only by meticulously pricing and aggregating the land and labor of the nation, Petty argued, could the king discover the resources he had at his disposal. Once people and nature had been priced and capitalized, Petty could reveal to the king what the English people could bear and how a significant portion of their potential market productivity was lost to the kingdom because of plagues, unemployment, or drawn-out dinners. Political arithmetic was a method not only for measuring existing wealth but for imagining new sources of revenue extraction as well. The purpose of Petty's calculations was not to passively quantify the world but rather to actively regulate it in order to increase the Crown's revenue. The manner in which one counted people greatly influenced the manner in which one then acted upon them, so once Petty had priced people like capitalized investments, it only made sense to try to maximize them as such.[48]

In Petty's mind, the greatest error a king could make was to tax one individual's wealth more than another's. "Now that which angers men most," he warned a king whose father had had his head chopped off only a generation prior, "is to be taxed above their Neighbours." Only by accurately pricing humans and nature, Petty argued, could a ruler impose his taxes equitably. After Petty concluded that labor produced £25 million of a total £40 million in annual national wealth, he declared that it would be only fair for landless peasants to shoulder an equal ratio (in this case five-eighths) of the state's tax burden. The language Petty used in his arguments was that of equality, yet the tax policy he envisioned was regressive. And yet Petty's desire for proportionality in taxation reveals a broader cultural and political development—the increasing need for the English king to legitimize his tax policies not with arguments of feudal hierarchy, customary tradition, or religious authority but rather with the cold, calculating numbers of an incipient bourgeois liberalism.[49]

The English Civil War led to a significant shift in the balance of power between the monarch and a Parliament dominated by a landed yet commercially oriented aristocracy and gentry. Prior to the 1640s, roughly 25 percent of the Crown's revenue was raised by Parliament. After the Stuart Restoration of 1660, that number would stand at roughly 90 percent, and it was Parliament, not King Charles II, that determined the scale and scope of the restored Crown's annual tax revenue. While the English monarch had never been a truly absolutist ruler, following Restoration the powers of the purse swung definitively toward a Parliament filled with market-oriented landholders like William Petty. For the king to receive the revenue he required for war, he would have to go through this ascendant class of landed elites.[50]

What Petty offered the king in his pricing of people and nature, therefore, was a legitimization of taxation that was based on practical reason, human individualism, legal equality, natural rights, and private property—a bundle of principles and ideas that we have come to refer to as "liberalism." In suggesting that taxation be perfectly proportionate to wealth, Petty was relying on the notion that landowners would be far more willing to pay their taxes if they knew that the tax system was based not on the arbitrary whims of an absolute ruler but rather on the rational and predictable notion that each citizen was giving up an equivalent share of wealth. Rather than allocating resources according to fixed classes, prescribed ranks, or aristocratic titles, Petty was envisioning a new society in which the gradations of society were determined by one measure and one measure only—money.[51]

While Petty sometimes clothed his political arithmetic in a commonwealth rhetoric in which money was metaphorically the lifeblood of the "body politic," the dominant theory of society behind his political arithmetic was liberal and individualistic. For Petty, "Publick good" was not some organic whole that equaled more than the sum of its parts. On the contrary, Petty's pricing of land and labor in units that could be aggregated into national income accounts was built entirely on the liberal notion that society was *precisely* the sum of its atomized parts. A rational and just ruler would run the kingdom by first breaking it down to its most basic components—the plot of land that earned 10 pounds a year and the human being who created 7 pence a day. After all, as one of the first mercantilists had put it as early as 1623, "what else makes a Common-Wealth, but the private wealth?"[52]

William Petty did not invent economic quantification or social measurement. Ever since domesticated animals and farm crops were first counted by Sumerian tax collectors on Mesopotamian clay tablets more than 5,000 years ago, the quantification of material life has been a hallmark of human civilization. The earliest example of writing known to date is an act of quantification: "29,086 measures barley 37 months." A quick glance at previous forms of economic measurement in Western history, however, demonstrates how Petty's political arithmetic was nevertheless a radical departure from previous forms of social quantification.[53]

Twenty years after William I conquered England in 1066, he commissioned a massive survey to discover "how many hundreds of hides were in the shire, what land the king himself had, and what stock upon the land; or, what dues he ought to have by the year from the shire." The final product was an enormous statistical survey that later became known as the Domesday Book, for its authority to settle any political dispute. A typical entry, regarding a manor in Wiltshire, read like this:

> Reginald holds RODBOURNE of Miles. Vigot held it [in the time of King Edward] and it paid geld for 5 hides. There is land for 4 ploughs. Of this 2 hides are in demesne. There are 3 villains and 5 bordars and 1 slave with 3 ploughs. There is meadow 6 furlongs long and 2 furlongs broad, and pasture 2 furlongs long and as many broad. It was worth 100s [in the time of King Edward], now 4 pounds.[54]

As the final sentence of this entry indicates, prices existed in medieval England. But in contrast to Petty's political arithmetic, monetary values were just one of several ways (hides, ploughs, furlongs) to evaluate land and were not viewed as the central unit through which social value should be measured. For example, it was the "hide"—not money prices—that were used to calculate the enormously important land tax known as the "geld." Defined as the amount of land needed to support a single household, the hide measured the value of land in a quintessentially feudal manner—according to the number of families it could sustain. "Ploughs" served a similar purpose, privileging need over productivity by gauging not the monied output of land but the number of tools required to work it. The careful counting of villains, bordars, and slaves reveals a hierarchical society of prescribed and fixed positions in which human beings could not be aggregated by means of the commensurable unit of money because they were not understood to have been created equal.[55]

The Domesday Book's marginalization of market prices as a measure of social value or economic progress was not unusual—it had been the norm for most of Western history. The Greeks had looked at market exchange with great suspicion and apprehension. They often viewed merchants as tricksters and thieves. Contractual market transactions (often referred to as "oaths" in antiquity) that put moneymaking before household management, kinship ties, or honor were not lauded for their consensual freedom but rather condemned for their swindling duplicity. The Persian emperor, Herodotus informs us, referred to the Greek market, or agora, as a "place in the center of the city where they assemble and cheat each other with oaths." Aristotle's writings contain similar thoughts regarding the "art of moneymaking," which he viewed as an improper, unnatural, unnecessary, and "justly censured" attempt to transform trade from a means to an end (the end being household management and material comfort) into an end in itself. In Aristotle's mind, the accumulation of money was "wealth of the spurious kind" and no barometer of progress.[56]

Following in the Greeks' footsteps, Roman law often distinguished market prices from the actual value or "just price" (*iustum pretium*) of goods. Basing legal decisions on the doctrine of "enormous loss" (*laesio enormis*), the imperial Roman government did not leave the valuation of land or basic goods to the market for fear of its exploitative practices. This conceptual divide between market price and moral value continued to be central to the medieval scholastic discourse surrounding the just price as well. By the thirteenth century, scholastic thinkers such as Thomas Aquinas were debating "whether a man may lawfully sell a thing for more than it is worth"—precisely the sort of question that becomes obsolete once prices are made synonymous with value. Also viewing markets as a site of potential exploitation and asymmetrical power relations, Aquinas defined a just price as a rate that did not take advantage of either buyer or seller's pressing needs or dire straits. In Petty's political arithmetic, such ethical distinctions ceased to exist, as power was removed from the discussion of market exchange and prices were simply assumed to measure the value of things.[57]

Because they could not be trusted, money prices remained somewhat marginalized measures of value throughout most of Western history. The market was purposely insulated and segregated from everyday life for the very same reason. Throughout antiquity and the Middle Ages, cultural, ritual, or architectural boundaries effectively separated markets from the rest of society. Be it through the construction of "market crosses" (structures used to demarcate the boundaries of market exchange in medieval towns) or the ringing of bells to announce the start of the haggling, markets were culturally confined and physically conscribed by space and time. As a result, they were understood not as abstract processes that permeated every aspect of one's life but rather as specifically delineated places. When you left these marketplaces—and you were sure to know when you did—you left the market along with it.[58]

The distinction between price and value in the quantifying minds of English rulers continued well after the Domesday Book and into the early modern era. By the late fifteenth century, the Tudor rulers could no longer ignore the social dislocation that followed the engrossment and enclosure of open fields and commons. Hoping to stem the tide of enclosure, under Henry the VIII the Parliament passed an act in 1515 demanding that enclosed lands that had been converted to wool-producing pasture in areas of depopulation should be returned to tillage and the abandoned and "decayed" peasant farmhouses be rebuilt. The Crown, however, soon realized that if this act was to have any teeth, it would have to collect data on enclosed lands, engrossed fields, and decaying homesteads. In 1517, one year after Thomas More famously lamented how sheep "devour men," a commission of inquiry was sent out to all but four northern counties in England in order to quantify what the capitalist revolution in the countryside had wrought. Quite fittingly, since these inquiries continued many of the quantification practices of medieval England, they have been referred to as the "Domesday of Inclosures."[59]

Both the Tudors' Domesday of Inclosures and Petty's political arithmetic set out to make sense of the enclosure revolution through measurements based on observation. Yet they could not have been more different. Petty ignored the social disruption brought on by enclosure and focused upon pricing the productivity of nature and people as factors of capitalist production. On the other hand, when the Tudors observed the county of Northamptonshire, they saw not bushels per acre, shillings per ewe, or seven-pence-per-day laborers but rather 14,081 enclosed acres, 345 "houses of husbandry decayed," and 1,405 people "displaced." Here was a statistical vision whose basic unit of measure was not monied productivity but social destruction.[60]

The rise of William Petty's political arithmetic, therefore, marked a sea change in English forms of social quantification. But his emergence serves only as the genesis of the pricing of progress, not its widespread acceptance. While Petty's data were often cited in the late seventeenth century, and an enumeration of the population of England and Wales was even undertaken, such acts of government quantification soon dissipated along with Petty's popularity. A second attempt to hold such an enumeration in the 1750s failed, and England did not institutionalize a national census until 1801. The "social tables" of Gregory King, Petty's finest protégé, were not published until 1802. The first statistical societies did not appear until the early nineteenth century. *The Wealth of Nations,* like most economic discourses of the era, was greatly influenced by Petty's economic theories, but it contained only a few statistics, and there is just a single direct reference to political arithmetic: "I have no great faith in political arithmetic," writes Adam Smith.[61]

Petty's popularity was limited because while he may have imagined English people and nature as an income-generating investment, it was hardly that. Many landholding aristocrats had indeed begun to see their land as a money-yielding asset, but they were still *aristocrats,* with privileges and powers that did not derive from market exchange or capital accumulation. Also, policies such as entail, primogeniture, and the Elizabethan poor laws ensured that the commodification of land and labor remained highly conscribed. In a society where, to borrow a term from Karl Polanyi, the "fictitious commodification" of nature and man had not yet become a fully modern fact, and where the capitalist revolution in the countryside was still embedded within an outer shell of traditionally feudal relations, there was little chance that Petty's radical way of counting the world would be institutionalized quickly. Revolutions of this magnitude do not occur overnight or even over the course of a single century. To make matters worse, Petty's lack of reliable data led to highly inaccurate estimates. The entry on "political arithmetic" in *The Universal Dictionary of Trade and Commerce* from 1744 focuses mostly on such faults, arguing that Petty was seeking to merely flatter the king by convincing him that England was far more powerful than its European rivals. "That this genius was mistaken in all these assertions," the dictionary noted, "we have ground to suspect he rather made his court than spoke his mind."[62]

The best—and most entertaining—piece of evidence proving that Petty's investmentality did not resonate with many eighteenth century Englishmen comes from the incisive and acerbic pen of renowned essayist Jonathan Swift. In a 1727 essay titled "A Modest Proposal for Preventing the Children of Poor People from Being a Burden to Their Parents or Country," Swift provided a biting satire of political arithmetic by revealing the absurdity of pricing people as income-yielding instruments and judging their value only according to their market worth and productivity:

> I am assured by our merchants, that a boy or a girl before twelve years old, is no saleable commodity, and even when they come to this age, they will not yield above three pounds, or three pounds and half a crown at most, on the exchange; which cannot turn to account either to the parents or kingdom, the charge of nutriments and rags having been at least four times that value. . . . I have been assured by a very knowing American of my acquaintance in London, that a young healthy child well nursed, is, at a year old, a most delicious nourishing and wholesome food, whether stewed, roasted, baked, or boiled; and I make no doubt that it will equally serve in a fricasie, or a ragoust. . . . I have already computed the charge of nursing a beggar's child (in which list I reckon all cottagers, labourers and four-fifths of the farmers) to be about two shilling per annum, rags included.[63]

Note that while turning children of the poor into two shillings' worth of fricassee, Swift mentioned "a very knowing American" who seemed to share the author's calculating sprit. There is much truth in any good satire, and this is no exception. By the 1720s, the pricing of progress may not have caught on in England, but it had made its first landing in colonial America. There too, however, it was far from an immediate hit. Nevertheless, when a gifted young man by the name of Alexander Hamilton tried to relight the flame of political arithmetic on the other side of Atlantic in the 1770s, he would use William Petty and his capitalizing calculations as kindling.

TWO

Seeing like a Capitalist

IN THE SUMMER OF 1791, U.S. treasury secretary Alexander Hamilton went hunting for data from which he could create some economic indicators. Preparing to write his soon-to-be famous "Report on Manufactures," Hamilton planned to augment his argument for the government subsidization of American manufacturing by gathering figures that would reveal to the American public the productivity of American "manufactories" in comparison to agriculture. Treating both farming and manufacturing not as callings, crafts, or lifestyles but rather as capital investments, he intended to measure and compare—in units of price—the annual yields of farm and factory. Plugging such standardized units of land and labor into equations of national wealth production, he hoped to prove that agrarian America's stubborn obsession with farming was preventing the nation from maximizing the "revenue of society," which Hamilton defined as "the aggregate value of the annual produce of the land and labor of the country." Half a year later, in the finished report, he made clear what his statistical objective had been that summer:

> The question must still be, whether the surplus, after defraying expences, of a *given capital,* employed in the *purchase* and *improvement* of a piece of land, is greater or less, than that of a like capital employed in the prosecution of a manufactory: or whether the *whole value produced* from a *given capital* and a *given quantity of labour,* employed in one way, be greater or less, than the *whole value produced* from an *equal capital* and an *equal quantity of labour* employed in the other way: or rather, perhaps whether the business of Agriculture or that of Manufactures will yield the greatest product.[1]

In his statistical search for the investment that would "yield the greatest product," Hamilton took advantage of the recently established web of federal tax collectors he had assembled across the nation. According to the much-despised "Whiskey Tax" Hamilton had recently pushed through, treasury officials were supposed to venture from town to town collecting an excise tax on domestically distilled spirits that would go to the funding of the national debt—yet another Hamiltonian innovation. Displaying his usual knack for overstepping official bounds, Hamilton wrote to the tax collectors requesting that while they were scouring the land for whiskey they also collect information on "the manufactures of every kind carried on within the limits of your district." More specifically, Hamilton instructed his men to collect data on "the Quantities periodically made" and "the Prices at which they are sold" and "whether they are carried on by Societies, Companies or Individuals." He then sent a similar letter to a number of leading manufacturers.[2]

To complete his statistical experiment, Hamilton needed to compare the annual revenue of a factory to that of a farm. "It has occurred to me," he wrote in a second letter to the tax collectors and several wealthy farmers, "that if the actual product on cultivated farms of middling quality could be ascertained with tolerable precision, it might afford as good a rule, by which to judge as the nature of things admits of." Enclosed with each letter was a "form with a number of columns," which he asked be distributed to a few local farmers in each district. Like the manufacturing data he had requested, the columns included the "actual quantity in cultivation" as well as the total cash revenue from these goods. "The price," Hamilton felt the need to explain, "ought to express the value of each article on the farm. Perhaps to determine this there is no better rule than to deduct the expense of transportation from the price at the nearest usual market."[3]

As the results began to pour in during the fall of 1791, Hamilton must have soon realized that he had grossly miscalculated the quantitative bent of the denizens of the new republic. In response to Hamilton's inquiries regarding manufacturing data, Silas Condict, an artisan from Morristown, New Jersey, wrote, "I can say that Industry and an attention to Mechanism is gaining Ground, tho' we have no established Companies or Manufactories carried on here," but he could not supply any quantitative information at all. He spoke of the "great many people" employed in the iron business, how the number of sheep was "fast increasing," and how the silk manufacturers had a "sufficient quantity of eggs" and a "considerable stock of worms." Peter Colt, a Hartford businessman who sensed the level of detail Hamilton was expecting, could only apologize. "I am not possessd of sufficient documents on which to ground any details or calculations as to the amount of the products of our different Manufactures or their annual value," he lamented in his letter. Boston merchant Nathaniel Gorham did not supply Hamilton with any quantitative data either, instead choosing to note that household manufacturing had doubled in the past generation and that a visitor to any New England home would find "cloth almost wholly made by [the family] themselves."[4]

To be sure, not every response was a disappointment. George Cabot, a prominent stockholder in the Beverly Cotton Manufactory, supplied Hamilton with impressive and detailed data on the annual costs and revenue of his business. However, such responses came from relatively large (and rare) manufactories. Another such reply came from O. Burr & Company, a hat-making factory in Danbury, Connecticut, that employed "seven journeymen and ten Apprentices." The divide between factories and artisanal or domestic production is a recurring theme in the responses Hamilton received. When speaking of proprietary, small-scale artisans, tax collector Chauncey Whittlesey of Middletown, Connecticut, noted that the "annual produce is not easy to determine" and "the subject as not to admit of very exact calculations." Yet when he turned his attention to the linen manufactory in town that had invested $250 in capital, Whittlesey was able to give fairly precise details regarding its revenue and produce. As another Connecticut revenue inspector who separated factories from small workshops aptly put it, "We have No regular Established Factories in this Town and therefore no pecuniary Incouragements. Our Domestick Are Considerable but to what amount is very doubtfull."[5]

Hamilton did not fare much better with the yeoman farmers of the mid-Atlantic states. A Bucks County, Pennsylvania, farmer replied that the best he could do was venture some rough estimates due to "the novelty of the subject—and never having kept any regular account of the annual produce of my lands—nor know any person to whom I could apply for such minute information." A tax surveyor in Pittsburgh responded that "in a new Country like this where farming is not yet reduced to system, it is difficult to form an Estimate as you wish." A Maryland farmer replied that his neighbors received Hamilton's forms with "hearty intentions," but they soon discovered "the impossibility of fulfilling their design & promise, for they kept no minutes, &

their attention to the bulk of the articles . . . had been trifling." The farmer did suggest that perhaps "if the value of things, especially of the Land, can be omitted, the quantities would be more readily . . . obtained."[6]

Timothy Pickering, a good friend of Hamilton's and a prolific land speculator, became most frustrated in his attempt to glean data from the other farmers in Pennsylvania. First off, Pickering complained, he could not calculate the true value of certain farms because "the residue of the country is without inclosures, where the cattle range at large and where . . . the people cut wood for timber & fuel for discretion without regarding their own lines of property." After sending Hamilton figures from only a single farm, Pickering concluded his letter by remarking, "It will be impossible to ascertain the requisite facts with precision: For I doubt whither one American farmer in a thousand has determined by actual admeasurement, the sizes of his fields and their produce."[7]

If Pickering was right, then one of those few farmers was Richard Peters, the president of the Philadelphia Society for the Promotion of Agriculture. Capitalizing even his cows by calculating that they annually produced £60 worth of butter, calves, and cheese, Peters sent in a detailed analysis of his farm's costs and revenues in which he concluded, after discounting the opportunity costs of his cows and other capital investments, that farming was "but a bad trade when Capital is calculated upon." As with the factories' data, however, Peters's response was exceptional, not representative.[8]

Letters from the South read much like those from the North, although Hamilton evidently did not send his agricultural form to any large-scale tobacco or rice planters. Silvanus Walker from western South Carolina noted only that "there is no manufactories carried on in the interior parts of this state, only in private families, and they in general manufactor as much as they commonly wear." Thomas Newton of Norfolk and Charles Yancey of Louisa County, Virginia, supplied no quantitative information. Virginia supervisor of revenue Edward Carrington did supply Hamilton with two detailed surveys of domestic manufacturing conducted by his regional inspectors, but the ambitious Carrington had pressed his subordinates for these estimates and it was he, not the households, who calculated and aggregated the monetary values.[9]

For Hamilton, these mostly disappointing results were only half the problem. His pursuit of income statistics had been not only a bold act of social quantification but also an unprecedented effort at state-building, an attempt to construct a centralized federal bureaucracy capable of monitoring the economic productivity of the American people. While largely unhelpful, at least the farmers and artisans who responded to Hamilton's queries exhibited an amicable desire to assist the secretary of the treasury. According to the revenue men, the same could not be said of all Americans. Surveyors complained that many people were highly uncooperative and "averse" to supplying information, likely fearing further taxes or an assault on self-rule. The surveyors further noted that quite a number of individual Americans acted as if they were "enemies of the government" and "got into such a spirit of Jealousy that they suspect some design unfavorable to them in every thing that is attempted of a public nature."[10] Later the Whiskey Rebellion would leave some of these same tax collectors tarred and feathered.

Hamilton's failed efforts at collecting the statistical data he wished for hinted at the general weakness of the government apparatus he had constructed and the dubious social legitimacy of the nascent federal state that commanded it. Sure enough, President Thomas Jefferson and the Democratic-Republican Party repealed the excise tax on whiskey in 1801, and any hope of using treasury officials for future data-gathering mission was quashed.[11]

Since Hamilton was unable to collect the price data he had wished for, his "Report on Manufactures" remained bereft of all statistical indicators. Few today even know that he had intended to include a statistical appendix in his famous report. His venture into the realm of political arithmetic and government-run economic data collection had not succeeded. Neither had his attempt to transform the United States into an industrial power: The manufacturing report was the only one of Hamilton's four reports that Congress did not rush to implement.[12]

Yet judging from Hamilton's own writings, it appears that he never put much thought into why his foray into political arithmetic had been so unsuccessful, nor did he ever link his inability to price American progress with his failure to bring large-scale manufacturing to the United States. While Hamilton acknowledged that the income statistics he needed to prove his case that factories were a better investment than farms required "numerous and complicated details" and an "accurate knowledge of the objects to be compared," he believed that his experiment in social quantification simply demanded "more previous inquiry and investigation than there has been hitherto either leisure or opportunity to accomplish."[13]

Hamilton was mistaken. He had failed in his attempt to bring both political arithmetic and industrial revolution to American shores because the manner in which he viewed and quantified the world did not mesh with the ideological principles upon which the United States had been founded, nor did they correspond with the political economy of the early Republic. In treating land and labor as factors of capitalist production and farms and factories as capitalized investments, Hamilton's investmentality ignored the fact that the basic social unit and ideological anchor of American society was the property-owning patriarchal household and not, as in eighteenth-century England, the troika of rent-seeking landlord, profit-oriented capitalist, and wage-earning laborer. In proposing that the worthiness of agriculture and industry should be measured by their priced output and capitalized efficiency, Hamilton assumed that the American people shared his belief that market productivity trumped other social considerations such as proprietary independence, material competence, patriarchal hierarchy, or white power. Most did not. In short, in believing that most Americans had the ability, inclination, and opportunity to price and aggregate their own household's human and landed productivity, Hamilton revealed how little he understood the enormous social, economic, and ideological chasm that had emerged between the burgeoning American Republic he had helped create and the capitalist British Empire he had experienced as an adolescent in the Caribbean and read about in his beloved books of political arithmetic.

———◆———

The "Report on Manufactures" paraphrased whole passages from Adam Smith's *The Wealth of Nations,* a book Hamilton had recently received, along with many other British economic treaties, from his sister-in-law in England. There is little doubt that Hamilton's notion of national wealth as "the aggregate value of the annual produce of the land and labour" was taken directly from Smith, who in numerous places in his magnum opus defined the "revenue" or wealth of a nation as "equal to the exchangeable value of the whole annual produce of its industry" or "the annual produce of the land and labour of the country." Since Hamilton made a significant effort in his report to discredit Smith's disdain for government intervention, the sharp ideological divide between the two men has often been underscored. Yet while Hamilton and Smith differed on how one should go about accumulating national wealth, they nevertheless were in agreement regarding what the ultimate goal of a nation should be: to squeeze the maximum amount of commodified output, measured in market price, out of its land and labor.[14]

Hamilton cited Smith's definition of wealth not because it was a novel contribution to economic theory but rather because it had become the conventional wisdom of eighteenth-century British political economy. Despite the long-standing liberal tendency to try to sever the ties between laissez-faire and earlier economic theory in England, Smith's portrayal of national wealth as the commodified stream that flowed out of the "fund" of labor and land was taken from the very English thinkers he mocked as mercantilist, chief among them William Petty. Hamilton likely recognized this intellectual genealogy, as he had become well acquainted with Petty's political arithmetic by the time he sat down to write his "Report on Manufactures" in 1791—an intellectual journey that began on the battlefields of the American Revolution.[15]

Among Hamilton's voluminous papers is a truly remarkable historical source: the "Pay Book of the State Company of Artillery Commanded by Alexander Hamilton." Open the pay book that the young Captain Hamilton carried with him in 1777 and it initially reads precisely as one would expect, containing the detailed accounts of Hamilton's artillery company. Yet after a few pages the accounts stop, and suddenly the pay book is filled with pages of economic statistics, divided geographically by nation. "The Dutch," Hamilton scribbles, "were computed by Sir Walter Raleigh to have 3000 ships & fifty thousand seamen employed in the herring fishery"; "the Kingdom of Bohemia," Hamilton notes, has "revenues [that] are computed at 12 or 14,000,000 [for] one year." Devoting the most space to England, Hamilton's notes include the number of men employed in the "coal trade," "hardware manufacturers," and "woolen manufactories," while adding that the wool industry's "consumption at home amounts to a million sterling per year."[16]

Where did these economic figures come from? Hamilton's cadre of biographers solved this puzzle long ago: when Hamilton headed out to war he took with him not only the pay book but also Malachy Postlethwayt's mammoth two-volume *Universal Dictionary of Trade and Commerce,* written in 1757, the premier encyclopedia of economic and business knowledge of the era. Around the time British ships off the coast of Manhattan started to bombard his company, Hamilton was busily jotting down economic statistics into his pay book. The fact that Hamilton must have lugged those enormous books with him from camp to camp suggests that the young man took such exercises in economic quantification very seriously.[17]

Postlethwayt first made a name for himself in England as a pamphleteer in support of First Lord of the Treasury Robert Walpole and the Royal African Company, a joint-stock company that yielded profits to English investors by transporting tens of thousands of slaves from Africa to the Americas. While Postlethwayt would go on to denounce slavery later in life, in the 1740s he was, as one historian has noted, "the chief propagandist" for the subsidizing of the trade in enslaved bodies. Postlethwayt has even been credited with coming up with the term "triangular trade" to describe the flows of slaves from Africa to the Americas, agricultural commodities from the Americas to England, and manufactured goods from England to Africa to purchase more slaves. His greatest claim to fame, however, was *The Universal Dictionary of Trade and Commerce*—parts of which were translated from a work written in French by Jacques Savary, the inspector general of manufactures to the French king—which served many in England as the master synthesis of eighteenth-century business accounting practices, economic thought, and political arithmetic.[18]

Postlethwayt's deep involvement in the slave trade led him to imagine human beings as human capital. In one pamphlet from 1746, Postlethwayt lobbied for government support of the Royal African Company by claiming that African slaves were an "inexhaustible fund of wealth." Referring to enslaved Africans as "an annuity" in a second pamphlet, he cited an assertion by political arithmetician and Petty enthusiast Charles Davenant that a slave produced £16 of income per year and then estimated that "the annual Gain of the Nation by *Negroe Labour* will fall little short of Three Million *per Annum*."[19]

In his dictionary published a decade later, Postlethwayt's investmentality spread from Africa and the Caribbean to the English mainland, as he frequently referred to human beings and nature as income bearing assets. In his entry for "people," he gushed how "the bodies of men are, without a doubt, the most valuable treasure of a country." In his entry for "landed interests," he presented calculations proving that each English laborer who produced woolen goods for the Turkish market generated £6 a year of income for English landowners. For his entry on "leases," Postlethwayt explained to landowners how best to capitalize their land, and thus maximize their rental income, through an array of complex years-of-purchase calculations. In his entries for "ledger" and "mercantile accounting" he showed how double-entry bookkeeping could be used to measure a business's profit and loss. Even in his entry on "saffron," Postlethwayt calculated that an acre of spice would earn £5 4s. yearly.[20]

Postlethwayt cites William Petty often, and Petty's work is clearly one of the theoretical pillars of the dictionary. For his entries on "revenue," "labor," and "landed interest," Postlethwayt espouses Petty's view of nature and people as factors of capitalist production whose moneymaking capabilities should be carefully measured. Quoting extensively from English mathematician John Arbuthnot's work in his entry for "mathematics," Postlethwayt argues that arithmetic is "the great instrument of private commerce" and that in its form of double-entry bookkeeping "ought to be, kept the public accounts of the nation." Postlethwayt made sure to stress "not only the accounts of the public revenue in all its branches, but those likewise that regard the whole state of a commonwealth, as to the number, fructification of its people, increase of stock, improvement of lands and manufacture." Quoting Davenant, he summarized the main principles of Petty's national income accounting and pricing of everyday life in his entry for "political arithmetic," celebrating this calculative technology's ability to determine what "the yearly income may be from land, and what from mines, houses, and homesteads, rivers, lakes, meers, ponds, and what from trade, labour, industry, arts, and sciences."[21]

As he would later note in a 1782 letter, Hamilton viewed Postlethwayt's book as a rich source of calculations by "the ablest masters of Political Arithmetic." He would return to it many times over his lifetime. After carefully copying a potpourri of Postlethwayt's data in his 1777 pay book, Colonel Hamilton neatly rehashed the national income calculations that William Petty had first performed a century prior:

> Out of 49.000.000 £ expended and consumed by our people at home, not more than four millions are of foreign commodities. There remain therefore 45.000.000 £ for an annual expense and consumption in home product and manufactures. Of these the landowner can expend and consume no more than his rents, and they are computed at no more than 14.000.000 of £. Sterling; therefore above two parts in three in home product and manufactures are expended and consumed by all other denominations of our people.[22]

This is one of the longest passages in the pay book, and it is a paraphrasing of Postlethwayt's entry on "political arithmetic." Pricing the annual "home product" of the nation according to the amount of commodities consumed and rent payments received, the young Hamilton was imbibing Petty's proto-GDP figures of national income with relish. Hamilton went on to note how "it is agreed by the best authors of Political Arithmetic that the rents of lands houses and mines are not more than 3/8 of the annual expenses of the nation, Davenant calculates them at 14 Millions Sterling." While Postlethwayt cites Davenant, this three-eighths was in fact the ratio first calculated by Petty. The following line of the pay book directly makes the connection with Petty's national income accounting and pricing of everyday life: "Sir William Petty," Hamilton jots down, "supposes every person in England upon an average spends £7 a head which supposing the nation to be 7 million makes the whole expense & consumption 49 Millions."[23]

There are more than 1,000 pages in Postlethwayt's encyclopedia. Hamilton's pay book, on the other hand, includes only a few dozen pages of scrawled notes. Since Hamilton likely recorded the bits that interested him most, it is apparent that he had become especially intrigued by the methods whereby Petty and his disciples had quantified England into a priced stream of revenue. Hamilton's failed statistical endeavor a decade later, therefore, was no whimsical, spur-of-the-moment exercise in social quantification but a clear and conscious attempt to import English political arithmetic and the pricing of progress to the United States.[24]

Hamilton's report from 1791 did not read like most American political pamphlets of the time. Framed not in the republican language of British Commonwealth writers John Trenchand and Thomas Gordon but rather in the economic vernacular of Petty and Postlethwayt, Hamilton does not rail against "luxury," yearn for "virtue," or exhibit distress at "corruption"—the common tropes of revolutionary America propaganda. Instead, Hamilton used terms such as "ordinary profit," "net surplus," "stock or capital of the farmer," and "rent for the landlord." While the unique circumstances of colonial America pushed many of its residents toward the classical republicanism and civic humanism of the English "country" party, Hamilton preferred citing the pamphleteer of Walpole's rival "court" party.[25]

Hamilton's political inclinations do not, however, challenge the claims of those who have argued for the centrality of republicanism in colonial American life, for one reason: Hamilton did not hail from colonial America. The widely heralded father of American finance, manufacturing, and capitalism was born and raised not on a Virginia plantation, in a New York merchant house, or on a Massachusetts farm but rather on a Caribbean island where 93 percent of the inhabitants were enslaved Africans producing sugar for the world and profits for European landlords. Alexander Hamilton's path to the pricing of progress, much like Malachy Postlethwayt's, was paved by the Atlantic slave trade.[26]

In England, Petty could quantify peasants as individual units of income-generating wealth only after enclosure had torn them from their land and from the traditions, relations, and obligations of feudal society. Caribbean sugar slavery shaped Hamilton's investmentality in similar ways, although in this instance there were not only conquered lands at work but confiscated bodies as well. African slaves were relatively easy to abstract, price, and capitalize because they had been, quite literally, ripped from the endless webs of social relationships that had constituted their previous social existence.[27]

Born on the British island of Nevis but raised mostly on the Danish island of St. Croix, a young and restless Hamilton felt he was living in a peripheral colony of a second-rate European power. In fact, however, he was growing up at one of the key nexuses of a burgeoning British capitalism. A neutral port ideal for trade, with its leading newspaper in English and a large majority of its planters and merchants of Anglo-Saxon descent, St. Croix was very much a part of the British West Indies. And like the British Caribbean, St. Croix was as central a site of eighteenth-century market expansion, capital accumulation, and industrial revolution as the financial markets of London, the ports of Liverpool, or the textile mills of Manchester.[28]

The story of St. Croix is the story of sugar, and during Hamilton's childhood 80 percent of the island's labor force was devoted to sugar production. The cultivation of sugar cane was labor and capital intensive and benefited greatly from economies of scale. As a result, sugar cane could not be grown on family farms. It required large, consolidated plantations to be profitable and a significant outlay of initial fixed capital. In the St. Croix of Hamilton's day, 65 percent of plantations had at least fifty slaves. These large plantations needed a good deal of capital, and London financiers were more than willing to oblige by supplying a steady dose of mortgages to the West Indies. In 1773, for instance, British capitalists invested no less than £37 million in Caribbean colonies, a majority of which flowed to sugar plantations.[29]

With their plantations financed by bankers, owned in large part by absentee landlords, inhabited almost entirely by commodified slaves, and frequently run by business-oriented attorneys or agents who had a rentier's eye toward profit maximization, St. Croix and similar Caribbean societies never developed into the full-fledged settler communities of colonial America. Indeed, Hamilton was raised on a giant capitalized investment. The island itself, in fact, had been purchased by the Danes from the French West Indies Company in 1733.[30]

Living on an island-turned-investment was all Hamilton knew growing up—and it showed. Most historians who have studied Hamilton's financial and industrial plans have downplayed his Caribbean roots, if not ignored them altogether. They usually explain his all-encompassing vision for American economic development by either crediting the influence of European thinkers or turning to the ahistorical argument that he was simply a farsighted genius. In this well-worn narrative, which has recently reached Broadway, the Caribbean serves merely as a prop to emphasize Hamilton's traumatic rags-to-riches journey and anti-slavery sentiment.[31]

Hamilton certainly was influenced by European economic thought, was no fan of slavery, and was unusually intelligent. Nevertheless, judging by the clear affinities between the capitalized society young Alexander Hamilton experienced as an adolescent and the investmentality he would later subscribe to as a young adult, the impact of his Caribbean upbringing appears to have run deeper than previously thought. Only when placing Hamilton in the context of Atlantic slavery can one begin to fully grasp the ideological assumptions that shaped his actions as the architect of American capitalism as well as his foray into political arithmetic and the pricing of American progress.

At some point in the late 1760s a teenage Hamilton went to work as a clerk for the mercantile firm of Nicholas Cruger and David Beekman, both members of prominent New York merchant families, in the port town of Christiansted, where he lived. In 1771 Hamilton was left in charge of the firm's importing and exporting business for five months while Cruger returned home. Trying to bring order to a whirlwind of market transactions,

Hamilton spent his days reading price currents, copying accounts, and haggling over the price of imported butter, flour, and mules.[32]

Unlike colonial America or even England, extreme monoculture islands such as St. Croix were dependent on markets in a manner unparalleled in world history. While less than 20 percent of the output of European agriculture during the seventeenth and eighteenth centuries went to the market, on Caribbean sugar plantations that figure stood at around 80 percent. In a society in which not only luxuries but also basic necessities came not from local households but from boat bottoms, Hamilton stood at the vanguard of an unprecedented commodification of everyday life. Small wonder, then, that a few years later Hamilton would be attracted to Petty's national income accounting, which assumed that markets were synonymous with society and all forms of value must take commodity form.[33]

Butter, flour, and mules weren't the only thing Hamilton and his employers were pricing, marketing, and selling. As the auction advertisements in the *Royal Danish American Gazette* show, Cruger and Beekman's firm was a central node in the Caribbean slave trade. On January 26, 1771, for example, Cruger advertised an auction of 300 slaves. Such transactions were not atypical. Eighty-five percent of the 60,000 slaves brought to St. Croix between 1747 and 1803 passed through Christiansted, and slave auctions were commonplace events in the compound of the Danish Slave Trading Company or the private yards of importers such as Nicholas Cruger. As Cruger's clerk, Hamilton witnessed and recorded the auction prices of this human chattel. After 250 slaves arrived from Africa, Hamilton wrote (Cruger may have been dictating) that the slaves looked "sickly and thin." Without missing a beat, however, he noted that at auction "they average about 30 [pounds]." A second letter in Hamilton's handwriting, although again it is not clear if these are his words, asks to have "two or three poor boys . . . bound in the most reasonable manner . . . to put on plantation."[34]

Later in life, Hamilton did not support slavery—although he did not do much to fight it either. But that does not mean slavery did not change him. When Hamilton first came across Petty's radical pricing of life and capitalization of human bodies in the pages of Postlethwayt's dictionary, he probably was not shocked, offended, or perplexed. He had priced people before.[35]

The sugar plantations on St. Croix were not only massive farms but giant factories. Overseers and slave drivers developed highly disciplined and unprecedentedly brutal systems of synchronized gang labor in order to ensure that the trenches for planting sugar cane were dug with maximum productivity and speed. Since ripe cane had to be ground soon after it was cut, there was little time for rest once it had been harvested. To process sugar, according to one contemporary Barbados planter, was "to live in a perpetual Noise and Hurry . . . the climate is so hot, and the labor so constant, that the Servants [slaves] night and day stand in great Boyling Houses, where there are Six or Seven large Coppers or Furnaces kept perpetually Boyling." Laboring by the light of a blaze that had to be kept up throughout the night, slaves often worked, according to Sidney Mintz, in shifts "lasting all day and part of the night, or the whole of every second or third night." In the grinding mills, hatchets were kept at close hand in case they were needed to sever the arms of half-asleep slaves who might doze off and get their limbs caught in the rollers.[36]

Someone as involved in the sugar trade and as observant as Hamilton—he described in great detail the destruction wrought by an island hurricane when he was only seventeen—must have witnessed the budding industrial revolution taking place on a Caribbean island that was only 82 square miles. As noted, Hamilton lived in the town of Christiansted, but plantations were not segregated from the port city. One of the island's largest and most productive sugar plantations, La Grande Princesse, was adjacent to Christiansted and included 726 acres and 379 slaves in 1792. It was common practice for Grande Princesse slaves to walk to town every evening in hopes of selling some fodder. Hamilton never had to work an industrial night shift, but he was constantly surrounded by those who did.[37]

Two decades later, while making his case for large-scale industrialization in the United States, Hamilton's report argued for factories in part because "labor employed in agriculture is in a great measure periodical and occasional, depending on the seasons, liable to various and long intermissions; while that occupied in manufactures is constant and regular, extending through the year, embracing in some instances, night as well as day." It has long been assumed that the Anglophile Hamilton was referring to English textile manufactories in this passage. Yet, judging by the 24/7 nature of slave plantations, it is just as likely that Hamilton's dream of nonstop production was inspired by events far closer to his childhood home.[38]

———— ◆ ————

Hamilton's 1791 inquiry was not the first American attempt to value American farms in monetary flows, as if they were capitalized investments. That honor belongs to early eighteenth-century planters in the South Carolina low country, a fact that further proves the strong link between Caribbean-style slavery and the investmentality required to price progress. Unlike tobacco planters in the Chesapeake region, these South Carolina planters grew rice. Due to the high costs of irrigation, rice cultivation required an economy of scale that, much like sugar production, led to the emergence of a few extremely wealthy planters who oversaw extensive plantations with a large number of slaves. It has been estimated, in fact, that on the colonial rice plantations along the South Carolina coast, the percentage of those enslaved often reached a St. Croix–like 90 percent. What is more, the South Carolina coast developed a distinct West Indies feel due to the fact that many of the planters immigrated to there not from England but from the Caribbean. Like their future fellow Caribbean immigrant Alexander Hamilton, they had been at the center of global British capitalism and were used to putting price tags on people, places, and things.[39]

In a 1710 pamphlet intended for English investors on "the manner and necessary charges of settling a PLANTATION, and the *Annual Profit* it will produce," South Carolinian Thomas Nairne displayed an investmentality that was absent from most of colonial America. At first the author's descriptions of South Carolina were similar to descriptions of Virginia, New England, and the middle colonies. Calculating the costs of "living comfortably" on a small family farm, the author noted how a 200-acre farm with two slaves could be had for £150. The author did not detail the annual revenue of such a farm, noting only that it would allow for a life of "tolerable Decency."[40]

When Nairne turned to low country rice plantations, however, his narrative changed abruptly. He began by estimating the initial capital investment required for a 30-slave, 1,000-acre farm at £1,500. He then went on to calculate that such a plantation could yield an income of £337 worth of rice per year. The author's business-savvy audience in England probably recognized on its own that South Carolina land yielded an impressive 20 percent annual return on capital, since it took but five years to pay back the initial investment. Nevertheless, the author spelled it out anyway, reminding his readers that "for the sum of £1000 laid out in *England* at 20 years purchase, will buy but £50 a year and here [£1500] settles £337."[41]

Nairne was treating plantations not as family farms but capital investments, and he was only getting started. In the next few pages he delved into a series of elaborate calculations to prove that it would be worthwhile for Carolina's lord proprietors to pay for the transfer of 100 men and 400 slaves to the region. His argument centered on the annual income of bodies. "The lowest computation usually made," the author explained, "is that each labouring Person here does, one with another, add £5 yearly to the Wealth of Great Britain." Aggregating this statistic in a speculative manner much like Petty's loss-to-the-kingdom figures, Nairne declared that natural multiplication would soon lead to annual revenues of no less than £36,000, with quitrents alone worth £1,209. Tellingly, Nairne's calculations priced not only slaves but planters as well.[42]

Within the slavery-fueled Atlantic network of London mortgage investors, South Carolina planters, Caribbean merchants, and slave trade pamphleteers, these kinds of capitalist calculations were becoming routine ways to gauge the viability of a slave-based plantation society. In yet another pamphlet from colonial South Carolina, titled *Profitable Advice for Rich and Poor,* South Carolina planter John Norris sought to prove the profitability of plantation slavery in his colony. "When they are imploy'd chiefly on planting rice," Norris explained, "a Slaves Years work may be worth [to] the Master 25 or 30 pounds." Using the same years-of-purchase logic as other early modern capitalists, Norris noted that "a Man's Slave will, by his Labour, pay for his first Cost in about Four Years at most." Judging by the fact that these planters were offering estimates not only of the market price of slaves but also of the annual income they would produce, Hamilton might have fared far better in his attempt to capitalize American agriculture had he sent his tables to the rice planters of South Carolina.[43]

A final example from South Carolina further demonstrates the connections among the pricing of progress, investmentality, Atlantic slavery, and British colonialism. James Glen arrived in South Carolina in 1743 to serve as governor. He would stay until 1756, when he would return to

Scotland. During his reign as governor, Glen produced the most cutting-edge political arithmetic of eighteenth-century colonial America. But he did not generate these data in a vacuum. Rather, he was constantly harried by the British Board of Trade and the lords commissioners for trade and plantations to provide market data that could value the productivity of the colony as an investment. For those in the British imperial core, this was nothing new. In 1720 the lords commissioners had already begun to send queries to the New World asking for information on the "annual produce of the commodities of the province." In 1739, among requests for land prices and rent revenues, they asked for a biannual report "of what number negroes . . . and at what rates sold."[44]

Yet in James Glen the lords proprietors finally had a man on the other side of the Atlantic who saw—and quantified—the world in the same manner they did. In the 1740s, Glen sent back to Great Britain not only a great deal of rice and indigo but also a steady stream of statistics. "The very freight of our produce," he noted in one letter, "brings in a profit of about one hundred thousand pounds sterling a year to the mother country." In other letters, he dutifully priced and aggregated all the exports from South Carolina. This included not only the major staple, rice, but also everyday goods such as walnuts, bacon, and turpentine. Glen's most impressive act of political arithmetic, however, came in 1751. After being asked by the lords commissioners to estimate "the value of South Carolina," Glen responded by generating the first national income accounts in American history. Likely mimicking the "social tables" of William Petty and Gregory King and their notion that market production could be gauged by measuring market consumption, Glen estimated the annual flow of income the colony generated by dividing its population into four classes, from rich to poor. Estimating that 5,000 inhabitants spent 2 shillings a day, 5,000 spent 1 shilling a day, 10,000 spent 6 pence per day, and 5,000 lived on a "bare subsistence," he priced the "value" of South Carolina at £40,000 of aggregated annual income.[45]

Glen's own experiences as a rent-seeking landowner in Scotland and a slave-owning rice planter in South Carolina shaped his investmentality. After returning to Scotland in the 1750s, Glen continued to oversee his plantation from afar by keeping up a frequent correspondence with his brother-in-law, John Drayton, who managed his colonial business affairs. This correspondence reveals Glen to be a shrewd businessman who collected the same kind of crop and income accounts for his own plantation that he had generated in his government reports.[46]

Glen's personal papers also show how he treated both land and labor like income-generating investments. In 1773, only a few years before his death, an aged Glen wrote up a summary of his annual income flows. Like any British elite, he began with his lands, noting that his estates yielded a revenue of £600 per year. He then moved on to his other financial assets, such as the annuity he was paid by a certain Mr. Bullock (£210) and the interest he was owed on loans given to, among others, John Drayton (£178). Under these income-generating assets, Glen added that "my slaves used to bring in 200 pounds per annum, but by death and desertion and by growing old they have not of late years provided one hundred." In his ledger he estimated that they currently yielded him £50 a year. Here, then, we see how Glen's assessment of South Carolina's "value" according to the income-generating abilities of land and labor was an application of his own capitalist mind-set as rentier, creditor, and planter. The calculations Glen the businessman made for his own account were very much like those Glen the governor generated for the colony as a whole.[47]

———————

In his letters to John Drayton, James Glen comes across as a man who treated familial debts as interest-bearing investments. Insisting that his brother-in-law begin to pay interest on the debts owed to him, Glen justified this demand by noting, "God knows it was for money that I had borrowed to serve your concerns, for which I was paying interest out of my own pocket." Glen's treatment of debt as interest-bearing credit would have been deemed unsavory by most Americans of the era, who did not charge their fellow farmers or planters—let alone family members—interest on their borrowing. It was not, however, something that Alexander Hamilton likely would have opposed.[48]

By the time Hamilton sent out his statistical questionnaires about labor and land as priced inputs of capital yields in 1791, he had taken part not only in the extreme investment society of the Danish West Indies but also, after his move to New York City, the nascent rise of American banking. As Hamilton penned his "Report on Manufactures," the United States was at the dawn of a "bancomania" that would see the number of banks in the country balloon from 6 in 1791 to 246 in 1816. As usual, Hamilton was ahead of the curve: in 1784, he was the driving force behind the founding of the Bank of New York, only the second bank in the United States and the first in New York City. By the summer of 1791, Hamilton had pushed his plan for a national bank through Congress and had become the undisputed architect of American finance. Constructing a novel and revolutionary system of finance and moneymaking practically from nothing, Hamilton had gone from living in a society where 90 percent of its inhabitants had been turned into capital to the very banking wizard who created capital.[49]

There were no banks in colonial America. That is, there were no privately owned, profit-oriented, joint-stock financial institutions that sought to earn a return on capital for their shareholders by lending out money to the American people and their business enterprises. Dominated by individual merchants and their kinship connections, commercial credit in colonial America was a limited and informal affair, as even the largest merchants dealt mostly in short-term debts (usually of thirty to ninety days' duration) that had a very specific purpose tied to the final delivery of particular mercantile goods. The absence of institutionalized, profit-seeking banks meant that when colonial Americans sought to inject money into their society, they turned to the state. This usually occurred in two ways. One option was for colonies to recompense residents who had provided services to the state with fiat paper money that could also be used for tax payments. A second popular option had the colonies lend out paper money in the form of low-interest mortgages from government-run land banks, known as "loan offices," which accepted the mortgaged land as collateral. The interest on these land loans was used to fund government services—an effectively nationalized financial system that allowed for a remarkably low tax burden in colonial America.[50]

While the issuance of colonial cash varied greatly from state to state, these government-run money-issuing systems shared one basic characteristic: unlike private banks, they were driven not by the desire to turn money into even more money but rather by the notion that money should facilitate the payment of debts and the exchange of useful goods in order to sustain the livelihood and autonomy of commodity-producing farmers, planters, and artisans. As the leading expert on early American banking has noted, Americans of that era believed that "money in this sense is not meant to stimulate economic activity" but rather to limit itself "to the needs of trade and legal payment." The purpose of money, in short, was solely to serve as a medium of value and infrastructure of exchange that would allow petty commodity producers to sell their surpluses, purchase consumer goods, and pay their taxes.[51]

Hamilton viewed money in a very different light. He belittled this colonial American approach to cash, arguing that when money was "employed merely as an instrument of exchange," it was "dead stock." According to Hamilton, only when deposited in banks did money "acquire life, or, in other words, an active and productive quality." By transforming otherwise dormant savings into credit lent out to active, profit-seeking entrepreneurs, Hamilton believed that private banks were by far the most "productive" moneymakers, enlarging "the mass of industrious and commercial enterprise" and serving as "the nurseries of national wealth." Ensuring that money would never rest, banks had the unique ability to transform money from a passive medium of exchange into capital, or as Hamilton referred to it, "*active* wealth."[52]

Hamilton's national bank was so radical, so controversial, and so bold that its most revolutionary aspects often get lost in the historiographical shuffle about monopoly privileges and constitutional legitimacy. First and foremost, Hamilton's Bank of the United States privatized the making of money, transforming it from a public service (or even government infrastructure) controlled by colonial legislatures into a private, profit-yielding enterprise directed by capitalists. Hamilton was not only aware of this crucial point but proud of it, and he addressed it explicitly: "To attach full confidence to an institution of this nature," he argued, "it appears to be an essential ingredient in its structure, that it shall be under a private and not a public Direction, under the guidance of individual interest, not of public policy."[53]

Most Americans of the era conceived of money from the point of view of an independent producer who wished to even-handedly exchange the fruits of his or her labor with that of other petty producers. In contrast, Hamilton's approach was from the point of view of a capitalist investor who had placed his money in a profit-oriented institution precisely so that it could be lent out to someone who would return more than had been initially invested. Whereas colonial Americans stressed the virtue of equivalence, Hamilton emphasized the glory of growth.

Associating monetized growth and capital accumulation with national progress led Hamilton to critique the notion that the dominant economic unit in the early United States should be the household of landowning farmers. Since family farms did not produce exclusively for the market or for profit, Hamilton complained, their ongoing westward expansion "diminishes or obstructs active wealth of the country" since it "not only draw[s] off a part of the circulating money and places it in a more passive state, but it diverts into its own channels a portion of that species of labor and industry which would otherwise be employed in furnishing materials for foreign trade."[54]

According to Hamilton, this yeoman economic policy was misguided because it was not maximizing returns on capital. Small wonder, then, that when Hamilton sought out a statistical indicator to measure the worthiness of farms versus factories, he adopted a mode of investmentality in which "the business[es] of agriculture and manufacturing" were compared and evaluated as a series of alternative opportunities for capital investment. Like a bank manager mulling over where he should lend out his clients' capital, Hamilton had concluded that the debate over the future of the American republic should, in part, be decided by measuring each alternative path's potential monetary return and then choosing the route that "yields the greatest product."[55]

Hamilton's investmentality was also bound up in his attempts to bring factories to America. Only a few weeks after Hamilton sent out his statistical inquiries to the revenue inspectors, he asked for significant amounts of other economic data from a man named Thomas Lowery. In this instance, however, Hamilton was acting not as the secretary of the treasury but as a private entrepreneur. Along with a few other American and European businessmen, Hamilton and assistant treasury secretary Tench Coxe were subscribers in the Society for Establishing Useful Manufactories (SUM). Their goal was to attract capital (some of which would come from Hamilton's own Bank of New York) and skilled craftsmen from Europe, charter a corporation, and establish an entire city of textile manufactories somewhere on the eastern seaboard. While the society would end up creating the city of Paterson, New Jersey, along the banks of the Passaic River, in the fall of 1791 Hamilton and his fellow investors were still searching for the most advantageous site for their project. Upon Hamilton's request, Lowery, the director of the society, supplied him with "the prices of the sundry articles of provisions, fuel [and] labor" in western New Jersey, noting that "the labor of an able bodied man may be obtained for 15 to 18 pounds per annum."[56]

Hamilton was in need of such data since his aforementioned official inquiries had requested information on the annual monetary yields from manufacturing and farming (the market outputs) but not the initial costs (the inputs). While William Petty and the classical economists who followed in his footsteps often priced the factors of capitalist production by equating productivity with compensation, Hamilton—like any good industrialist—did not. He understood that in order to imagine future returns on capital one needed to see within each worker or piece of land *both* its productive capacity and its monetary costs, as it was between these two prices that an investor's precious profits lay. Textile industrialist George Cabot exhibited this "double vision"—a hallmark of how manufacturers viewed the world— in his response to Hamilton's statistical inquiries, noting that "while our artists have been learning their trades at our expense, their work is now worth more than it costs." Hamilton, therefore, was interested not only in pricing the productivity of the average American but also in determining the amount of money it took to keep that worker alive and laboring. He would not be the last American industrialist interested in collecting such cost information.[57]

Manufacturing promoter Tench Coxe, Alexander Hamilton's business partner, assistant at the Treasury Department, and kindred ideological spirit, was also interested in trying to price everyday American life. When Coxe was a merchant in Philadelphia during the 1780s, the only economic numbers that he seemed to care about were the prices of consumer goods. "Our present markets are high in the extreme," he noted in a typical correspondence, "rum is 58, sugar 40." Requesting that a British merchant send him a "monthly price current," from which he hoped "to get profitable information," Coxe focused on commodity prices because he knew that his profits were largely dependent on the arbitrage between markets. Interested solely in international commercial exchange, Coxe sought the prices of commodities such as sugar or coffee, and little else. As commercial newspapers of the era confirm, Coxe was acting like a prototypical early American merchant. The pages of such mercantile papers as the *New-York Commercial Advertiser* contained commodity price currents and money exchange rates but little other data. With their attention turned to far-flung port cities such as Canton, Marseille, and

Havana, most merchants did not appear very interested in the priced productivity of American land and labor.[58]

By the 1780s, however, Coxe had caught the manufacturing bug and soon became the most prolific proponent of British-style industrialization in America. Such industrial visions manifested themselves not only in the SUM project but also in a near obsession with land speculation. Something of a prophet of American capitalism, Coxe began to buy up great swaths of land on credit in Pennsylvania, New York, North Carolina, and Virginia in the mid-1780s in hopes that they would eventually yield either coal or cotton for the factories of the future. Once Coxe shifted his capital and attention to manufacturing, where one had to purchase not finished consumer goods but labor power and raw materials, his quantitative focus shifted to pricing people and land. Here we see the main difference between a strictly commercial mentality and a capitalist one.[59]

By the 1790s, Coxe was no longer situated solely in the realm of international commerce, skimming profits off the fringes of American society, and he began to seek out the tiniest scraps of data that might allow him to price the potential productivity of the American household and the land that sustained it. In western Pennsylvania, one of the areas where Coxe had bought up land, he gauged the productivity of distilleries on the banks of the Susquehanna by estimating the number of gallons of whiskey heading downstream. In upstate New York, where Coxe had inherited land, he recruited his esteemed business associate William Cooper of Cooperstown to help him determine the flow of income maple trees yielded in the form of syrup (Cooper estimated the annual syrup revenue from Otsego Township at $15,000). In Virginia, Coxe took full advantage of one of the few useful responses Hamilton had received on domestic manufacturing in order to conclude that the average American household annually produced $83.50 worth of "home-made hosiery and cloths of wool, flax, hemp and cotton." As these examples and many others make plain, Coxe the industrialist was no longer satisfied with the price of coffee or silk—he also wanted the price currents of natural resources and human labor. By 1810, Coxe would deservedly gain a reputation as the leading expert on industrial data in the early United States and was chosen to organize the mess of information better known as the 1810 census of manufacturing.[60]

Anticipating eastern capital's colonization of the western frontier in the mid-nineteenth century, Coxe went so far as to envision entire cities as capitalized investments. After purchasing a large tract of land on the banks of the Susquehanna River with the hopes that it would become "a town or city for inland trade and manufacturers," Coxe carefully planned the city of his dreams, noting that the streets would be "sixty feet wide, in oblongs of five hundred feet, fronting the southwestern or prevalent summer winds." What is more, he calculated the return on capital such a city-builder would receive by pricing every aspect of the town, from the 510 stone and brick houses (totaling $153,000), six blacksmith shops ($3,000), two bakehouses ($1,000), and four lumberyards ($100) to the four schoolhouses, "part to be German" ($3,200), one church "for all denominations" ($4,000), two taverns ($7,000), and two printer's offices ($800). Coxe then happily concluded that while the costs of building the city were great—half a million dollars—the resulting increase in real estate values would make the city worth $1,008,540 upon its completion, more than double the initial investment.[61]

The pricing of American progress was relevant not only to the objectives of Hamilton the banker and Hamilton the industrialist but also to those of Hamilton the treasury secretary. In 1790, Hamilton managed to convince Congress that the federal government should assume all state loans from the war and convert them into a permanent sovereign debt financed by federal bonds that would repay creditors not in depreciated paper money but rather in specie at near par value. In so doing, he made a conscious and controversial political decision that the primary goal of his financial system would be to transform U.S. taxing power into a capitalized investment that offered safe and steady returns to the minority of creditors and speculators who, by 1791, had scooped up most American war debt for pennies on the dollar. Inspired by England's groundbreaking decision to finance much of its public expenses through sovereign debt loaned by private capitalists, Hamilton's reasoning behind this momentous decision has been well documented: in ensuring that the United States would remain a sound investment at all costs, he was creating a modern state whose financial foundation lay not in the hands of state legislatures but in the capital gains that fused the interests of the federal government with those of its wealthiest inhabitants.[62]

Placing the sanctity of contract and the promise of steady returns above all else, however, was dependent on the American government having the taxing power to repay its creditors in a manner that would not trigger something like a second Shays' Rebellion. Hamilton turned to Petty's political arithmetic in part because he realized that capitalizing the federal government's fiscal power into safe, income-yielding bonds would be far easier if one could measure the American people's capacity to yield, through the collection of taxes, a continuous flow of interest payments. By the summer of 1791, Hamilton had plenty of experience in viewing Americans as a source of government revenues. In getting his fiscal feet wet as the congressionally appointed tax receiver for New York State in the early 1780s, and then spending most of his first days as treasury secretary poring over tomes of customs and tax data in order to work out his intricate financing schemes, Hamilton had—much as William Petty had done—come to recognize how national income measurements could aid centralized fiscal policies. "There is no part of the administration of government," Hamilton would note, "that requires extensive information and a thorough knowledge of the principles of political economy so much as the business of taxation."[63]

Yet the imperatives of Hamilton's fiscal policies were distinctly different from those of William Petty a century and a half earlier. Prior to the founding of the Bank of England in 1694, the English state had not yet turned to sovereign debt as its central source of financing. As a result, Petty only had to worry about ensuring that annual tax revenues covered annual expenses. Hamilton's crucial decision to make sovereign debt the basis of government finance, on the other hand, forced him to put an emphasis on generating profitable returns on bondholders' capital. He had to make certain that the American economy would be capable of returning not only the principal of the debt but also the interest payments. Hamilton didn't need to just balance the budget; he needed to turn money into more money. He needed, in other words, what we now refer to as "economic growth." It is only in this fiscal context, therefore, that we can fully understand Hamilton's fixation with productivity and his desire to collect statistical evidence that would prove his contention that industrialization would offer "a positive augmentation of the Produce and Revenue of the society." Such increased market production was especially crucial to Hamilton because he had made the capitalization of U.S. taxing power the anchor of his entire financial system. Since specie was so scarce in the United States, Hamilton had rather brilliantly decided that three-quarters of the capital needed to open the Bank of the United States could be paid not in gold or silver but in federal bonds. As a result, government bonds became the stabilizing stock of wealth with which the Bank of the United States could issue currency and accumulate capital.[64]

Besides Hamilton, no American demonstrates the link between capital investment, sovereign debt, and political arithmetic in this era better than Samuel Blodget Jr. The son of a successful New Hampshire merchant, canal investor, and entrepreneur, Blodget was a man of capital through and through. In 1791 he founded the Boston Tontine Association, a life insurance scheme in which wealthy individuals pooled their capital and received annuities until they died (survivors kept dividing the dead's annuities between them until only one lucky investor remained). When sales soured, Blodget and the other investors used this capital to organize the first joint-stock company in the United States—the Insurance Company of North America. Selling 40,000 shares in only eleven days, Blodget used this windfall to purchase 494 acres of land on a site along the Potomac River planned for the nation's future capital—months before the official sale of lots actually began. Throughout the 1790s, Blodget became a fixture in the District of Columbia as he speculated in lots, raised funds through lotteries, and founded the Bank of Columbia. In short, where capital was being raised and investments were being made, you could find Samuel Blodget Jr.[65]

An enthusiastic supporter of Hamilton's economic and financial policies at a time when the recently elected president, Thomas Jefferson, was planning to get rid of the permanent sovereign debt and the national bank, Blodget published a truly extraordinary article in 1801 titled "Thoughts on Increasing Wealth and National Economy of the United States." It has become commonplace for historians to assume that "the economy" was a twentieth-century invention. In general this argument is sound, as the word *economy* did usually mean "thrift" or "frugality" in nineteenth-century parlance. But Blodget's use of the term was exceptional. When he thought of "national economy," he conceived of it as the aggregate wealth of the United States. What is more, he was interested not in cutbacks but in continuous growth that would—Blodget was not one to mince words—transform America into "THE GREATEST AND MOST POWERFUL NATION OF THE UNIVERSE."[66]

Blodget opened his article by citing William Petty. Translating Petty's pricing of people from pounds to dollars, he noted that the average American was worth $400. Adding real and personal property to the sum of human capital, Blodget calculated the wealth of the young American nation in 1790 at "two thousand million dollars." Blodget then concluded that economic growth—he referred to it as "net amount of increase of wealth"—should remain steady at 3 percent a year. Equating rates of human reproduction with rates of compound interest, Blodget made these growth estimates by imagining people as capital and exponential population growth as a "natural sinking fund."[67]

Blodget opened with these calculations because he wanted to prove that instead of reducing its borrowing of capital, American society could afford to take on far more sovereign debt thanks to its robust growth rate. Explicitly and repeatedly associating national progress with capitalized growth, Blodget exclaimed that such an increase in wealth was "the only requisite to American prosperity and greatness." "Like a dog in the manger," Blodget warned, Jeffersonians had "endeavoured to starve our young country, ever craving, from its vigorous and rapid growth, for increasing supplies of CAPITAL STOCK." To further his argument, Blodget priced American citizens as factors of wealth production. He computed that to cover the sovereign debt in 1791 each American had contributed $19 a year to bondholders—which amounted to nineteen bushels of wheat or thirty-eight days of labor. Blodget then calculated that due to an increase in both grain prices and population, the number of days Americans needed to work in order to pay off the sovereign debt in 1800 had dropped to only twelve a year. Capital accumulation was not keeping pace with population or inflation, Blodget argued, which meant Jefferson could afford to issue more bonds—not fewer.[68]

In 1806, Blodget expanded upon his argument in a book titled *Economica* that he published—and apparently wrote—while in debtor's prison. (It seems that Blodget had miscalculated the number of investors interested in his District of Columbia lottery and was unable to compensate the winner with the promised $50,000 prize.) Endeavoring in his book to "embrace every statistical point yet in our power," Blodget developed even more intricate ways to price progress and capitalize life. In chart after chart, he measured the wealth of the nation by pricing, among other things, exports, homes, churches, dockyards, timber, shops, tools, mills, furniture, carriages, and animal stock as well as the capital invested in turnpikes, canal, bridges, and banks.[69]

One of Blodget's most creative statistical creations was a diagram that he referred to as a "financial money-meter." At the bottom of the money-meter, marked at $1 of capital per person, Blodget wrote "extreme distress, universal distrust, government in danger." If one moved up the meter dollar by dollar, as capital flowed into the country, things got brighter and the nation slowly improved from a situation in which "idleness abounds" to one where "commerce flourishes, everything improves." At the highest level of prosperity on the meter, the United States finally reached the "average of commercial Europe in 1805"—$25 of capital per capita.[70]

Most people in the early United States did not think capital per capita should serve as the measure of national growth, and so Blodget's book did not catch on. He would have been completely forgotten were it not for a few twentieth-century economic historians. Identifying with Blodget's desire to price American progress by measuring market productivity rates, these "cliometricians" kept Blodget's memory alive mostly through a single table in *Economica*. In that book, Blodget had sought to mimic William Petty and the "social table" of his greatest disciple, Gregory King. Just like King's table from 1694, which Blodget almost certainly came across in George Chalmers's *An Estimate of the Comparative Strength of Great Britain*, Blodget divided the American public into different social classes and then priced them according to their supposed income-bearing productivity. Sticking to his previous pricing of the American "free planter and agriculturalist" at $400, Blodget echoed the racist beliefs of the era by valuing slaves at only half that amount, $200. Multiplying each class of Americans by their estimated population and aggregating it all together, he concluded that the total capitalized value of the American people stood at $2.8 billion. More than a century and a half later, economic historians would hail Blodget as one of the key American forefathers of GDP.[71]

For-profit business enterprises in the early United States were dependent on two fundamental prerequisites: persuading investors both foreign and domestic that the United States was a site of safe and profitable investments, and convincing American legislators and the broader public that these endeavors would lead not only to private profit but also to public good. Hamilton, Coxe, and Blodget believed that economic indicators could help with both goals.[72]

In using statistics to whet the usually conservative appetite of American and European investors, Hamilton and Coxe hoped to show that the United States was not a decentralized agrarian republic of self-sufficient farmers incapable of even paying off its war debts, but rather a commodity-producing wonderland teeming with the cheap labor power, abundant natural resources, and investment-friendly institutions needed to yield tremendous returns on capital. Most of Coxe's early statistical work, which often sought to show the untapped potential in transforming American homespun into capitalist manufacturing, appeared in a set of newspaper articles written largely for London investors, which had as a main goal to disprove an English lord's claim that the British needn't be concerned with the future of American industry.[73]

Whether it was Blodget's "money-meter" or Hamilton's claims that "the more capital . . . the greater the blessings of the community," both men consistently framed their investmentality not only in a calculus of personal profit but in a republican language of public good. Oftentimes the need to convince legislatures that investment-friendly policies served a public good acted as the driving force behind data collection. In 1817, for instance, the Philadelphia Society for the Promotion of American Manufacturers sent out a detailed statistical survey to manufacturers "for the purpose of . . . strengthening our applications to the legislatures by the most powerful means—a well digested statement of facts." Fishing for flattering statistical tidbits they could present to the state legislature, surveyors asked for the "national gain" each manufacturer added to the Republic.[74]

These attempts to price American progress, however, ended in failure. Hamilton was unable to collect the data he requested. Early attempts by the federal census did not fare much better. When presenting the data he had collected for the 1810 manufacturing census, the head marshal of South Carolina (much like the marshals of Rhode Island, Kentucky, Georgia, and Pennsylvania) felt the need to add that the data accounted for "not more than one half of the real value and that, in general, the manufacturers are much more considerable." As a result, Coxe's 1810 census digest included almost as many blanks as numbers. In the only slightly more successful 1820 manufacturing census, the disgruntled compiler of Louisiana's data added a disclaimer: "The above returns are in such a confused state that it is impossible to reduce them to the form required by Congress."[75]

In a rare moment of honest despair after he had failed once more to collect the data he desired, Coxe suggested that "foreigners, who sincerely desire information, take up the Philadelphia directory and learn . . . by this simple but authentic document, the ingredients of which our towns are composed." Admitting that he "found himself restrained in the statement of facts concerning the United States, by the want of that accurate and various information," in the end the best Coxe could offer the foreign investor was the 1790s version of the yellow pages. Hoping to use the wonders of money to aggregate American labor and nature, Coxe had to settle for descriptions such as this:

> That produce, manufactures, and exports of Pennsylvania are very many and various, viz. wheat, flour, midlings, ship-stuff, bran, shorts, ship-bread, white water biscuit, rye, rye flour, Indian corn or maize, Indian meal, buckwheat, buckwheat, meal, bar and pig iron, steel, nail rods, nails, iron hoops, rolled iron tire, gun-powder, cannon ball, iron cannon, musquets, ships, boats, oars, handspikes, masts, . . . shingles, wooden hoops, tanners' bark, corn fans, coopers' ware, bricks, coarse earthen or potter[s]' ware, shoes, boots, foal-leather, upper leather, dressed deer and sheep skins, and gloves and garments thereof, fine hats, many common, and a few coarse.

A similarly rambling list of tangible, incommensurable things—likely written by Coxe—appeared in the appendix to Hamilton's "Report on Manufactures" precisely where his statistical calculations ought to have been.[76]

Without proper funding or subsidies, the manufacturing town of Paterson foundered. By the time of his tragic death in 1804, Hamilton had trouble getting investors to pay their installments, and the few existing mills closed down. Coxe did not fare much better. Despite purchasing giant tracts of land in southeastern Pennsylvania that sat upon the largest deposits of anthracite coal in the country, he never succeeded in creating the manufacturing base that would make such an investment profitable. Coxe died depressed, almost penniless, and in heavy debt; only his grandchildren would reap the tremendous rewards of his vision of industrialization. As for Blodget, he was never the same after his stint in debtor's prison. As one biographer noted, "His optimism frequently outran his prudence, for which he ultimately paid a heavy price."[77]

As for these men's statistical work, their inability to collect data led to sharp criticism. In an article in the *North American Review* in 1816, Blodget was criticized for being too "speculative" and "deficient in the details." In 1819, the same magazine censured Coxe in much the same way. It likely would have been little consolation for both men to know that their statistical failures should have been attributed not to their own calculating abilities but rather to the fact that the American public could not supply them with the data they requested. But *why* did these men fail to collect the statistics they desired? To answer this question, we must turn to the political economy and ideology of the early United States.

THREE

The Spirit of Non-Capitalism

HAMILTON'S FORAY INTO THE pricing of progress did not fail because Americans rejected markets, money, or commodity exchange. Along with selling their agricultural surpluses in the market, most Americans purchased a fair amount of consumer goods, as probate records from the era show. Furthermore, they were not shy about evaluating their property in money prices. The 1743 inventory of Benjamin Tower of Attleborough, Massachusetts, reveals that local assessors priced everything from cows and linens to pillowcases and pots. In the South, Americans put price tags not only on trinkets but also on human beings. In the 1801 probate lists of Daniel Mc-Neil of Jefferson County, Georgia, one can find alongside the $10 "painted cubbard" and $15 "walnut tables" the $200 "Negro girl Cate" and the $150 "Negro girl Rose."[1]

Early nineteenth-century account books reveal that everyday American life consisted of a whirlwind of "book credit" exchanges in which not only goods but also labor tasks were given money values. Connecticut farmer Russell Sackett was once paid 60 cents for a day and a half of work, and 10 cents for killing a hog. In 1808, Sackett paid Daniel Yemans 40 cents to chop wood and another 40 cents to "look after my cattle." New Hampshire farmer Matthew Patten was paid 2 shillings to write a neighbor's will. Maine midwife Martha Ballard received money payments for many of her deliveries. In order to collectively set their labor rates, artisanal guilds such as the House Carpenters of Pittsburgh published yearly "books of prices" that priced everything from the cost of grooving door panels to installing circular shutters.[2]

Early American land policy, meanwhile, was fast transforming the United States into one of the most commodified environments on earth. By 1732, real property could be used to pay back commercial debt, a crucial step toward the commodification of land. Shortly after the Revolution, American legislatures abolished primogeniture, entail, and other forms of feudal tenures to ensure the unencumbered exchange of real estate. Following the Northwest Ordinance of 1785, land surveys and cadastral maps became a cutting-edge form of land commodification technology as they sliced, diced, and priced nature into freehold grids of private property that could be bought, divided, or sold with relative ease. By the turn of the nineteenth century, land was far easier to truck and barter in the United States than in England.[3]

Yet despite Americans' day-to-day interaction with cash exchanges, slave labor, land markets, and the commodity form, when Hamilton, Coxe, or the census marshals requested that the American people price the income generated on their farm, plantation, or workshop, almost none could supply such information. Even when partial wealth or income data were collected, Americans did not seem very interested in the findings. A search of the newspapers of the era in the period following publication of the 1810 and 1820 manufacturing censuses reveals neither disdain nor enthusiasm for such statistical endeavors but rather an almost complete indifference. Coxe's digest of the first manufacturing census was published in January 1814. Few newspapers bothered to report its findings in the upcoming months. "At the last census the marshals were required to enter every family," one southern congressman complained in the debates over whether there should be a second census of manufacturers in 1820, "but what benefit was it to the nation?" It appears that most Americans shared this sentiment. The manufacturing census was eliminated in 1830.[4]

If the American farmer, planter, and artisan lived in a commoditized, commercial, market-oriented society, why could they not supply Hamilton or the census marshals with the price data requested? Why didn't they know how much cash was annually produced in their households or on their land? Why didn't they care to know the costs and productivity rates of their family members, slaves, and cows? The answers to these questions are rooted in the great structural and ideological divide that developed between colonial America and British Empire in the seventeenth and eighteenth centuries. By examining the key economic, intellectual, and cultural differences between England and the United States around the time of American Revolution, it becomes evident that extensive market and commodity exchange is not the only prerequisite for a capitalist society and the pricing of progress. While there is little doubt that early America was a commercial society deeply committed to market transactions, it was, nevertheless, decisively non-capitalist.

This was largely because, unlike in England, a relatively wide swath of households owned the most important means of production, land, and chose to organize and control its production not as an income-generating capitalized investment.

That said, historians such as Carl Degler were not completely off base when they argued that "capitalism came in the first ships." America was indeed born as a British investment. What Degler and others have forgotten to add, however, was that save for a few capitalist pockets such as the South Carolina low country, British capitalism soon foundered on American shores.[5]

As early as the late 1500s, English colonial promoter Richard Hakluyt saw the New World as an opportunity to "inlarge the revenewes of the Crowne very mightily and inriche all sortes of subjectes in generally." A few decades later the Virginia Company, a profit-seeking joint-stock corporation, established the first English settlement in American history in 1607. The company's investors hoped to earn a handsome income by importing laborers to America and having these workers mine precious metals or grow cash crops on company-owned American lands. This would not be English colonialism's only attempt to turn American lands into a profitable asset. Along with such corporations, throughout the seventeenth and eighteenth centuries many English gentlemen who had received generous land grants from the Crown—such as Lord Baltimore in Maryland, William Penn in Pennsylvania, and the lord proprietors in South Carolina—hoped to enrich themselves by replicating the burgeoning agrarian capitalism of Ireland and England in the Americas. Often referred to as "projects" by contemporaries, these colonizing endeavors were far more ambitious than engrossing an Irish field or enclosing an English pasture, but they were not fundamentally or ideologically that different. In both instances English elites were imagining land and labor as income-bearing investments.[6]

For example, William Penn's marketing of Pennsylvania to 600 British investors in the 1680s was greatly influenced by his previous experience as an absentee landholder of 12,000 acres in Ireland in the 1670s, where he earned more than £1,100 in annual rent by leasing out his lands to twenty-four tenant farmers. By the time he received the American land grant from Charles II as satisfaction for a debt of some £16,000 owed to his father, Penn's Irish experience had accustomed him to viewing land as an income-bearing asset. Along with his religious objectives, Pennsylvania was a bold attempt by Penn to expand his already booming real estate business. Lord Baltimore also owned a great deal of income-generating Irish lands when he received his own massive land grant in the Americas.[7]

Once projectors and proprietors realized that there was little gold or silver along the Atlantic coast, most attempted to import the English agricultural system to the New World. Much like Hartlib Circle "improvers," they sought out productivity statistics that could be used to control, allocate, and monitor their colonial workforce from afar. Recall that it was the lords commissioners of trade and plantations who pushed South Carolina governor James Glen to price his colony and estimate its annual income in 1751. Such requests began well before the 1750s. The Virginia Company's instructions to Sir Thomas Gates on the eve of his departure for Jamestown in 1609, for instance, read much like the Hartlib Circle's later improvement tracts and make plain that an analogous, productivity-maximizing worldview was behind not only English enclosure but American colonization as well. The directors instructed Gates that after dividing laborers into groups of "tennes, twenties & so upward," he must "appointe some man of care . . . to oversee them and to take daily accounte of their laboures." Each overseer would supervise the work of his group and "deliver once a weeke an accounte of the wholle committed in his charge."[8]

Despite such detailed instructions, however, the Virginia Company's managerial vision for an income-bearing America failed miserably. By 1619, the company lands were "without one penny yielde." Unprofitable despite the discovery of a cash crop in tobacco, the company dissolved by 1624.[9] It was a sign of things to come. For while subsequent English proprietors and projectors hoped to transform colonial America into a second Ireland, they mostly ended up replicating the Virginia Company's failure. William Penn's investment in Pennsylvania, for instance, ended in disaster—he wound up in debtor's prison having lost £10,000 and his estate. In South Carolina, the lord proprietors had great trouble controlling settlers and collecting rents, and so the colony was eventually turned over to the Crown. English elites "saw these grants as an opportunity to turn private estates into personal incomes," summarizes one historian of colonial American settlement, "but the tenant system failed to take hold and proprietors were forced to adapt by simply selling the land to settlers."[10]

Simply selling the land to settlers—rather than extracting continuous rent from tenants as in England or Ireland—would have revolutionary

THE PRICING OF PROGRESS

repercussions for American society. British colonizers succeeded in transforming land in America into a far more alienable commodity than in
England, but they mostly failed to capitalize it into an ongoing, rent-earning
asset, as they had done in their home country. As a result, most of those who
purchased American land as an investment eventually liquidated their holdings. By the American Revolution foreign capital investment (including
land) in the United States stood at a "trivial 1 percent" of colonial wealth.
The British sell-off, however, would have even more radical implications
for the structure of American society: by 1776, a whopping 70 percent of
Americans who could, by law, own land (this would include white and free
black men as well as unmarried women) were landowners.[11]

The entire social hierarchy in England was based on the fundamental
fact that only a minute group of elites owned land, the most important factor
of economic production. When modern landownership figures in England
were finally collected for the first time in 1871 (landed elites had been smart
enough to know that some things were better left unquantified), it was discovered that some 7,000 families in England owned 80 percent of the
country's lands. In mid-eighteenth-century America, on the other hand, if
a man was white and worked the soil, he more than likely owned it. It is
estimated that by the time of American independence, only a sixth of farm
operators remained tenants their entire lives. Before 1700, the percentages
of land ownership were even higher. In the mid-seventeenth century, less
than a tenth of free household heads in eastern Massachusetts and roughly
a twelfth of farmers in the Chesapeake region leased land instead of owning
it. Even on the Hudson River manors, where the experiment in tenant
farming would succeed on an unprecedented scale, manor lord Jeremiah
Van Rensselaer was not pleased, noting in 1671 that it was "no longer possible to get any tenants for the farms."[12]

European visitors to the United States quickly recognized this stunning
social development. Speaking of the American immigrant, the observant
Hector St. John de Crèvecoeur wrote in 1783:

> He is become a freeholder, from perhaps a German boor . . . from nothing
> to start into being; from a servant to the rank of a master; from being the
> slave of some despotic prince, to become a free man, invested with lands,
> to which every municipal blessing is annexed! What a change indeed! It
> is in consequence of that change that he becomes an American.[13]

The Spirit of Non-Capitalism

What a change indeed. Around 1750, 70 percent of lands in England were leased out to tenants and 30 percent were worked by owner-occupiers. In America those figures would be reversed. Exorbitant costs of settlement, Native American resistance, and high mortality rates all played an important role in this revolution. But perhaps the key to English proprietors' failure to transform America into a steady, income-yielding investment lay in the most basic of economic facts: while land in England and Ireland was scarce and labor plenty, in colonial America the situation was reversed. With land so plentiful and therefore so cheap, it was a great challenge to maintain for more than a few years—let alone reproduce—a steady population of tenant farmers and wage laborers who would agree to work lands they did not own. As a result, both absentee proprietors and local landlords were often forced to change their initial plans and sell their lands outright rather than earn a continuous income from lease or rent. As one commentator noted as early as 1712, to make money in South Carolina required one to become a planter, not a rentier. "The profit thereof is according to the stock he keeps, and the family of servants or slaves to work thereon, to raise Corn, Rice or other grain," the planter explained, "for people are not yet populous enough to rent land." Not much had changed a century later. The land tax book of Caroline County, Virginia, in 1802 reveals that of the 181 landowners sampled in one district, only 25—a mere 13 percent—received payment in rent.[14]

Trying to turn Pennsylvania into enclosed, capitalist England, William Penn had hoped to earn money from his land grant by selling it off in major chunks of 500,000 acres to large landowners who would then rent it out to tenant farmers. But things did not go as he planned. Because labor was so scarce and land so plenty, Penn ended up selling his land for a measly 2s. 6d. an acre, which is less than what he received from one year's rent on a single acre of Irish land. The level of quitrents was even more pathetic. According to accounts from 1703, Penn was charging James Atkinson 90 shillings for 300 acres—which comes out to roughly 3 pennies an acre. To make matters worse, Penn often failed to collect even this pittance from the colony's inhabitants. As a result, Pennsylvania was soon filled not with absentee rentiers, entrepreneurial managers, and a landless proletariat but with yeoman farmers and their families occupying lands they owned.[15]

The reversed ratio of land and labor made the reliance on wage labor problematic, since the scarcity of able bodies in the New World increased

· 79 ·

labor prices to the point where even those who could not purchase land at first could fairly quickly acquire the money needed to become a landowner or artisan. As John Winthrop lamented as early as 1641, freed indentured servants "could not be hired, when their times were out, but upon unreasonable terms." By 1789, tax ledgers show that even in Philadelphia—the most urbanized area in colonial America—only 6.5 percent of residents were listed as unskilled laborers, while 50.7 percent were considered artisans. The number of indentured servants, meanwhile, had dropped rapidly in the city as freed servants became their own masters. Since most white indentured servants became property owners, colonial Americans keen on maintaining consistently controllable workers who would not leave to start their own farm or workshop were forced to turn either inward to their own families or outward to the African slave trade. An unprecedentedly egalitarian and free society for white males but almost no one else, it soon became evident that the most effective way to get someone to work for you in early America was to get married, have children, or purchase slaves.[16]

———————

The emergence of proprietary households of patriarchal producers, as opposed to tenant farms of wage laborers, created a schism between America and England that was not only structural but ideological as well. In setting the theoretical foundation for a century of classical economics, Adam Smith contended in *The Wealth of Nations* that "wages, profit, and rent, are the three original sources of all revenue as well as of all exchangeable value." This argument was based on the notion that the aggregated income stream of a nation—as well as the price of every individual commodity—was made up of three components: the rent earned by landlords, the profits earned by tenant farmers or manufacturers, and the wages earned by laborers. (While Petty had concentrated on only two factors of production, land and labor, by Smith's time the nascent rise of capitalist manufacturing had led to a third: the entrepreneurial profits earned from investing capital in the purchase, organization, and management of wage labor and raw materials for industrial or agricultural production.)[17]

The three revenue flows that made up Smith's definition of national income (rent, profits, wages) mirrored the class structure of English society (landlords, bourgeoisie, laborers) and the respective factors of production that each owned (land, capital, labor). This holy trinity of factor inputs served as the basis of modern British political economy, political arithmetic, and, unsurprisingly, Hamilton's "Report on Manufactures." This social model and theory of value, however, gained very little traction in early America, as it made no sense in a world of yeoman farmers and slave-owning planters in which most white men worked the land they owned, received no wages, paid no rent, and earned no profits on capital. Interestingly, Smith himself recognized this incompatibility:

> A gardener who cultivates his own garden with his own hands, unites in his own person the three different characters, of landlord, farmer, and labourer. His produce, therefore, should pay him the rent of the first, the profit of the second, and the wages of the third. The whole, however, is commonly considered as the earnings of his labour. Both rent and profit are, in this case, confounded with wages.[18]

To Smith, the American producerist desire to earn a full return on one's labor—the cornerstone of American economic ideology throughout the nineteenth century—was such an alien way of thinking that he could only assume it was rooted in a misunderstanding of basic economic principles.

If this was indeed the case, then Benjamin Franklin was the most "confounded" of all. In 1729, a young Franklin sought to convince the British that they should allow for the printing of paper money in the colonies by publicly owned land banks. Fresh off a visit to England, where he had read William Petty's corn-into-silver narrative in the "Treatise of Taxes," Franklin used the very same story—and even the very same words—in order to offer up his own theory of value:

> Suppose one Man employed to raise Corn, while another is digging and refining Silver; at the Year's End, or at any Period of Time, the compleat Produce of Corn, and that of Silver, are the natural Price of each other; and if one be twenty Bushels, and the other twenty Ounces, then an Ounce of that Silver is worth the Labour of raising a Bushel of that Corn.[19]

While it may appear at first glance that Franklin was merely regurgitating Petty's theory of value, he was in fact Americanizing it in revolutionary ways. Petty had used the corn-into-silver model to argue that the landlord's appropriation of monied rent was equal to the natural productivity of his land. Franklin, in fittingly American fashion, ignored rent and landlords alto-gether. Arguing that only labor was productive, he offered a very different theory of value—a producerist, labor theory of value befitting an American society in which the dominant social unit was the yeoman farmer or planter who reaped what he (or his dependents and slaves) had sown.[20]

The political ramifications of this labor theory of value were enormous. In creating a tripartite theory of value that added together rents, wages, and profits, Adam Smith had legitimized and naturalized a class-based society of landlords, entrepreneurs, and wage laborers in which income derived not solely from one's toil but also from the ownership of capital, land, or the means of economic production. In creating a theory of value that equated wealth only with labor, on the other hand, Franklin developed an economic theory that challenged the moral foundation of capitalist relations by rejecting the notion that one can justly earn income simply by owning a scarce resource such as land or money.[21]

If the structure of American society made English political economy irrele-vant, nonsensical, and unjust, it also made Petty's political arithmetic unquanti-fiable. In attempting to measure the moneymaking productivity of American land and labor, Hamilton tried to import William Petty's political arithmetic to America. The radically different structure of American society, however, made such calculations impossible. Recall that William Petty's pricing of the money-making capacities of land and labor was based on two crucial market observa-tions. First, as Hamilton made sure to note in his trusty pay book, Petty measured the overall income of the nation by estimating the amount of basic necessities (food, housing, etc.) that the average laborer purchased in the market. Second—and this too appears in the pay book—Petty separated the income yields of land and labor into two distinct revenue flows by as-suming, with the help of his trusty corn-into-silver model, that the rent rates he saw in the English market were equal to the productivity of the land. That Pet-ty's calculations were creative and his estimates dubious is not particularly rel-evant, for the way people make sense of the world around them need not be based on accurate information. What is relevant, on the other hand, is the fact that on the basis of these two simple market observations Petty could convinc-ingly claim that the English laborer was worth 7 pence per day.

As Hamilton must have recognized, replicating Petty's market observa-tions was not possible in the United States. Since most of the goods consumed by Americans were produced within the confines of their own household, there was no way to use market consumption as a means to estimate the aggregate flow of income produced annually in the United States. Petty could somewhat credibly imagine England as a complete market society in which all wealth had been reduced to commodity form. Hamilton could certainly do the same while in the Caribbean. Such an argument, however, was untenable in homespun-dominant America.[22]

Since most American farmers owned the land they worked and did not have to rent it out, it also would have been odd for Hamilton to use rent figures to capitalize the moneymaking value of American lands. Leased to rent-paying tenants, English land could be quantified as a dynamic, income-generating asset through the use of such capitalizing calculations as "years of purchase." Directly cultivated by its owners and their dependents or slaves, American land could not. It should come as no surprise, therefore, that in dower cases and other instances where American land was to be priced, its value was not determined by capitalizing future rental revenues.[23]

In fact, with "years of purchase" methods so rare in colonial America, most local governments there tried to avoid the prickly problem of land valuation altogether. Quitrents were levied at a flat rate per acre, regardless of value. Save for New England, land was rarely priced in probate records or tax lists even though it was, by far, the main source of colonial wealth. Although the Continental Congress decided in 1781 that each state would pay taxes "in proportion to the value of all land within each state," the pricing of land was found to be so bureaucratically unfeasible that by 1783 Congress suggested a head count of inhabitants instead.[24]

Hamilton would not be the last American to be frustrated by an inability to price early American progress. By the mid-twentieth century, a sizable cadre of economic historians seeking to calculate American GDP back to the colonial era faced the very same difficulties, leading one of their ranks to describe the era before 1840 as "a statistical dark age." Much like Hamilton, these economists' attempts at calculating the moneymaking productivity of the nation were stifled by an American society dominated by proprietary producers who owned the means of production, an economic development that made estimating the income flows of land, labor, and capital impossible. As one leading economic historian lamented, "While a good deal of information is available concerning commodity prices in the colonies, much less is known about the relative costs of the basic factors of production—land (i.e., raw materials), labor, capital, and managerial skills." As a result of these structural obstacles, in order for Hamilton in the eighteenth century or economists in the twentieth century to price land and labor as inputs of capitalist production, they would have to turn directly to the American people for data. Here too, they would face great difficulties, since most early Americans did not view or quantify the world in the same manner they did.[25]

One fruitful way to uncover how American farmers and planters made sense of their economic lives is to read their account books. Hundreds exist from this period, and they are remarkably similar. Each page of each book was devoted to a fellow patriarchal proprietor in the community. The left-hand side of the page recorded transactions in which the book owner was the debtor. On the right-hand side appeared the transactions in which he was the creditor. Usually valued in units of money, some exchanges were for goods, other for specific tasks. Debts and credits slowly accrued over time, often over a span of several years, until sometimes—although certainly not always—the two men (and they were almost always men) would meet to balance the books. At that point, both sides of the account would be added up, a balance would be taken, and a reckoning made. After the account was balanced, it would be marked as "settled" and both parties would sign. At no point during this process, no matter how many years had passed, would interest be charged on debts.[26]

Perhaps the most revealing thing about these account books is what did not appear in them: an aggregation of total incoming and outgoing flows of money across the different personalized accounts they kept. It would have been rather easy for the American farmer to go page by page and add up the total inflow and outflow of goods and labor every year, summing together the $23 he owed to farmers Smith and Johnson with the $49 owed to him by farmers Carter and Jones. But almost none did. The American producer was interested only in keeping a running tab with his neighbors, not in calculating his annual net revenue. In this regard, he was different from many merchants of the era, who often did (albeit loosely) keep track of their aggregated income and outgo, usually through the use of double-entry accounting. In fact, as early as 1659, Puritan merchants were using a special book "in which is the sum of most of my accounts."[27]

In a thoughtful article on the historical usefulness of early American farmers' account books, economic historian Winifred Rothenberg lamented the fact that these sources "record only *transactions*—flows—there are no stocks, no aggregates, no acreages, no yields, no outputs." Rothenberg wondered "why per acre yields and seed / yields, why outputs and inputs and the relationship between them were of so little interest to Massachusetts farmers, why these magnitudes so important to us [economic historians] are so elusive." She pondered why it was that early American producers saw no point in collecting the type of aggregated, proto-GDP productivity and income statistics that Hamilton had requested and "cliometricians" adored. Trained in neoclassical economics, Rothenberg had been taught that human behavior could be modeled because it shared certain inherent, natural constants that transcended geography, culture or time. Yet in colonial account books she was being confronted with the disturbing fact that early Americans showed no interest in the type of maximizing mind-set that formed the foundation of both macroeconomic indicators and microeconomic modeling. As a result, Rothenberg seems to have been coming around to the troubling notion that the entire project of pushing national income measurements back in time—the raison d'être of most "growth historians" (as E. P. Thompson called them)—might be not only "elusive" but anachronistic as well.[28]

American farmers were not interested in aggregate revenues, incoming and outgoing cash flows, household productivity, or land yields because they had little reason to be. Not only did they not view their farms or plantations as capitalized investments, but also they did not have to worry about the drive for higher and higher rents that had pushed many early modern English landowners to maximize the income of land and labor. This, combined with the relatively low rates of indebtedness, land prices, and property taxes, meant that early American farmers usually were not forced to devote their efforts to producing a consistent cash flow. When on the rare occasion that Americans were obliged to organize their household production to maximize income, they fought vigorously to stop this encroachment of the cash nexus on their daily lives—as Shays' Rebellion in western Massachusetts and the War of the Regulation in North Carolina poignantly demonstrate.[29]

American proprietary producers, therefore, weren't merely disinterested in treating their productive property as an income-generating investment;

they dreaded it. They saw such subordination to income maximization as a direct challenge to their economic autonomy, which was their ultimate social objective. The central purpose of land or other forms of productive property was not generating cash flows but maintaining self-rule. Wary that those who lived only by market sales would, as Jefferson nicely put it, become victims of "the casualties and caprice of customers," even southern planters like Jefferson who produced tobacco for export nevertheless practiced mixed farming and did not organize their household exclusively around commodity production, purposely allocating their energies between the market and the household. For them, revenue-maximizing behavior flew in the face of Jeffersonian notions of proprietary independence, since such "dependence" on the market "begets subservience and venality, suffocates the germ of virtue." While market-oriented Americans certainly may have timed the slaughter of their hogs by responding to price incentives—as Rothenberg has demonstrated—such a finding obscures the far more important fact that the notion of investing all of one's property in pig breeding in order to generate more income was unthinkable to most Americans, since it left them at the mercy of the pork market. Hamilton and Blodget tried to convince yeomen that the key benefit of manufacturing and banking was that it maximized market output and made for a more efficient capital investment than the family farm. But they failed to realize that this was not the top priority of the American patriarch. "Secure our independence by impoverishing, discouraging and annihilating nine tenths of our sound yeomanry?" Virginian John Taylor asked in response to Hamilton's manufacturing scheme. Such an approach, he believed, would turn Americans into "swindlers" and make them "dependent on master capitalists for daily bread."[30]

Widespread ownership of the means of production offered yet another reason capitalist investmentality was a rarity in Early America. As the lord commissioners' requests to James Glen demonstrate, spatial distance is often a harbinger of the emergence of capitalizing statistics, as far-off investors required monetized data on inputs and outputs if they were to make sense of an investment they owned but did not control. There was, however, little need for such investmentality in America, since such acts of distant investment were few and far between. Unlike in the Caribbean, an "absentee mentality" did not take hold in colonial America, as most Americans worked the land they owned alongside their families or slaves. Even the wealthiest of southern planters in this era, who did not work the fields themselves, nevertheless remained nearby and did not diversify their wealth by investing in spatially distant forms of property outside their own household. As Elizabeth Blackmar has argued, in early America "wealth derived not from claims to income generated by intangible assets but rather from real property that sustained direct productive activity."[31]

Even if a few Americans had wanted to collect the data Hamilton requested, such an endeavor would have been almost impossible, since much economic production in the early Republic remained outside the marketplace and therefore was not priced. Take, for instance, a typical entry in Matthew Patten's diary on the day of the rye harvest:

> We carted in 27 stooks and 8 sheaves that we Reapt in this field and in the afternoon I went to James Moors in Goffestown and I got 3½ Gallon of Rum from him and I gave him a dollar toward it which paid 3 gallon of it.

As this diary entry suggests, only when farmers stepped out of the household and into the realm of market exchange—in this case to buy a drink—could they record market prices. The revealingly opaque "we" Patten used in his account, moreover, demonstrates that while exchanges among fellow farmers, artisans, or producers were carefully personalized and priced in account books, the internal workings of the farm, plantation, or workshop were not.[32]

From New England to Virginia, the disappointing responses Hamilton received in 1791 reveal that most American families shared the same homespun approach: they could not price their productivity because the bulk of manufacturing was done either by "individuals," "white females in poor families," or "under the eye of the mistress . . . by female slaves." Census marshals ran into similar difficulties. As one disgruntled marshal in Lincoln County, North Carolina, explained in 1820, he could not supply any of the requested data on priced inputs or outputs because "the manufacturing establishments in this county being carried on principally by negroes of the owners and so intimately connected with other branches for their support, in no instance was it practicable to obtain any definite answer to the questions." Artisan households appear to have been just as problematic as slave-based plantations. "Carriage makers, blacksmiths, hatters, shoe-makers, tailors, domestic makers of garments and other manufacturers known to exist among recent improvers and in old establishments, are omitted, or did not appear to the officers," complained Coxe in his summary of the 1810 census.[33]

The designers of the 1820 manufacturing census sought to solve the impossibility of pricing homespun production by declaring that only data on "manufacturing establishments" would be collected, not "household production," since such labor was merely "incidental." Instead of lamenting the inability to price household production, census planners adopted a rule that modern economists, by the very nature of their discipline, are often forced to follow: if you can't price it, ignore it. According to this statistical approach, if you did not produce money, you did not count—or get counted.[34]

This put much of the onus for the American household's disappointingly low income revenues on women's labor. Men such as Coxe came to believe that the solution to the United States' seemingly low productivity rates was to send women to work in the factories, where "the time of housewives and young women . . . could be profitably filled up." Assuming that women's labor was unproductive because it did not yield money, Hamilton wholeheartedly agreed with Coxe, arguing that the move to the factory would benefit everyone since the patriarch would "experience a new source of profit and support from the increased industry of his wife and daughter." The pricing of everyday life, in short, led to an erasure of women's labor, and it caused Hamilton and Coxe to construct narratives of the "unproductive housewife" that legitimized such glaring statistical absences. As twentieth-century feminist economists noted in their critiques of GDP and mainstream economics, not much had changed in this regard since the early nineteenth century.[35]

———————

The emerging ideological gulf between British investmentality and American non-capitalism is best articulated by tracing exactly what happened when American farmers and planters encountered England's leading political arithmetician in the 1790s, and how this confrontation deteriorated into an anti-British rant against capitalist calculation. Arthur Young was the editor of the English *Annals of Agriculture* and the preeminent political arithmetician of his day. Traveling across England and continental Europe, he enjoyed pricing the countryside as a series of capitalized assets. One of his favorite pastimes was to collect data on the monetary inputs and outputs of English farms in order to measure their annual revenue and return on capital. In one typical calculation, Young used rent rates to capitalize the value of a 300-acre farm at twenty-eight years' purchase (interest rates had dropped since Petty's time), and then went on to compute that its return on capital, after rent, was around 5 percent.[36]

Young was eager to deploy his investmentality on American agriculture, and so he sent his favorite American pen pal—President George Washington—a questionnaire in the summer of 1791 that was similar to, yet completely independent of, what Alexander Hamilton had sent American farmers only a few weeks prior. Much like Hamilton's circular, only more detailed, Young asked for data on the annual costs and revenues of a middling American farm. Hoping to calculate the return on capital, he also requested information on land values and rent rates.[37]

After receiving from Washington the best revenue and cost estimates that Pennsylvania, Maryland, and Virginia had to offer, Young—somewhat impertinently—responded by questioning why he had not received any data on labor costs, a crucial matter if he was to succeed in calculating a farm's profit. "Labor is so slightly touched on," Young complained, "that I know not how to estimate it." Always the perfect gentlemen, Washington politely wrote back explaining that Young must ascribe such omissions "to the habits and values" of the American people. Southerners did not know their labor costs because "hired labour is not very common . . . the wealthier farmers perform [labor] with their own black Servants whilst the poorer sort are obliged to do it themselves." Laying out one of the key differences between the proprietary, household economy in America and the wage labor system in England, Washington added that, in general, no American could provide this information, since "our modes—system we have none—are so different from yours, generally speaking, and our business carried out on so much within ourselves, so little by hiring, and still less by calculation."[38]

Sensing Young's disappointment, Washington then did two things. First, he sent Young a collection of the best responses that Alexander Hamilton had received from his own inquiry into the productivity of agriculture, including the work of Richard Peters, who had capitalized even his cows for the sake of the secretary of the treasury's data. Second, he sent Young's questionnaire to Thomas Jefferson in hopes that the Sage of Monticello might have better luck pleasing the political arithmetician from London.

A quintessential child of the Enlightenment, Jefferson was not bashful about counting things, and his obsession with quantification went far beyond the usual account books of the era. Hoping to supply Young with the data he desired, Jefferson tried to mimic Young's own profit estimates on his 300-acre farm in Virginia. Displaying a decent grasp of British political arith-metic—he had four of William Petty's books in his massive library—Jefferson estimated that a farm that hired labor would earn a return of 10 percent, while a farm that owned slaves would earn about 14 percent.[39]

Jefferson's and Peters's calculations were the most intricate estimates of agricultural profitability ever attempted in early America. Young, however, remained entirely unimpressed and responded that their figures were so way off that he did not need to visit to "to know that this is simply impossible." Not one to mince words, Young could not hide his disappointment: "Your information has thrown me afloat on the *high seas*. To analyze your husbandry, has *the difficulty of a problem*. Is it possible, that the inhabitants of a great Con-tinent, &c. can carry on farming as a business, and yet never calculate profit by per centage on capital?"[40]

Writing back in an apologetic yet now subtly annoyed tone, Jefferson ex-plained that his estimates were inaccurate because he "had never before thought of calculating what were the profits of a capital invested in Virginia agriculture"—a significant statement when we consider that Jefferson was a walking calculator who once dealt with the death of a friend by measuring the dimensions of his tombstone. Jefferson then added that he did not believe anyone in America made such calculations. Peters's response was not nearly as diplomatic as Jefferson's, and even more revealing. Testily noting that he "know not where to land Mr. Y. from his Sea Voyage," Peters went on to forcefully explain "why our Farmers need not make Calculations about per centage." In doing so, he articulated the various tenets of American eco-nomic ideology and its rejection of both investmentality and English agrarian capitalism.[41]

"Added to our Situation as a new Country, where much Land is to be had for little money, our political Arrangements contribute to our Happi-ness, & to our moderate, but competent, Wealth," Peters began. He cele-brated the fact that in the United States, unlike in England, there was no hierarchical, class-based exploitation, "no over-grown Nobles to wanton on the hard Earnings of an oppressed Yeomanry." and no "pampered Priests . . . who fatten on the Property of the People." Peters then lashed out against the English enclosure of the countryside into large assets that earned aristocrats "enormous Rents, made necessary by their Dissipation & Extravagance, & by their capricious Terms of leasing Lands, of which they are the principal Engrossers."[42]

Shifting to his beloved United States, Peters argued that, as opposed to English tenants, American proprietors had no need for Young's calculations because they were not pressed to run their farms like income-maximizing investments. "Free . . . from the pressure of heavy Rents, *Church Dues* and Taxes, our Farmers are the Proprietors of the Soil they Cultivate: they gather the Honey, shear the Fleece, and guide the Plough for themselves alone." Since American wealth came from one's direct working of the soil and not from claims to rent flows generated by tenants, Peters believed, returns on investment were meaningless figures in a republic in which farmers "do not indeed *receive* an annual Interest or Revenue on their Capital, but they *pay* none." Arguing, as Washington had done, that the realm of production remained firmly within the American household, Peters also pointed out that Americans did not keep track of their labor costs because "the Children Assist in the Labour of the old Farm, or in the establishment of the new one. This supercedes the Necessity of calculating on hired Labourers, the Work being chiefly done within themselves."[43]

In his concluding remarks, Peters tied all the strands of his argument together, emphasizing the American desire not for capital gains or monied income but rather material contentment from the fruits of one's own (and enslaved) labor: "We have here innumerable Instances of Farmers who get forward, without ever spending a Thought on per Centage, or other nice Calculation. . . . The easy Situation of an industrious, full handed American Farmer is the pleasing Result of a Combination, produced by all the causes I have mentioned. Instead of calculating, he labours & enjoys."[44]

While not enthused about capitalizing statistics or British investmentality, the everyday American farmer did not discard the notion that quantification could be used to measure a nation's progress and prosperity. The Ball family, for example, worked a modest farm in the hill country of Vermont and only traveled to Boston once a year to exchange dairy products for some finished goods. Nevertheless, they owned a copy of Jedidiah Morse's *The American Geography, or A View of the Present Situation of the United States of America,* as did many Americans. Like other statistical gazetteers and almanacs of the era brandishing titles such as *Picture of New York* or *A Statistical View of Maine,* Morse's statistics allowed readers to transcend space and catch a glimpse of the larger world.[45]

At a time when facts did not need to be numerical to be deemed objective, Morse's book was incredibly verbose, including thick, wordy descriptions of rivers, capes, islands, natural history, bridges, lighthouses, "colleges and academies," "mines and minerals," "revenues and taxes," and "charitable and medical societies," as well as a copy of the Constitution and a timeline of American history. Nevertheless, the book also had its fair share of statistics. Opening the state-by-state section, for instance, reveals a detailed table of each county that includes figures on the number of inhabitants and acres of improved and unimproved land, as well as the number of horses, cattle, fighting men, townships, congregational places of worship, and various religious denominations. The Balls were interested in such a potpourri of figures because these statistics—unlike Hamilton's calculations or the censuses of manufacturers—resonated with their own social, economic, and cultural values, interests, and goals.[46]

No measure of progress was more central to early Americans than population growth. That said, they had very mixed feelings about whether they would like to see this metric rise or not. At times, their proprietary, noncapitalist worldview led them to celebrate American population growth. In other instances, it made them dread it. In the harrowing first decades of American settlement in the mid-seventeenth century, death had been ever-present and head counts became a marker of survival. A century later, the multiplication of people had come to serve as an indicator not only of mere survival but also of the thriving success of a uniquely American way of life. In his second stab at the Americanization of political arithmetic in 1751, Benjamin Franklin used local church and municipal records to estimate that the American people were increasing at an astonishing rate, doubling their population in roughly twenty years. Arguing that the number of people increased "in proportion to the number of marriages," Franklin went on to put forth a theory as to why the American people were multiplying so rapidly:

> Land being thus plenty in *America,* and so cheap as that a labouring man, that understands husbandry, can in a short time save money enough to purchase a piece of new land sufficient for a plantation, whereon he may subsist a family; such are not afraid to marry; for if they even look far enough forward to consider how their children when grown up are to be provided for, they see that more land is to be had at rates equally easy, all circumstances considered.[47]

Encapsulated in this seemingly simplistic measure of population growth, Franklin argued, lay the barometer for American progress. Hewing not to the tenets of income maximization or capital accumulation but rather to principles of social mobility, material equality, generational sustainability, and propertied independence, Franklin viewed rapid population growth as an effective indicator of whether the American objective of competence—the ability to support a family comfortably without working for others—was being met.

This is not how many English economic thinkers or businessmen viewed population growth. Arguing "that the demand for men, like that for any other commodity, necessarily regulates the production of men," Adam Smith agreed that population growth was a sign of progress, but he credited it to capital accumulation and entrepreneurial moxie. Before Smith, English merchant-manufacturers had come to recognize that a rising population meant that people would no longer be able to find employment solely from the land. Pushing people off farms and into factories, population growth would not only feed the manufactories' insatiable demands for labor but also ensure that wages did not rise. "Numbers of people are the Wealth of a Nation," one English mercantilist noted in typical fashion in 1753, "as where they are plenty, they must work cheap, and so manufacturers are encouraged for a foreign market."[48]

By contrast, American statistical works of the era shared Franklin's sentiment, transforming demographic growth into a key metric of American society's overarching goal: the production and reproduction of free, independent, republican citizens. Seeking to explain the state's impressive population explosion, a statistical history of New Hampshire explained that "a young man who has cleared a piece of land, and built a hut for his present accommodation . . . attaches himself to a female earlier than prudence dictates." David Ramsay of South Carolina associated population growth with economic and political freedom, noting that American reproduction rates "varied more or less in proportion to the degrees of liberty that were granted to the different provinces."[49]

Yet Americans like Benjamin Franklin also came to fear continuous population growth in the United States for the same reason that British elites celebrated such human multiplication: it led to an industrial, capitalist society filled with unfree, propertyless wage laborers who no longer owned the means of economic production and thus were forced to work for another. "Manufactures are founded in poverty," Franklin remarked in 1760. "It is the multitude of the poor without land in country, and who must work for others at low wages or starve, that enables undertakers to carry on manufacture." As New England farmers came to recognize as early as the 1780s, an acute lack of arable land for their increasing numbers of offspring was beginning to seriously threaten the future of their yeoman way of life. In direct opposition to English mercantilists, these New Englanders came to view population growth as a sign of an oncoming nightmare rather than ongoing progress. Down in Virginia, Thomas Jefferson was reaching similar conclusions. Projecting that in a century the number of inhabitants per square mile in America would reach 100—the same unfortunate level as in England—Jefferson used population statistics to push for westward expansion and challenge Hamilton's desire to open the floodgates of immigration. As Jefferson noted to James Madison from France, where he had witnessed the social problems that population growth could bring, "it is not to soon to provide by every possible means that as few as possible shall be without a little portion in land." With these anti-growth statistics serving as their ideological compass, President Jefferson would go on to carry out the Louisiana Purchase while the proprietary American yeoman who voted for him would shift his eyes not toward statistical growth charts but rather toward the frontier.[50]

———•◆•———

If slavery played such a central role in pushing Malachy Postlethwayt, Alexander Hamilton, James Glen, and South Carolina low country planters toward the pricing of progress, why did it not thrust most American southerners onto a similar ideological path in the early years of the Republic? The answer to this question appears to lie, in part, in the difference between Anglo-Caribbean and early American slavery, or to put it another way, the difference between rice and sugar, on one hand, and tobacco, on the other.[51]

While the high fixed costs, economies of scale, and grueling labor discipline required to produce sugar transformed Caribbean plantations into highly capitalized enterprises that only the (often absentee) wealthy could afford to own, the major slave crop in colonial America—save for rice in South Carolina—was tobacco. Unlike rice or sugar, tobacco required little capital investment and few slaves, and it was relatively easy to plant, grow, and sell. It was not a plant well suited for routinized gang labor and offered no important economies of scale, so small households as well as large plantations could grow it profitably. The Virginia Company, in fact, became unprofitable not because it failed to grow tobacco but rather because *everyone* could and so white men were not forced to work as tenant farmers on company lands.[52]

There was, therefore, good reason for Adam Smith to claim that he had "never heard of any tobacco plantation that was improved and cultivated by the capital of merchants who resided in Great Britain." While the basic social unit in the Caribbean was the absentee, highly capitalized, large-scale plantation, in the early American South it was the proprietary household. On the eve of the American Revolution, the average Caribbean slave lived on a plantation with 240 other slaves. In Virginia and Maryland that number stood at five, and less than 25 percent of Chesapeake planters had more than twenty-five slaves. On Caribbean plantations, absentee landlords treated their plantations as capital investments (in part because they had mortgages with London financiers), paying revenue-maximizing managers to oversee an extreme form of monoculture that led to an almost complete market society with relatively few settlers. On the contrary, the typical American slave owner lived in close proximity to his slaves and sometimes worked among them, practiced mixed farming, and was not nearly as dependent upon the market for his sustenance. Lacking the investmentality of many Caribbean planters, even the biggest American plantations weren't abstract investments—they were home. As a result, even the wealthiest tobacco planters did not collect the kind of aggregated revenue figures Hamilton had sought.[53]

A closer look at how slaves were priced and valued in colonial Virginia demonstrates how tobacco slavery—much like early American society at large—oscillated between market and household. On one hand, when slaves were the object of an auction, they were treated as commodities and priced as such by both private proprietors and public institutions. Colonial Virginia, for example, charged an ad valorem tax on newly imported slaves based on their market price. Yet once slaves in colonial America and the early United States (as opposed to antebellum times) were bought, they mostly—though never completely—left that cash nexus behind. In early America, most planters did not keep track of their slaves' market price because they were fairly infrequently sold. When asked by Arthur Young what was the price of labor, all George Washington could reply was, "I am not able to give you the price of labour, as the land is cultivated wholly by slaves."[54]

The state ceased to price slaves as well, as ad valorem taxes came into play only at the point of importation. Avoiding any and all attempts to price a slave owner's property, colonial Virginia, as Robin Einhorn has shown, "never asked its tax officials to measure the value of anything"—including slaves. From colonial times until 1840, Virginia and the federal government taxed slaves at a flat rate that did not require their monetary valuation. In 1781, for instance, the flat rate stood at 10 shillings a slave, 2 shillings per horse, 3 pennies per cow, and £15 for a billiard table. These rates of taxation, which did not distinguish between a twenty-five-year-old male field hand and a sixty-year-old female house slave, suggest that once slaves had entered a household, most white Americans viewed them much like land or cows—not as income-yielding, capitalized assets but rather as pieces of property whose direct use was rooted deeply within the household mode of production. Scottish-born James Glen, one of the first to price progress in colonial America, spoke out in frustration against this non-capitalist approach to property valuation, complaining that taxes on slaves were laid "indiscriminately, by which means a negro who brings 25 and 20 pounds sterling a year to his master pays no more tax than one who is worn out with labour, bed ridden, and instead of being a benefit becomes a heavy burthen upon his master." Other British observers also recognized how slaves were not being valued according to their productivity. Touring the American countryside for the British Board of Trade, one astute observer noticed how "the price of a slave is no test of his value as a labourer."[55]

The threat that slaves could, at a moment's notice, be sold surely existed, yet in early America it was not nearly as omnipresent as it would become in the antebellum cotton-growing South. The internal slave trade did not really take off until after the War of 1812 and the rise of King Cotton. The domestic slave markets, advertisements containing prices for slaves, slave-backed mortgages, and slave life insurance policies that would capitalize the American slave into the financial centerpiece of the antebellum South had not yet come to dominate the economic landscape or slaveholders' minds. Since in the time of the early Republic most increases in the slave population were the result of domestic reproduction as opposed to international import, and since many slaves were passed on to the children of slave owners as an inheritance, a significant number of slaves in Revolutionary America (it is impossible to estimate how many) could enter and leave this world without ever being priced. An ad from a Virginia planter in 1827, just as the internal slave trade was beginning to ramp up, revealingly notes that he will sell "to the highest bidder . . . 120 negroes, all of them born and raised on the plantation." Before the 1830s, in short, the chattel principle was surely present, but not yet ascendant.[56]

The primacy and preeminence of the household over the market in the shaping of early American slavery reveals itself most clearly in debates regarding the expansion of the "peculiar institution" and the closing of the international slave trade. In 1792, the Virginia legislature required immigrants from other states to swear that they had not brought slaves into the state "with an intention of selling them." In that same year, South Carolina decided that the only slaves allowed into the state would be those who came with their masters. Georgia and Kentucky passed similar laws a few years later. The legitimacy of the international slave trade was also fast eroding in the 1790s. By the time the trade was officially banned in 1808, every state but South Carolina (again we see how the state was in many ways an outlier) had already made it illegal. As Adam Rothman has argued, it was a "patriarchal defense of slavery" that shaped these decisions, as southerners created a moral divide between slave trading and slaveholding in their attempts to "domesticate" the institution of slavery and insulate it from the cash nexus.[57]

Yet despite all this, early American slavery played an important role in the eventual pricing of American progress. We have seen how Caribbean-style slavery helped bring British investmentality to American shores, especially in the rice-growing areas of South Carolina. But slavery set important precedents in other areas of the United States as well, helping to legitimize and normalize the first inklings of a capitalization of people and the pricing of everyday life. For on the rare occasions when early Americans did seek to price social developments in monetary values, slaves served as their main source of both inspiration and data. After discovering, for instance, that forty-four African Americans had died in 1705, the editor of the *Boston News-Letter* priced the "loss to the country in general" at £1,320 by calculating that each dead slave had been worth £30. Uncharacteristically seeking to price American population growth in the 1790s, the *Weekly Magazine* could do so only if it turned to slavery, as it noted in typical racist fashion that by "calculating the value of each person, in a pecuniary view, only at the price of a negro," one could estimate that the nation's wealth was "equal to nearly one hundred million sterling." Even Benjamin Franklin used the chattel principle in his political arithmetic. In 1731, Franklin analyzed Philadelphia's smallpox deaths in the *Pennsylvania Gazette.* The total number of dead included sixty-four African Americans. Not bothering to note whether some of these blacks may have been free, he calculated their loss at £30 each based on the going price of slaves. In another article, Franklin treated slaves as capitalized assets, explaining that one could estimate their annual productivity simply by observing the interest rate on such human capital.[58]

When Thomas Jefferson was asked by Arthur Young to calculate the labor costs of an American plantation or farm, he too drew upon the fact that slaves could be not only priced but capitalized. "Suppose a negro man, of 25 years of age, costs £75 sterling," Jefferson began. "He has an equal chance to live 30 years, according to Buffon's tables, so that you lose your principal in 30 years." Discounting both the annual interest on £75 of capital as opportunity costs (the capital invested in a slave, after all, could have been invested elsewhere) as well as the annual depreciation that accrued because the slave was to die in roughly thirty years, Jefferson reached the conclusion that, in addition to the £6 a year it cost to keep a slave alive and working, the total annual cost of slave capital stood at £12.50 a year. Since the labor of whites could not be capitalized in the same way as that of blacks, Jefferson used slave prices to gauge the profitability of all American workers. He made sure, however, to note that "there must be some addition to this, to make the labor equal to that of a white man, as I believe that the negro does not perform quite as much work, nor with as much intelligence." Along with his racism, Jefferson's calculations show how slavery allowed Americans to imagine all human beings—not just those who were enslaved—as human capital.[59]

While Jefferson had never before felt the need to price the costs of his slaves or calculate his plantation's return on capital, slavery nevertheless enabled him to put British political arithmetic into practice. However, Jefferson was not through just yet. "I allow nothing for losses by death, but on the contrary shall presently take credit 4 pr. cent pr. annum, for their increase over & above keepg. up their own numbers," Jefferson continued. He added this additional return on his slave investment because he recognized that slaves were a very rare and special kind of capital, as they had the power to not only produce profits but reproduce ever more productive capital. As he explained, Jefferson had added this 4 percent increase in capital growth because "he had observed that our families of negroes double in about 25 years, which is an increase of the capital, invested in them, of 4. percent over and above keeping up the original number."[60]

In his return-on-investment calculations, Jefferson was accounting for the reproduction of slaves as the reproduction of capital. He had done so before. "I consider a woman who brings a child every two years as more profitable than the best man of the farm," he had explained in an earlier letter. "What she produces is an addition to the capital, while his labour disappears in mere consumption." While Ben Franklin and other Americans had utilized the very same statistic—that Americans tend to double their population in a generation—to celebrate the virtues of white American proprietary independence, slavery had led Jefferson to transform black population growth into a metric for calculating capitalized gains.[61]

Despite Jefferson's intricate calculations, however, such a slave-based investmentality remained on the margins of early American society. Nevertheless, its future, precedent-setting impact would be substantial. In 1837, as cotton expansion and the internal slave trade had begun to turn slave bodies into capitalized assets that could be bought, sold, mortgaged, insured, or securitized, Edmund Ruffin's *Farmer's Register*—a leading journal for the profit-minded cotton planter—reprinted Jefferson's calculations so as to teach American enslavers how best to value their slave capital.[62]

FOUR

The Age of Moral Statistics

ON A CHILLY FEBRUARY DAY in 1844, a heated argument erupted on the floor of Congress regarding a letter that Secretary of State John C. Calhoun had sent to a British diplomat a few months before. "So far as that letter goes to impute to the people of the Free States a desire to oppose the progress of human rights," Ohio representative Joshua Giddings declared, "I regard it as a base slander upon Northern character." At that moment, South Carolina representative Armistead Burt interrupted:

MR. BURT: I want to know if the member from Ohio meant to say that the Secretary of State has done, or is capable of doing, anything base?

MR. GIDDINGS: I am a little surprised at your question.

MR. BURT (MUCH EXCITED): That was your language.

MR. GIDDINGS: I hardly know how to understand this southern dialect.

MR. BURT (AMID CRIES OF ORDER, AND THE RAPPING OF THE CHAIRMAN'S MALLET): Do you understand your own language?

MR. GIDDINGS: If gentlemen will keep cool I shall soon be through my hour. . . . I was humbled and mortified at seeing a weak and loosely penned lecture in favor of slaveholding made the subject of an official communication to the British government by an American Secretary of State; particularly as the whole argument against human liberty was based upon errors in our late census, which were palpably obvious to any person who would examine the official returns. Those errors relate to the numbered of insane colored persons reported to be in our free states.[1]

In the letter that triggered this angry exchange, Calhoun had argued that "in all instances in which the States have changed the former relation between the two races, the condition of the African, instead of being improved, has become worse." Calhoun contended that blacks who had been freed from the bonds of slavery in the North had "invariably sunk into vice and pauperism, accompanied by the bodily and mental inflictions incident thereto—deafness, blindness, insanity, and idiocy—to a degree without example." Calhoun then went on to substantiate his claims with an array of statistics. These figures showed, for instance, that the proportion of northern blacks "who are deaf and dumb, blind, idiots, insane, paupers and in prison" was "one out of every six," while in the South it was "one of every one hundred and fifty-four."[2]

Examining how Americans wielded statistical indicators in their debates over slavery serves as a useful lens into how they measured progress more generally. By the 1850s, northern and southern elites often fixated on wealth and income statistics in order to censure or legitimize slavery. In the 1830s and 1840s, however, Americans rarely priced progress when arguing over the ownership of property in people. Rather, they turned, as did John Calhoun, to a series of "moral statistics" on crime, education, religion, insanity, health, pauperism, and prostitution.[3]

It was the emerging bourgeoisie in the industrializing cities of the North who imported, collected, and disseminated most of the moral statistics that circulated in Jacksonian America. Nevertheless, these figures soon gained wide acceptance among most upper- and middle-class Americans—even southern slaveholders—as worthy measures of progress and prosperity. By the 1840s they had become a widespread statistical trope, as elites on both sides of the Mason-Dixon line frequently cited an array of moral statistics in order to prove the superiority of their respective society.

Ohio congressman Joshua Giddings, therefore, was not upset that John Calhoun viewed insanity and pauperism statistics as barometers of social progress. Quite the opposite: he had a great deal of respect for the ability of such moral statistics to gauge the well-being of American civilization. The problem, he believed, was that there existed grave errors in the 1840 census figures regarding the propensity for insanity among free blacks in the north. These census errors made for one of the biggest political scandals of the era. Mere census statistics could cause such a ruckus only because both sides of the slavery debate recognized the immense power that moral statistics had over the American imagination. Tensions ran high that February day in 1844 because, with moral statistics being bandied about, the stakes were high.[4]

The controversy over black insanity statistics was but a single battle in a much larger statistical war between North and South that broke out in Jacksonian America. Anti-slavery almanacs and northern politicians often critiqued southern society by citing varying moral statistics collected by the 1840 census, such as the number of children who went to school or knew how to read. "Ohio has one half of the population of the eight slave states," one Ohio representative noted in a speech to Congress reprinted in the *Anti-Slavery Bugle,* yet the state had "815 more colleges, academies and schools, and sends to school 131,000 more children." As Calhoun's letter reflects, southerners were quick to respond with moral statistics of their own, citing not only insanity statistics but also northern figures on paupers, prisoners, criminals, and the disabled.[5]

The debate over slavery was hardly the only instance in which moral statistics were used in Jacksonian America. In fact, wherever Americans grappled with significant economic change or social dislocation, moral statistics could be found. As a result, such figures spread across the rapidly industrializing North in the 1830s and 1840s but also, albeit to a far lesser extent, through the rapidly expanding cotton kingdom of the South. Whether cited by New England medical journals or southern literary magazines, the *New York Tribune* or the *New Orleans Daily Crescent,* temperance tracts or women's reform movements, evangelical sermons or Alabama medical studies, Sunday school unions or an attorney general's crime reports, the American Statistical Association or the superintendent of the poor, moral statistics were everywhere.

In the North, as industrialization, immigration, transiency, wage labor, and a rambunctious democracy led the traditional binds of the patriarchal household and the communal village to slowly disintegrate, moral statistics supplied a nascent American bourgeoisie with a novel instrument of social and paternalist control. As individuals with newly loosened social ties and obligations rushed pell-mell into a brave new world, wreaking havoc on the hierarchical social orders of the past, anxiety-ridden northern elites looked to moral statistics as a means to transform such rootless Americans into quantified objects that could be observed and monitored—and disciplined and governed. While genuinely seeking to ease the suffering of industrialization's victims, they also hoped that these statistics would instill in American workers their own middle-class work ethic of self-control and self-improvement.[6]

In the South, moral statistics circulated far less frequently and for different reasons. After all, southerners had far simpler, more direct, and more violent ways to control and discipline their enslaved workers than novel statistical surveillance techniques. Nevertheless, moral statistics became a useful trope for the legitimization of slavery among southern elites, and were often used to contrast the viciousness of northern industrialization with the supposed safety and stability of slaveholder paternalism. Desperate to revitalize such paternalist self-narratives in a world where the mounting internal slave trade was tearing plantations and their slave families apart at ever-increasing rates, many slaveholders embraced moral statistics in an attempt to downplay the commodification of African Americans and prove that slavery was a benefit not only to whites but to blacks as well.[7]

The place of moral statistics in the long history of the pricing of progress is an ambiguous one. On one hand, moral statistics were clearly an important precursor to modern economic indicators. For the first time in American history, moral statistics succeeded in injecting quantified measures into everyday American discourse, newspapers, politics, government bureaucracies, and civil society. In an age when traditional forms of social control, which had emanated from the hierarchy of the patriarchal home and deference to political elites, were quickly falling victim to industrialization, immigration, individualism, labor commodification, and democracy (the last for white men, at least), moral statistics offered a new path. They showed American elites how statistics could step into such power vacuums and serve as tools not only of mass surveillance but of mass governance.[8]

On the other hand, while moral statistics were used to discipline the public into accepting and internalizing a nascent set of bourgeois norms and values regarding everything from sexuality to mental normalcy to work ethic, the northern reformers who created them often also sought to quell disease, stamp out prostitution, and improve living conditions. While these statistics were far from innocent, at their heart nevertheless lay a vision that placed humanity, not money, at the center of society. In focusing on the human condition, these figures differentiated themselves from future economic indicators that would treat the American people as income-generating means to a wealth-accumulating end.

The rise of moral statistics, therefore, reflects the fact that money was not yet the central unit of social measure in the calculating minds of most Americans during the Jacksonian era. In an age of rising inflation, counterfeit currency, and wildcat banking that led many Americans to view paper money as nothing more than dubious "rags," both northerners and southerners displayed an acute distrust in the market's ability to assign a dollar value to basic commodities, let alone their nation. Still very much rooted in their local communities, American elites of the era preferred more concrete and corporeal measures of progress, such as life expectancy and Sunday school attendance, to the airy abstractions of exchange value. In an age before the corporate form and the stock market took off, capital was still mostly locally embedded, and so American businessmen were forced to witness firsthand the communal effects and social dislocation wrought by their industrial investments. As they fretfully watched the crumbling of the hierarchical order, an effect they had helped to unleash, these elites concerned themselves not with abstract flows of faraway capital but with developing new means of local control and social legitimization. Counting paupers, prostitutes, lunatics, drunks, and scholars, they focused on the physical, mental, and social condition of the lower classes, not their priced productivity. The basic unit of measure for moral statistics was bodies and minds, not dollars and cents.[9]

In 1836, pauperism statistics appeared for the first time in the best-selling *American Almanac*, the leading statistical compendium of the day, whose professed goal was to "advance the moral civilization and improvement of the country." The initial figures the almanac cited were from Europe. They showed that the proportion of paupers in Great Britain was one in six, in Holland and Belgium one in seven, in France one in twenty, and in Prussia and Spain one in thirty. By 1838, however, the *Almanac* had added the number of American paupers to the statistical tables it collected on each state, reaching the final conclusion that "paupers in all the States are few, compared with the number found in most European countries."[10]

This importation of pauperism figures from overseas was no outlier: most moral statistics originated not in the United States but in Europe. Initially European moral statistics would circulate in the United States. A few years later, similar figures would be generated for the U.S. population, and American moral statistics were born. Even the term "moral statistics" had been imported from Europe. So to gain a better understanding of the making of moral statistics we must begin on the other side of the Atlantic.[11]

As the prescribed hierarchies of the ancien régime gave way to liberal individualism, Europe's emerging bourgeoisie turned to social statistics to try to make sense of their changing world. Unlike the aristocrats who ruled before them, these liberal elites imagined society not as a feudal ladder of fixed positions but rather as a collection of individuals that could be statistically classified, aggregated, or compared as various, far less rigid social groups or "populations." As individuals became an object of scientific and quantitative inquiry, men such as Belgian astronomer Adolphe Quetelet, widely regarded as the father of modern social statistics, began to turn their statistical gaze and mathematical tools away from heavenly bodies and onto human ones. As in the natural sciences, social statisticians believed that quantification could uncover the natural laws of society and thus the causal logic according to which it operated. More important for this book, however, they came to believe that these figures could be used as a measure of social progress. William Petty's political arithmetic anticipated some of these developments, but it was only in the early nineteenth century—historians seem to agree that the 1820s was a crucial decade—that the word *statistics* suddenly came in vogue.[12]

While Americans were influenced by moral statistics from across Europe, the numbers coming out of Great Britain had the largest impact. By the nineteenth century, the British government was coming around to the advantages of social quantification. The first census was held in 1801, and the first collectors of social statistics were overseers of the poor, schoolmasters and clergymen. The government's Home Office began to collect crime statistics in 1810. The first major statistical survey on education was conducted in 1818 by the Select Committee on the Education of the Lower Orders, a name that reflects just how the English bourgeoisie were imagining the people they so carefully counted. The first government health statistics, also clearly linked to class politics, were gathered by the Select Committee on Children Employed in Manufactories. By the 1830s, these somewhat ad-hoc acts of social quantification were being formalized and institutionalized. The London Statistical Society was founded in 1834. In 1837 the General Register Office was established, following an act of Parliament. William Farr, one of its first heads, would go on to become—along with poor-law reformer Edwin Chadwick—the leading disseminator of moral statistics in England in the 1840s. Hinting at the continuities between moral and monied statistics, Farr would later play a central role in the pricing of English progress.[13]

English moral statistics were, first and foremost, a bourgeois response to industrial revolution. The first statistical society in England, in fact, was founded in 1833 not in London but in Manchester, the manufacturing capital of the world. Run by a coterie of industrialists who would later align themselves with the Liberal Party, the Manchester statistical society employed statistical analyses in order to bring order to urban chaos, stabilize class conflict, discipline laborers, improve living conditions, increase productivity, and legitimatize factory labor. One of its first major studies, written by James Phillips Kay, was titled *The Moral and Physical Condition of the Working Classes*. As Kay bluntly noted in this work, he hoped to educate and discipline workers by allowing them to see "their political position in society and the duties that belong to it."[14]

The Manchester Society rarely collected statistics on the goings-on within factory walls, choosing to avoid controversial data on wages or labor hours. Rather, they sought out data that would allow them to infiltrate the working-class home, body, and mind. Thanks to their charitable donations to the city, men such as Kay believed that Manchester's industrial elite had "the right of inquiring into the people's arrangements—of instructing them in domestic economy—of recommending sobriety, cleanliness, forethought and method." According to the Manchester society, the purpose of its statistical surveys was "to assist in promoting the progress of the social improvement in the manufacturing population." Such statistical inquiries were part of a larger reform movement in the city. The Gregs, a family of leading textile industrialists in Manchester, not only helped found the statistical society but also established Sunday schools, gymnasiums, and libraries in an attempt to inculcate within the city's working classes their own middle-class values. If looms helped manufacture textiles, statistics were intended to help manufacture "good labourers, good fathers, good subjects."[15]

Members of the Manchester society went around town counting how many children were going to school and how many books they had in their homes, how many crimes had been committed and in how many of those alcohol had played a role. What people count reveals a great deal about what people want, and these Manchester statisticians dreamed of a clean, orderly city, with no crime or drunkenness, in which healthy, self-reliant, yet docile workers would happily go off to the factory to work hard for twelve straight hours. These statistical reports placed a special emphasis on Sunday school attendance, likely because these church-run institutions preached the gospel of self-reliance (so as to make dependence on poor relief a disgrace) while also instilling Victorian values of self-improvement, self-control, and self-discipline. When the final reports weren't blaming the worker's own character for their suffering, the statistical organization made sure to lay the blame for society's ills not on the factory but on the city. "The weakly children are fatigued by twelve hours' labour," one report concluded, "but the healthy ones are not." To these men, the problem in Manchester was not the work (or pay) but the outer environment and inner morals.[16]

The Manchester society was soon overshadowed by its London counterpart, but the nature of moral statistics remained very much the same throughout the 1840s, only entering into a decline in the 1850s (as happened in the United States also). Beginning in the 1830s, men such as Farr and Chadwick became international celebrities as they collected data on disease, literacy (they were the first to determine how many English people could sign their names), sanitary conditions, crime, education, religion, insanity, and death. In most instances the link between moral statistics and industrial productivity remained implicit, but on occasion it came to the fore. William Farr, for example, argued for public health policies that would "reduce the annual deaths in England and Wales by 30,000 and to increase the vigor (may I add the industry and wealth?) of the population in equal proportion."[17]

Similar statistical developments took hold in other industrializing European nations, especially France. The wave of moral statistics that washed over Europe soon reached American shores. When the *American Mechanics Magazine* cited moral statistics for the first time in 1834, the figures cited were from Europe. When Francis Lieber (himself a European immigrant) pushed for the inclusion of crime statistics in the 1840 census, he noted the value of French crime reports. The American Statistical Association (ASA), founded in 1837, was purposely designed as a carbon copy of the London Statistical Society. Bostonian Lemuel Shattuck—the founder of the ASA and a leading proponent of moral and vital statistics in America—remained in frequent correspondence with the register general of England and British actuary Thomas Rowe Edmonds as well as Adolphe Quetelet, Hamburg cholera mapper J. N. C. Rothenberg, and many others.[18]

The importation of European moral statistics to the United States marks a crucial turning point in the history of social quantification in America. Up until the 1820s, Americans mostly rejected English forms of social quantification. By the 1840s, this was no longer the case. American newspapers such as Vermont's *Green-Mountain Freeman* chose to cite "statistics of evil" from London and Glasgow that told of "23,000 drunkards reeling through the streets . . . 500 temples of debauchery and 150,000 sabbath-breakers." Even though these moral statistics came from Europe, they nevertheless struck close to home by the 1830s, resonating with middle-class Americans who could identify with the fears and anxieties of the European bourgeoisie. "Europeanization"—a drawn-out process that whittled away at early American exceptionalism—was under way, and the United States was discovering that industrialization and protelarianization were making the country's social structure, and thus its social problems, more and more similar to class-torn Europe's. For the rest of the century, the statistical divide between the New World and the Old would continue to diminish, and by the 1850s Americans would become stalwart attendees at international statistical conferences in Europe.[19]

As in Europe, the main impetus for the rise of moral statistics in America was the industrial revolution, although religious fervor certainly played a central role as well on both sides of the Atlantic. Until the 1820s, American manufacturing had largely been organized under the auspices of the patriarchal household. With no real divide between home and work, apprentices and journeymen subjected themselves to the patriarchal authority of their master. Apprentices and journeymen would not only work alongside skilled masters, learning the tricks of the trade, but also usually live under the same roof and eat together (and, perhaps more important, drink together). Work was irregular and personal, as most workshops were modest affairs adjacent to the master's home, and produced a smattering of unstandardized goods mostly for the local market. Even when manufacturing was not conducted in the artisanal workshop, it remained within the confines of the patriarchal family, as it was outsourced to women who worked in their homes.[20]

In the 1820s and 1830s, things began to change. Faced with increasing competition, a greater demand for standardized goods, and growing pressure to reduce costs, master artisans began to centralize production in small factories that stood separate from their homes. A far more acute division of labor led some masters to rely less on the skilled labor of the apprentice or journeyman and more on the unskilled labor of wage-earning day laborers—many of whom were migrants or immigrants. These workers ceased to live in their bosses' homes or even their neighborhood, and a social as well as spatial distance developed between them. Many masters came to feel that they owed little to their workers other than their wages, and so labor became an estranged, flexible "variable cost" that could be hired and fired according to the rhythms of the market. A market-mediated relation between manufacturer and wage laborer came to supplant the traditional patriarchal relation between master and apprentice.[21]

Within the confines of their new factories, manufacturers tried to instill a bourgeois work ethic and industrial discipline by implementing clock bells, attendance books, and a strict set of rules and regulations. But once work was done for the day and laborers went off to their own homes in their own neighborhoods, manufacturers felt their social power slip away. The breakdown of the patriarchal social order was creating a crisis of control among middle-class denizens of industrializing towns, as laborers ceased to live, work, eat, drink, or play under the watchful eye of their masters. With immigration and transiency on the rise, the cultural conformity that was part and parcel of life in small villages dissipated as well, and urban life slowly became a society of strangers. To make matters even worse for middle-class Americans, the rise of Jacksonian democracy brought a contentious and populist form of urban ward politics that often left elites feeling that they could no longer rely on local governments as a means of social control. Anxious for new methods of social discipline that could transcend the emerging class divide between owners and workers, the northern bourgeoisie turned, among other things, to moral statistics.[22]

The development of the Lowell textile mills offers a unique look into the intersection of moral statistics and industrialization. While the Brahmin Boston Associates who built the mills were eager to develop British-style manufacturing in the United States, they were reluctant revolutionaries, wary about what these economic changes might do to the patriarchal fabric of homespun America. Horrified by the social dislocation he witnessed during a visit to England, Lowell industrialist Nathan Appleton believed that social progress could not simply be measured by money. " 'Tis true that in this country money will purchase a thousand conveniences and attentions we are without in America," he noted in his diary, "but as these are in great measure the consequence of the debasement of the lower classes of society—for the happiness of our country at large I could with it long without them."[23]

To avoid the "debasement" of American society and the rise of a European wage-laboring proletariat, the Lowell manufacturers famously employed local farmers' daughters for only a few years and housed them in carefully regulated boardinghouses. Nevertheless, the boardinghouse was not the family home, and Lowell elites now needed to keep an eye on far more girls than just their own daughters. Among other practices, they began to utilize moral statistics. After visiting the Lowell mills in 1841, for instance, English Quaker and abolitionist Joseph Sturge cited "the moral statistics of the place" at length from a "pamphlet published by a respectable citizen of Lowell." Regurgitating the data he had been fed during his visit, Sturge noted that Lowell contained "14 religious societies, 4936 scholars, 433 teachers," and that most of the scholars were mill girls. Sturge then went on to quote statistics regarding public schools, Sunday schools, and pauper rates. A component of what Lowell Unitarian minister Henry Miles referred to as "the moral police of the corporations," moral statistics were used by Lowell managers to improve both living conditions and profit margins. As Miles explained in one of his sermons, "The productiveness of these works [the textile factories] depends upon one primary and indispensable condition—the existence of an industrious, sober, orderly and moral class of operatives. Without this, the mills in Lowell would be worthless. Profits would be absorbed by cases of irregularity."[24]

———————

Part and parcel of the Second Great Awakening that swept across the Northeast, a steady stream of moral statistics also erupted from the hundreds of reform associations cropping up in industrializing towns. By 1828 in the upstate New York town of Utica, which was home to one of the largest textile manufacturers in the country, there were twenty-one religious or charitable societies, three reform societies, five benefit associations, six fraternal orders, six self-improvement associations, and plenty of moral calculating. As one moral reformer of the city asserted, statistics on sexual offenses could "move public opinion" and, like "mounted pieces of artillery, pour upon the lines of licentiousness a stream of fire, spreading terror and dismay through the camp."[25]

Steeped in a Calvinist theology that centered on God's will, most colonial Americans did not devote much time or effort to collecting moral statistics, since social phenomena such as poverty, prostitution, and crime were understood to be unavoidable. The Jacksonian Era's middle-class men and women who joined moral reform associations in droves, however, no longer believed in the inexorable depravity of man or woman; rather, they believed in humans' moral free agency and thus their potential for perfectibility. Instead of placing their faith in an inscrutable predestination, religious reformers focused on the individual's ability to better him- or herself. Appearing frequently in sermons and reform associations' annual reports, moral statistics came to be seen as a key medium with which to spread the millennial gospel of self-improvement. As the twentieth annual report of the American Tract Society explained, "A moral census of the United States would be a document of invaluable interest to the Christian philanthropist. It would serve as an incentive and guide to benevolent effort, and lead to more intelligent, well-directed and comprehensive plans of evangelization."[26]

The life of Lemuel Shattuck, founder of the American Statistical Association, reflects how religious change played a key role in the making of moral statistics. Typical of the fatalistic Christianity of early America, Shattuck's first diary entry in 1812 opens by noting that "this day 19 years ago I was born into this world a sinner, possest of that principle which is opposed to God and his government; totally depraved in all my actions, desires and affections." By the end of that decade, however, Shattuck had headed west, founded a school in Detroit based on the highly disciplinary Lancasterian system that was all the rage at the time, and had opened the first Sunday school in the state of Michigan. As school principal, Shattuck began to emphasize self-improvement, not inherent depravity. Already exhibiting his future fondness for statistical surveillance, he proudly noted in an 1819 *Detroit Gazette* article that 75 of his 170 students had made definite improvement in reading; 114 had been taught to write on paper and 69 on slates; and 61 had made progress in simple rule arithmetic, 15 in reduction, and 13 in "the rule of three."[27]

By the 1840s, after moving back east to open a shop in Concord, Massachusetts, Shattuck's spiritual transformation was complete, and he no longer dwelled on humankind's propensity for sin but rather its possibility for perfection. His 1845 census of Boston delved into the world of health and moral statistics as a "means of ameliorating the mental, moral and physical condition of man." A serial do-gooder, by 1848 he was proposing laws that would force owners to muzzle their dogs and by 1850 he was pushing for a cleaner city as head of the Boston Sanitary Commission. That year he tried to start a magazine titled *The Philanthropist,* which would focus on "educational institutions, pauperism, prison discipline, hygiene and statistics" and "give a correct account of the condition, government and statistics of all the charitable, punitive, disciplinary, educational and moral institutions."[28]

Christian do-gooding and moral statistics went hand in hand. Reformers viewed such figures as a powerful instrument for discipline, surveillance, and self-improvement that could help cut crime, improve health, end prostitution, stifle alcohol abuse, and make America a better place to live. By the 1840s, many organizations answered the American Tract Society's call for the taking of a "moral census." In 1840, the *Minutes of the General Assembly of the Presbyterian Church* contained more than thirty pages of moral statistics. In 1841, the American Temperance Society calculated that of all the paupers in America, "seven-eights became so by intemperance." The annual reports of the Utica Female Missionary Service—of which Mary Ryan estimates that 70 percent of the members were the wives of merchants—featured a precise accounting of the number of child salvations. Sunday school journals regularly kept an eye on the working classes, and counted the number of conversions as well.[29]

Even Lewis Tappan's Mercantile Agency—the first credit reporting company in America, founded in 1841—can be seen as a data-generating institution for moral reform. An ardent abolitionist and temperance reformer, Tappan applied the logic of moral statistics to credit relations by imposing market discipline through moral surveillance. Reports made by local informants of their neighbors' deviancy or immorality were funneled to a central office and made available to paying customers. At a time when businessmen were beginning to believe that "good moral character" was their "most valuable capital," Tappan's credit agency supplied a nascent bourgeoisie with the moralizing data they felt they needed to make good in the marketplace. As such, the early entries in Tappan's Mercantile Agency contained very little monetary measurements and a great deal of gossip. In 1862, Morgan Frost of Oswego County would be priced at $10,000 "worth." But in 1846 he was simply "very industrious and attentive." Freeman Phillips, a hatmaker, was first priced in 1869. In the 1840s, he was "honest, attractive, home-owner, prudent cautious."[30]

Moral statistics were being collected not only by reform societies and mercantile agencies but also by insane asylums, prisons, poorhouses, and hospitals. In early America, such institutions had been scarce, with little regimented scheduling of the inmate's day and few statistical reports. With the crumbling of the household order, however, came the rise of these custodial institutions. The first state prisons opened in New York in 1823, Pennsylvania in 1826, Massachusetts and Maryland in 1829, New Jersey in 1830, Tennessee in 1831, Georgia in 1832, Louisiana in 1835, and Alabama in 1841. Jacksonian America was also the heyday of the construction of insane asylums, houses of correction, and poorhouses. In 1830 there was one public insane asylum in the entire country. By 1860, twenty-eight of the thirty-three states had public institutions for the insane. Between 1820 and 1840 sixty towns in Massachusetts constructed new almshouses. One in-depth statistical study of the poor in New York State done in 1824, a study that never would have been undertaken a few years prior, demonstrated that only 30 towns in a sample of 130 had an almshouse. By 1835, 51 out of 55 counties had at least one.[31]

American prisons, poorhouses, and insane asylums reflect the reformist dreams of American elites. Seen as "a grand theatre, for the trial of all new plans in hygiene and education, in physical and moral reform," asylums were conceived as utopian islands of total bourgeois order, in which the messiness of real life could be superseded by regimented systems of complete discipline and control. Statistics played a central role in this new system of regulated order. The annual reports of insane asylums, prisons, and poorhouses became a never-ending wellspring of moral statistics. Along with moral reform associations, religious organizations, and state censuses, asylums inundated the United States with an array of data on paupers, drunks, prostitutes, scholars, lunatics, and criminals. To gain a better sense of how these figures were used, we must take a closer look at each.[32]

American towns had been collecting information on the poor since colonial times. Colonial reports mostly kept track of the number of paupers and their expense to the community. They lumped together all those in need, be they orphans, widows, or invalids. Often the only distinction made, which demonstrates the communal life of colonial America, was whether the person in need was a stranger to the town or not. But in Jacksonian

America, when pauperism became an indicator of societal well-being, new statistical categories emerged in government reports seeking to track *why* a given person was a pauper. The 1845 report of New York's secretary of state, for instance, which contained data collected by the various superintendents of the poor, listed "intemperance," "idleness," "idiocy," "lunacy," "blindness," "lameness," "sickness," "decrepitude," "old age," "destitution," "misfortune," "mute[ness]," "orphan[ed]," "illegitimate," "abandoned," "debauchery," "total debauchery," and "cause not given."[33]

Such categories were often used to divide the deserving poor from the undeserving. Lemuel Shattuck quantified the poor in such a manner in his 1845 city census, classifying paupers according to whether they could work or were "unable to labor." By the end of the 1840s, this approach was reaching the federal government as Boston Brahmin and statistical dabbler Nahum Capen wrote a letter to the Senate Census Committee head, John Davis, suggesting that a table separating paupers with "physical disability" from those with "bad habits" should be added to the 1850 census.[34]

Some Americans, however, did not view pauperism figures in such a way. In their hands, these statistics underwent a republican transformation. "I should be very unwilling to make the British Government a model for our legislation in republican America," a young James Buchanan declared on the floor of Congress in 1839. "Where is the country beneath the sun in which pauperism prevails to such a fearful extent?" Using England as a stand-in for capitalist relations rather than as an exemplar of moral statistics, Buchanan transformed pauperism into an indicator of societal well-being. He was not alone. In 1834, for instance, a popular labor newspaper edited by the Workingmen's Party's George H. Evans echoed Buchanan's argument regarding the degradation of American society by showing how in one American city of 80,000 people there were more than 5,000 paupers. Yet unlike their middle-class employers, most working-class Americans never took to moral statistics and rarely incorporated them into their writing. Jacksonian Democrats such as the journalist William Leggett had a flair for the melodramatic, and dry statistics did not further their populist agenda. As a result, moral statistics remained an elitist pastime.[35]

Jacksonian America was also filled with a "striking" amount of intemperance statistics. Amherst College president Herman Humphrey used statistics to prove that the prevalent use of ardent spirits in the United States was "a worse evil at this moment than the slave-trade ever was, in the height of its horrible prosperity." Seeking to compare the "aggregate of misery" brought on by intemperance and that caused by the slave trade, Humphrey filled numerous pages with complex calculations based on intemperance data mostly taken from Unitarian minister John Gorham Palfrey's sermons at Brattle Square Church in Boston. In doing so, Humphrey reached the conclusion that while the slave trade brought 25,000 to 30,000 people "into bondage," intemperance brought 36,000. While 10,000 to 15,000 annually had died due to the slave trade, he claimed, 36,000 lost their lives to alcohol each year. "Thus, where the slave trade opened one grave," Humphrey concluded, "hard drinking opens three."[36]

Humphrey's calculations were hardly unique. At some point most temperance sermons or reports of the era cited statistics. In 1831, religious leaders in Boston created a table that tracked the number of church members who had been excommunicated because of intemperance. Reverend Charles Walker kept a record of the deaths in his community during the six years he spent as minister of East Rutland, Vermont, and concluded that of the thirty-nine men who died, more than half were intemperate. Such temperance statistics usually appeared in industrializing areas and were undoubtedly intended to instill in urban journeymen and laborers, who no longer lived or worked alongside their bosses, the same industrial discipline that their masters-turned-manufacturers had begun to internalize in the 1820s.[37]

Another popular moral statistic was prostitution. In 1830, Reverend John McDowall moved to New York City to do missionary work in the slums of Five Points. Going from brothel to brothel, he began to collect statistics on the number of prostitutes. At the end of the year, McDowall founded the New York Magdalen Society and published his astonishing findings, which claimed that there were 10,000 prostitutes in the city and that their clientele included some of New York's finest gentlemen. While the controversy over McDowall's figures led to the closing of his society, his report became the initial drop in a torrent of prostitution statistics. A "census of prostitutes" became a frequent occurrence in cities such as New York, Cincinnati, and Philadelphia, whether they were conducted by government institutions such as the New York Board of Aldermen, moral reform organizations such as the Magdalen

Society, local police departments, magazines such as the *Journal of Public Morals,* sensationalist journalists, or crusading individuals such as John McDowall.[38]

For some reformers, prostitution figures were viewed simply as indicators of "licentiousness" and "moral depravity," and the women themselves were usually blamed for having "fallen." Depicting prostitutes in his diary as having "thief written in their cunning eyes and whore on their depraved faces," financier George Templeton Strong, like many men of capital, tended to explain the rise of prostitution with arguments that focused on the intrinsic weakness of women of the lower classes. Other New Yorkers, however, viewed prostitution as a structural, economic problem. After reading McDowall's stunning statistical reports, a writer for the *Sun* linked sexual exploitation to economic exploitation, noting that the increase in "licentiousness" was due to the low wages of female servants and the "unjust arrangement of remuneration for services performed." In his sensational book *New York Naked,* George G. Foster voiced the same conclusion: "Female prostitution is the direct result of the inadequate compensation for female labor."[39]

The idea that prostitution could serve as an indicator of societal well-being led some reformers to greatly expand the scope of McDowall's initial project, in hopes of uncovering the reasons behind the social phenomenon. Written as an official report to the New York City Board of Almshouses Governors, William Sanger's mammoth *History of Prostitution* included a wide-ranging statistical survey that included data on prostitutes' health, literacy rates, age, life expectancy, place of birth, average weekly earnings, trade or calling prior to prostitution, and even their father's occupation or business. Discovering that prostitution was the "only means of support" for 85 percent of the women he spoke with, and that roughly half had been working beforehand as domestic servants under conditions that "would bring a blush to the cheek of the southern slave driver," Sanger turned prostitution statistics into an indicator of economic exploitation. He also placed the brunt of the blame on the importation of British forms of capitalist social relations to America. "Study the moral statistics of any of the manufacturing towns in Great Britain or on the Continent of Europe," he concluded, "and the same results are presented, but in more alarming degree."[40]

In 1840, information on level of education—another staple of moral statistics—appeared in the U.S. census for the first time. The census marshals were instructed to count the number of students in primary, grammar, and common schools as well as universities, colleges, and academies. Along with literacy rates, these education figures soon became a leading benchmark for measuring progress. *The Liberty Almanac,* a key source of anti-slavery statistics in the Jacksonian era, made sure to point out in an article titled "Slave Power—Morally" that in Connecticut 1 out of 568 people was illiterate, while in Virginia it was 1 in every 12.5. "Ohio alone had 51,812 scholars—more than are to be found in thirteen Slave States!" What the almanac did not point out, however, was that literacy and education data had been collected only for whites. Apparently no one in the Census Bureau had felt the need to check the educational status of African Americans, be they free or enslaved.[41]

A main stimulus for the rise of education statistics was the work of Boston education reformer Horace Mann, who in 1837 was appointed the secretary of the newly created Massachusetts Board of Education—the first such institution in the United States. With no real regulatory or funding power, yet required to submit an annual report, Mann turned to statistics. Traversing the state, he counted the number of libraries, mechanics' institutes, reading rooms, lyceums, literary societies, and public lectures.[42]

Mann's reports often emphasized the importance of free education in a republican society that strived for social and economic equality. But he also saw schools, and hence school statistics, as instruments of social discipline. "The increased means for education for the last sixty years," Mann lamented to a friend in 1840, "have not kept pace with the increasing obligations, duties and temptations of the community." The connection that Mann made between education statistics and social control also came to the fore in a lively debate in European and American elite circles regarding whether increased education led to a reduction in crime. This was the key question at the heart of André-Michel Guerry's 1833 *Essay on Moral Statistics of France,* a groundbreaking work of social science in which Guerry used statistical maps of crime and education to prove that there was in fact a positive correlation between the two.[43]

Guerry's findings were widely reported in such periodicals as the *American Annals of Education,* a foreseeable development given the rising popularity of crime statistics in the United States. During a passionate sermon in Baltimore on "spiritual destitutions," Presbyterian pastor T. J. Shepherd stopped to apologize to his crowd for apparently being as yet unable to back his claims with "accredited criminal and pauper statistics." In his regret, Shepherd expressed what his crowd already knew: crime statistics packed a powerful punch as indicators of societal well-being. The pro-manufacturing *Niles National Register* used statistics on Swedish incarceration rates to prove that industrialization did not necessarily lead to the "demoralization" of the people. Horace Greeley's *New York Tribune* was especially fond of statistics that listed crimes committed, conviction rates, sentences, and the impact of intemperance. In reviewing a state report, the *Tribune* noted that "the most valuable and interesting portion of the report is its statistics of crime and corruption," which reflected the glaring need "for the suppression of licentiousness and other vices."[44]

Shattuck's 1845 Boston census reveals how statistics and prisons became entwined in the city's rampant industrialization. Citing data from the directors of the Massachusetts House of Reformation, Shattuck noted that of the 685 boys and 128 girls committed to the House of Reformation since 1826, 323 had been sentenced for "theft or petty pilfering," 216 for being "stubborn and disobedient," 191 for "vagrancy," and 45 for being "idle and dissolute." Yet thanks to the institution's strict and regimented policies, many of the "vagabonds" who had challenged bourgeois property rights and work ethic had been successfully absorbed into the labor market: of the 800-plus criminals, 442 had successfully been "indented to farmers, seamanship and various trades" with "girls instructed in housekeeping."[45]

Crime statistics could not have circulated in daily newspapers, city censuses, and Sunday sermons were it not for the increased bureaucratization of the American state and the numerous annual reports thus generated. The Ohio attorney general, for example, first published an annual crime report in 1846. The report found that in 363, or one-sixth, of the state's prosecutions "intemperance is set down as the cause of the offence." It was these reports, moreover, which allowed Americans to take part in the debate surrounding education and crime that Guerry had first set off. A New York State report, for instance, held that of 27,949 convicts, only 1,182 had received "common education"; 414 had received a "tolerably good education," and 128 were "well educated." "What an argument for free schools!" exclaimed one of the many newspapers that printed the findings.[46]

Insanity statistics were also a central component of the moral statistician's toolbox. Mental health was a hot-button issue in Jacksonian America, as the establishment of dozens of asylums would suggest. That insanity rates were at the center of the biggest antebellum scandal surrounding the American census, therefore, should not be surprising. The story behind the scandal is straightforward enough: Edward Jarvis, a struggling physician from Massachusetts with a penchant for statistical analysis, published an article in a leading medical journal in 1842 in which he revealed that, according to the 1840 census, the proportion of blacks suffering from insanity was far higher in the North than in the South. In Maine, for instance, a stunning 1 out of 14 African Americans was listed as "insane" or "idiotic," while in Louisiana it was 1 out of 4,310.[47]

At first Jarvis accepted these census figures and explained them with the typical racist and paternalist tropes of the day, noting that "slavery has a wonderful influence upon the development of moral faculties and the intellectual powers" of blacks since it insulated their feeble minds from the "responsibilities which the free, self-thinking and self-acting enjoy and sustain." Apparently, however, Jarvis was still unconvinced that such striking differences were accurate, and he decided to go over the actual data. Much to his surprise, Jarvis discovered enormous discrepancies. He quickly published a second article in the same journal and announced that the figures were all wrong. By then, however, it was too late.[48]

Recognizing the powerful sway that moral statistics had in both the North and in Europe, southerners did not miss an opportunity to stake a claim for the moral superiority of their "peculiar institution." First, an anonymous writer sent a short article to *Hunt's Merchants' Magazine* revealing the stunning discrepancies in northern and southern black insanity statistics. (The fact that a business magazine was interested in such figures is further evidence of the widespread authority moral statistics had in the early 1840s.) Then, in the summer of 1843, the influential *Southern Literary Messenger* published a detailed article that reveled in these statistical findings. "Insanity arises," the journal argued, "most frequently from moral causes." Citing 1843 *American Almanac* statistics generated by newly established insane asylums in Massachusetts, Ohio, and Western Virginia, the *Messenger* asserted that of the 1,284 men and women who had been committed, 879 had been driven insane from "moral causes," which included "domestic affliction, religious feeling, grief for loss of property, fright, disappointed affection and jealousy." "Dreadful indeed are the evils," the article concluded, convinced that it had effectively linked insanity to morality, "that produce a maniac in every 34 of the population." The census figures, according to the article, proved that blacks were "not only happier in a state of slavery than of freedom, but we believe the happiest class on the continent."[49]

The seemingly objective conclusions of the *Southern Literary Messenger* reverberated through American society like a tidal wave, proving once more the power of moral statistics. From that point on, southern leaders such as John Calhoun would endlessly cite the 1840 census insanity figures, while northerners such as Edward Jarvis and John Quincy Adams, as well as the newly founded American Statistical Association, battled tirelessly to have the errors of the census officially acknowledged.[50]

By the 1830s, there was widespread agreement that mental illness was a by-product of the stress that accompanied market relations and the demise of traditional hierarchical societies. Such arguments became especially popular following the Panic of 1837, an event whose very name (much like the twentieth-century use of the term "economic depression") reveals the mental anguish that accompanied a sudden contraction in credit and output. Worcester Lunatic Hospital head Samuel Woodward, one of the leading experts on insanity statistics in America, concluded that the United States was fourth among all the countries in the world in the proportion of lunatics. Why was America ranked so high? Writing in the aftermath of the Panic of 1837, Woodward provided a clear answer, which was cited in the leading "magazine of moral science": "overtrading, debt, bankruptcy, sudden reverses, disappointed hopes."[51]

Jarvis argued for similar causes. Recall that he had initially thought that it was totally plausible that black insanity rates in the North would be much higher than in the South since southern slaves (according to Jarvis) lived in a stress-free, paternalist world, while northern blacks were forced to deal with the pressure that came with "self-acting" free labor. "In this country," Jarvis once noted, "where no son is necessarily confined to the work or employment of his father, but all the field of labor, of profit, or of honor are open to whomever will put on the harness, all are invited to join the strife for that which may be gained by each." As the theories of Woodward and Jarvis reveal, every time insanity statistics were cited, mentioned, or used, an implicit argument was brought to the fore: market freedom was stressful, and it could drive you mad.[52]

As the scandal over census insanity statistics demonstrates, northerners were not the only ones ensuring that moral statistics would become the dominant social indicators of the age. It was, after all, an article in the *Southern Literary Messenger*—a Virginia magazine for southern elites—that transformed Jarvis's statistical discovery from a minor observation in a little-read medical journal into a full-blown sectional conflict. The *Messenger* article that broke the story, meanwhile, demonstrated that while the magazine's editors took advantage of erroneous insanity statistics, southern elites were up to speed on all the leading moral statistics of the day. Shifting effortlessly from insanity to crime statistics, the magazine noted how "of every nine convicts in the eastern penitentiary [in Philadelphia] in 1831, four were negroes; of every nine in 1841, seven are blacks!" Comparing these figures to the population of Virginia Penitentiary, where there were "nearly three times as many whites as colored," the article concluded that black slaves "are a more respectable class than persons of their race in the free states."[53]

The uglier the scandal surrounding the 1840 census got, the more often southerners exhibited their proficiency in moral statistics. After Jarvis and the ASA wrote a memorial to Congress arguing that the 1840 census was filled with errors, William Weaver—superintendent of the census and a proud Virginian—provided Congress with a lengthy response. Gathering data from "the keepers of jails and houses of correction" as well as on the number of "inmates in the houses of industry or almshouse," Weaver calculated that the percentage of "confined" blacks in Boston was 6 percent, in New York 4 percent, and in Philadelphia 3.35 percent. Shifting to the South, Weaver then showed that the number of "confined" blacks in Richmond was 2 percent and in Charleston 1.57 percent.[54]

Southerners were especially fond of using the northern elites' love of reform associations, prisons, and asylums—and the statistics they generated—against them. In response, northerners pointed to the fact that moral statistics made the South look good because a slave society did not need to collect such figures. "We have a full record of the northern crimes," one northern newspaper complained, "but not of the southern. The crimes and punishment of slaves, short of felony and hanging, are not recorded. Minor offences such as drunkenness, fighting, disorderly conduct in public spaces, are in most parts of the South scarcely noted, and in no part, so strictly dealt as in the Northern cities, where they have vigilant police." The northern commenter had a point. Living in a largely rural slave society where most laborers remained unfree and the state did not have a monopoly on violence, southerners had not needed to develop the kind of bourgeois institutions of social policing that served as the mainspring of moral statistics. As reformer and abolitionist Theodore Parker recognized, it was only in the "free states" where "men originate societies for the Reform of Prisons, the Prevention of Crime, Pauperism, Intemperance, Licentiousness, and Ignorance."[55]

That said, while the South's use of moral statistics was certainly strategic, it was not completely cynical. There was a genuine interest in such figures among southern elites. In one instance, the *Southern Literary Messenger* praised the figures included in the *American Almanac,* "especially the account of the principal benevolent institutions in the United States." In another piece on education, the magazine cited a Virginia legislative report that the state had 58,787 illiterates while Massachusetts only had 4,448, and that Massachusetts had 160,257 scholars attending primary schools while Virginia only 35,321—disturbing differences. Finally, it was Francis Lieber, professor of history and political economy at South Carolina College, who wrote a memorial to Congress in the 1830s suggesting that the moral statistics section of the census be dramatically expanded.[56]

As the *Messenger*'s interest in moral statistics demonstrates, while southerners enjoyed making northerners look bad, this was not the only thing that had led them into the comforting arms of moral statistics. As historian James Oakes has shown, "Prosperous planters and mistresses reared their children according to the precepts lad down in guidebooks written by and for the northern middle class." What is more, it seems likely that southern slaveholders were genuinely attracted to northern moral statistics because they understood the disciplinary power of institutionalized surveillance. There may not have been as many asylums or poorhouses in the South, but there were plenty of open-air prisons in which dreams of total social control played out every day. They were called plantations.[57]

As a result of the general interest in moral statistics, the city censuses of Charleston and New Orleans mimicked the quantification techniques of Shattuck's groundbreaking Boston census, as did Mobile, Alabama, physician and statistician Josiah Nott. Nott also kept abreast of all the leading European moral statisticians of the day, and corresponded with Shattuck throughout the 1840s. Much like Calhoun and other southerners, he enjoyed legitimizing slavery through a statistical comparison of the condition of free and enslaved blacks. In one typical instance, he used vital statistics in order to show that while one in twenty-six blacks died in Philadelphia each year, in Charleston it was one in forty-one. Arguing that in Africa, "the average longevity of blacks (as in all barbarous nations) will be less than among slaves," Nott couched his argument in the paternalist language of moral statistics to make the claim that "history cannot point to any epoch, or spot on earth, where the condition of the negro race, either physical or moral, has been at all comparable with that of the slaves of the United States." Cynically or not, southerners such as Nott and Calhoun wielded moral statistics in order to play up their own paternalist self-narrative that slavery was morally better for slaves than free labor. "We must satisfy them that slavery is of itself right," declared John Calhoun, master of the statistical spin, "that it is not a sin against God—that it is not an evil, moral or political."[58] Such paternalist statistical arguments were badly needed in Jacksonian America, as the internal slave trade ramped up and tore apart countless plantations and their black families.[59]

Moral statistics did not measure social welfare in units of money, as the American people's general disdain of the pricing of progress held strong through the 1840s. Further evidence for this can be found in the sudden explosion in the use of the word *priceless* in the 1830s and 1840s, a linguistic development that reflected the widely held belief that some things could not—and should not—be measured in money. According to one historical database, the frequency with which the word appeared in published texts quadrupled from 1810 to 1840. According to another, the term appeared 29 times in American newspapers between the years 1805 and 1815 and 668 times between the years 1835 and 1845. Between 1815 and 1825, not a single article in the *New Hampshire Sentinel* contained the word *priceless*. In the 1840s, the word appears 21 times.[60]

As an increase in market relations—in both the industrializing North and the cotton South—began to pull more and more aspects of society into a monetizing vortex, Americans reacted by trying to create isolated pockets of life

that would not bow to the power of exchange value to render all things commensurable. These pockets were deemed "priceless," and they came to include far more than precious works of art. Addressing a crowd of Jacksonian
Democrats in New York City, one labor activist rhetorically asked his fellow
workers whether "the priceless legacy of a Jefferson [would] be wrested from
us." The *Illinois Free Trader* spoke of the priceless "right of suffrage," and
the *Rutland Herald* wrote of the "priceless privilege" of youth. Early American patriarchs tended to segregate women from the market. They continued
to do so in the Jacksonian era, declaring "women's virtue" and "love" to be
priceless. Childhood, as novel a bourgeois invention as moral statistics, was
also deemed impossible to price. "Sport on! Sport on!" cried a poem for
children in the *Jefferson Republican*, "for your priceless worth is wealth un-
told at the household hearth." Abolitionists were especially fond of declaring
the priceless value of "life," "liberty," and "freedom." *The Emancipator* condemned slavery for doing its "utmost to cheapen human life, when the proof
of its priceless worth lived in his own nature." Despite the fact that hundreds
of thousands of the state's residents were being priced and sold, even
Virginia's *Southern Argus* described the soul as a "priceless and unfading
jewel."[61]

Jacksonian Democrats were especially vocal in their disapproval of the
equation of progress with money. Anti-banking reformer William Gouge criticized New York businessmen for considering "wealth as the only means of
happiness," and then went on to compare them to "the magpie, [who] in
hiding silver spoons in its nest appeared to act with as much reflection as they
do in piling money-bag on money-bag. They have no object in view beyond
accumulation." Gilbert Vale, a New York labor radical, rejected the materialism of classical English economics and argued that the government "should
regard the *happiness* of the people, while political economy only regards the
wealth of the nation." Vale urged American economic thinkers to not "merely
regard the accumulation of wealth at the expense of moral principles, health
or rational refinement of the family."[62]

While Jacksonian America's distrust of price statistics and wealth figures
was, in part, a continuation of early American ideas, there was also something
novel in their rejection of monetized metrics: a rapidly diminishing faith in
the representative powers of money. While Americans of an earlier era had
spurned the pricing of progress, many of them had still believed that com-

modity prices were an accurate representation of labor value. This was a fitting worldview for the property-owning yeoman farmer or artisan producer, who experienced the market mostly as an even-handed mechanism of exchange. By the Jacksonian era, however, fractional-reserve banking, rising inflation, and the emergence of a dispossessed class of wage laborers seriously undermined the representative association between labor and price. "Every dollar of a bank bill that is issued beyond the quantity of gold and silver in the vaults," John Adams declared as early as 1809, "represents nothing and is therefore a cheat upon somebody." Adams was not alone. Urban laborers who were seeing their cost of living rise yet their bargaining power be whittled away began to attack the representative ability of cash. Led by the likes of labor leader Langdon Byllesby, a nascent labor movement began to organize unions in an attempt to bypass market valuations and fix wages "according to the average time required for the making of an article."[63]

Some Americans went so far as to reject the idea of money completely. Josiah Warren opened a "time magazine" in Cincinnati, a cooperative that disposed of goods according to their labor-time costs. Much like the "labor notes" used in New Harmony, Robert Owen's utopian community in Indiana (as well as the "equitable labor exchange" Owen founded in London in 1832), Warren's customers paid for goods with pieces of paper inscribed with statements such as "three hours' labor in Carpenters Work." Walk into Warren's time store, and you would find a sign on the door:

> All hail to the era of knowledge divide!
> When the value of Labor by Time is displayed,
> When money the bane of mankind must decline
> Since time, peerless time, forms the medium of trade.[64]

Yet urban laborers and cooperative-store owners were hardly outliers in their rejection of such money measures. Even Boston's elite joined in the chorus. Horace Mann mocked English political economy's "heathen standards" of progress, which focused not on republican equality but on material growth. "Political Economy which busies itself about capital and labor, supply and demand, interest and rents, favorable and unfavorable balances of trade, but leaves out of account the element of a wide-spread mental development, is naught but stupendous folly," Mann declared. Shattuck also wholeheartedly denounced the pricing of progress in his Boston census:

> Others have objected to any investigation which might show one section of the city to be more unhealthy than the other, because it would *impair the value of real estate!* . . . In proportion as we view human life, with all the manifold consequences of its perseveration, to be more valuable than the few dollars and cents, more or less, which a landlord may receive from a tenant in an unhealthy locality. . . . The private, social or public consequences of sickness and mortality cannot be measured in money. This is a matter of great magnitude, compared with it, all other investigations are unimportant.[65]

Many Southern elites also rejected the pricing of progress. Josiah C. Nott, for example, showed little interest in monetized measures. This was partly due to his virulent racism. In the lead-up to the 1850 census, Nott successfully lobbied Congress to add not market statistics, in which he showed little interest, but rather the racial category "mulatto." Nott had done so because he wanted to statistically prove that "mulattoes" were physically weaker and less fertile than "pure" blacks or whites. He believed that such a finding would confirm his theory of racial polygenesis, which held that blacks and whites were not of the same species. Nott was horrified that Shattuck had not bothered to statistically separate blacks and whites in his Boston census, and his main goal was to use data in order to segregate, not aggregate. Since one of the main benefits of money is that it makes everything—even blacks and whites—commensurable, one can see why Nott did not care for the pricing of everyday life.[66]

Nott's writings on life insurance, however, suggest that racism was not the only reason he cared little for market measures. As policies insuring the life of a slave became more popular in the 1840s, the southern business magazine *De Bow's Review* asked Nott, an expert on slave life expectancy, to pen an article on the topic. Southern planters had begun to hail life insurance as a godsend, as it significantly lowered the risks involved in buying slaves. Yet instead of supplying *De Bow's* with actuarial tables, slave prices, or age-based productivity figures that would have allowed slave owners to calculate the depreciation rate of slaves or determine whether a particular premium was a good value, Nott stood steadfast against the very practice of slave insurance.

The argument he gave was a moral one. Today, in fact, his point about the incentive problems brought on by insurance is known as "moral hazard":

> As long as the negro is sound, and worth more than the amount insured, self-interest will prompt the owner to preserve the life of the slave; but if the slave becomes unsound and there is little prospect of perfect recovery, the underwriters cannot expect fair play—the insurance money is worth more than the slave, and the latter is regarded rather in the light of a super-annulated horse. Would not many be like the Yankee Captain with the insured ship, "damn the old hulk, let her sink—I am safe"? "The Almighty Dollar" would soon silence the soft, small voice of humanity.

In the 1840s, even despicably racist, emphatically pro-slavery demagogues such as Josiah Nott had their misgivings about the cash nexus destroying what they saw to be the traditional social relations that tied a master to his slave.[67]

Yet as the sectional crisis became more and more rancorous, and the United States became more and more capitalist, the American elite's way of quantifying the world would undergo a dramatic change. By the 1850s, the wealthy and powerful on both sides of the Mason-Dixon line would come to embrace the evaluative powers of "the almighty dollar"—a term that exploded onto the scene in that decade, after Washington Irving had first used it in 1836 to describe "that great object of universal devotion throughout our land."[68]

FIVE

The Hunt for Growth

FOR THE BUSINESSMEN OF St. Louis, June 19, 1880, was a date that would live in infamy. That was the day the municipal results of the 1880 census were released and the prominent citizens of the River City discovered, much to their horror, that the population of their fair city had only increased from 310,804 in 1870 to 333,570 in 1880. "The city," the *St. Louis Post-Dispatch* noted, "is considerably agitated today over the apparent imperfections in the taking of the census." "The public," wrote *St. Louis Globe-Democrat* editor Joseph McCullagh, "seem to have grown somewhat restless concerning the results of the present census . . . and are beginning to be frightened that the figures will not reach, or at any rate go beyond, 400,000." The result, the *Illinois State Register* added, "is alarming to the soul of the average citizen of the 'Future Great' and curses loud and deep are escaping the throats of the people."[1]

While these newspapers framed the census results as a crushing blow to "the city," "the public," "the average citizen," and "the people," in practice only the city's newspaper editors, merchants, manufacturers, bankers, and real estate owners seemed to be upset by this statistical development. One such businessman feared that the census results "will materially depreciate our real estate, and injure the trade and commerce of St. Louis, as such an extent as will be felt by all classes of our citizens." The editor of the *Post-Dispatch* exclaimed that the census was "a libel on our growth" and warned that St. Louis "will appear as a decaying, retrograding city," the consequences of which would be disastrous: "It will dishearten our people. It will discourage capital. It will decrease the value of real property and choke up prosperous industries." McCullagh explained to his readers that the disappointing population count "is not merely a sentimental grievance, it is a blow to the prosperity of St. Louis and to the welfare of every business interest. Our trade, our real estate, our railroads, our municipal and private credit, all are injured by a defective census."[2]

Less than a week later, the St. Louis bourgeoisie were dealt another devastating statistical blow. The census results had been tabulated in Chicago, that archnemesis to the north, and the Windy City had announced that it had surpassed the vaunted half-million mark. The businessmen of St. Louis were stunned: this was not how things were supposed to play out for an urban elite who had earnestly believed that continuous population growth would one day lead to St. Louis replacing Washington, D.C., as the capital of the nation. Only ten years before, in the census of 1870, they had ranked as the third-largest city in the nation. A few months before the 1880 census, the St. Louis papers were still confident enough in their city's growth to joke that "the newly appointed census taker for St. Louis should understand . . . that he must beat Chicago or leave town." After the news of Chicago's population explosion reached St. Louis, the mood was far more somber. The people of St. Louis, McCullagh wrote, had been "hopeful of a showing in population that would cause Chicagoans to rush towards the Lake front with overwhelming unanimity to throw themselves headlong into the water." Instead, it was St. Louis who "must take a back seat for the next ten years." To make matters even worse, "the Cheeky Chicago People" were reveling in their newly found statistical dominance, with Chicago papers mockingly arguing that perhaps the discrepancy between St. Louis's outrageous boasts and their dismal statistical reality was due to a sudden loss of population caused by the city's stench.[3]

A few days after the bad news broke, a group of "prominent citizens" met at the Lindell Hotel to decide what to do about the census. Despite the fact that "the heat in the room was murderous," the St. Louis hotel was packed with so many flour and commission merchants, bankers, manufacturers, grocers, dry-goods wholesalers, and other men of business that the crowd spilled into the hallway. As those present shouted out their grievances, a plan was hatched to send a coterie of leading businessmen to Washington to demand a recount from Francis Amasa Walker, the census superintendent. This was the second census Walker had supervised, and he was already well versed in these situations. In 1870, he had agreed to administer a recount in New York, Philadelphia, and Indianapolis. Meeting with St. Louis's leading men in Washington, Walker said he would call a recount. After a month of tense waiting and daily coverage by the newspapers, the new results finally came in. The census had been off—but barely. Instead of 333,570 people, the new census counted 350,518. St. Louis's economic elites were crushed.[4]

Since St. Louis's businessmen seemed to have been genuinely convinced that the initial census results were incorrect, it appears that they were less concerned with the *actual* population growth of their city and far more with the abstract statistical *image* the census had produced. From their laments and frustrations, we can surmise that their panic-stricken reaction to the 1880 census results stemmed from their assumption that a city's perceived population growth had a direct effect on its ability to attract capital. As they noted, a disappointing census return would lead to injured credit, discouraged capital, choked industry, and depreciated real estate. We can also deduce that these population statistics were not serving as some barometer that gauged the ability of hardy American pioneers to survive the harsh winters of the Midwest. Despite the rather frantic tone of its businessmen, the city of St. Louis had not undergone some horrific calamity that had decimated the population. It had even grown—just not enough, apparently. No, this was not about survival; it was about capitalism. Why did booming census figures serve as a magnet for attracting investors to a city? What was the connection between population gains and capital gains, human growth and pecuniary growth? In short, what did counting people have to do with counting profits?

To answer these questions, we must travel back nearly a half century prior to explore the statistics-laden pages of *Hunt's Merchants' Magazine,* the first national business periodical in American history. Seeking to rationalize capital investment into a "science of business" following the Panic of 1837, Freeman Hunt launched a magazine that would play a decisive role in the transformation of urban population growth into an economic indicator that could help his readers decide in which western American cities they should purchase urban lots and invest their capital. With the help of a western booster and a southern economist, Hunt inundated his readers with population figures that linked the spatial concentration of the American people with future returns on westward-flowing capital. In so doing, *Hunt's* changed the way eastern capitalists envisioned the inhabitants of the United States by teaching them to recognize the vast profitability embodied in the American people's productive labor and material needs, especially those urban dwellers who did not own land, their home, or productive property. Before *Hunt's,* investors rarely analyzed data concerning the American people when deciding where to put their capital. By the Gilded Age, aggregated body counts could make or break any capital-hungry town, all the while helping to reimagine the American citizenry as the source of vast potential profits.[5]

Embedded within this statistical vision was a novel set of social and cultural values. Rather than prioritize landed independence, as early American measures had done, the figures in *Hunt's* figures extolled population growth, urban concentration, capital accumulation, and wage labor by landless urban dwellers. Fearful of an ever-increasing population in which independent farmers would be forced off the land and into city factories as dependent, propertyless wage laborers, most early Americans were wary about celebrating population growth as the ultimate engine of industrial progress and national prosperity. *Hunt's* displayed no such fears or trepidations, as it consistently equated more people and more cities with more markets and more progress. "It is not agriculture," Hunt declared, "it is commerce that has multiplied with such marvelous rapidity the cities and towns of the United States, and made them grow with such marvelous growth—which has built Chicago in twenty years and San Francisco in five." Portending the dawn of a new age of unabashed American capitalism, *Hunt's* celebrated not yeoman virtue, patriarchal independence, and moral reform but national markets, increasing urbanization, capital gains, and economic growth.[6]

American infatuation with economic growth statistics has largely been seen as a twentieth-century development. Yet it was in the mid-nineteenth century that American businessmen first fell in love with the idea of quantitative growth. *Hunt's Merchants' Magazine* played a crucial role in this statistical courtship. It is in the often bland pages of a mostly forgotten business magazine that some of the origins of our contemporary growth-obsessed polity can be uncovered. It is also here, in these profit-minded body counts, that the first significant move toward a pricing of American progress can be found.[7]

Unlike the abstract economic growth figures of today, which aggregate the prices of all commodities produced and consumed, the first growth statistics in America were far more corporeal. Just like the moral statistics they would eventually come to outshine, the magazine's growth tables counted mostly bodies, not money. Such a focus on population growth, however, did not mean that human beings were at the heart of this statistical vision, as they were with moral statistics. Quite the opposite, in fact. Serving as a crucial bridge between two distinct regimes of social quantification—moralizing statistics and capitalizing ones—the population growth statistics in *Hunt's* were used as a financial tool that could indicate the location of profitable investments. Transforming the American people into a statistical means to an accumulative end, *Hunt's* was not interested in whether the urban bodies it so meticulously counted belonged to scholars, prostitutes, paupers, or prisoners. It cared only about the rate at which their number grew.

Different economic, social, and cultural settings lead to different statistical visions. The governmentality of American moral statistics was the product of local businessmen, still very much entrenched in their community, trying to cope with industrial change in their own backyard. The investmentality of *Hunt's,* on the other hand, was the product of far-flung currents of national and international capital being invested by people who might never visit the towns they bought. Because of this social and spatial distance between investor and investment, *Hunt's* audience worried little about the local or social impact of their capital. They cared only about their return. And their return, *Hunt's* assured them, would only grow if the number of people who populated the city did too.

———————

While working as a young reporter for the *American Traveler* in 1836, Freeman Hunt decided to take a tour of the Hudson River and send back to his editor "plain, matter-of-fact epistles" on the region. In his first letter, Hunt began not by describing the city of Poughkeepsie or its surroundings but by pricing it. "The gross products of the country, from its soil, its mines, and its manufactories," Hunt noted, "are believed by persons best qualified to judge, to approach very near to *five million dollars* per annum." As it continued, Hunt's statistical narrative quickly got swept up in the speculative fever of the times. "Lots which were sold eighteen months ago for $600 have been sold for $4000," he wrote with exuberance, while "a farm in the vicinity, which was offered twenty months since for $22,000, has lately been sold for $68,000."[8]

Most travelers' literature of the era read nothing like this. *The Fashionable Tour in 1825* described Poughkeepsie simply by noting that "the village is about the same size of Newburgh, handsomely located, and a place of considerable trade." It did not list land values or gross products but rather spoke of "the sublime and romantic scenery" of the Hudson River valley. Hunt's letters, on the other hand, replaced romanticism with numbers—even on the seemingly most romantic of subjects. "If you have any young men in your goodly city in want of wives . . . some of the fair are certainly very beautiful," he reported. "I advise you to send them forthwith . . . as there are in the village, according to a census just completed, one thousand one hundred and thirteen unmarried young ladies."[9]

Always self-conscious of his statistical ramblings, Hunt made a point to explain to his editor the reasoning behind his unique writing style and viewpoint. "I consider the general diffusion of the statistical, commercial and geographical knowledge of interesting portions of our wide-spread republic," he wrote, "of vast importance to enterprising Yankees." Hunt had begun his career in journalism by founding and editing the *American Magazine of Useful and Entertaining Knowledge,* a typical Jacksonian Era magazine that contained a fair share of moral statistics. But in this journey down the Hudson, Hunt didn't bother to cite the number of paupers or drunks in Poughkeepsie. He was looking at the town not through the eyes of the local elite but rather through the eyes of Yankee capital. On this trip Hunt had discovered his life's calling: to assist financiers in their search for far-off profits by serving them a healthy portion of economic facts, figures, and charts.[10]

It would take Hunt only three more years to transform this vision into reality. In 1839 he began publishing *Hunt's Merchants' Magazine,* a monthly periodical whose mission it was to supply American businessmen with all the information they needed to capture new markets, assess their real-estate holdings, or pick railroad securities or bank stocks—in short, turn money into more money. In the following two decades, which ended with Civil War and Hunt's untimely death (according to the *New York Times* obituary, he had a "foible for the drink"), *Hunt's Merchants' Magazine* became the journal no serious investor interested in America, whether American or European, could afford not to read.[11]

The fact that Freeman Hunt's data-gathering career began with a visit to towns along the Hudson River was no accident. The Erie Canal, which had opened a decade prior and connected the Hudson to upstate New York and the Great Lakes, would play a central role in the rise of the magazine's statistical frontier. Until the Erie Canal opening, most eastern businessmen were international merchants who focused on agricultural exports and manufactured imports. Besides investing in federal bonds or the occasional speculation

THE PRICING OF PROGRESS

in agricultural land, the gains merchants accumulated were almost always plowed back into further mercantile pursuits. Even when they were investing in bank stocks, a common practice among eastern merchants following the bank boom of the early 1800s, these businessmen were still funneling most of their cash into mercantile endeavors, since nearly all the money loaned out by the notoriously conservative early U.S. banks was in the form of sixty- or ninety-day "commercial paper." This short-term credit flowed into the western or southern hinterlands, helping wheat farmers and cotton planters finance the cultivation and shipment of their staple crops, but it didn't linger in the West or the South very long. Once the wheat or cotton was sold, the loans were repaid and the capital flowed back east. Such short-term commercial capital greased the wheels of an agrarian market economy but did not upend it.[12]

One reason early American businessmen dabbled mostly in short-term commercial capital was that they had few other investment options. Given the abundance of cheap land, the dearth of cheap labor, and the American patriarch's goal of proprietary independence, most attempts to reap consistent returns from large-scale tenant farming failed. The basic unit of the early American economy, the family farm, was not a capitalized asset in which one could purchase a claim to future income yields. American agriculture remained a small, proprietary endeavor in which wealthy rentiers could not directly invest, let alone profit from. As a result, there was not much capital in the early United States. Between 1805 and 1840, only 6.5 percent of the annual national product congealed into investment capital. (By the end of the century, capital formation would make up 20 percent of the economy.) Despite Hamilton's efforts, foreign countries did not see the young United States as a particularly good investment either. From 1820 to 1830 the net amount of international capital that flowed into America was just about zero. While British banks lent short-term capital to farmers and planters, the United States had not become a site of long-term capital investment. How could it? Once Jeffersonians had done away with Hamilton's federal debt, there were few financial assets in the American capital market in which a foreign investor could safely place money.[13]

By the time Hunt took his tour of the Hudson River in 1836, however, the Erie Canal had triggered a sea change in the political economy of the American Northeast as millions of dollars in long-term capital began to flow westward into revolutionary new channels such as western bank stocks, government canal bonds, trust-funded farm mortgages, and urban space. Backed by the taxing power of New York State, nearly half of the Erie Canal bonds issued by the state government were quickly snapped up overseas, mostly in London. As a result, $4 million worth of Barings-backed capital poured into the canal between 1825 and 1835, much to the glee of its American underwriters—the firm of Prime, Ward, and King, which can probably stake the best claim for being the first investment banking company in America.[14]

The incredible success of the Erie Canal brought a tidal wave of foreign (still mostly British) capital crashing onto American shores in the 1830s—"the most significant inflow of capital during the nineteenth century," according to one historian. After breaking about even in the 1820s, the net flow of incoming international capital ballooned to a whopping $173 million in the 1830s. Despite the Panic of 1837, the money kept coming. Between 1835 and 1858 the rate of capital accumulation in the United States increased at the breakneck speed of 50 percent per decade. America was, slowly but surely, becoming a significant site for capital investment.[15]

But where did all this capital go? Foreign investors mostly bought, as with the Erie Canal, state-backed canal bonds from Ohio, Illinois, Michigan, and Wisconsin. About a third was invested in the state banks that cropped up by the hundreds following Andrew Jackson's attack on the Second Bank of the United States. Even American cities borrowed money overseas, with Washington, D.C., floating municipal bonds in Amsterdam, and Philadelphia and Baltimore doing the same in London. By the time the Panic of 1837 hit, $222 million in American securities were held abroad, a majority intended for canals.[16]

An investment in canals, however, was also a bet on the rise of American cities, industry, and national markets. Creating the infrastructure necessary for the rise of urban nodes of commodity trade, canals and cities were intricately linked. This is why the first real estate map (known as a plat) of Chicago was drawn for none other than the commissioners of the Illinois and Michigan Canal. Canals would become profitable only if shipping, trade, and manufacturing centers—in short, cities—emerged at their endpoints and along their banks. While European investors stuck to government-backed canal bonds, a new breed of American businessmen turned to investments in city space. As one historian explained, "There was an urban as well as a rural frontier, and to these rising communities gravitated the lawyer, the newspaper proprietor, the town planner, the note shaver and moneylender, the lands speculator and the land agent acting for eastern capitalists."[17]

Investment in urban space first began in large port cities such as New York City. By the early nineteenth century housing was becoming a capitalized venture in Manhattan as the thriving international port transformed the city into a bustling metropolis that required a large influx of porters, jobbers, clerks, retailers, merchants, sailors, artisans, wholesalers, and domestic servants. In colonial times, as Elizabeth Blackmar explains, artisan builders had "created their product for a known customer" in "a local economy of simple commodity exchange." In other words, the person who wanted a building hired someone to build it. Housing was often commodified in colonial New York—you paid someone to build you an alienable structure you could then use as your home or sell to someone else—but it was not a capitalized, income-yielding investment. Things began to change in the early nineteenth century with the emergence of entrepreneurs who built numerous houses even though they did not have a known buyer and did not intend to live in the homes themselves. "What determined [this] new construction," Blackmar explains, "was not the social need for housing but the rate and security of profits."[18]

Few exemplify this critical shift in housing better than John Jacob Astor. While Astor had begun as a merchant and made his fortune in the fur trade, by the 1830s he was also one of the largest real estate rentiers in New York City. For the first time in American history, businessmen were succeeding in turning urban space into a steady, income-yielding investment. By the Panic of 1837, this urban real estate business had spread like wildfire. In 1831, for instance, Kittredge and Maynard were typical Boston merchants of the era. Their account book that year records the exchange of 134 boxes of cheese, 25 barrels of cranberries, and 30 bushels of potatoes. By the mid-1830s, however, these merchants had neglected the foodstuff business and had turned much of their attention to buying and selling town lots in Boston and Billerica as well as in Goffstown, New Hampshire.[19]

The rent-seeking spatial logic of English enclosure was finally beginning to take hold on American shores. When New York City real estate mogul Samuel Ruggles agreed to sell five of his many houses on Third Avenue to a

man by the name of Henry Betts, the two men used the same "years of purchase" calculations that had emerged in seventeenth-century England in
order to determine the present asset price of future rent gains. As the contract signed by both men demonstrates, Betts had agreed to purchase the lots
for $22,500 largely because he thought he could earn $2,000 in annual rental
fees. Ruggles and Betts had effectively agreed upon only eleven years' purchase, which comes to roughly 10 percent interest—a far higher rate of
return than in England and one that reflects how high risk and a scarcity
of capital made the burgeoning American real estate market exceptionally
profitable.[20]

In early America, the abundance of land and the paucity of people spoiled
English proprietors' attempts to capitalize the New World into a rent-yielding
asset. They simply could not monopolize space. Canals changed all this
thanks to their unprecedented ability to turn unremarkable slices of land into
scarce, privileged resources. Astor, Ruggles, Betts, and other rent-seeking capitalists could begin to profit nicely from New York City space in large part
because the Erie Canal, having only one endpoint, had created an extreme
form of spatial scarcity on the island of Manhattan and its surroundings.
Anyone who wanted to gain from the canal's ability to cheaply ship or receive European goods or western crops would have to pay dearly for spatial
access to this unique service.[21]

The Erie Canal also transformed New York City into a concentrated
node of trade and manufacturing that served as the physical and spatial infrastructure for the production, circulation, exchange, and reproduction of
an abundance of wealth. Wheat needed to be stored, cotton needed to be
shipped, clothes needed to be sewn, imports needed to be sold, and labor
power needed to be reproduced—all near or around the Erie Canal. As a
result, whether New York City lots were destined to become warehouses, de-
pots, homes, retail shops, dry-goods stores, factories, distilleries, or banks made
little difference. Thanks to the canal, the ownership of city space now allowed
one to siphon off a great deal of the wealth produced in or around it.[22]

The writings of Samuel Ruggles help demonstrate the role that statistics
played in the rise of canals and cities. As he was building his real estate empire, Ruggles also became New York State's canal commissioner. There he
learned the importance of market statistics as he compiled reports of the

aggregated product and toll revenues that headed downstream. After the Civil War, Ruggles would use this experience as the U.S. representative to the 1869 International Statistical Conference. For that conference he would produce an impressive "tabular statement" of the "bushels per head" output of America, which became the pride of the conference and a symbol of New York's prosperity.[23]

Along with such market growth, the correlation of urban population increases and rising rents was not lost on Samuel Ruggles. Asked to supply "some statistics in regard to interests in the city of New York" by New York congressmen Benjamin Tallmadge, Ruggles replied with a lengthy letter on population growth that gives us a rare glimpse into the calculating mind of one of the first real estate capitalists in the country. Comparing New York to London, Ruggles began by noting that "1000 acres will not accommodate more than 100,000 inhabitants." Using this equation as his guide, he pointed to the streets south of 24th Street and concluded, "The whole of our next increase must be thrown upon this section." Seeing as these streets were precisely where Ruggles had spent $180,000 to transform swampland into the new Gramercy Park neighborhood, one can assume that Ruggles had made these exact calculations prior to choosing a location for his investment in urban space.[24]

This was not the only way Ruggles used urban growth statistics to imagine future profits. New York City's population was growing at a clip of 15,000 souls per year, Ruggles explained to Tallmadge. As a result, the city would require an additional 1,500 houses a year, "which at 2000 dollars each will cost three million annually." Ruggles noted that most of the capital for building construction would have to be borrowed, and he remarked that in New Orleans such financing was lent out at 10 percent interest. This information was not lost on Tallmadge, who had been president of the Phoenix Branch Bank. Nor was it trivial to Ruggles: throughout the 1830s, he did very well for himself by providing credit to fellow real estate developers.[25]

The transformation of urban space into investment capital spread quickly outward from the canal endpoints to the entire canal corridor. By the time the Erie Canal was finished, the urban real estate business was booming not only in New York City but in lots from Buffalo to Brooklyn as well. Inspired by the Erie Canal's success, when Illinois and Ohio began planning their own canals to the Great Lakes in the 1820s and 1830s, eastern investors were more than willing to funnel great amounts of capital into potential cities along these future canal routes. In the developed Northeast, urban investment often meant constructing new buildings. In the frontier West, it meant constructing whole towns—at least on paper. After purchasing a swath of land with supposedly wonderful urban potential, investors would plat a city by drawing a map that divided the town into lots. Similar to the process of cadastral land surveying, once the plat had been drawn, space could become a commodity (but not necessarily capital—that required the ability to continuously extract rent). Using the plats as their guides, investors could buy or sell urban lots at will.[26]

Buy and sell they did. Going wherever the canal might lead, investors all along the eastern seaboard rushed to invest either directly in urban lots and joint-stock land companies or indirectly in local banks and other mortgage-supplying financial institutions such as the Ohio Trust and Insurance Company. By 1833, lots in the small, nondescript fur-trading town of Chicago (population 350) that had sold for $33 in 1829 were going for $100,000. "Town lots were the staple of the country," one western onlooker wryly remarked in retrospect in 1854, "and were the only articles of export." Within less than a decade investment in urban American space went from being a novel curiosity to a national craze. Even previously conservative commercial banks became far more willing to accept an undeveloped town lot as security for a mortgage that would go to finance urban construction. As a result, those who invested in bank stock were indirectly investing in cities. With the bankers' stamp of approval, urban space had been capitalized.[27]

Similar to the competition in English land rents that first sparked the capitalist revolution, rising real estate prices in American cities pushed city residents to be more productive, so that they could cover the high costs of space. Single-family homes became tenements, casual workshops became frenetic factories, and small shops became giant emporiums. The real estate boom increased not only market productivity but inequality as well, as new urban migrants were quickly priced out of the property-owning circles. The faster cities grew, in fact, the more unequal they became. In 1800, 40 percent of Philadelphians owned real property. Sixty years later that number had plummeted to 10 percent. Young western cities that had been born as capitalist land investments were even more unequal. In 1848, seventeen people owned 40 percent of San Francisco. It is no wonder that Henry George's *Progress and Poverty* was written in the Bay Area: by 1860, the wealthiest 10 percent of the city's residents owned 90 percent of the real property.[28]

Freeman Hunt's entrepreneurial instincts kicked in after his Hudson River letters were warmly received by business elites in Boston and New York. By 1837 he had devised a plan to edit and publish a monthly magazine intended specifically for men of capital. In 1838, he made his pitch at the New York Mercantile Association, an organization designed to educate clerks in the intricacies of business. "There is at present no work to which the merchant can refer for a record of many facts that might be important aids to him," Hunt told his audience. "Besides the information which he gathers from the columns of newspapers . . . there is a great deal to be collected from the history and *Statistics of Commerce*." The board of directors of the New York Mercantile Library Association approved, voting unanimously to "lend an individual and united support in recommending [Hunt's magazine] to public patronage; and further, that it be made as far as practicable the organ of this Association."[29]

Their enthusiasm was not surprising. Eastern businessmen were hungry for data to help them manage this new investment frontier. New York Mercantile Association member Arthur Bronson, one of the biggest investors in urban lots and western mortgages in the country, was always on the lookout for information to help him make investment decisions. Moreover, he had learned firsthand from his own land agents the important connection between population and profits. "There is a great movement of people to the south and west from this country and they drain the country of money," one North Carolina agent wrote Bronson. "The drift of people going to the south west makes it hard doing business," he explained in another. "People are leaving the area in droves," the agent warned in a third note. "I do not think that land is as high as it was six years ago in this country."[30]

Yet despite his awareness that population statistics could be useful, when Bronson set out for his western reconnaissance mission in 1833 to purchase city lots, he had only a farmer's "emigrant guide" at his disposal. While such guides may have sufficed for the yeoman farmer looking for a place to settle, their lack of statistical detail was a liability for the eastern capitalist looking for a place to invest. Local newspapers had also fallen behind the times and were filled mostly with the kind of mercantile figures (price currents, exchange rates, international shipping news) and moral statistics that would not do for a land speculator like Bronson. As a result, Bronson and his partner Charles Butler had to get creative. In one instance, they estimated the size of the village they visited by counting how many children were in the local school. With such a dearth of reliable data, it is not surprising that stories abounded after the Panic of 1837 of investors who had purchased lots in towns they thought had buildings, paved streets, and hundreds of residents but in reality existed only in one convincing booster's dreams.[31]

It was, in fact, out of the ruins of the 1837 panic that Hunt's statistical frontier would arise. Hunt's first edition came out in 1839, a year that had little resemblance to 1836, when Hunt's first travel articles had been published. The rampant investment in canal bonds and city lots that had characterized the roaring 1830s had come to a crashing halt with the Panic of 1837. By 1839, most American capitalists were not out west seeking investment but back home licking their wounds. The panic was a boon for Hunt, however, as he played on businessmen's trauma from 1837. Stressing the need for a rationalized, data-driven system of capital investment, he warned that "operations are often begun in a reckless spirit of speculation, and end, as might have been anticipated, in defeat, simply because some element necessary to success, or some piece of information essential to the adventure, had, in the ardor of pursuit, been disregarded."[32] Rightly dismissing commercial newspapers for providing only "ephemeral accounts of the state of trade," Hunt later proclaimed that the magazine's goal had been to "construct the Science of Business" by supplying the merchant with a diverse array of articles and statistics on "the study of the resources of nations, Commercial Geography, the processes of production, and the Laws of Wealth, or Political Economy."[33]

Turning business into a science was not the sole purpose of Hunt's magazine. Hunt repeatedly reminded his readers that until his magazine appeared on the scene "there was not a single Magazine . . . to represent and to advocate the claims of Commerce." Hunt extolled the general prosperity brought on by American businessmen, reminding his readers that "next to religion," business was the most "active principle of civilization, of knowledge and refinement," and "liberty has always followed in its steps." Throughout the pages of the periodical as well as in special supplements, subscribers to *Hunt's* were presented with glowing, hagiographic accounts of the "lives of American merchants." Hunt also wrote a personal advice book for young businessmen on the make, one of the earliest in the genre. In this how-to manual, fittingly titled *Worth and Wealth,* Hunt taught his young readership that they should measure their self-worth and success in units of money. "In a republic . . . there remains but one basis of social distinction, namely, wealth," Hunt explained. "In society at large, gradations of social position are measured by stock-certificates, rent-rolls and bank-accounts." As this quote reveals, Hunt's idea of economic progress was not old-fashioned mercantile trade but rather new-style capitalist investment in the form of urban real estate and financial securities.[34]

Hunt's was the first business-related journal to be of national scope both in its content and in its distribution. Even the *Economist,* the British equivalent of *Hunt's,* was only founded in 1843. Before *Hunt's,* most men of business got their news from the local paper. As a nationally distributed magazine that covered both traditional mercantile issues and such novel business interests as manufacturing, railroads, mining, and land speculation, *Hunt's* quickly became a forum where men from different regions and trades could unite under the banner of business and forge the ties needed to turn the decentralized and fragmented American economy into a single, expansive national market. Hunt envisioned that his magazine would "form a connecting chain and become the repository of the various mercantile associations throughout the country," and by the end of the 1840s his self-conscious effort at bourgeois class formation had borne fruit, as all the most important Mercantile Library Associations of the nation, including the branches in New York, Philadelphia, Boston, Baltimore, Louisville, Charleston, and Cincinnati, pledged allegiance to *Hunt's Merchants' Magazine* and made Hunt an honorary member of their institutions. The New York, St. Louis, and Cincinnati Chambers of Commerce and the Baltimore, Chicago, Pittsburgh, and Philadelphia Boards of Trade also passed resolutions extolling the virtues of the magazine as well.[35]

While no subscription records survive, it appears that by the mid-1850s most men in the upper echelons of American society were reading Hunt's periodical. The leading businessmen and politicians of the era, including Supreme Court justice Levi Woodbury, Missouri senator Thomas Benton, and

Massachusetts capitalists Nathan Appleton and Patrick Tracy Jackson, all had subscriptions to the magazine, and some even contributed articles. Senator Henry Clay praised the magazine for collecting "a large amount of valuable statistical and other information, highly useful, not only to the merchant, but to the statesmen, to the cultivator of the earth, to the manufacturer, to the mariner, in short, to all classes of the business and reading community." After commenting on how he read *Hunt's* not only at home but on his business trips, Boston manufacturing magnate Abbot Lawrence deemed "this periodical of value not only to the merchant, but to the statesman, diplomatists, jurist, manufacturer, mechanic, agriculturalist, and national economist." Even President Millard Fillmore commended the magazine as "one of the most valuable periodicals that were ever published."[36]

Newspapers heaped even more praise upon Hunt and his magazine, while noting its widespread circulation. In a special piece for *Godey's Magazine* in 1846, none other than Edgar Allan Poe devoted an entire article to Hunt. "The journal is regarded as absolute authority in mercantile matters," Poe gushed, "circulates extensively not only in this country but in Europe, and even in regions more remote." Not stopping there, Poe noted that *Hunt's* was "glorified in the Hong Kong Gazette, is regularly complimented by the English mercantile authorities, has every bank in the world for an eager subscriber, every consul, every ship-owner and navigator; is filed away as authority in every library, and thought of in half the countries of the world as early as No. 3 in their enumeration of distinguished Americans." When French engineer Charles Minard decided in 1844 that he wanted to create a global statistical map of cotton commodity flows, he derived the data for his map not from French or British periodicals but rather from *Hunt's*. The magazine, it appears, was not only changing the way American capitalists viewed the United States but influencing the vision of businessmen across the world as well.[37]

Hunt's was filled with an array of groundbreaking statistical charts that reflected businessmen's shift in interest from short-term, often international market exchange to long-term domestic capitalist investment. Early editions of *Hunt's* were still dominated by traditional mercantile statistics such as global commodity prices, maritime insurance premiums, bank stock figures, gold quantities per country, public debt comparisons, import/export trade balances, and foreign exchange rates. Seeing the world more through the eyes of an importer than a manufacturer, in these early years Hunt published just as many statistical tables on European manufacturing as he did on American production. Within a few years, however, Hunt began to supplant these traditional tables with never-before-seen statistics regarding the dividends of Lowell mills, New York rental returns, Pennsylvania coal mining proceeds, Buffalo canal receipts, and Western railroad earnings. The proportion of traditional commercial statistics dropped from roughly 70 percent between 1840 and 1842 to 47 percent between 1850 and 1852.[38]

The magazine's greatest statistical innovation, however, was its use of population figures. In early America, few merchants took much interest in population statistics. Census results were rarely seen in papers such as the *New-York Commercial Advertiser*. With their capital invested mostly in international trade rather than domestic expansion, businessmen had little reason to examine such figures. Viewed mostly as a tool for determining congressional representation—not capital gains—newspapers focused far more on the political ramifications of census figures than on the economic ones. Statistical gazetteers of the time that were written explicitly for merchants, such as Timothy Pitkin's *Statistical View*, were filled with pages of international import and export data but included only a few, rather meager population tables.[39]

Hunt's changed all this. From the very first volumes of the magazine, Hunt included a fair amount of population tables under the title "Miscellaneous Statistics." By the fourth volume, he had given population statistics its own segment in the statistical section of the magazine, alongside the figures on manufacturing, commerce, and banking. In a move unprecedented in commercial literature, Hunt's featuring of population data signaled to his readers that the whereabouts, concentration, and number of American people mattered to businessmen. Soon enough, Hunt became a leading expert on population flows. When Bostonian Jesse Chickering desired information on immigration for his own statistical study of American population growth in the 1840s, one of the first people he turned to was Freeman Hunt.[40]

Yet Hunt himself was but one player in his magazine's demographic education of America's investors. To see why businessmen in the 1820s largely ignored population growth while those in 1880 were obsessed with it, we must shift our focus toward two of the most important contributors to Hunt's magazine: western booster Jesup Scott and southern economist George Tucker.

Born and raised on a Connecticut farm to a wealthy family of old New Haven stock, Jesup Wakeman Scott headed west to Ohio in 1831 in order to oversee his father-in-law's investment in land on the southern shore of Lake Erie. In 1825 the Ohio state legislature had chartered the dredging of a canal that would link Cincinnati to Lake Erie, and many speculators, including Scott, had scrambled to buy up the land along the lake in hopes that, in the future, the canal's terminus would fall upon their plot. Along with a few other investors, Scott helped plat the city of Toledo on the banks of the Maumee River. Toledo was a capitalist enterprise from the start, and even its name was chosen for marketing reasons; as one investor noted, it "is easy to pronounce, is pleasant in sound, and there is no other city of that name on the American continent." In an era Scott would later recall for its "memorable speculation in wild lands and wild cities," he and his fellow Toledo investors competed with other towns along the lake in the 1830s for the canal's endpoint in a high-risk game of geographical roulette. As Scott's father-in-law understood well enough, the stakes were high: "Wherever your great city is located, the fortunate holder of the land," he wrote to his son-in-law, stood to "make a great profit."[41]

By 1836 the canal had not yet reached anywhere near the lake, but Scott had still managed to accumulate $400,000 worth of real estate in northwestern Ohio. Or so he thought at the time. When reality finally caught up to the runaway lot prices in the Panic of 1837, Scott was forced to liquidate nearly all his holdings, including the family mansion in Connecticut. Still willing to take risks, however, Scott decided to hang on to his plots of land in Toledo. It was the right decision. In 1843 the Wabash-Erie Canal finally opened for business—with Toledo as its outlet to the great lake. If Scott could convince eastern capitalists that the Toledo canal was destined for greatness, he would become a very wealthy man. That year he wrote the first of many articles for *Hunt's*.[42]

As was the case with many men who invested in cities that mostly existed on paper, Scott's desire to attract capital turned him into a newspaperman. Shortly after he arrived in Ohio, he founded *Miami of the Lake,* the first weekly in northwestern Ohio. Later he briefly became the editor of the *Toledo Blade,* the town's leading daily paper. Throughout his writing career, however, Scott's main audience was never local farmers but eastern capitalists, as he hoped to convince them to divert their capital to the soon-to-be global empire of Toledo by "disabusing the public mind at the east, if our sheet shall have the fortune to circulate there, of the numberless false impressions in regard to this section."[43]

As Scott understood, in order to convince eastern capital to invest in Toledo, he needed to reach into the investors' homes, their parlors, their inner circles. While the local newspapers he edited never reached New York, Boston, or London, Scott succeeded in having his voice heard on the East Coast and even Europe by becoming a frequent contributor to *Hunt's*. Beginning with his first article in 1843 and over the next decade, Scott published numerous essays praising the economic potential of the western frontier, carving out a niche for himself as the magazine's expert on urban investment and westward expansion. While some town boosters of the era used geographical determinism to prove that the future capital of the American empire lay in Alton, Illinois, or in Flat Rock, Michigan, Scott was one of the first town promoters to lean on population statistics to further his arguments—and his sales pitch.[44]

In his first set of articles for the magazine, Scott provided a lengthy analysis of urban population statistics that would become his trademark. In order to explain what the future held for the American people (and American capital), Scott began by quoting the census returns of England. Pointing to the fact that "the proportion of people engaged in agriculture has decreased decidedly with every census," Scott cited an English report that concluded that in England "those engaged in manufacturing and mechanical occupations, as compared with the agricultural class, were 6 to 5 in 1801; they were as 8 to 5 in 1821; and 2 to 1, in 1830." By calculating the rate of increase in American urban populations with the help of the 1830 and 1840 censuses, Scott went on to show that similar demographic patterns had commenced in the United States and that the percentage of people who worked the land was already dropping.[45]

As he did in almost all of his articles, Scott used his own state, Ohio, as the best example for this rise in urbanization and industrialization, illustrating that even though the population of the Buckeye State as a whole had grown 62 percent in the past decade, population in its largest urban centers had risen 138 percent. Projecting his calculations forward, Scott predicted that by the year 1890, only a third of the population would be farmers. In the future, Scott contended, there would be a complete division of labor in the West, as most Americans would live in cities and work in manufacturing. Their industrial products would be exchanged with the small number of rural farmers still needed to supply the food and raw materials cities depended upon. Most Americans would no longer depend on the land to survive but the market. Instead of being scattered across the Great Plains, they would gravitate toward great cities.[46]

But where would these great cities be? "How are we to know beforehand with reasonable certainty," Scott rhetorically asked, "which are to be the favored cities destined to show forth such wonderful augmentation?" Again, Scott's answer lay in body counts. "Of the sixty-nine cities . . . which doubled their numbers in ten years and under, sixty-one are in the Western plain," Scott wrote, concluding that New England's "ascendency as a manufacturing region is temporary, waiting only the development of the new country about the lakes and the upper Mississippi to be superseded." Illustrating to the readers of *Hunt's* that population statistics could be used to signal exactly where they should invest their capital, Scott's articles often included charts that calculated the number of years it took for a city to double its population. Through these statistical rankings, Scott transformed urban population figures into an economic indicator, helping eastern investors to decide which cities to invest in by "indicating the direction to which the industry of our people tends, in those portions of the west, where population has attained a considerable degree of density." As William Cronon has pointed out, charts like this were deceptive: the smaller the town, the easier it was for it to double its population. Such a table, however, provided Scott with exactly the statistical effect he desired, as it put Toledo among the ten most profitable cities in America, far above more accomplished cities in New England or on the Atlantic coast.[47]

Implicit in all of Scott's statistical analyses was a simple argument: landless people made for big profits. By convincing his reading public that Toledo's population was on the rise, that American yeomen would soon be moving en masse from country to city, and that the new manufacturing centers of America would be out west, Scott hoped to prove to eastern investors that the West was not simply a land of self-sufficient farmers off whom it would be impossible to make sustained profits. On the contrary, Scott's statistics demonstrated that there already existed a landless population out west that could be funneled into an array of manufacturing enterprises, much like Lowell and Lynn in Massachusetts. Thanks to these demographic changes,

Scott argued, the time was fast coming when American capitalists could safely invest in western cities, knowing full well that the supply of labor needed to construct buildings, keep factories humming, dredge canals, and fill the urban lots of tomorrow would be available.

With the help of his population statistics, Scott also taught the American investor that picking a real estate lot required far more than just knowing the location of the canal endpoint. It required knowing the "direction to which the industry of our people tends." Following canal flows was not enough— American capitalists needed to follow the flow of laboring people as well, statistically monitoring how they moved through space. As a man who thought he had made $400,000 only to see it dissipate in a moment, who had won the game of canal roulette yet still owned a town that existed largely on paper, and who would make his fortune only if his lots became factories, warehouses, and tenements, Scott understood that the monopolization of space alone could not make him rich. What determined the value of urban spaces was not only their spatial scarcity but the potential profitability they held for the manufacturer, retailer, landlord, or real estate developer. Investing in urban space, Scott had come to realize, depended on the rise of an industrializing, capitalist society. You needed the labor power and material needs of people—and not just any people. You needed people who could work in factories and live in rented apartments, people who did not own productive property or their homes. In short, you needed a big dose of landless people. For urban lots to become profitable capital investments, Scott's statistical message implied, the platted cities on paper would have to come alive—and the yeoman political economy of Jeffersonian America would have to go.[48]

The notion of national progress Scott projected in *Hunt's* diverged greatly from that of early America, a shift that was evident even in his own personal development. When Scott initially arrived in the Midwest, the first work he edited was the *Ohio and Michigan Emigrant Guide and Farmers Register,* a typical periodical of the era and one intended not for eastern capital but for pioneering farmers. In his *Register,* Scott sounded downright Jeffersonian, telling eastern farmers to go west so that they would not become "daylaborers, with no prospect ahead but of bare subsistence." Utilizing a very different sales pitch, he focused on the "virtuous and temperate habits" of agriculture and made family relations—not market ones—a top priority, arguing that "where land is cheap, the sons of farmers generally settle near their fathers."

When he gave a lecture at a local lyceum, he sang a similar tune. In this venue, Scott not only emphasized population growth but stressed that Toledo should aim to become the "moral and intellectual rallying point to the nation." What is more, he was far less optimistic with his figures. "Altho' it has very many streets rejoicing in high sounding names," Scott remarked, "to be candid we must admit—that up to this time . . . we are but the meager skeleton of a great city." He described Toledo with adjectives such as "littleness" and "insignificance" while challenging his audience to "lift this shame city out of its native mud." Only a few years later, the draw of capital would lead Scott to tell a very different story.[49]

As Gilded Age economist Richard Ely once noted, it was common knowledge among antebellum intellectuals that "the South led the North in economics before the Civil War and up to that time Virginia was ahead of Harvard." If we take Ely at his word, this would have made George Tucker—the first-ever professor of political economy at the University of Virginia—the leading economist in the country. Freeman Hunt apparently agreed with Ely's later assessment, for he filled the pages of his magazine with Tucker's economic theories and growth statistics. Beginning in the magazine's second volume, Hunt tapped Tucker as his magazine's "house economist" and published a chapter of Tucker's *The Laws of Wages, Profits and Rent, Investigated* each month. A few years later, Hunt serialized Tucker's *Progress of the United States in Population and Wealth in Fifty Years*—a groundbreaking statistical analysis that not only stressed the link between urban population growth and capitalist profit but also contained the first-ever income and wealth statistics in American history based on market output data collected by the census. Hunt soon decided to publish it in book form as well.[50]

As the dominant voice of economic theory and statistical growth in the magazine throughout the 1840s and early 1850s, Tucker had a lasting influence on how *Hunt's* readers made sense of their economic world. Since British political economy was not yet taught at most colleges or universities, and most Americans did not go to college anyway, a generation of business-minded Americans first encountered the invisible hand of Adam Smith or the marginal rent theory of David Ricardo through the writings of George Tucker in *Hunt's*. What is more, by portraying urban population and market productivity statistics as the ultimate markers of social advancement, Tucker imparted to the readers of *Hunt's* not only the wonders of human proliferation but also the notion that progress could, and should, be priced.[51]

George Tucker offers further proof that modern-day growth statistics, the capitalization of everyday life, and the pricing of American progress have deep roots in the history of Caribbean slavery. While Tucker would spend most of his adult life in Virginia, the first American to derive proto-GDP indicators from the federal census was born and raised on a Bermuda sugar plantation his family had owned for nearly two hundred years. Tucker hailed from an elite planter dynasty that could be traced back to the first British settlers on Bermuda. His ancestors served as leading slave merchants, sugar planters, and island governors. The name Tucker, in fact, was one of the first six slave surnames to appear on the island. Much as was the case for Alexander Hamilton, treating people as income-generating inputs and society as a capitalized investment probably came naturally to Tucker thanks to his Caribbean upbringing, even though he—like Hamilton—did not support the expansion of American slavery.[52]

Tucker never found his place in antebellum Virginia. He seemed more interested in investing in canals, cities, and banks than in slaves, tobacco, or cotton. When tasked with managing the estate of another, he looked into buying not slaves nor land but bank stock, noting in confidence that "the stock in the Girard Bank of Philadelphia or the State Bank of New York would, at the present prices, yield more than 8 per cent annual profit." In his voluminous and eclectic writings, which ranged from science fiction and plantation romance novels to satiric humor and standard economic prose, it is clear that Tucker's heart was set on transforming the South into an industrial powerhouse with large cities, big factories, plenty of wage laborers—and no slaves.[53]

In *Letters from Virginia Translated from the French,* an anonymous satire of the South, Tucker critiqued slavery's "genteel laziness" and argued that canals would promote economic progress and urban growth in the South, especially in Norfolk. (Tucker was heavily invested in the Roanoke Canal and owned lots in Norfolk.) In *The Valley of Shenandoah,* the precursor to the classic American plantation novel, Tucker presented plantation culture as far too focused on virtue, honor, and public spirit while lacking any prudent, rationalized business sense. In *Voyage to the Moon; with Some Account of the*

Manners and Customs, Science and Philosophy, of the People of Morosofia, and Other Lunarians, one of the first science fiction books in American literature, Tucker describes a utopian lunar civilization that began a lot like early America but developed (properly, in Tucker's eyes) into an unequal, industrial, and urbanized society where landholders earned "extraordinary profits."[54]

It was, however, in his economic writings that Tucker left his mark. A Malthusian thinker who tended to "out-Malthus Malthus," Tucker the economist was infatuated with population growth. In 1798, Thomas Malthus had famously argued that because populations grew exponentially but food production grew only geometrically, the niggardliness of nature would condemn mankind to a life of subsistence, poverty, and want. Pursuing Malthus's line of thought, Tucker agreed that as the population of a nation grew, wages would have to drop due to an "increased competition of the laboring classes in consequence of the increase in population." Unlike Malthus, however, who painted an especially grim picture of mankind's fate, Tucker celebrated these immutable laws of population because thanks to this drop in wages, capitalists finally would be able to profit from the labor of Americans without having to enslave them. Tucker's message was clear: growth was great.[55]

In the New World, Tucker noted, since "land is plenty, and population thin, raw produce will commonly exchange for the amount of labor expended in producing it." Much like Ben Franklin, Thomas Jefferson, and other early American thinkers, Tucker recognized that low population density was what gave white American farmers the bargaining power to receive a full return for the fruits of their labor. Yet unlike those early Americans, Tucker saw this as a terrible development. He was, however, optimistic about the future for the very reason Jefferson had been pessimistic: as the population of the United States would increase, this egalitarian wonderland of widespread proprietary ownership would come to an end. Many yeoman farmers would be forced off the land and into cities, where they would see low wages due to competition in the labor market. This would be a boon for the owners of land and other means of production, as population growth would lead not only to diminishing wages but also to stronger demand for foodstuffs and other manufactured consumer goods. The profits generated from the emerging gap between low wages and high commodity prices would "continue to rise with every successive increase of numbers."[56]

This population growth would end slavery as well. When "labor will finally attain a price so low, that the earnings of a slave will not repay the cost of rearing him," he argued, "then, of course, his master will consider him as a burdensome charge rather than a source of profit." The expansive growth of landless urban residents would put an end to slavery not because slavery was exploitative, Tucker seemed to be saying, but rather because—compared to wage labor—it would not be exploitative enough.[57]

When the 1840 census was published, Tucker quickly moved from theory to practice, as he began poring over census statistics in order to see what the future held for the American republic. The final outcome of this analysis was Tucker's *Progress of the United States in Population and Wealth.* In this work, Tucker created a complex array of never-before-seen statistical indicators, which compared rates of increase in the American population by region, race, state, and city. Like Scott, Tucker compared the proportion of Americans laboring in agriculture to those working in manufacturing, as well as those living in rural areas to those dwelling in cities, in order to see if his theories were already bearing fruit and the number of urban, landless workers was rising. As the word *progress* in the book title suggests, Tucker was pleased with the results. Using such indicators as the percentage of Americans who worked on farms and lived in cities, he concluded that urbanization was on the rise. Soon, it appeared to Tucker, his utopian moon colony of urban development, wage labor, and large profits would become a reality on earth.[58]

Next, Tucker took the revolutionary step from measuring population growth to measuring economic growth. In his next-to-last chapter, Tucker took advantage of the newly collected agricultural and industrial figures from the 1840 census in order to price the annual income generated by American inhabitants and resources. With some creative calculations, Tucker provided a state-by-state analysis of the income-yielding capacity of farm, factory, forest, fishery, merchant house, and mine. This enabled any reader of *Hunt's Merchants' Magazine* to quickly see, for instance, that while Maine forests yielded an annual income of $1,877,663, Pennsylvania pigs generated $4,518,192.[59]

Tucker priced not only trees and hogs but also the income-generating capacity of the American people. After aggregating each state's revenue flow, Tucker divided the total market output by the number of total inhabitants. A reader could now, in a single chart, compare the per-capita productivity of different states. As always, however, statistical choices required political ones, and Tucker needed to decide whether to count slaves as people. Would *Hunt's Merchants' Magazine* legitimize the chattel principle or admit to the humanity of African American slaves? In the end, Tucker decided he did not want to alienate any of his readers and placed both indicators side by side. As Tucker's double chart makes clear, the question of whether slaves should be counted as human beings had a dramatic effect on antebellum per-capita growth figures. For example, Mississippi produced a paltry $79 per inhabitant if slaves were treated as people—far less than the $102 generated by Massachusetts. But if only Mississippi whites were deemed people, that figure leapt to a near-record $164 per capita.[60]

Tucker did not settle for a mere statistical snapshot of American market productivity based on the 1840 census. Viewing time as a never-ending process of capital accumulation, his final chapter, titled "The Increase of Wealth," aimed to show how the "small excess of annual income over annual expense is constantly adding to the mass of capital, which is so efficient an agent of production." Tucker's logic became a staple of nineteenth-century economic thought. Treating the nation like a business, he argued that the difference between national revenue (market production) and expenses (market consumption) yielded profit, which was then added to "the national-stock of wealth." Income statistics could show the annual profit flow of the business that was America, while wealth statistics could show the total amount of profit, congealed into capital, that accumulated over time.[61]

George Tucker did not live to see the Civil War, which would end slavery and propel wage labor to greatness. A slave owner who sought to kill slavery with the mechanisms of the market, in the end died because of those very things. On March 21, 1861, while he was waiting to board a steamboat in Mobile, Alabama, a bale of slave-picked cotton fell off a barge that was heading upriver, striking Tucker in the head and killing him. Tucker's work in *Hunt's,* however—especially his population and economic growth metrics—would have an enduring impact on Americans. "The little work on the Census," Tucker wrote in his autobiography a few years before his death, "had more circulation, and was more read and used than anything which I had previously written." Scott's urban population charts found their way into other publications, most notably *A Practical Guide on Business,* a widely read how-to book intended for businessmen and investors. Even as far away as England, books such as *The Progress of America from the Discovery of Columbus to 1847* were republishing Scott's statistical writings on population growth.[62]

Local newspapers from the 1850s demonstrate how businessmen began internalizing *Hunt's* emphasis on population statistics well before the existential crisis that gripped the city of St. Louis in 1880. In the lead-up to the 1850 census, the *Ohio Daily Statesmen* reminded its readers that population figures were "important," since they "indicate the proper direction for the investment of capital." After the results were in, tables upon tables of urban population statistics began to appear in dozens of papers across the old Northwest, as the booster-editors of every ramshackle town in Ohio seemed to be claiming that their town had grown the most rapidly. Perplexed by this burst of municipal patriotism, in 1870 one onlooker puzzled over the "universal but after all inexplicable municipal pride which glories in a rapid growth of population above everything else."[63]

One of the most frequent tables to appear in American newspapers from 1850 and throughout the Gilded Age was a ranking of American cities by population. Such rankings quickly became a decennial tradition, as editors supplied the color commentary as to why Boston had fallen from third to fifth or Cincinnati had risen from twelfth to sixth. Oftentimes these articles read more like accounts of exciting sporting events than bland economic statistics. "Cleveland, Columbus and Dayton started even in the race in 1840," one Ohio newspaper pronounced. "Since that time each has more than doubled its population. The census of 1850 will soon determine their relative standing." Decades before the cities of the Midwest competed for the baseball pennant, they battled for growth.[64]

Conjuring up images of a collective race against other cities allowed newspaper editors to frame these growth figures as indicators of not just potential profit but overall progress as well. In all these articles there existed an underlying assumption that the interests of urban residents and urban capitalists were one and the same. Seeking to transform growth into a citywide, cross-class goal, by 1880 St. Louis businessmen were typically equating the "prosperity" of the city with the "welfare of every business interest," while assuming that the unwelcome census results would not only "discourage capital" but "dishearten the people."

The impact of *Hunt's* was not limited to midwestern cities and eastern capital. An overlooked advocate of capitalism living in perhaps the most overlooked capitalist city in American history, New Orleans, James De Bow began his long and influential career as statistician, slave apologist, imperial booster, and business journalist by dreaming of becoming the South's Freeman Hunt. When he started his own magazine in the mid-1840s, the young De Bow wrote a letter to Hunt stating that he planned on publishing a southern version of *Hunt's Merchants' Magazine*. De Bow would go on to do just that, and a comparison of *Hunt's* and *De Bow's Review: Agricultural, Commercial, Industrial Progress and Resources* reveals a pair of worldviews that are far more similar than different, even if Hunt was a proud anti-slavery "Free Soiler" and De Bow a proud pro-slavery "Fire Eater."[65]

In an early issue of his own magazine, De Bow restated Hunt's vision of a data-driven "science of business." Linking statistical analyses to capital gains, he declared that without statistical data "it is impossible that any previous calculations can be made, whether an adventure will turn account or not." In another article he warned that "to the ignorant, commerce is but a game of chance but to the accomplished merchant it is a science where skill can scarce fail of its reward." Like Hunt, De Bow saw his role as that of an educator who needed to teach southerners to become rational businessmen by mastering the art of statistical analysis. "There is among the cotton planters no dissemination or concentration of professional knowledge and practice," De Bow complained. "Every farmer lives in an agricultural world of his own."[66]

De Bow's attempts to mimic Hunt can also be seen in his editorial choices. Oftentimes, he would publish letters from far-flung southern boosters on the Texas frontier who were trying to convince slave owners to push westward with their slave capital. Using population growth statistics as their main pitch, these letters sounded a lot like the *Hunt's* articles by western urban boosters such as Jesup Scott. "There are now about 3,000,000 slaves in the southern states increasing at the rate of nearly thirty percent every ten years" wrote one

Texas booster to De Bow in a letter he later published. "Within that time," warned the booster, "a home and lands to cultivate must be found for another million of them."[67]

⸻

Sparked by *Hunt's Merchants' Magazine,* by the mid-nineteenth century urban growth statistics became an omnipresent part of American culture and society. But support for these figures was far from unanimous. Many American farmers were hardly enamored of a future in which increasing population growth caused their children to become landless wage laborers. Such Americans displayed their disdain for population growth not only in public statements but also in the privacy of the bedroom. As demographers have recognized, antebellum Americans initiated one of the most intense repressions of human fertility in human history. It is almost impossible to glean from historical sources what everyday, non-elite antebellum women thought of population growth, but the increased use of female contraceptives in this era strongly suggests that many American women were not too enthused with the gospel of growth promoted in *Hunt's.*[68]

Perhaps the loudest anti-growth voices in the era, however, belonged to members of the anti-immigrant nativism movement that took the country by storm in the 1850s. Prioritizing Anglo-Saxon purity, proprietary independence, and high wages for whites, nativists rejected Hunt, Tucker, and Scott's love of numerical growth. An 1844 political pamphlet by New York City's American Republican Party, the precursor to the Know-Nothing Party, dealt with this topic head on:

> It is the whim of the enthusiast that delights many of our countrymen at seeing our country filling up with such rapidity and our public lands absorbed by foreigners, the exclusion of our sons, who are thus cheated out of every foot of good soil for their industry and of their political rights and privileges. It is a whim, we say, to be thus delighted with the idea of *numbers* and with the latitude given for boasting our numerical strength.[69]

Fearing that city growth brought with it licentiousness and a lack of social control, moral statisticians did not cheer Hunt's love of growth either. Continuing a tradition that had begun with Jefferson's population density calculations in *Notes on Virginia,* Horace Mann was wary of a population increase in Massachusetts because "density of population has always been one of the proximate causes of social inequality." By 1845, Lemuel Shattuck knew how important urban population growth was to Boston manufacturers. Yet this did not stop him from painting an ugly statistical image of the suffocating density in the Eighth Ward in his city census, nor did it preclude him from openly criticizing the exaggerated boosterism that had led to a massive influx of immigrants "deluded from their homes by wrong impression given them." In a move that must have made competing cities smile, Shattuck went out of his way to prove that Boston's results in the 1840 census were too high, since all sailors in town at the time had been counted rather than just those who lived there.[70]

Future president James Buchanan represented a similar view in his correspondence with statistician Jesse Chickering in 1847. A Bostonian with close ties to the Brahmin manufacturing elite, Chickering published a groundbreaking book in 1848 on population growth that included the first serious attempt to measure the number of immigrants entering the nation. In this book, Chickering found that most urban population growth in Massachusetts was due to immigration. In his analysis, he demonstrated how critical this influx of foreigners was to the manufacturing and real estate interests of the state. "In some places," Chickering noted, "it is thought that the factories can hardly be carried on without them." Chickering also documented how the effect of immigration "has been to raise the price of real estate in certain localities, in which before it had but little or no value; for they must have space for their dwellings, and houses must be multiplied and extended for their accommodation; and prices, as is well known, increase with the demand." Judging by these pro-growth comments, it should come as no surprise that Chickering was a fairly frequent contributor to *Hunt's*.[71]

Buchanan was not nearly as accepting of foreigners. "The landholders and speculators in the interior will be glad of settlers to raise the value of their lands," Buchanan responded to Chickering, and "this consideration will influence many real estate owners in great cites." Yet in Buchanan's eyes, such a growth-fueled real estate boom was no sign of progress: "On the whole it appears to me that this country is to be the receptacle of the worst species of population of the old worlds, namely, of paupers becoming so in part from causes beyond their control but mainly super induced by intemperance, laziness, incapacity."[72]

Even by 1880, Hunt's gospel of growth was hardly mainstream. In the midst of his distress over the census results, St. Louis editor Joseph McCullagh pointed to the businessmen of the city and admitted that "most of the complaints against the present enumeration come from this class of citizen." He then went on to pin blame for the disappointing results on the majority of St. Louis residents, who for some odd reason did not care about the census nearly as much as city elites. "Thanks to the absence of any public-spirited zeal or interest in the affair," he snapped, "the reported population is from fifty to a hundred thousand less than the real population."[73]

Further evidence that *Hunt's* statistical frontier of urban growth had not yet become hegemonic by the Gilded Age can be found in one of the most famous statistical tropes in American history: census chief Francis Amasa Walker's 1874 population maps. The key catalyst of Frederick Jackson Turner's frontier thesis, Walker's *Statistical Atlas of the United States* depicted a decade-by-decade snapshot of American population growth based on nearly a century's worth of census figures. These maps, however, displayed a quantitative interpretation of the frontier dramatically different from what could be found in *Hunt's*.

As head of the census and arbiter of city recounts, Walker knew a thing or two about American businessmen's obsession with urban growth. Nevertheless, the vision he chose to present to the American people in his atlas— which was disseminated to schools and libraries across the nation—was something of a negative image of the statistical frontier as seen in *Hunt's*. Rather than celebrate the great increase in urban populations and landless wage labor, Walker's maps—through classification decisions that focused on counties and not cities—greatly downplayed the stunning surge in American urbanization. Rather than depict a growing nation of propertyless urban wage workers, Walker drew his readers' attention toward the "frontier line" of "solitary ranchmen, the trapper and the fisherman, the small mining party and the lumbering camp." Framing America as the same yeoman republic it had always been, Walker titled these maps "The Progress of the Nation." It was very popular in its day, but at its heart was a notion of progress that soon would be made obsolete.[74]

SIX

The Coronation of King Capital

IN THE LATE 1850S, statistical indicators once again found themselves at the center of a bitter sectional dispute over slavery, a dispute that led to the longest speakership battle in American congressional history. At the heart of the matter was a book, *The Impending Crisis of the South,* whose publication and dissemination had been supported and funded by Republican members of Congress. Written by a North Carolinian by the name of Hinton Helper, the vehemently anti-slavery tract had become the Republican Party's most effective piece of political propaganda. Its impact was made possible thanks to the lobbying power of *New York Tribune* editor Horace Greeley and some of the wealthiest and most powerful men in New York City, who bankrolled the second edition of the book in 1859. By the fall of 1860, more than 200,000 copies had been distributed, making Helper's book one of the greatest best sellers in American history. The direct association of Republican congressmen with the funding of the book caused a tremendous controversy over who would be elected Speaker of the House, as southern congressmen refused to vote for any politician who had endorsed the controversial book.[1]

Referring to Helper's book as a "rehearsal for the secession crisis," historian George Fredrickson suggested that *The Impending Crisis* may very well be "the most important book, in terms of political impact, that has ever been published in the United States." Southerners certainly understood the power of Helper's creation, as they arrested any distributor of the book and even hanged three men in Arkansas for possession of it. What has sometimes been overlooked, however, is the fact that Helper's book consisted mostly of a lengthy series of economic indicators derived from 1850 census data. Driven by a belief that Harriet Beecher Stowe's moralizing *Uncle Tom's Cabin* would not resonate with rational men of business, Helper concluded his preface by noting that while "Yankee wives" had offered readers "the fictions of slavery," it was time that "men should give the facts."[2]

Associating masculinity with economic quantification, Helper's book was dominated by one particular form of "fact": market output statistics that priced the American people's capacity to produce commodities. Rather than focus mostly on moral statistics—as both northerners and southerners had done in prior decades—Helper's first chapter, which was more than a hundred pages long, measured the "progress and prosperity" of the North and the South by tabulating the cash value of agricultural produce that both regions had extracted from the earth. In so doing, he calculated that in 1850 the North had produced $351,709,703 of agricultural goods, the South only $306,927,067. Throughout the rest of the book, Helper went on to concoct a dizzying array of similar progress-pricing indicators. To give but a few examples (Helper was nothing if not repetitive), he demonstrated that the North had generated more cash from slaughtered animals ($56,990,237 vs. $54,388,377), more money from manufacturing ($842,586,058 vs. $165,413,027), and more bank capital ($230,100,058 vs. $165,078,940).[3]

Assuming capital accumulation, market productivity, urban development, and industrial manufacturing to be the leading barometers of human advancement, Helper heaped extravagant praise on northern capitalists, some of whom would later fund the book's second edition. In one passage, he pointed to the Massachusetts textile industrialist Abbott Lawrence, who, according to Helper, was "always solicitous to invest his capital in a manner calculated to promote the interest of those around him." Lawrence, Helper claimed, was eager to build textile mills in Virginia, but the inefficiencies of slavery made him think otherwise, and he ended up keeping his money in New England, where "he employed his capital in building up the cities in Lowell and Lawrence, either of which, in all those elements of material and social prosperity that makes up the greatness of states, is already far in advance of all the seedy and squalid niggervilles in Old Dominion." Virulently racist, Helper was one of the first Americans to use economic data as a way of masking his own prejudices. He would not be the last.[4]

As the uproar surrounding Helper's book demonstrates, the anti-slavery cause—and the statistics harnessed to bolster it—underwent a dramatic change in the 1850s. If the most oft-heard arguments against slavery in Jacksonian America had a moral basis, and thus cited mostly moral statistics, by the 1850s northerners were shifting the weight of their claims against slavery toward economic arguments, and thus cited mostly monetized output figures. As one skeptical Bostonian of the era remarked, the typical Free Soil speech consisted of "one-third disjointed facts, and misapplied figures, and great swelling words of vanity to prove that the South is, upon the whole, the very poorest, meanest, least productive." With the focus of the debate shifting away from the plight of slaves, the words that came to be used to define the South (and its African American inhabitants) in mainstream Northern discourse were *unprofitable, sluggish,* and *inefficient.* In his speech to Boston and New York capitalists, businessman Nathaniel Banks—who would later head the Senate's Special Committee on the Census—referred to the South as the "foe of all industrial progress and of the highest material prosperity."[5]

The North's turn toward "economic anti-slavery" in the 1850s must be seen in part as a response to a discursive shift that had already begun to take place in pro-slavery narratives by the late 1840s. A decade before Helper would ignite the tempers of southern congressmen with his market productivity statistics, the situation had been very much reversed: Massachusetts congressman Horace Mann became enraged when he found Virginian Elwood Fisher's pro-slavery lecture "profusely scattered about the House." An influential yet forgotten precursor to Helper's best-selling work, Fisher's short pamphlet used an array of market output and economic growth figures—which he referred to as "landmarks of progress"—to argue that the South was far more advanced than the North. Once again it appears that slavery was ahead of the curve in pricing American progress.[6]

Arguing in the opening pages that "the first object of civilized life is to accumulate wealth," Fisher assumed that in order to undertake "a comparison of the progress of the white people of the respective sections," all one needed to do was compare per capita wealth. Fisher then spent dozens of pages doing precisely that, as he compared the amount of property the average white man owned in Maryland ($531) versus Massachusetts ($406), Virginia ($758) versus New York ($260), and Kentucky ($456) versus Ohio ($276). Of course, what Fisher neglected to emphasize in these comparisons was that he was quantifying African American slaves not as people but rather as capital. This statistical choice made the South's per capita wealth figures look especially impressive, since in states such as Virginia, Fisher proudly noted, slaves were worth "about $100,000,000." While northerners would claim that Fisher's numbers game was a sham, the sad truth is that from the point of view of southern slave owners, in which African Americans were treated as wealth, Fisher's statistics were accurate. As such quantification decisions reveal, there was nothing objective about the numbers being flung around in antebellum America—each data point was ingrained in the ideology of its creator.[7]

By the time Helper had written his response in the late 1850s, Fisher's pamphlet had been reprinted in the pages of *De Bow's Review* and the South was awash in a "cotton is king" literature that sought to legitimize slavery by demonstrating its incredible economic productivity and profitability. These narratives were based predominantly on cotton output statistics designed to prove the value of slavery to American society. The amount of cotton exported from the South in the previous thirty-nine years, southerner David Christy noted in 1855, "has exceeded in value the exports of breadstuffs and provisions to the extent of *fourteen hundred and twenty-one million dollars!* Verily, Cotton is King!" Figures collected from Louisiana's government reports, declared southerner Samuel Cartwright, "speak in a language too plain to be misunderstood by any one, and prove conclusively that . . . a dense slave population gives the highest value and greatest productiveness to every species of property."[8]

As the statistics wielded by both sides in the sectional debate over slavery demonstrate, a slow, uneven, yet clearly discernible statistical revolution was taking place in the decade leading up to the Civil War. The 1850s, in fact, serve as a kind of watershed decade for the pricing of progress, a hinge upon which the entire narrative of this book turns. Before 1850, the use of prices to measure societal well-being was infrequent and marginal. Market, capital, and profit statistics appeared only in narrowly construed economic policy debates such as the 1832 manufacturing survey commissioned by treasury secretary Louis McLane to determine the effectiveness of federal tariffs. Moral statistics dominated the more burning social issues of the day, serving as the central measures of social progress. After 1860, however, the trickle of monetized data droplets burst into a consistent torrent that only grew stronger as the years went by. While moral statistics certainly did not disappear overnight, economic productivity, market output, and per capita income or wealth statistics began to stake their claim as the premier indicators of American progress and prosperity.[9]

The eclipse of moral statistics by money metrics helped separate the economic from the moral, as the wonders of market growth and capital accumulation came to be reified as an objectively positive development regardless of one's personal opinions on ethics, politics, or society. "It has been no part of my purpose to cast unmerited opprobrium upon slaveholders, or to display any special friendliness or sympathy for the blacks," Helper explained in his preface. "I have considered my subject more particularly with reference to its economic aspects as regards the whites—not with reference, except in a very slight degree, to its humanitarian or religious aspects." Later he added that it was not his purpose "to draw a broad line of distinction between right and wrong, to point out the propriety of morality and its advantages over immorality." For Helper, in short, slavery had to go not because it was immoral but because it was "unprofitable." Slave labor should be replaced by wage labor not because of natural rights or moral imperatives, or because of a need to take into account the physical and mental well-being of African Americans, but because American society would get more bang for its collective buck.[10]

Yet while Helper sought to separate money from morality, other Americans in the 1850s were coming to see monetary gains as the ultimate indicator of ethical integrity. Such a monetizing of morality seems to have been at work in the Mercantile Credit Agency. After ardent moral reformer Lewis Tappan retired in 1849, the agency was eventually purchased by businessman R. G. Dun. Dun renamed the company after himself, but the name was not the only thing that changed. As the company pushed into the latter half of the nineteenth century, much of its moralizing gossip was replaced with cold, hard prices that measured the "worth" of the businessman in question. Hotel owner John Mooney, for instance, began his career as a "prudent, steady young man." By 1869, however, he had gone out of business, and the final entry on him noted that he "never was worth a cent, never will be." Morgan Frost was simply "very industrious and attentive" in 1846. By 1862, however, he was "worth" $10,000. Robert Green, a sailmaker, was said to "own a good house and lot" in 1849. By the 1860s, Dun and Co. was pricing the lot.[11]

Regardless of whether price statistics marginalized morality or monetized it, their political impact—especially on the sectional conflict—was enormous. As Robert Fogel has recognized, the shift from moral to economic anti-slavery arguments "transformed the antislavery movement from a minor political factor into a political force that could control the national agenda." As Helper's book demonstrates, economic indicators played a key role in bringing northern elites into the anti-slavery fold, thus helping to transform a marginal movement into the Republican Party and Abraham Lincoln into a president.[12]

Historians have mostly explained the northern shift to an economic argument against slavery by noting its pragmatic nature. While it was undoubtedly so, a crucial question still remains: why is it that by the mid-1850s, American political elites had come to believe that the American public would be more susceptible to capitalizing statistics than moralizing ones? Why could economic growth figures "control the national agenda" in mid-nineteenth-century America but moral indicators no longer could?[13]

To answer these questions, we must take a closer look at the two major historical developments that triggered the pricing of progress in the 1850s: the expansion to the West of capitalized railroads and of capitalized slaves. Although investments in railroads and cotton plantations were drastically different, they led to surprisingly similar quantitative visions. While the westward flow of capital into railroad corporations greatly altered the way northern elites looked at (and quantified) rural farmers and urban laborers, the westward flow of capital into cotton plantations altered the way southern elites looked at (and quantified) their slaves. In both instances, new social relations were being forged in which it became only natural to see the American people—slave or free—as capital goods, society as an investment, and progress as monied growth. The governmentality of moral statistics was giving way to the investmentality of economic indicators.

While there is little doubt that slavery's principle of property in human beings was incompatible with liberalism's principle of self-ownership, or that the basic social relation *between* master and slave was not mediated by the contractual relations of the market, examining this era through the historical lens of social quantification complicates the notion that the Civil War was a battle between a capitalist North and a neo-feudal, non-capitalist South. In both the North and the South, moral statistics were losing their dominant cultural grip on elites in favor of priced productivity and economic growth statistics. In both the North and the South, well-to-do white men were turning to worship at the statistical altar of market productivity, capital accumulation, and profit maximization. The similarities in how elites on both sides valued

their society, therefore, suggests that the Civil War was more of a battle between two conflicting forms of capitalist development: one driven by property in rails and iron, the other by property in people and cotton, but both
by the coronation of King Capital.[14]

In 1798, and again in 1815, the fiscal imperatives of war forced the American
federal government to do something it really did not want to do—implement
a "direct," federal property tax. Such property taxes naturally included human
property and so, as the law of 1798 made clear, "all slaves, whether negroes,
mullatoes or mestizos above the age of 12 and under the age of 50 . . . shall
be assessed at fifty cents." Here is a typical example of how a non-capitalist
United States valued and conceived of slaves: while there was little doubt that
these men and women were property, they nevertheless were all assessed
at the same amount and lumped under the same vague category of "tithable" Such a way of classifying slaves was also used in daily life. "I have a
plantation about five miles from this place," noted Virginian Robert Carter,
who ran one of the biggest slave plantations in early America, "whereon
are 16 blacks—9 of them tithables." What mattered to Carter and the tax collector was not the income-generating productivity of the slaves nor their
market prices, but only that they were of an age to labor. In a Virginia dominated by tobacco planters, all slaves were deemed pieces of property—but
few were quantified as pieces of capital.[15]

Following the cotton boom and the western expansion of slavery in the
mid-nineteenth century, the notion of slaves as property changed and slaves
became capitalized. That is, they came to be treated, organized, and valued
less as patriarchal property that provided their owners with republican virtue,
material competence, paternalist identity, and proprietary independence, but
more as mobile, productive assets that provided their owners with a steady
stream of income that could always be exchanged in a highly liquid capital
goods market known as the internal slave trade. Not unlike the shift that occurred with early modern landed property during the time of English enclosure, a slave's value was no longer ingrained in past traditions but rather was
a function of future income flows. As slaves were priced, sold, insured, mortgaged, leveraged, rented, and securitized, old ways and old social relations

dissolved quickly. As Fogel has noted, "There was very little difference between the way in which planters priced their slaves and the way they priced their other capital assets."[16]

By the 1850s, slaves had become a dream investment. Their earnings were fairly stable, the markets for them were quite liquid, their value was constantly on the rise, and unlike machines or land, they could both reproduce themselves and be easily transferred from place to place. Southerners understood all of this. "The peculiar institution," one southern commentator noted in *De Bow's*, "had become the most profitable and safe investment in the whole country." James Henry Hammond reveled in the fact that slaves earned profits for their owners both in the field and in the marketplace, noting how "the very negro who, as a prime laborer, brought 400 dollars in 1828 would now, with thirty years upon him, sell for 800." As historians of capitalism have dug deeper into the antebellum South, the evidence for the widespread capitalization of slavery has become overbearing. Whether the transactions involved slave insurance, slave mortgages, or slave rentals, African American bodies were constantly being financialized.[17]

Frederick Douglass, the first great historian of American capitalism, recognized one aspect of this process as early as 1846. "I will give you an invariable rule," he noted. "When cotton gets up in the market in England, the price of human flesh gets up in the United States." Economic historians long ago corroborated Douglass's comment. Prices of slaves began to move in tandem with the prices of cotton because slave owners were starting to value their slaves as income-bearing capital. Like the price of any income-bearing asset— be it a textile machine, an urban lot, or an acre of land—the market value of slaves was coming to be determined by the future revenue streams that slaves would yield their masters. In the antebellum South, such a revenue stream was determined by the price of cotton.[18]

By the eve of the Civil War, the notion that each slave, whether fifteen years old or forty-five, could be valued at roughly the same "tithable" rate would have been considered ridiculous. If early modern England had its "years of purchase" multiplier to make capitalizing land a quick and easy calculation, southern slaveholders had the "hand," a metric that elegantly quantified the income-generating capacity of slaves, thus making for easier market exchanges (slaves, for instance, were often measured as "full," "half," or even "quarter" hands). Business-oriented slave owners, however, took far more into account than just that one rough measure. More and more cotton planters began to keep track of their slaves' labor output through a daily routine known as the weighing of the cotton. "When a new hand, one unaccustomed to the business, is sent for the first time into the field," escaped slave Solomon Northup explained, "he is whipped up smartly, and made for that day to pick as fast as he can possibly. At night it is weighed, so that his capabilities in cotton picking are known." A crucial method of both labor discipline and capitalized calculation, the daily meeting of slave and overseer included not only a whip but also a slate that carefully documented the number of bales that each slave picked.[19]

A slave's price reflected not just productivity rates but also physical as well as (supposed) character traits. At a slave auction in Richmond, Virginia, in 1853, for instance, an enslaved boy who was five feet tall was worth $850 to $950, while a boy who was only four feet eight inches was worth only $700 to $800. James Coles Bruce, one of the largest slave owners in the South, included in his slave inventory the slave's age, productivity in "hands," market value, temperament, and health. Claiborn West, a twenty-eight-year-old "full-hand," was listed as a "good negro" and was worth $800. Bob Scooner was also a twenty-eight-year-old "full-hand" but was worth only $700 because he was "well disposed but sloe." Bruce, apparently, had estimated that Scooner's inferior pace was worth roughly $100. Finally, John Miller was another twenty-eight-year-old "full-hand," and there is nothing to suggest that he was not a productive worker. But Miller was listed at only $600 because he had run away in the past. The $200 Bruce knocked off his market value was apparently the risk premium associated with the possibility he would do so again.[20]

The vast paper trail left by antebellum slavery—bills of sale, slave inventories, slave trader account books—provides the historian with an endless number of mundane documents that affixed prices to people. That fairly precise prices, and not just round numbers, often appear in these archives allows one to imagine the haggling that must have gone on before Isaac was sold for $675, Caroline for $655, Charles for $420. As the chattel principle ascended to the heart of southern society, southerners began to converse about slave prices much as they talked about the weather. "I have attended a great many auction sales of slaves," one southerner wrote to an acquaintance in 1851 from New Orleans. "I was at one yesterday where about 100 were sold, Men, Women and Children. I thought it a very hard sight the first sale I attended, as many of them would feel so hurt at being separated." Apparently, though, such hard sights had become routine for the man, since in the very next sentence he added, "I will give you an account of the prices for which they sold yesterday." Talking about slave prices became the way in which planters professed their authority as slave owners and masculinity as patriarchs. Meanwhile, the entire South was filled with a never-ending flow of price currents. "We beg leave to give to you the state of our Negro market," wrote slave auctioneers Betts and Gregory of Richmond, Virginia. The Sears catalogs of the antebellum South, these listings included such detailed prices as "No. 1 men" ($1,550–$1,620) and "second rate girls" ($900–$1,100).[21]

As planters came to treat their slaves as capital, they also began to view not only their plantations but all of society as an investment. On the day that the future senator of South Carolina, James Henry Hammond, arrived on the plantation he had received through his wife's inheritance, he conducted a "slave census." Later he calculated what the capital returns of the previous plantation owner had been and discovered that it was less than 1 percent. As a result, he shifted his slaves from task-based labor to the far more productive and industrial form of "gang labor." He also began to keep careful track of how much cotton his slaves picked and often used contests to try to boost their productivity. He calculated that he earned a profit of $215 a year from each slave. Keeping close tabs on his overall revenue, in 1841 he noted that his annual income averaged $12,500. A few years later, Hammond returned to the same profit-oriented calculations—only this time for the United States as a whole instead of just his plantation. "There is not a nation on earth," Hammond declared in his famous "Cotton Is King" speech, "that can compete with us in produce per capita. It amounts to $16.66 per head." Hammond went on to carefully compare northern and southern market output to show that the South produced $220 million a year and the North only $95 million.[22]

De Bow's Review, the self-proclaimed *Hunt's Merchants' Magazine* of the South, further demonstrated how the capitalization of slaves was rapidly changing the way southerners measured not only their slaves or plantations but society writ large. In the late 1840s, when his magazine was just getting started, James De Bow published a few articles citing moral statistics, many of which he penned himself. By the early 1850s, however, he had turned wholeheartedly to the pricing of progress, as he imagined the entire South as one giant, profit-maximizing plantation:

> The best cotton lands will not yield more than three hundred pounds per acre, and the general average from year to year probably does not exceed two hundred pounds. Suppose, however, the quantity to be two hundred and fifty pounds, there is required 1,794,807 acres of land to produce it; and as the product will not average more than 2,500 pounds per hand, it will require about 195.480 hands for its culture. The land, at $25 per acre, is worth $44,870,175. The hands (slaves) at $500 each are worth $97,740,000. Thus, the land and slaves together, would amount in value to $142,610,000. . . . In order to make the estimate high enough for the planter, we will suppose his net receipts to be 6 cents per pound. At that price, the quantity, 480,000,000 pounds, will return him, say, in round numbers $29,000,000.[23]

De Bow turned to these calculations not only to legitimize slavery but also to attract far-flung capital to the South. He made this point explicit when he convinced the Louisiana state legislature to create the first state statistical bureau in the nation—with him as its head. Following Hunt's playbook, he noted how the bureau would generate statistical indicators that could be used to draw capital to Louisiana by "contrasting each period of her Growth and comparing the results with those presented by other states of the Union."[24]

The southerners most interested in De Bow's economic indicators were those pushing westward into the cotton frontier of the Deep South. Between the years 1849 and 1851, for instance, the states that added the most subscriptions to *De Bow's Review* were Mississippi and Alabama. Apparently De Bow's endless array of priced statistics resonated with this new breed of cotton planters far more than it did with the genteel slave owners of Virginia tobacco plantations.[25]

In an article in *De Bow's* titled "The Future of the South," De Bow used statistics in order to prove that the French abolition of slavery had been an unmitigated disaster. "In 1836," he argued, "4,932 hands produced in Martinique 6,056,990 pounds of sugar or one hogshead each. In 1849 [following the French abolition of slavery in 1848], the proceeds averaged one hogshead for 34 hands." Hinting at what might happen if African American slaves were freed, De Bow reminded his readers that "75 percent of the exports of the union are the product of slave labor" and that $1.23 million in capital created by northern textile factories had been "reared upon the frail foundation of black labor." "The thread of cotton has gradually enveloped the commercial world and bound the fortunes of American slaves so firmly to human progress," De Bow concluded, "that civilization itself may almost be said to depend upon the continual servitude of the blacks in America."[26]

De Bow's arguments did not go unnoticed. Four years later, David Christy's article "Cotton Is King or Economic Relations of Slavery" repeated, in far more statistical detail, many of the arguments Nott had made. Christy argued that the global reliance on slave productivity had transformed slavery into an "institution that was no longer controlled by moral or physical force but had become wholly subject to the laws of Political Economy." Rejecting the notion that freed blacks working for wages could possibly pick cotton as productively as slaves—as many northern capitalists at the time were claiming—the pamphlet concluded that "the products of slave labor are in such universal demand . . . that it is impracticable, in the existing condition of the world, to overthrow the system." Seeking to prove the immense and ever-growing productivity of slavery, the pamphlet contained a table revealing that while the exported-cotton-to-slave ratio in 1820 was 83 bales per slave, by 1853 it was 337 bales.[27]

Alabama physicians and southern periodicals were not the only ones making these pro-slavery economic calculations. In 1835, while in the midst of utterly revolutionizing how Americans would receive their news, *New York Herald* editor James Bennett hired former merchant Thomas Kettell to write the "money columns" in his paper. While Bennett has been credited with inventing sensational journalism and the daily penny press, this too was a groundbreaking move, as Kettell became the first-ever financial editor of a daily American newspaper. As one nineteenth-century Wall Street investor later recalled, it was Kettell "who gave that journal [the *Herald*] a reputation among financial men." Kettell would go on to contribute numerous articles to *De Bow's* and *Hunt's Merchants' Magazine* while editing the much respected *United States Magazine and Democratic Review* in the 1840s and the *United States Economist* in the 1850s. In his writings Kettell became famous for using monied metrics to make his arguments. Particularly fond of per capita wealth statistics, Kettell would frequently use such figures in a before-and-after comparison to empirically prove the benefits that a bank, railroad, or manufacturing company provided to a city or town.[28]

In 1856 Kettell published a book that sent shock waves through the country. Titled *Southern Wealth and Northern Profits,* the book used "statistical facts and official figures" to show the "necessity of union to the future prosperity of and welfare of the republic." In his plea for reconciliation between North and South, Kettell used economic indicators as his barometer for "welfare" as he set out to prove that an institution as incredibly profitable as slavery should not be abolished. "What will the future historian say of the North," Kettell asked rhetorically in his opening remarks, "which destroyed its source of profit for a mere trivial pretense?" Rejecting the notion that the South was unproductive and backward, and referring to the issue of human bondage as a "trivial pretense," Kettell used his patented array of before-and-after wealth statistics to prove how wonderful slavery truly was. "From a market value of $250, [slaves] have risen to $1500 and $2000. This simple fact alone would show not only the great value that their labor is to the Christian world, but that their owners have thus, as it were, come under bonds in the sum of $1200 and $1800 each hand, to give them the best moral and material care." Incredibly, Kettell was using slave prices to measure not only the well-being of the enslavers but that of the enslaved as well.[29]

Firmly in the "Copperhead" branch of the northern Democratic Party, Kettell's tract was adamantly pro-slavery. But railroad journalist Henry Varnum Poor's approach to the sectional crisis reveals that anti-slavery northern elites who supported the Republican Party were using very similar statistical measures and economic arguments when dealing with slavery. In 1860, with the threat of civil war looming, Poor was asked by the editor of the *New York Times* to write a series of articles on the impending crisis. Poor was not a political analyst or public intellectual but rather the editor of *American Railroad Journal,* a business magazine filled with financial statistics designed to help investors decide in which railroad lines they should place their capital. That Poor was even asked to pen these articles reveals how

American political discourse was shifting from moral imperatives to financial ones.[30]

Like so many middle-class Americans of his generation, Poor had dabbled in moral statistics when he was a young man. In a visit to England, he even asked to meet with Edwin Chadwick, the great moral statistician of Great Britain. By the time he produced his *New York Times* articles in 1860, however, Poor had changed with the times. Years of editing a journal intended for railroad investors had shifted his statistical outlook to one completely fixated on monetary yields.[31]

In his articles for the *New York Times,* which had titles such as "A Businessman's Look at the Political Crisis," the anti-slavery Poor began his argument against secession by treating slaves like fixed capital. "The South must continue to produce Cotton, not only as a means of existence, but because they can put their labour to no other use," he noted. "According to their estimate, they have $4,000,000,000 invested in labour, chiefly engaged in the culture of this staple. The interest, at 6 per cent, on this sum is $240,000,000. If there were no other motive, they are not going to let this vast investment lie idle." Poor went on to argue—in this article and others—that due to their dependence on the North's far more advanced society of industry and finance, the South could ill afford to secede. To prove the advantages of the North, Poor used the same kind of wealth statistics as Helper, Fisher, and Kettell. Citing *De Bow's Review* (revealingly, he and De Bow were close friends), Poor demonstrated that the average person in South Carolina generated $41 a year, while in Massachusetts the average person produced $172 worth of goods annually. Pricing the income-generating capacities of free northerners in a manner similar to how planters valued their slaves, Poor concluded that such figures proved that the North was the more advanced society and had little to fear from secession.[32]

Henry Varnum Poor of Massachusetts and Thomas Kettell of New York were using the same per-capita wealth statistics to measure progress as James Henry Hammond of South Carolina and Josiah Mott of Alabama. That Poor made his main point by discounting the opportunity costs of slaves at the going rate of interest demonstrates that the capitalization of men did not stop at the Mason-Dixon line and that slavery served as a crucial stepping-stone, in both South and North, toward an investmentality that imagined people as capital and progress as monetary growth. Slavery, however, was not the only major force leading northerners to price progress. Poor, after all, had not spent his days buying slaves or weighing cotton. Rather, he had dedicated his life to the railroad.

The year was 1851, and the wealthy railroad investors of Boston, a city at the heart of antebellum railroad finance, decided to organize a celebration in honor of the "completion of various lines of Railway, which connect the Canadas and the Great West with the Tide Water at Boston." To prepare for the celebration, a number of committees were organized. There was one "to arrange for the meeting of the merchants," another for "fireworks," and yet another to organize a "harbor excursion." A separate committee was charged with producing "tabular representation of the present condition of Boston in relation to railroad facilities, foreign commerce, population, wealth, and manufacturers." Hoping to include in these statistical tables an accurate estimate of daily passenger traffic, the committee paid a private police force of fifty-five men to spread out across the city from 6:30 A.M. to 7:30 P.M. on September 6, 1851, in order to count the number of passengers who came in (41,729) and out (42,313) of the city. As the results of the report proudly demonstrated, a great deal of people now used the railroad to enter the city: 11,963 came by train, 14,310 by foot, and only 127 by horseback. The committee, meanwhile, quickly translated human traffic into dollars and cents by calculating the railroads' gross earnings from passengers and freight. "The net income," the statistical report assured its readers, "was more than 6 per cent." As the committee's tables made plain, railroads had the power to reduce space to price, people to profit, and, as Richard White has argued, everyday life "down to money."[33]

Comparable in their wide-ranging social impact only to the invention of the Internet in the late twentieth century, the railroad revolutionized American society in many ways. Railroads were the first large, multi-unit, for-profit corporations in American history; they developed novel forms of corporate management, bureaucratic hierarchy, and cost accounting; they attracted massive flows of capital from the richest men in the world, single-handedly turning the American stock market from a negligible backwater into a global institution; they had a devastating effect on the natural environment and Native Americans; they forged a national market consisting of urban nodes and rural satellites; they were the largest employer of men for most of the nineteenth century, and the cradle of the American labor movement; they were pivotal in the making of the Knights of Labor, accident insurance, the Granger and Populist movements, the Sears catalogs, and Chicago. Often the monopolistic gatekeepers to the world (again, only the power of Google seems a worthy comparison), they radically altered American politics, government regulation, and power relations. They not only "annihilated time and space" but privatized it. When railroads crashed, as they often did, many people died. When railroad stocks crashed, as they often did, the entire economy went with them. Railroads overshadowed every other enterprise in their scale, scope, and power; for most of the nineteenth century, when Americans spoke of "the corporation" they were referring to railroads.[34]

That Boston capital chose to celebrate these new railroad lines not only with fireworks and harbor tours but also with "tabular statements" points to yet another, often overlooked aspect of the railroad revolution: railroads radically changed the way American elites valued and quantified the world around them, playing just as central a role as cotton slavery in the decline of moral statistics and the rise of capitalizing ones. As William Cronon has recognized, railroads "generated vast new quantities of statistics which themselves helped revolutionize the American economy by making possible increasingly intricate analyses of trade and production." To this one must add that railroad statistics also made possible increasingly intricate trade and production analyses of people and progress. For the privatized ribbons of incorporated iron that spread across the country in this decade, colonizing western towns with eastern capital wherever they went, gave birth not only to a national market and corporate capitalism but also to a new statistical regime in which American communities and their residents were reimagined as abstract units of income-generating wealth.[35]

It is, therefore, no coincidence that the 1850s were the crucial decade for both the pricing of progress and for the American railroad. "Pay particular attention to the 1850s," Alfred Chandler advised in his analysis of railroads, and for good reason. In 1847, 263 miles of railroad track were laid in the United States. In 1857, that number would jump to 2,077. In 1850, there were 172 chartered railways. In 1860, there were 474. In the 1840s, 6,000 miles of track were laid. In the 1850s, that figure would balloon to 21,000, and by the end of the decade the major lines between East and West had come into being.[36]

More important than sheer scale, however, was the changing nature of railroad investment. Up to 1850, much of the capital invested in railroads came from local citizens, nearby counties, and proximate municipalities who purchased railroad securities not to earn a return but rather to link their communities to the emerging national market. The direct goal of these early railroads was less profit than infrastructure. All this changed in the 1850s when eastern and European investors came to recognize the profitability of railroads and began to pour enormous amounts of capital into lines outside of the regions in which they lived. By the end of the decade, railroads were mostly being financed not by local businessmen and regional governments but by national and international capital markets. By 1856 railroad securities outnumbered bank stocks on the New York exchange, becoming the leading investment in America. In 1850, $318 million was invested in railroads. By 1860, that figure had more than trebled to $1.149 billion, and any urban booster interested in raising capital to furnish a railway to their city would now have to go through Wall Street investment banks to secure funding. As early as the 1790s, Hamilton dreamed of capitalizing the westward-expanding labor of American yeoman households and artisanal workshops into priced streams of interest-bearing eastern capital. It took the railroads to make this dream come true.[37]

The changing investment portfolio of eastern elites in the 1850s reveals these changes. Take, for example, the account books of Henry Grew and his wife, Jane Wigglesworth Grew. Bostonian Brahmins to the core, the Grews were rich because Jane's father was the successful Boston merchant Thomas Wigglesworth. An agent for the East India Company in Boston, Wigglesworth had become wealthy through international commerce. Yet as Henry's account books make clear, by 1851 the Grews had funneled nearly half of their net worth into a dozen railroad securities, including the Vermont Central, the Vermont & Canada, the Boston, Concord & Montreal, and the Northern Railroad. Rich Bostonians were not the only ones moving their capital into iron rails. Samuel Finley Vinton moved from New England to Ohio in the 1820s, where he would go on to become a successful lawyer and member of Congress. At first, the majority of Vinton's wealth was held in urban lots and Ohio Company land. Two years after his death in 1863, however, his estate account revealed that 85 percent of his annual income from capital ($11,114) was in the form of thousands of shares of railroad securities, while only 15 percent ($1,955) was from real estate holdings.[38]

Railroads had not always been viewed mostly as a means for capital accumulation. Befitting an era in which progress was often measured in moral statistics, Boston physician Charles Caldwell titled his 1831 speech to the Lexington Lyceum "Thoughts on the Moral and Other Indirect Influences of Rail-Roads." In this piece, Caldwell asserted that railways would lead "to an improvement in common school education" and to "the promotion of sound morals, as well as of enlightened taste and becoming manners." Arguing that railroads would make it easier for poor urban dwellers to go West and become yeoman freeholders, Caldwell believed that an America with railroads would be "exempt from such of the poverty, wretchedness, and concomitant vice and no little of the sickliness of large cities." Many agreed with him. In 1839, the Pennsylvania House of Representatives determined that railroads would lead to an increase in "intelligent freemen . . . skilled in the arts of civilization, and refined moral and religious virtues." Viewing the railroads as an engine for public good more than an asset of private investment, the New York state legislature concluded that their positive moral impact was "a prospect more pleasing to the philanthropist and patriot, than the mere anticipation of profit."[39]

These Jacksonian Era Americans conceived of railroads as they conceived of all corporations: as institutions whose main goal was to increase social welfare, not private incomes. Referring to railroads as "democratic institutions," the editor of the *American Railroad Journal* who preceded Henry Varnum Poor told his readers in 1845, "We are not those who think a railroad to be profitable must pay a large dividend. Many railroads would be profitable to a large portion of the people, if they never paid 5, or even 3 percent." By the early 1850s, Poor's predecessor's claim that railroads need not yield even 3 percent would have been deemed absurd. Purchasing the *American Railroad Journal* in 1849 and soon refashioning it as a magazine devoted almost exclusively to helping capitalists earn a healthy return, by 1852 Poor was openly admitting that railroads were "merely commercial enterprises and are to be conducted upon commercial principles."[40]

Poor's comment reflected a larger shift in American approaches to railroads and corporations. By the mid-1850s, *Hunt's Merchants' Magazine* enthusiast and U.S. president Millard Fillmore was celebrating the New York & Erie Railroad not as a great public works project but as "the great private enterprise of the age." Meanwhile, western boosters began to praise railroads (many through the pages of *Hunt's*) less as a purveyor of a higher civilization than as the cause of higher real estate prices. By 1856, a member of the New Jersey legislature demonstrated the "prosperity" of the railroads through "a comparison of the wealth of the counties having railroads with other parts of the states." These were exactly the kind of price statistics Thomas Kettell had used to measure the pros and cons of slavery. In fact, Kettell loved to write about the wonders of the railroad almost as much as he liked to write of the benefits of slavery. "Why the railroads of Massachusetts have cost $50,000,000, and the wealth of the state has increased $300,000,000 or six times the amount in ten years," Kettell gushed in a typical article. "That is to say, from the land at Plymouth to 1840, two hundred years elapsed, in which the wealth of Massachusetts reached $299,878,327. Ten years of railroads have added a sum equal to the whole results of those two hundred years. Is that not a railroad pace?"[41]

When capital-hungry railroad boosters from across the nation wrote up a prospectus to convince investors in New York, London, and Berlin to pour their savings into a railroad between St. Louis and Milwaukee or Louisville and Baltimore, they realized that their investor audience cared little for the kind of information on these towns' churches, schools, vices, prostitutes, or moral associations that had interested locals. Boosters knew that in order to convince eastern and European capital to finance railroad lines they might never ride, in communities that were thousands of miles from their home, one could not speak of civilizing or moral improvements. Wall Street, in short, had little need for moral statistics. On the contrary, to attract capital one had to speak in the pecuniary language of costs and benefits—and back it all up with a steady stream of earnings statistics.[42]

The prospectus made sure that the railroad's pricing of progress would commence before a single iron rail was laid. Railroads earned income from two main sources: passenger fares and freight traffic. Capitalists picking and choosing which railroad securities to buy knew this, so when they examined the possibility (and profitability) of connecting two communities with a railroad, they were primarily interested in gaining a sense of the potential volume of passengers and freight that would flow between the rail's endpoints. In a typical prospectus that sought to fund a railway between Hartford and New York, railroad boosters statistically projected "the amount of business, transportation and travel in the immediate vicinity of the line, and the annual income it is reasonable to expect on the first opening of the railroad." As explained in yet another prospectus peddling a railway between Providence and Worcester, these statistics were designed to "exhibit the inducements it offers for capitalists to subscribe the means necessary for its construction."[43]

A closer look at the prospectus for the Providence-to-Worcester line reveals that such "inducements" included an array of statistics on population, agricultural output, and industrial productivity. Offering a village-by-village breakdown of all the communities en route, here is how a typical town, Valley Falls, Rhode Island, was described in the prospectus:

> Population including Home Print Works adjoining: 1500.
> This is a manufacturing village, in which are 5 cotton mills, with 22,340 spindles, 627 looms, making 101,970 yards of cloth per week, and working 2,543 bales of cotton per annum, and 3 machine shops. There are 276 females, and 205 males employed.
> Estimated annual tons of merchandise: 1900.
> Estimated Annual sum paid by passengers in stages: $2,400.
> Estimated annual sum paid by freight of merchandize: $1,900.

Hoping to present their calculations in the most digestible manner possible, the authors of the prospectus ended their report by consolidating all these village-by-village descriptions into a single table. Readers could now instantly compare the income-bearing potential of Valley Falls ($4,300 total from passenger and freight traffic), Pawtucket ($40,465), Waterford ($5,450), Uxbridge ($7,119) and dozens of other communities.[44]

Once a railroad was up and running, a second round of market statistics ensued, as income figures regarding freight and passenger traffic were no longer estimates but actual earnings that appeared in annual stockholder reports. In the 1840s, many reports—such as that of the Boston & Maine Railroad in 1849—provided little information on passenger and freight traffic, choosing only to assert rather vaguely that "net earnings of the road, over and above its expenses of operation and repairs, have been . . . an average of 8 per cent per annum." A year later, however, the Boston & Maine president added to the 1850 report a more detailed chart of income from passengers and freight, and in 1851 he included a chart that allowed readers to compare year-to-year earnings. That report also included a novel and elaborate month-by-month and town-by-town income analysis so that readers could instantly see that while the "passengers, rents and mails" from Malden had paid $416.66 in March, Somerville had generated only $118.40 that month. A second table included a similar town-by-town / month-by-month earnings chart, only this time for freight. This table reveals the statistical power of the railroad: with, for example, $2,539.40 in freight for commodities generated by Lawrence in April and $1,423.70 by Haverhill, the Boston & Maine railway succeeded in pricing the market output of the American people, precisely where the likes of Hamilton had failed a half century earlier. The table became a staple of shareholder reports across the nation, as securitized returns on railroad investment came to be closely intertwined with the market output of iron welders in Worcester, dry-goods merchants in Cincinnati, seamstresses in Chicago, or wheat farmers in California.[45]

With such data at hand, one could begin to extract all sorts of novel economic indicators from railroad reports. This is precisely what Henry Varnum Poor did as the editor-in-chief of the *American Railroad Journal,* and it was a huge success. In the 1850s alone, five weekly and two monthly railroad periodicals were born. Poor, however, led the way. The *American Railroad Journal*'s subscription list increased from 12,000 in 1849 to 30,000 in 1854, reflecting the sharp uptick in demand for financial data by American elites such as the Grews and the Vintons. Processing huge amounts of data on railroads' operational costs and earnings, which he collected either from annual reports or by sending out circulars to rail managers, Poor translated these figures into easy-to-read metrics, be it "cost per mile," "debts more than surplus," "net earnings," "net earnings per mile," "rate of dividends," "price of shares," "gross earnings," or "capital stock paid in." These tables allowed investors to quickly develop an opinion of a railroad by, for instance, comparing capitalization and cost, gross to net earnings, or percentage of net earnings to the dividend.[46]

As the market productivity of American villages, towns, cities, and counties was made legible and visible by railroad statistics, Americans began to use this data to conceptualize not just railroad traffic but the American economy as a whole. Take, for example, the annual stockholders' report of the Chicago, Burlington & Quincy Railroad Company from 1855. Not only did this report provide a window into the railroad's earnings and expenses, it also allowed readers to see the previously invisible scale and scope of the Chicago market. Thanks to the railroad, Americans could now see that 132,598,578 pounds of wheat, 9,062,243 pounds of "sundries," and 13,347,130 pounds of live hog had entered the city in 1855, while 195,766,120 pounds of lumber, 22,603,980 pounds of shingles, and 7,568,672 pounds of iron had exited.[47]

Recognizing that the railroad allowed Americans to catch a rare glimpse of the emerging national market, Poor came to believe that "the railroad system may be regarded as the barometer of the entire industrial system." While admitting that he dealt "with but one subject or department of national industry or life," Poor argued that this one "department, however, goes far to include all as the greater part of the products of our industries are moved from producer to consumer by our railroad. The amount of such movement is consequently a pretty accurate measure of the productiveness of the industries of the country of the progress made in them from year to year and of the national wealth." Here we see how Poor transitioned from specific analyses of certain railroads to a far more general statement regarding national wealth and progress. Poor echoed these sentiments in his private correspondence with his wife, exclaiming that his railroad statistics "will be the record of a great achievement— of the greatest material development the world has yet seen."[48]

———— ⚬✦⚬ ————

Years after his book had become a huge best seller, Hinton Helper suggested that it was the 1850 census that had triggered his turn against slavery:

> In the process of my conversion from the pro-slavery opinions and pre-judgments in which, if I may so speak, I was born and bred, nothing influenced me so much, nothing so whetted my desire for closer scrutiny into the two conflicting systems of society, nothing so hastened my espousal of the cause of white free labor, and certainly nothing so strengthened and confirmed me in my utter detestation of negro slavery, as the thorough perusal of a certain public document . . . the Seventh Census.[49]

There is a certain irony to Helper's claim, since the "public document" he is referring to was tabulated and disseminated by none other than James De Bow. In 1853, De Bow parlayed his statistical expertise into the most coveted position of the numerically minded: chief of the Census Bureau. While De

Bow arrived in Washington after the 1850 census had already been designed and executed by Joseph Kennedy, it was he who summarized the census findings in the mass-published compendium that would go on to be cited endlessly by northerners and southerners alike. If Helper had been enthralled by these nicely organized tables of market productivity, he had slavery and its most ardent advocate to thank, at least in part, since the Census Bureau published an unprecedented 320,000 copies of the census compendium.[50]

Helper's comments, meanwhile, reveal a larger truth: the rise of the pricing of progress would have been impossible without the government's decision to allocate a sizable amount of resources to the systematic collection of market output data in the 1840 and 1850 censuses, the latter being regarded by most historians as the first "modern" census in American history. Such state-collected market statistics allowed Helper and others to transform the sectional dispute over slavery into an exercise in the pricing of the North's and South's productive capacities. As is apparent in Thomas Kettell's 1845 letter to Senator Samuel Tilden requesting census data and other numerous "public documents of a commercial and financial nature," even the keenest believers in private capitalist enterprise were dependent on the state for market statistics.[51]

Return to the Jacksonian Era and it becomes evident just how difficult it was to whet the appetite of potential railroad investors without census data that charted the productivity of the American people. When renowned newspaper editor Nathan Hale became one of the first Americans to call for the construction of railroads in the 1820s, few listened. Hale recalled in his memoirs how his closest friends left his house "with expression of pity" after he had tried to convince them of the railroad's practicality. One newspaper in Boston referred to Hale's proposed Boston & Albany Railroad as "a project which everyone who knows the simplest rule of arithmetic to be impracticable, but at an expense little less than the market value of the whole territory of Massachusetts; and which, if practicable, every person of common sense knows would be useless as a railroad from Boston to the moon."[52]

Desperate to develop a new "rule of arithmetic" that challenged the conservative calculations of merchants who had been taught to focus on international commerce rather than internal development, Hale tried to convince Boston elites of the "practicability" of investing in his railroad by calculating "the business of the country lying between Boston and Albany." Yet with no census data to show, for instance, the annual tonnage of wheat produced by the average New England farmer, Hale's attempt to create the first railroad prospectus in American history failed. Forced to employ private "agents" to do a job that required the capacities of the state, he was unable to "attain that degree of certainty which is desirable."[53]

Hale was not alone in his frustrations. As one Pennsylvania railroad booster grimly noted a decade and a half later, "All who, as holders of stock, capitalists, and dealers, are pecuniarily interested in the financial history and condition of the Commonwealth, have long felt and lamented the want of necessary and accurate information. To learn anything, an examination of various and scattered documents was required; and the statistics there given were always dubious and often most incorrect." Prior to the 1850 census, even the state relied on private data collection. "In the absence of statistical statements published by national authority," noted one 1853 Treasury Department report, the most "valuable information" before 1850 had to be culled from "the publications called *Hunt's Merchants' Magazine, De Bow's Review,* the *Banker's Magazine,* and the *American Railroad Journal.*"[54]

As calls for government production of market statistics increased, so did demands that the census devote resources to their collection. The central voice in this regard was Archibald Russell's. Russell made a name for himself in 1839 when he authored a book that described in great detail the types of industrial and agricultural statistics the decennial census should collect in the upcoming census. Writing during the heyday of moral statistics, Russell made his alternative statistical objective very clear in the opening pages of his book, declaring that he was "anxious to procure the opinion of businessmen upon the form most suitable for returns from the various manufacturing and agricultural interests."[55]

Beginning with manufacturing, Russell soon ran into the same problem that Alexander Hamilton and Tench Coxe had experienced decades prior: American artisans and yeoman households saw their manufacturing as an extension of their proprietary livelihood and not as a for-profit enterprise. Russell, however, came up with a useful narrative to solve this problem:

> If a village shoemaker is called a manufacturer, what sort of return can he make, he knows not how many boots he has made, nor the value of those he has repaired, but working for minute gains he does not keep accurate accounts of the progress of his business. On the whole therefore

we believe that the term manufacture ought strictly to be applied to articles intended for *wholesale or export trade,* and that those avocations which merely supply the locality where they are made are more properly the product of trades than manufactures.

Russell worked out these contradictions by simply defining his statistical categories according to his own ideology: if manufacturers do not earn a substantial monetary income, they should not be counted as manufacturers. Implicit in his argument was the notion that the goal of manufacturing was not to make things but to make money.[56]

While in this instance Russell chose to ignore anything he could not price, his work was often quite exacting. Russell was wary of the perpetual danger of "double counting"—a fear that future advocates of gross national product (GNP) would lose a great deal of sleep over as well. "If we include this wool in any estimate of the agricultural produce of the country," he warned, "we must exclude it from its manufactured produce, for if we do not it will be reckoned twice over." Russell's focus on the minutiae of the census gave his statistical vision an impression of objectivity, precision, and rigor that the work of previous economic statisticians, such as Samuel Blodget, had lacked. Russell also anticipated one of the central goals of modern economic indicators by placing a newfound emphasis on efficiency. While earlier manufacturing censuses tracked only total industrial output, Russell believed one could gauge labor efficiency by making per-day productivity measures available. As such, he recommended adding a category on the "aggregate time of work in a year."[57]

In what would become his most lasting legacy, Russell believed that the government should collect data not just on manufacturing, as previous censuses had done, but on agricultural statistics as well. Save for a few ad hoc attempts by the likes of the New York state census and the federal patent office, the gathering of crop and livestock statistics had not been undertaken by the American state up to 1840. Russell argued that in a largely agrarian society, such a statistical blind spot was unacceptable. Here too, Russell proposed that the census collect not only aggregated yields on such staple crops as wheat, cotton, and barley but also "average return per acre" figures, which would enable one to gauge the relative efficiency of American land and labor. "One of the most interesting features of such returns," Russell asserted, "would be to show the exact progress of improvement . . . and to exhibit the increasing wealth of the country at large."[58]

A year after Russell's book saw light, the 1840 census brought back the manufacturing census and also began to collect data regarding the quantity of livestock, cereal grains, cotton, hay, and other agricultural produce. Comparing the census to Russell's writings, it becomes evident that whoever was responsible for the addition of agricultural questions to the 1840 census (it is not clear) had a copy of Russell's book open as those questions were being written: the order of grains in the census—wheat, barley, oats, rye, buckwheat, corn—is identical to that in Russell's book. This unprecedented market output data would not go unused for long. It soon allowed George Tucker to generate the first-ever aggregated wealth and income statistics in the pages of *Hunt's Merchants' Magazine*. A few years later, Michigan native Ezra Seaman would follow in his footsteps. "The prosperity of any people, the comforts they enjoy, and their wealth and power, depend entirely on their productive industry," Seaman declared in his book *Essays on the Progress of Nations,* which would go on to see numerous future editions. Now able to add together the total dollar value of products such as cotton, fabrics, hats, boots, pork, beef, wheat, rye, milk, cream, and eggs, Seaman priced "prosperity" at $865,269,561, or $59 per person.[59]

The 1840 census, however, was considered by contemporary Americans (and future historians) highly unreliable, in part because in one key instance it did not follow Russell's recommendations. Rather than base their data on farm-by-farm surveys, the architects of the 1840 census decided—probably because it was a lot cheaper—to rely on per-district estimates made by the assistant marshals. The real leap in the collection of credible agricultural productivity data, therefore, came with the 1850 census. Assistant marshals were now instructed to gather their information directly from "all farms and plantations." In addition to output questions regarding bushels of wheat or pounds of cotton, these schedules also addressed "the cash value of farms" and the number of acres of improved and unimproved land. Just as Russell had prescribed a decade prior, one could now make per-acre efficiency calculations. But it is little surprise that the agricultural schedules of the 1850 census followed Russell's instructions: he drew them up himself.[60]

The census was not the only institution through which Russell pushed for market statistics. He was also a founding member of the American Geographical and Statistical Society (AGSS). On a cold October evening in 1851, Russell and a coterie of businessmen met in the well-regarded library of John Disturnell in New York City. Originally trained as a mapmaker, by the early 1830s Disturnell had shifted to compiling information for enterprising businessmen, especially those interested in railroad investment. He wrote the first American railroad guide in 1840, and his *New York as It Is* series and statistical gazetteer were widely read among New York businessmen.[61]

The men who gathered on that October night and for future society meetings fit right in with the statistical gazetteers on Disturnell's shelves. Some of the leaders of New York business soon became members, including Henry E. Pierrepont, shipping magnates Alexander Isaac Cotheal and Henry Grinnell, transatlantic telegraph cable promoter Cyrus W. Field, and merchant S. DeWitt Bloodgood. Along with Russell, the top business journalists and economic statisticians in the country also came to meetings, including Freeman Hunt, Henry Varnum Poor, Dr. J. Calvin Smith, and Cincinnati editor, railroad booster, and all-around statistical wizard Edward Mansfield. Demonstrating how business statistics were entering the mainstream media, some of the top newspaper editors of the nineteenth century joined as well. This list includes Charles Dana of the *New York Sun,* Hiram Barney of the *New York Evening Post,* and Henry Raymond of the *New York Times* (a strong proponent of business statistics and the man responsible for publishing Poor's widely read economic analysis of the sectional crisis).[62]

Knitting a national market required both far-reaching railroads and far-seeing statistics, and none knew this better than the men who made up the American Geography and Statistical Society. By 1859 the society had founded a statistical journal, edited by Henry Varnum Poor, and created one of the best libraries for economic statistics in the world. As for the papers presented at their meetings, most were intended for the profit-seeking American capitalist: "Statistics of Agriculture," "Growth, Trade and Manufacture of Cotton," "Railroads from the Atlantic to the Pacific Ocean," and "Statistics and Geography of Iron." In one of the earliest expressions of a budding American imperialism, many of the talks were not on the United States at all, but rather on the economic potential of South Americans regions such as Paraguay, Chiriquí, and New Granada.[63]

No passive organization, the AGSS pushed federal and state governments to collect more and more business-related statistics. It was the AGSS, for instance, that convinced the New York state legislature to add industrial and agriculture statistics to the 1855 state census, as the society's members did not want to wait an entire decade for their precious output figures. Judging by the society's library catalog from 1857, which is filled with an assortment of statistical reports by banking comptrollers, canal commissioners, and state treasury departments, the AGSS had a great deal of success convincing state governments (especially in New York, Wisconsin, and Ohio) to increase their data-collecting capacities. The prodigious representation of railroad statistics in the AGSS library makes plain the way many members put this sudden wellspring of data collection to use.[64]

AGSS members did not only serve as outside lobbyists. Like Russell with the 1850 census, many went on to play an official role in the collection of government economic data. Cincinnati booster and *Railroad Record* editor Edward Mansfield was made commissioner of statistics for the state of Ohio in 1857. Henry Varnum Poor contributed to a groundbreaking Treasury Department report regarding trade traffic on the Great Lakes. Perhaps most influential of all, Joseph Kennedy was a leading AGSS member as well as the superintendent of both the 1850 and 1860 censuses.

Thanks in part to AGSS efforts, by the mid-1860s businessmen could turn to a plethora of statistical data when investing their capital, be it the *Chicago Daily Tribune*'s annual compilation of railroad, banking, lumber, warehouse, and packing house figures, West Virginia's "industrial statistics" on oil wells, data from the newly founded Minnesota Bureau of Statistics on the state's "progress and capabilities," or the Boston Board of Trade's impressive collection of cotton manufacturing data. The coordinated efforts of private interests and state bureaucracies were responsible for this burst of economic data, but such statistics also received quite a boost from the outbreak of Civil War.[65]

———————

In the fall of 1864, well before he became the most widely read economic writer in Gilded Age America, a young and unheralded man by the name of David Ames Wells gave a lecture to a group of businessmen from the rapidly industrializing city of Troy in upstate New York. The atmosphere in the room was tense, and for good reason: the Civil War was both a military nightmare and an economic one. In his speech that evening, Wells did not touch on the enormous human costs of the tragic war, choosing to focus solely on its financial expenses. They were staggering. In 1860, the U.S. national debt had been $64.8 million. By 1864, it had surpassed $2 billion.[66]

The national debt was increasing by a million dollars a day, and it had become a well-acknowledged fact among northerners that if the national debt hit the $3 billion mark, the war would have to come to a close—whether slavery's westward expansion and the South's rebellion ended or not. The fate of the Union was not the only thing on the line. Thanks largely to Jay Cooke's impressive marketing abilities, middle-class Americans across the North—including the Troy men who served as Wells's audience—had poured much of their life savings into a single financial asset: government war bonds. With war expenses snowballing into financial catastrophe, these men were terrified that they would never see their precious savings again, let alone a return on their investment.[67]

The purpose of Wells's speech was to calm the American bondholder so "that anxiety and fear may be, in a degree, banished from their hearts." Using a mind-boggling array of population and wealth statistics in unprecedented ways, Wells set out to prove that thanks to "the increase of the population of our country and its wondrous development in wealth and resources," there would be no problem financing the war or paying back bondholders. Citing population censuses, fire insurance records, state bank commissioners' reports, and even the estimated national increase in sheep, Wells painstakingly proved his point by envisioning the United States—and its inhabitants— as one big capitalized investment. Meticulously pricing everyday life into a series of wealth and revenue streams, Wells sought to soothe the anxieties of his audience by calculating both the overall capital stock of the United States and the annual income flow that would be generated from this capitalized wealth. "The re-united nation will start anew on its era of peace with a capital of twenty thousand millions," Wells confidently concluded, "and an annual increase of wealth which certainly cannot be estimated at less than $2,000,000,000." Even when taxed at a fairly low rate, Wells explained, such an ever-expanding pool of capital could pay off the government's war debts.[68]

After writing up his talk into a pamphlet titled *Our Burden and Our Strength,* Wells saw his lecture became an overnight sensation, especially among richest and most powerful men in America, who had already come to see their nation as an investment. Railroad capitalist John Murray Forbes spoke of the pamphlet with great enthusiasm, noting how "a great many people will pay for a thing like this which they approve," including "the Banks and Insurance Presidents and other semi-patriotics who want our credit kept up to par." Corresponding with Wells more than thirty years later, *Nation* editor Edwin Godkin could "still remember how remarkable and comforting was your expedition at the time of hardest pressure in the War."[69]

A year after his lecture went viral, Wells's statistical abilities got him hired as special commissioner of the revenue, in one of the last moves of Abraham Lincoln's life. Lincoln wanted Wells to reproduce his lecture's intricate economic calculations in the form of an annual report on the main trends in the American economy. At Wells's disposal was a new institution, the Bureau of Statistics in the Treasury Department, which was supposed to help him collect all the data he required. The annual release of Wells's report would quickly become an influential event in postbellum America and the fulcrum of many political debates. Such government involvement in the world of economic quantification was unprecedented. Yet the war had changed everything, as it led to a significant expansion of the federal state's administrative capacities—and data collection was no exception.[70]

Quintessential exhibitions of American investmentality, Wells's reports imagined the history of the American nation as a never-ceasing process of capital accumulation. The aggregate amount of propertied wealth in the United States, he argued, "represents the surplus of accumulation over expenditure which had resulted up to that date from all the labor and economy of all the people who have inhabited the territory of the U.S. since its first discovery and settlement by Europeans." (In his view, Native Americans were clearly incapable of creating value, since they did not create money.) Reading the nation like an income statement and balance sheet, Wells assumed that the difference between "national production" and "national consumption" was what determined "the accumulation of new capital." Anticipating GDP and national income accounting, Wells calculated in his fourth report, for 1869, that the "value of the annual product" had risen to 13.4 percent per year and that the "value of the annual product of each person" stood at $121.03. Nevertheless, Wells believed that American capital was accumulating "much slower than it ought to be" and that "not to increase, is to retrograde." In later years, this would lead Wells to believe that American laborers were not efficient enough, since their productive output lagged behind their consumption inputs.[71]

It is not surprising that Abraham Lincoln hired David Ames Wells, nor that he was the president who presided over the vigorous expansion of the American state's statistical capacities. From his first years in politics through the final days before his death, Lincoln leaned on quantitative economic information as a tool for public policy and social change. In 1848, he advocated that the federal government collect more market statistics so that it could choose the internal improvement projects that would have the greatest economic impact. After the Civil War erupted, President Lincoln turned to the collection of price data in order to carry out his plan for the compensated emancipation of slaves in the District of Columbia. To execute the emancipation bill he signed into law in 1862, Lincoln established a commission whose job it was to assess the price of every slave in the city so that the government could determine how much federal money would be needed to compensate slave owners loyal to the Union. To head the committee, Lincoln chose Daniel Goodloe, a statistic-wielding critic of slavery who, just like Helper, had made a name for himself by using economic indicators to prove that slavery "retarded the accumulation of wealth." Unsure how to value the slaves of the city, Goodloe hired Baltimore slave traders as consultants. Over the course of ninety days they priced more than 3,000 slaves at around $300 per head.[72]

Lincoln's many biographers have mostly overlooked his propensity for quantification. Few have reminded us that minutes before he dazzled Congress at his second State of the Union Address in 1862 with his declaration that the American nation was in the midst of a "fiery trial," Lincoln had just spent the bulk of his speech citing population growth statistics in order to prove that the moneymaking capacity of future American citizens could easily pay for his plans for gradual compensated emancipation and voluntary African American colonization of Africa. Using the term *economical* five times in one speech to legitimize his plans and concluding that "labor is like any other commodity on the market," Lincoln effortlessly synthesized an array of census data in order to show that the income-generating capacities of the America people were more than capable of covering the 6 percent bonds of capital that would be given to slaveholders in exchange for their slave's freedom. "If with less money, or money more easily paid, we can preserve the benefits of the Union by this means than we can by the war alone, is it not also economical to do it?" Lincoln asked in his speech, balancing war and emancipation in cost-benefit analysis. This language was not nearly as rhetorically inspiring as his closing cry that Americans not "meanly lose the last best hope of earth," but by the 1860s such earthly calculations of capital flows and income-generating population growth packed perhaps the very same punch in the capitalizing minds of middle- and upper-class Americans.[73]

SEVEN

State of Statistical War

On March 3, 1893, Rhode Island senator and millionaire industrialist Nelson Aldrich—head of the powerful Senate Finance Committee and future architect of the Federal Reserve System—submitted a report to Congress titled *Wholesale Prices, Wages, and Transportation.* Known at the time as the Aldrich Report, it has become a mere footnote in American history. One glance at the report immediately reveals why. After a brief introduction, the 658-page government document consists of a seemingly endless series of tables marking the price fluctuations of every major commodity, including labor, in American society from 1840 to 1891. Behind these tedious price charts, however, lay a dramatic social upheaval. It is often in the most mundane details that one can best grasp great historical change, and few documents portray the economic, political, and ideological transformations of the late nineteenth century better than the banalities of the Aldrich Report.[1]

The report included no fewer than eleven statistical appendices. Appendix A alone included eighty-four statistical tables. In generating a fifty-year time series on food prices, the report tracked the price of fifty-three articles, from "Boston crackers" to nutmeg. For the "Cloths and Clothing" section, the report charted the price of twenty-eight articles, from "bleached sheetings" to "Ohio fine fleece." In creating a half-century time series on the price of labor, the report tracked the changing wages of more than 500 occupations, from textile "waste sorters" to "bricklayers' helpers." In unprecedented fashion, the Aldrich Report had taken on quite the technocratic project: the pricing of everyday American life.[2]

A task of epic bureaucratic proportions, the report's sheer size reflected the nascent expansion of the American state from a decentralized, antebellum system of "courts and parties" into an extensive, centralized, administrative government. The two state institutions that collected the data—the Department of Labor and the Department of Agriculture—had not even existed prior to the Civil War. The report also heralded the birth of the modern, state-sanctioned economic indicator. The commensurability of money meant that the reams of price data in the Aldrich Report's countless tables, charts, and appendices could be indexed and aggregated into a few basic metrics. New statistical constructs such as "cost of living," "purchasing power," "standard of living," and "price levels" were given life. They would go on to have a lasting effect on American society.[3]

While the data on wages were gathered, organized, and tabulated by Carroll Wright, commissioner of the recently formed Department of Labor and leading labor statistician of Gilded Age America, the Aldrich Report also received a great deal of statistical assistance from businessmen and their own developing institutions. Professor Roland Falkner of the Wharton School, the first business school in American history, indexed the messy price data into a few neat categories such as "food," "clothing," and "cost of living." The Manufacturing Chemists' Association supplied the price series on drugs, the National Association of Wool Manufacturers that for wool, and the Bostonian Arkwright Club the data on cotton textiles. When trade associations were not available, the Aldrich Report turned to the heads of private companies. The American Screw Company gave the price of screws, Roxbury Carpet Company the price of carpets, New York Knife Company the price of pocketknives, and Nicholson File Company the price of files. If the Aldrich report was a product of the federal government's increasing administrative capacities, it also reflected how dependent the state was on the good graces—and good data—of American business. Based mostly on prices jointly collected by cartels and corporations, the Aldrich Report was a coordinated product of bureaucratic expertise and bourgeois consolidation.[4]

Applying a novel statistical methodology to a century-old political debate, the Senate Finance Committee had commissioned the Aldrich Report because it believed that a statistical time series of commodity prices could finally settle the question of whether protectionist policies and high tariffs were good for America. In the past, politicians such as William "Pig Iron" Kelley had leaned on old anti-British tropes in order to legitimize the tariff, arguing that anyone who supported free trade was "in the pay" of English capitalists. By the 1890s, however, the state had begun to supplant such populist rhetoric with a new form of governance, one in which prices were implemented to assess and evaluate not only commodities but policy and prosperity as well. Without the report's price data, Nelson Aldrich explained, "it has been impossible to judge even with approximate accuracy the progress of the people of the country and the changes which have taken place from time to time in their condition."[5]

This was an epoch-making turn of events: while the state had played a crucial role in the mid-nineteenth-century shift toward the pricing of progress by expanding the reach of the federal census and other data-collecting bodies, most monetized indicators had nevertheless been molded and disseminated by private hands, not public institutions. As the Aldrich Report makes plain, however, by the end of the nineteenth century the notion that money could accurately measure American progress—and thus direct American policy—was being institutionalized in the halls of the expert-run administrative state.

Following Aldrich's lead, the Senate Finance Committee had instructed government bureaucrats "to ascertain through accurate and adequate statistics of prices and wages, the changes which have taken place in the condition, as shown by the relative purchasing power of their earnings, of the great mass of people in the country for the half century which has just closed." Imagining Americans—not only in 1890 but also in 1840—strictly as market consumers and wage laborers, the basic premise of the Aldrich Report was that in order to measure the prosperity of the American people, all one had to do was compare wages to cost of living.[6]

For those who measured progress in such a manner, the results did not disappoint. Constructing weighted cost-of-living indices (so that the price of bread would matter more than, say, the price of cinnamon) from the household consumption surveys of 2,561 "normal families," the Aldrich Report declared that while the cost of living had dropped roughly 5 percent since the mid-nineteenth century, wages had risen at roughly a 60 percent clip. Future analyses proved that these estimates were too optimistic, as they conveniently focused on skilled labor. Regardless, what mattered here most were not the actual results but the implementation of a very specific measure of social progress. "The relative standard of life at the different periods," the report explained, as if it were obvious, "can, of course, be obtained only from a combination of prices with average earnings or wages."[7]

There was nothing obvious about the Aldrich Report's "standard of life," however. Like all forms of social quantification, it was based on a number of ideological principles, value judgments, and cultural preferences. First off, in choosing to measure the social "condition" by calculating whether wages purchased more or fewer consumer goods than they used to, the Aldrich Report reflected the consumerist turn that had overtaken great swaths of Gilded Age thought in the prior two decades. In contrast to the producerist "free labor" theories that dominated much of the nineteenth century, the Aldrich Report cared little about whether American laborers had control over their work rhythm or daily output, whether they were bosses or bossed, whether they received a full return on the fruits of their labor, or whether the very institution of wage labor was even a legitimate one in a nation that viewed widespread ownership of productivity property as the centerpiece of freedom. Rather, the Aldrich Report was animated by a fairly new yet rapidly growing consumerism that defined the good life as one in which permanent wage laborers could enjoy the material fruits of industrial progress regardless of what power their employers held over them on the shop floor.[8]

Such a consumer-oriented worldview did not forsake the welfare of workers—material life was certainly better for American laborers if their wages bought more goods. Nor was it the sole product of top-down elite hegemony. Postbellum laborers articulated the idea of a "living wage" well before the Aldrich Report was conceived, and by 1890 it had become a staple of the American labor movement and would remain so throughout the twentieth century. Nevertheless, in focusing on material things that could be procured in the act of shopping, living-wage metrics played an important role not only in the pricing of American progress but also in the legitimization of industrial capitalism. Earlier Americans associated wage labor with subordination, exploitation, lack of proprietary freedom—even slavery. In 1860, American opinion of wage labor was still so low, in fact, that wage statistics were relegated to a single page in the census report alongside pauperism and crime. By the 1890s, however, wage statistics rose to the status of a central government indicator of the human "condition" as the contractual wage relation between employer and employee became the epitome of freedom.[9]

The state's equation of consumption with well-being and wages with freedom echoed the social relations emerging on the shop floor, where workers were taught by their employers to focus not on what they made but rather on how much they earned. Take, for example, the following excerpt from famed efficiency expert Frederick Winslow Taylor's *Scientific*

Management in which Taylor seeks to grab control of an immigrant worker's pace and output by using wage incentives to hawk a priceable selfhood:

"Schmidt, are you a high-priced man?"

"Vell, I don't know vat you mean."

"Oh yes, you do. What I want to know is whether you are a high-priced man or not."

"Vell, I don't know vat you mean."

"Oh, come now, you answer my questions. What I want to find out is whether you are a high-priced man or one of these cheap fellows here. What I want to find out is whether you want to earn $1.85 a day or whether you are satisfied with $1.15, just the same as all those cheap fellows are getting."

"Did I vant $1.85 a day? Vas dot a high-priced man? Vell, yes, I vas a high-priced man."

Taylor goes on to micromanage the worker, telling him how he should load pig iron so as to maximize his output. "Well, if you are a high-priced man," Taylor barks, "you will do exactly as this man tells you tomorrow, from morning till night. When he tells you to pick up a pig and walk, you pick it up and you walk, and when he tells you to sit down and rest, you sit down." One only needs to hear Taylor's obnoxiously authoritarian tone to understand that for men like Schmidt, there were clear social costs to becoming a "high-priced man." But those social costs were invisible not just to the Taylorist efficiency studies cropping up in the 1890s but to the Aldrich Report's cost-of-living figures as well.[10]

Another assumption implicit in the Aldrich Report was the construction of a conceptual barrier between labor and capital. In American producerist thought as well as classical economics, wages and profits emerged out of the same pool of surplus wealth created during the production process. According to this zero-sum worldview, wages and profits were in an inverse and conflicting relation to each other, since capitalists accumulated wealth by expropriating much of the surplus. To determine whether wage levels were just or fair, therefore, required an examination of profit rates as well as wage rates. In the Aldrich Report, however, capital is all but invisible. By perusing the hundreds of wage tables in the Aldrich Report one can gain a great deal of knowledge about labor costs—but very little about profits. One can trace the fluctuating price of almost every commodity known to humankind but learn nothing about wealth distribution or economic inequality. Much like the rapidly spreading neoclassical economics and subjective utility theories concomitantly being developed by the likes of John Bates Clark and Irving Fisher in the 1890s, the Aldrich Report supplanted a producerist labor of theory value with a consumerist theory of value, and it depoliticized economic life by presenting a world in which wages and profits were two utterly distinct factors of economic production generated by completely separate market forces.[11]

This leads to yet another basic assumption behind the Aldrich Report: the abstraction of labor into a factor of industrial production. If one looks at cost-of-living statistics from the point of view of an industrial capitalist rather than that of a consuming laborer, the Aldrich Report had much to offer American businessmen. This is no coincidence. Cost-conscious manufacturers played a key role in the rise of such cost-of-living figures. Manufacturers actively pursued such data because they realized that by using household surveys to record the amounts of commodified goods (food, clothing, housing, etc.) consumed by workers, they could calculate the overall cost of keeping productive laborers alive and working.

Yet the state did not invent this data-laden surveillance of labor costs—managerial capitalism did. In the mid-nineteenth century corporations such as the Pennsylvania Railroad pored over "cost sheets" in search of opportunities for increasing productivity, and by the 1880s industrialists such as Andrew Carnegie were doing the same. Such cost sheets, which Carnegie demanded on a weekly basis no matter where he was in the world, allowed him to see the operational costs of all factory inputs, be they coke, coal, ore, or men. "I see that costs of labor in ingots is 4.5 per ton, more than twice the cost of Bessemer," wrote Carnegie to one of the managers of his newly opened Homestead plant in 1888. Examining the payroll, he demanded to know why "we are paying 14 cents an hour for labor, which is above Edgar Thompson prices. The force might perhaps be reduced in number 10 percent, so that each man getting more wages would be required to do more work." A crucial tool for monitoring workers and maximizing productivity, such cost accounting techniques led Carnegie to believe that for his Homestead plant to undercut the competition he would have to wrest control of the shop floor from unionized skilled labor so that he, and he alone, controlled industrial output. By the 1890s, Taylor's theory of scientific management was reaching the same conclusions.[12]

Just as cost accounting techniques could help manufacturers reduce costs through a close monitoring of the priced inputs that went into the processes of mechanized production, so too could cost-of-living figures help reduce costs by a close monitoring of the priced inputs that went into the process of human existence. Many Gilded Age reformers, businessmen, physicians, economists, and even chemists came to believe that just as one gauged the fuel costs and energy efficiency of an iron furnace, so too could one price the cost of living and calorie intake—another statistical invention of the era—of laboring people. In short, cost-of-living statistics reveal how cost-accounting techniques spread out of the corporation and into everyday life, coming to play a central role in the forging of economic policy.[13]

Few men exemplify the mechanization of man better than Edward Jarvis, longtime president of the American Statistical Association and the ante-bellum leader in the field of insanity and public health statistics. As a driving force behind the rise of moral statistics in the 1840s, Jarvis had focused his statistical work on Americans' physical and mental condition. Yet as mechanization picked up steam and American laborers became, to quote President Grover Cleveland, a "mere appurtenance to a great machine," so too did Jarvis's statistical imagination undergo an industrial revolution. In response to the chair of the Census Committee (and future U.S. president) James Garfield's request for advice on improving the 1870 census, Jarvis recommended collecting data that would allow one to calculate the "value of life" by determining "the cost of development of a man, or building the productive machine, and his worth to the body politic."[14]

Price indices also allowed American businessmen to see the world not as separate, competing, proprietary individuals but as a consolidated, corporate class. While one could open to page 67 of the Aldrich Report and see the changing price of flannel shirts over half a century, this had not been Nelson Aldrich's or the Senate Finance Committee's main objective. Rather, the Aldrich Report's indices were intended to allow the reader to rise above the petty details of a single commodity or industry and gain a glimpse of something American businessmen had never before been able to see: the price level of society writ large. Suddenly cotton manufacturers, cattle ranchers, and steel magnates could transcend the politics of their given industry and get a sense of the shared advances or common challenges they faced with their fellow businessmen, be it rising labor costs or decreasing commodity prices.[15]

For Senator Aldrich, such an aggregated, indexed, macro view of society was a novel departure from the micro politics he had previously practiced. As head of the Senate Finance Committee throughout the 1880s, Aldrich left behind personal papers that are dominated by his endless dealings with narrow sectoral interests. This correspondence contains a fair amount of price statistics, but all revolve around very specific commodities. For instance, some manufacturers tried to use price data to raise the tariffs on buttons and china clay, others in order to lower the rates on hemlock bark and licorice paste. This was the workings of a fractured, decentralized business class rather than a consolidated one.[16]

On the contrary, the Aldrich Report took Boston crackers, nutmeg, and fifty-one other edible items and indexed them into a single category, "food." It then took "food" and indexed that into a metric including other indexed categories such as "clothing" and "fuel" in order to calculate the overall price level of society. Rather than have button merchants and snap manufacturers maneuver for special treatment, the Aldrich Report sent American businessmen the message that, in the end, they were all in the same boat: a boat that rose and fell according to the fluctuating waves of aggregated, averaged, and indexed price.[17]

While cost-of-living indices made legible the general price waves upon which businessmen's fortunes often rose and fell, they also came to serve as anchors of value in the storm-tossed world of modern capitalism. Prices are exchange values, and exchange values can be notoriously slippery things. The reason the Aldrich Report did not simply collect wage data in different eras— what economists today would refer to as "nominal" prices—was that such data would not have told a reader very much. Wages are worth only as much as a worker can buy with them. The inflationary spike of government-printed greenbacks through the 1870s and then the deflationary spiral that came with the return to gold drastically affected the purchasing power—and value—of the American dollar. As a result, the only way to turn nominal prices into "real" ones at any given historical moment was to compare them with other nominal prices. Cost-of-living figures do precisely this by creating a quantitative anchor of value that makes it clear whether the relative price of a given good, including wages, is in fact going with the flow or swimming against it.[18]

The Aldrich Report demonstrates how the managerial and consumerist values of corporate capitalism were coming to be canonized by the American state as general barometers of social progress by the 1890s. Such statistical hegemony did not come about naturally or easily, however—it was the product of a series of hard-fought political struggles. For when the Civil War ended, another war erupted—a war over how the state would measure social progress in an industrializing America. In general, this statistical war pitted those who were firmly entrenched in the early American ideology of proprietary producerism (rebranded "free labor" in the mid-nineteenth century but otherwise not much changed) against those Americans who jettisoned such ideas in favor of the consumerist and managerial principles portrayed so effectively by the price tables of the Aldrich Report. While these groups disagreed mightily with each other, neither was particularly laissez-faire or anti-government. On the contrary, both believed that the state should play a central role in determining how American progress was to be measured. The statistical battle was waged, therefore, not over whether the government should quantitatively evaluate American society but how.[19]

The soldiers of this numerical war came from many walks of life. On the free labor side were a motley crew of union organizers, eight-hour-day promoters, Radical Republicans, populist farmers, Single Tax enthusiasts, Knights of Labor statisticians, rogue graduate students, and more midlevel government bureaucrats than one might suspect. Rather than gauging progress by comparing the price of labor to the price of consumer goods, these men and women sought to measure inequality, exploitation, debt, tenancy, homeownership, independence, profiteering, leisure time, social mobility, power, poverty, and even Henry George's notion of unproductive "rent." On the other side stood textile manufacturers, government statisticians, Brahmin reformers, robber barons, bread-and-butter unions, railroad moguls, a few presidents, a census chief, and the chemist who invented the calorie. These men (and on this side they were pretty much all men) believed that price statistics should become the central barometer of American progress. They pushed for such data in order to control labor costs, stabilize society, and maintain business profits, but also because they genuinely saw such statistics as a reflection of the American laborer's material comfort and hence his or her well-being.

The opening salvo in this statistical war was fired in postbellum Boston. Much to the horror of Massachusetts's manufacturing elite, the newly founded Labor Reform Party garnered a surprising 10 percent of the vote in state elections in the late 1860s. Panicked by this emerging political threat, the Massachusetts legislature hastily sought a way to assuage the anger of the working classes. On June 23, 1869, a resolution originally initiated by Radical Republican Wendell Phillips calling for the establishment of a state bureau of labor statistics was passed. It was the first such bureau in the world.[20]

Along with Ira Steward, a skilled mechanic, labor intellectual, and leader of Massachusetts's eight-hour-workday movement, Phillips had been lobbying for a bureau of labor statistics that would serve as a political platform to raise awareness of the "labor question" and convince workers, the public, and the state to legislate an eight-hour work day. At one of the conventions of Steward's Eight Hour League in 1865, Phillips declared that since "the country was ruled by its brains," laborers needed "something" through which they could "break into that debating society up in the State House and make them discuss the eight-hour day." Four years later, that something turned out to be the Massachusetts Bureau of Labor Statistics (MBLS), as it was decided that Phillips would be allowed to appoint the bureau's chief and deputy. In collaboration with Steward, Phillips chose two labor advocates to staff the bureau: Henry K. Oliver, a known education reformer, and George McNeill, a wage-earning machinist and the president of the Boston branch of the Eight Hour League.[21]

In the mid-nineteenth century, for information to be perceived as factual it was expected to "separate between the descriptive and the interpretive" because of the agreed-upon supposition that "systematic knowledge should be derived solely from non-interpretive descriptions." The first report of the MBLS did nothing of the sort. Most of the quantitative information on wages and hours was supplied via personal worker testimonies. Arguing that its mission was "far greater in importance than figurate returns of industry," the bureau made it clear that it would not be a "collector of mere facts." Envisioning the bureau as a political tool and moral compass, Oliver and McNeil hoped that when the people of Massachusetts read their reports "a cry of mingled surprise and shame and indignation will arise that will demand an entire change of the methods of earning and pay." Mixing heart-wrenching descriptions of urban poverty and factory conditions with eye-opening statistics on such topics as social mobility, economic independence, and seamstresses' meager wages, the bureau harnessed the data it collected to prove that "factory life any way is a bad life, physically, morally, socially and intellectually," and that wage labor was nothing more than "the modern facilities of burglary."[22]

Unlike the future architects of the Aldrich Report, the original founders of the MBLS also did not believe that it was possible to put a price tag on progress. "The real and ultimate value of [manufacturing] to the true prosperity and abiding good of the commonwealth," they wrote, "can only be learned, by placing money in one scale, and man in the other." As a result, they sent out questionnaires in order to collect data on a number of issues that could not be priced, including home ownership, time for dinner, "moral and intellectual improvement," libraries, social mobility, hours of sleep, schooling of children, number of rooms in the home, sufficient drainage, daily commute, recreation time, life expectancy, cooperative associations, and miles a child had to walk to work.[23]

As eight-hour activists, the MBLS's staff believed that a leading indicator of social progress was the number of hours one worked. Choosing spare time as a central evaluator of society may not appear like much at first, but it was a radical denunciation of industrial ideals because it rejected the gospel of growth by suggesting that less market output was sometimes better than more. "Although manufacturing undoubtedly increases the material wealth of the nation," the bureau noted, "it does it, as now managed, at the expense of its manufacturing people." The demand to reduce hours of work also carried with it sharp producerist critiques. The heads of the MBLS did not read Marx's chapter on the working day in *Das Kapital*, published only two years before, but it did not take Marx to conclude that fewer hours at the same wages meant decreased exploitation. Small wonder, then, that Marx himself requested and read a copy of the MBLS report and found it to be "very valuable."[24]

It is important to note, however, that the MBLS was also interested in market statistics—it just saw them as yet another tool in the statistician's toolbox. In its first two reports, the bureau collected reams of data on wages and even a smattering of cost-of-living figures. It also sought to measure inequality and exploitation by comparing these wages to profit figures. This, however, proved impossible because not a single questionnaire sent out to businesses regarding profits or manager salaries was returned. Irate, Oliver turned to the state legislature and demanded that he be given the legal power to summon business owners. His request was denied.[25]

On the other side of town, Brahmin Boston's manufacturing and financial elite were utterly aghast at the bureau's first two reports. They initially tried to silence the bureau by cutting its budget or abolishing it completely—but to no avail. The problem, it seemed, was that the MBLS was gaining quite a following among not just laborers but Americans of all walks of life. While the business-minded *Boston Daily Advertiser* continuously slammed the bureau for its questionable findings, many Americans found the first reports compelling. The *Lowell Daily Citizen* believed that the bureau's statistical reports were "the best thing . . . [the] state had done since the War," since "information is the real want of the laborer and the chief requisite to the success of his cause." *Chicago Tribune* editor Horace White hailed it as the "virtual inauguration of the church of economists" as "statistics take the place of texts, while facts and figures supersede psalms and prayers." Comparing its statistics to Charles Francis Adams Jr.'s "systematic investigation" of the railroads, even the *New York Free Trader* congratulated the bureau for its "admirable method" and "extraordinary accumulation of facts." From renowned authors to professors of political economy to members of the various Mercantile Library Associations, the list of people who wrote in to commend the MBLS on its work read like a veritable who's who of postbellum middle-class reformers.[26]

Others focused more on the report's troubling conclusions, but with no less enthusiasm. A Cincinnati paper exulted at how the report "shows how completely the Lords of the Loom have the workmen under control." In an article in the *Atlanta Constitution* titled "Massachusetts Decaying," the southern author gleefully proclaimed that the "labor statistics show a downgrade in civilization . . . that would stimulate any other people to drop for a while the management of the universe and attend to home concerns." Even the well-regarded *Nation*—the center of the staid, mugwump universe if ever there was one—joined in the chorus. "It is difficult to exaggerate the value of such labor as is so intelligently done by the Bureau of Labor Statistics," noted J. R. Hodgkins, the magazine's leading economic correspondent. He continued:

> The proofs are numerous and unmistakable to the almost incredible fact that the condition of the working-classes throughout Massachusetts is a declining one, that the contrast between the relative positions of employer

and employed is steadily becoming greater, that the number of men who emerge from the condition of workingmen is extremely small, and that the relations between employers and employed are becoming more and more hostile and defiant. . . . When we read such things as these, we are introduced to a condition of affairs the existence of which is far from generally known.[27]

As the *Nation* recognized, the bureau had uncovered a most disturbing truth: it appeared that the widespread belief that wage labor was only a temporary stop for white men on the route to proprietary independence, social mobility, and republican equality had become a myth. In 1854, Abraham Lincoln could stand on the steps of Independence Hall and credibly declare, "There is no permanent class of hired laborers among us." By 1870, the bureau's statistics made such statements ring hollow.[28]

That the MBLS gained such widespread middle-class support demonstrates that postbellum Americans had not yet accepted the notion that the United States should become an industrial nation of wage-laboring employees. Even an elitist Massachusetts labor commission headed by the founder of the American Social Science Association and dead set against government intervention in the labor market was more than willing to admit in 1867 that "man should be the master, not the servant of his work" and that through the "practice of economy" wage workers could "become their own capitalists" and once again "be masters of their own time and their own terms." Such a contrast between wage labor and freedom would never have emerged from an official state commission in the 1890s. By that time, the notions of freedom and wage labor would go hand in hand, with consumerism as the bridge between them.[29]

For the manufacturing interests in New England, the widespread rejection of a permanent wage-laboring class was obviously dangerous. Having midwestern periodicals or southern newspapers question the notion of industrial progress in Massachusetts was one thing. Hearing it from the most respected of New York publications such as the *Nation* was quite another. For Massachusetts businessmen—especially those involved in textile manufacturing—this was unacceptable. Something had to be done. A reading of the *Nation* reveals that something was done quite quickly: Hodgkins's editorial praise of the MBLS would be his last contribution to the magazine. Unsatisfied solely with this move, however, Bostonians made sure to call in their own statistical cavalry. A harsh response to Hodgkins's article was sent to Edwin Godkin, the editor of the *Nation,* by the eminent Edward Atkinson, a well-known Boston cotton manufacturer, economic thinker, and statistical expert on everything from tariff reform to cotton yields. Pointing to the "rapid increase in savings banks deposits" as evidence that factory wages were high enough to allow operatives to accumulate wealth and one day open their own business, Atkinson insisted that the bureau's arguments had "no foundation in fact."[30]

Atkinson's letter would come back to haunt him, for the third annual report by the MBLS, published in the spring of 1872, centered on none other than a statistical analysis of Massachusetts savings banks. Taking a careful look at savings bank records, the bureau discovered that over 50 percent of the deposits were of more than $300—a sum that clearly no wage laborer could have attained. Aggregating these mysterious deposits, the bureau calculated that one-seventh of the savings accounts held around half of the total wealth deposited in the banks. Not only had the bureau disproved Atkinson's oft-heard argument regarding laborers' ability to save, but it had created the first inequality statistics in American history. To add insult to injury, the bureau accused Massachusetts capitalists of using the savings banks to evade taxes, since deposits were taxed at a much lower rate than other forms of property.[31]

Again Boston's bourgeoisie moved fast. Before the report was even presented to the legislature, it was swiftly turned over to the state's financial and banking committee for an investigation into the bureau's statistical methods. Called in to testify at a closed hearing, the bureau chiefs were surprised to discover that a number of bankers had been placed on the commission. Following a quick investigation, the commission concluded that the bureau's "inferences and conclusions . . . are based upon insufficient returns and data." Desperate to rid themselves of the MBLS, Boston elites tried to get the legislature to pass a resolution that would abolish the bureau. With the *Advertiser* as their mouthpiece, they declared that when they had read the bureau chief's "unspeakably mischievous" report, they were "astonished at [his] audacity" and accused him of lending "himself at the outset to a false and indefensible theory of labor, which made it next to impossible for him to collect statistics except such as favored his theory."[32]

The middle-class majority in Massachusetts, however, was against the abolishment of the bureau and still trusted its statistical findings. The Springfield *Republican* wrote that "each successive year increases, perhaps we may say doubles the value" of the bureau's reports. The *Boston Commonwealth,* the paper of choice for the petty bourgeois, defended the bureau from attack as well. Turning the tables on the *Advertiser*'s questioning of the bureau's motives, the paper retorted that "capital . . . was objecting to investigation of its methods," since "the rich man hugs his money, and objects to change." In the end, even the banking committee's accusation of unsubstantiated claims in regards to the savings banks statistics was rejected by the state legislature.[33]

With the situation quickly spinning out of control, the time had come for the best of Boston's "best men." Fresh off his damning indictment of Jay Gould's nefarious railroad schemes in *Chapters of Erie,* Charles Francis Adams Jr. was the most admired reformer in the state. Furthermore, as chairman of the Massachusetts Railroad Commission, he was viewed as an expert on apolitical statistical analysis. Devoting more than ten pages to the bureau's third report in the elite *North American Review,* Adams charged the MBLS with not deducing its conclusions solely from the statistics at hand. "We have facts of great interest and opinions of no value what so ever," snapped Adams, "tumbled together with disputed industrial theories, here advanced as settled facts, and garnished with specimens of the worst rhetoric." Unlike other Bostonian businessmen, however, Adams was against the abolishment of the bureau. Much like Atkinson and Godkin, Adams was an active leader in the newly founded American Social Science Association, an organization that lamented the fact that statistics were not used more in legislation by civil servants as an "efficient," bureaucratic alternative to partisan politics.[34]

By claiming that statistics were wholly objective facts that should be severed from any political interest, liberal reformers such as Adams gained the upper hand by transforming the dispute over the MBLS into a seemingly depoliticized affair of science and empiricism. With their journals of social science and Harvard diplomas, men such as Charles Francis Adams Jr. had the institutional prestige, cultural clout, and intellectual capital to convincingly undermine the work of the bureau in the eyes of most middle-class Americans. Naturally, the fact that men such as Adams and Atkinson were part of a social circle that included the richest and most powerful men in the state didn't hurt either. The "public opinion" of the middle class was often the determining factor in class conflicts between labor and capital in this era, and Brahmin businessmen were about to tip the scales in their favor. Less than a year after their controversial report, the Massachusetts governor relieved the bureau chiefs of their duties and appointed Carroll Wright, a former state senator who had voted numerous times against legislation that would limit the workday to ten hours, as director of the Massachusetts Bureau of Labor Statistics.[35]

Constantly repeating the mantra of nonpartisan objectivity with mottos such as "Figures don't lie and liars don't figure," Wright soon gained the respect and trust of both the economic elite and the middle class at large. He would remain the head of the Massachusetts bureau until 1885, when he would be appointed chief of the newly established U.S. Bureau of Labor. In 1894, the middle class's perception of Wright as the embodiment of nonpartisanship led him to chair the commission that investigated the Pullman strike in Chicago. In short, within a few years Carroll Wright became the most important government statistician in American history. While the founders of the Massachusetts Bureau of Labor Statistics have been relegated to a historical footnote, Wright has widely been regarded as the father of American labor statistics—and correctly so. It was Wright's statistical vision, centering largely on wage and cost-of-living statistics, that would be institutionalized by the federal government in the Gilded Age.[36]

Before his arrival, Wright would later recount, "the manufacturers of the State were, to a considerable extent, afraid of the Bureau, and in some sense, inimical to it." Continuing, he noted with pride that "today, they are, as a rule, friends." Massachusetts's manufacturers had good reason to view Wright as a friend. In his first report, in 1875, Wright compared wages in the United States to those in Europe, a comparison in which the American laborer fared very well. Turning to the question of legislating an eight-hour workday, Wright contended that the "hours of labor will take care of themselves." For the remainder of his career he would consistently prefer expert-led commissions and arbitration hearings to statist labor legislation. By his second report, Wright had concluded that wage labor was a legitimate economic system and that "the iconoclasm that strives to break it down, will be devoid of fruitful results or permanent benefits." As for the savings banks, Wright did look into the matter in his first report and discovered that the bureau's original calculations had largely been on the mark. He never investigated savings banks again.[37]

<hr />

In the first few years as head of the Massachusetts Bureau of Labor Statistics, Wright issued reports on schooling, sanitary conditions, literacy rates, hours of leisure, "fallen women," women's health, cooperatives, pauperism, crime, convict labor, and factory safety. By the 1880s, however, such moral statistics were appearing less and less often in his reports. Instead, Wright turned almost exclusively to a comparison of wage and cost-of-living statistics. His 468-page report in 1884, for instance, included 334 pages on wage and cost-of-living figures. The original MBLS founders had also collected some cost-of-living data, especially in their later reports. They viewed cost-of-living statistics as one indicator among many, a means of measuring whether workers had the ability to save and become their own bosses. For Wright, on the other hand, comparing cost of living with wages stood at the center of his statistical work. Furthermore, he saw it mostly as an indicator of consumer comfort, not social mobility. "No comparison as to the prosperity of industrial communities can be just," he explained in one of his reports, "that does not take into consideration the relative ease with which the workingmen in those communities may procure the means of subsistence, and the relative amount of comfort attainable for a given outlay of time and effort."[38]

As these comments attest, Wright was not simply a statistical yes-man for bourgeois elites. His concern for the material well-being of workers, as reflected in his living wage measurements, was genuine, and he supported labor unionization. While Wright was "friends" with the manufacturing elite, he was also close to skilled-labor organizations, who played an active role in the shaping of his statistical vision. In fact, Wright never would have been able to advance his cost-of-living agenda were it not for the strong support he received from American Federation of Labor (AFL) leaders Samuel Gompers and George Gunton. Pushing for "bread-and-butter unionism" that focused exclusively on higher wages, Gompers and Gunton not only accepted the institution of wage labor but viewed the wage labor market as a sign of progress. According to Gompers, wages were "the barometer which indicates the social, political, and industrial status" of a society. Dismissing free-labor skepticism regarding the very legitimacy of wage labor, AFL pamphleteer

Gunton agreed with Gompers that wages were "a necessary and continual part of social progress."[39]

Allergic to most statist forms of economic intervention (such as minimum-wage legislation) and labor strikes (he had a habit of pricing their "cost" to society), Wright supported a corporatist society in which wages would be set by collective bargaining between big labor and big business with the assistance of government-collected statistics and expert-led commissions. He never bothered to measure inequality or wealth distribution, yet he believed that wages should be high enough to ensure laborers a life of comfort and that the government should play a role in providing the data that would make this possible.[40]

Perhaps the best way to summarize Wright's worldview is through his experiences with one of the most explosive—yet also illustrative—sites in Gilded Age America: the town of Pullman, Illinois. In the early 1880s, Wright organized an annual conference for all the commissioners of the state bureaus of labor statistics in the country (by then there were quite a few), and in 1884 he decided that these commissioners should all go on a joint field excursion to Pullman, outside of Chicago. While visiting George Pullman's unprecedented company town, the commissioners were hosted by Duane Doty, the town's official statistician, who, along with other accountants, kept detailed reports on everything that went on in the town, from water consumption to shopping trends to rent payments. These men treated Pullman not as a city but as an investment. In 1894, for instance, the "profit on investment" on "capital invested in dwellings including Arcade, market, church, school house, brick yard cottages, etc. and improvements such as streets, parks" was calculated to be 3.82 percent.[41]

Awestruck by Pullman's statistical reach, and enthralled by the shopping arcade, running water, and other material comforts, Wright wrote a glowing report on the town, praising it as the model for a new America. Not once did Wright bother to note the clearly authoritarian nature of the town's governance, nor did he mention the profits George Pullman was accumulating in running a private city. As with his entire body of statistical work, questions of power, corporate concentration, labor independence, inequality, and coercion were rarely addressed, as his statistical gaze was firmly set on issues of economic stability and consumer comfort. That same focus on consumer comfort and cost of living, however, eventually led him to harshly criticize Pullman's managerial techniques. A decade later, when Wright was made head of the inquiry into the vaunted Pullman strike, Wright scolded George Pullman for lowering workers' wages yet not their rents. After that report, many workers across the country viewed Wright as a supporter of their cause.[42]

In his groundbreaking reports written in the aftermath of Civil War, revenue commissioner David Ames Wells consistently noted that the biggest problem in America was that the prices of consumer goods were too high. While Wells gave a number of reasons for these high prices, such as paper money, tariffs, and high taxes, the first cause he listed was the problem of the country's labor force. Lamenting the increased cost of labor, Wells believed that American laborers earned too much money for too little work. "The universal testimony of manufacturers," he noted with concern in his first report, "is that the operatives who entered the army from their establishments have not, as a general thing, returned to their old employments." While Wells briefly noted that this was partly because many of those men were dead, killed during the war, he gave other explanations for this troubling development as well:

> Some have engaged in the cultivation of cotton, and in various other industrial pursuits in the south; a much larger percentage have sought new homes and new employments at the extreme West, or on the Pacific coast; while others, taking advantage of the capital made available to them through the payment of bounties and previous savings, have become principals rather than subordinates in business.[43]

To most Americans of the era, Wells's laments must have sounded quite odd. Instead of celebrating the fact that more people were finding self-employment and proprietary independence, Wells seemed upset by it. Horace Greeley famously told the young laborers who had managed to survive the Civil War to "go West!" but Wells very much preferred that they head to the nearest factory. "During the summer of 1866," he noted, "the product of the cotton mills of New England was variously reduced from five to twenty-five per cent through the inability to obtain female operatives, even with the inducement of the highest rates of wages ever paid in this branch of manufacture." According to Wells, this "independence of labor over capital" had dire ramifications that damaged American economic growth. In his opinion, the government needed to find ways to help employers cut labor costs without sacrificing America's overall market output. To even begin to enact such policies, however, the government first needed to know what these labor costs consisted of. It needed to know the cost of living in America.[44]

It was this drive to reduce labor costs that led Wells into the home of the American worker in search of data. In one report, he estimated the cost of living by using data from a New England boardinghouse catering to factory operatives, many of whom were French Canadian immigrants. Noting that these families were "frugal and simple," Wells reported, for example, that the "average consumption of butter amount[ed] to about $16.51 a year for each person, including women and children." He then included an appendix that included "the quantity and cost of food and other necessaries of life consumed in the New England factory boarding-house." Concluding his remarks, Wells proudly noted how "no similar investigation, as respects accuracy, has ever before been instituted in the United States." Wells was right: such detailed cost-of-living statistics had never been collected before. It was the dawn of a new statistical age.[45]

Just as a steel mill sought to lower the costs of the coal it needed to keep a furnace firing, so did Wells hope to lower the costs of food, clothing, and housing needed to keep laborers alive. This was a form of cost accounting—but at the level of society rather than a firm. And while Wells's turn to cost-of-living statistics did not emerge from his personal experiences in manufacturing, of which he had none, the factory floor, capital-labor relations, and managerial techniques had no doubt shaped Wells's views, albeit indirectly. As Wells's personal correspondence in the late 1860s clearly demonstrates, the cost-of-living statistics he cited, and the economic vision that animated them, came from one specific source: Boston textile manufacturer Edward Atkinson (the same Atkinson who would attack the Massachusetts Bureau of Labor Statistics). The key to understanding the rise of cost-of-living statistics lies, therefore, not only in the works of government statisticians such as Carroll Wright and David Wells but also in the cost-conscious minds of businessmen such as Edward Atkinson.

Edward Atkinson was first and foremost a cotton manufacturer, a manager, an accountant, and a capitalist. Born in Brookline, Massachusetts, he became treasurer of the Ogden textile mills in 1851, and within a few years he was managing six mills from Maine to Rhode Island, including the Lincoln, Cohoes, Kennebec, and Indian Orchard facilities. In his correspondence with factory owners, it is clear that Atkinson was running the show: he oversaw all the books, including payroll; he calculated profits and determined dividends for the stockholders; he made the decision whether to shut down a mill if expenses were too high; he bought the raw cotton from the South; he decided how many spindles each factory should construct. In his role as mill manager, Atkinson quickly became infatuated with cost cutting. When he was hired to manage a mill in 1858, for instance, he immediately requested that reports on costs be sent to him monthly instead of semiannually, as had been done prior. Over the years, Atkinson expressed a particularly keen interest in labor costs and carefully examined the payrolls of all his mills. In 1861, he even wrote a best-selling book titled *Cheap Cotton and Free Labor,* which argued that the elimination of slavery would not be the end of American textile manufacturing since the labor costs of growing cotton could be reduced under a regime of wage labor. When Wells once asked Atkinson, a self-proclaimed profit maximizer, if he was willing to help employees purchase the factory homes they were presently renting, he retorted, "I do not believe in philanthropy toward the able-bodied that does not pay six percent."[46]

Atkinson's intense interest in costs emerged directly from his work in a textile factory. While the birth of cost accounting is generally associated with railroads, such techniques were preceded by more rudimentary calculations in New England textile factories of the 1850s. For example, Lyman Mills, a factory much like the one run by Atkinson, was calculating cost per yard for labor and cotton by 1850.[47]

While Atkinson always had textile manufacturing on his mind, he was also a one-man political juggernaut. As illustrated by the stunning breadth of his personal papers, which span seventy-eight volumes and 50,000 pages, while Atkinson never officially entered politics he was, without a doubt, one of the most powerful political forces in America for nearly a half century. Publishing an amazing 291 pamphlets, articles, and books in his lifetime and corresponding at a dizzying rate with the most powerful men in the country, from businessmen John Murray Forbes and Andrew Carnegie to Presidents Grover

Cleveland, William McKinley, and James A. Garfield, Edward Atkinson was—as historian James Livingston has put it—a "ubiquitous" presence in the most important political disputes of the era, be it money and tariff reform, the labor question, or foreign policy.[48]

Atkinson was especially adept at transforming impressionable men in key political positions into agents of his own interest. His voluminous correspondence with David Wells is a textbook case. In 1865, Wells had been hired by Lincoln to write but one revenue report. It was Atkinson who helped make the job permanent. After securing the position for Wells, Atkinson began to use him as his political eyes and ears in Washington, requesting that he dig up information on bills that had yet to be made public or influence the latest tariff laws that were in the works. Wells became very dependent on Atkinson, constantly asking for his help and advice. As a result, Atkinson's influence on Wells's statistical reports was vast. While Wells had arrived in Washington as an ardent supporter of high tariffs, Atkinson soon convinced him that the biggest problem in America was high labor prices. Lower tariffs and free trade, Atkinson explained to Wells, would reduce the cost of basic consumer goods and therefore labor's wages. As his long correspondence with Wells reveals, Atkinson's concern with high labor prices was clearly a product of his own cost-cutting concerns. In a letter written to Wells as the latter was preparing to write his first report, Atkinson hammered home his main points:

> In consequence of the forced division of labor into unnatural channels and the withdraw of labor into the army, labor advanced and has become too independent. The wages of a large portion of the labor in the country are now unnaturally high and the laborers do not do a full day's work. The prices of commodities, of all material and manufacturers are therefore unnaturally high yet they may pay no profit and in many cases a loss.

If the line about the independence of labor sounds familiar, that is because Wells used the same expression in his final report. And Atkinson was feeding Wells statistics as well as lines. The cost-of-living data Wells used in his revenue reports were supplied by Atkinson, as was much of the statistical information on labor that found its way into Wells's writings. Wary of showing the clear linkage between these numbers and his own manufacturing interests, however, Atkinson requested that the names of the mills be left out of the final report.[49]

The Panic of 1873 allowed Atkinson to stop worrying about labor costs since, as he noted excitedly to Wells, the crisis produced "an excess of laborers willing to work at low wages." By the mid-1880s, however, he was back at it. In the fall of 1884, Atkinson gave a talk to the American Social Science Association titled "What Makes the Rate of Wages?" "The true cost of any given article is the quantity of labor or the human effort expended in its production," Atkinson told his esteemed audience, articulating the conventional wisdom of a labor theory of value that had ruled American thought since the days of Benjamin Franklin. In the following sentence, however, Atkinson took the logic of this theory to a place that Franklin would not have dreamed of. "Now, if we consider a human being as an automatic machine, similar to any other mechanical power or force," he argued, "the true cost [of any given article] is the quantity of food and fuel expended in the conversion of a given amount of material substance into human force." Treating people like one of his textile machines, Atkinson assumed that the cost of human labor, like the cost of his spindles, was determined not by what the machine produced but rather by what it cost to keep the machine producing.[50]

Treating people like machines and their lives as an ongoing process of capitalist production, Atkinson then did what he did best: he turned to cost accounting, which in this instance amounted to cost of living. After spending the summer of 1885 sending out numerous requests to various manufacturers for statistics on the food their laborers consumed, Atkinson finally hit the jackpot when the Maryland textile mill Hooper and Sons sent him figures regarding the consumption and cost of food. Atkinson was ecstatic, noting that it was "difficult to obtain a detailed statement of the real cost of subsisting working people until you gave me this extremely valuable one. It will be the nucleus for a great deal of work in all the bureaus of statistics."[51]

By 1885 Atkinson had already worked his charm on the state bureaus of labor statistics, especially Massachusetts chief Carroll D. Wright. A few months prior he had written a letter to Wright about his failed attempts to gather information on food costs, explaining the "great difficulty for an unofficial person to explore the subject." Sure enough, the seventeenth report of the Massachusetts Bureau of Labor Statistics, published a year later, included a long, statistically detailed section on the cost and efficiency of food consumption among the working class. With generous government funding and a fairly large workforce of data miners at its disposal, Wright's bureau succeeded in generating dozens of "dietary schedules" from factory boarding-houses in Lowell, Lynn, and Lawrence as well as detailed data on the cost of living in working-class families from East Cambridge and Boston. Atkinson was proud that he had managed to shape the MBLS's inquiries and often bragged about his ability to influence the state statistical bureaus. "I have prepared the interrogations for all the Bureaus of statistics and for Carroll Wright," he noted in one correspondence. "Carroll Wright will adopt my formula," he noted in another, showing optimism "that Bureaus of statistics in thirteen states" would soon follow suit as well.[52]

As the MBLS's statistical tables that year reveal, a novel aspect had been added to Atkinson's cost-of-living calculations: a comprehensive breakdown of how much protein, carbohydrate, and fat laborers consumed for each cent of food they ate. Atkinson was the architect behind this statistical innovation as well. In May 1885, as he was reaching out to Carroll Wright, Atkinson also wrote a letter to Wilbur Olin Atwater, a chemistry professor at Wesleyan University interested in questions of human nutrition and metabolism. "You have entered upon an inquiry as to the necessary elements of food . . . from the stand point of the naturalist or biologist," Atkinson wrote. "I have been investigating the whole subject as an economist and there is an extraordinary dearth of accurate information." Atkinson suggested that the he and Atwater work together, along with Carroll Wright, to create nutrition-based cost statistics. Atwater enthusiastically agreed. A year later, in an article for *Century*, Atkinson explained why he had become so interested in food costs. Speaking of the American laborer, he noted that "his food is his fuel, and his physical exertion must be sustained by a sufficient supply with the same regularity and certainty that the boiler of the steam engine must be fed with coal."[53]

Atkinson's foray into nutritional cost accounting did not end with the MBLS report. In 1888, he requested that Atwater come up with a suggested ration of food that manufacturers could use when feeding their workers. While the 1885 report had found that workers spent roughly 24 cents a day on food, or $1.50 a week, Atkinson urged Atwater to come up with an equally nutritious formula that would cost only a dollar a week. A few years later, in his book *The Science of Nutrition*, Atkinson proudly noted how, thanks to the magic of his latest invention—a lamp-heated "Aladdin Oven"—he had managed to serve several friends at his whist club a seven-course dinner with a fuel cost of just 13 cents a serving, which was less than the cost of the after-

dinner cigars. With his own obsession for cost cutting, it comes as little surprise that Andrew Carnegie, who had begun to correspond frequently with
Atkinson in the 1890s, decided to purchase 3,500 copies of Atkinson's book
in order to donate them to every major library in the country.[54]

Thanks to some generous funding from the Department of Agriculture
that Atkinson managed to obtain, Atwater was able to construct the world's
first respiration calorimeter in 1896. As the newspapers of the day described,
the respirator was an airtight chamber "about as large as an ordinary convict's
cell" whose interior was visible through a triple-paned glass window. While
something similar had previously been used to measure the combustive efficiency of an engine, this newly designed chamber was for people, not machines. Once a person was placed inside, all of his inputs and outputs
could be registered through a barrage of instruments that measured the
amount of food he ate and the amount of excrements he passed. The first subject who entered the chamber was the school janitor, who was asked to lift
dumbbells while thermometers measured the rise and fall of temperature
within the house of glass. From the beginning it was clear that the calorimeter was designed for a certain class of men.[55]

As the Gilded Age gave way to the Progressive Era, Atkinson's dietary
schedules also spread through middle-class reform organizations. The Hull
House settlement, the New York Association for the Improvement of the Condition of the Poor, the Industrial Christian Alliance, and even the Tuskegee
Institute replicated the studies done by Atkinson, Wright, and Atwater. Not
everyone was pleased with this new fad, however. "As labor will be forced to
a new level," the *Philadelphia Inquirer* decried, "we are to have chemical apparatus and half-weight scales and frugal diets, and dyspeptic inspectors
travelling around and telling us that we eat too much." Eugene Debs wrote a
personal letter to Atkinson denouncing these studies as "scientific degradation" that would reduce the American worker's labor to "a cost as low as
Chinamen are subjected to." A Boston labor leader argued that the savings
would go to the employer's profit, not the workman's wages.[56]

When approached, many workers refused to answer questions regarding their cost of living. A Pittsburgh artisan's wife who had refused to
say how much food her family bought and ate explained how "the neighbors were convinced that it was a scheme to see how much it actually cost
for a man to live, in order that his wages might be reduced." Some workers

at boardinghouses purposely stuffed themselves with twice as much food as usual on the day the inspector came to measure their cost of living. If they could no longer influence the kind of labor statistics the state bureaus collected, American labor could still manipulate the actual numbers.[57]

———◦—◦—◦———

Carroll Wright had not been the only man competing for the coveted job of commissioner of labor, a position that essentially entailed being the head of a federal bureau of labor statistics. Terence Powderly, the grand master of the Knights of Labor, spent much of his time and energy in 1884 seeking the appointment as well. While labor historians have mostly ignored bureaus of labor statistics (except as valuable source material) in favor of strikes, unions, and party politics, from its humble beginnings the Knights of Labor saw these bureaus as one of the institutional centerpieces of their social movement. In 1878, for instance, the third demand listed in the preamble to the Knights' constitution called for the establishment of bureaus of labor statistics that would help Americans "arrive at the true condition of the producing masses in their educational, moral, and financial condition."[58]

It is therefore not surprising that when Powderly applied for the job of labor commissioner in person to President Chester A. Arthur in the summer of 1884, he brought with him 1,567 petitions calling for his nomination that had been signed either by branches of the Knights of Labor or by other worker organizations. He also presented clippings from 37 labor papers and 115 daily papers that supported his appointment. In response, however, Arthur handed Powderly a document of his own, one that had been sent to him by a group of manufacturers, which read:

> It is feared by the employers of labor that if Mr. Powderly is appointed by your Excellency he will exert his influence in opposition to the interests of employers. It is also feared that he is in sympathy with the communist element, and that he will be influenced and guided largely by that class.

And so the job went to Carroll Wright instead of Terence Powderly.[59]

The battle over the Massachusetts bureau was perhaps the most prominent struggle over the political power to shape government labor statistics, but it was hardly atypical. Beginning in the 1870s and continuing into the 1880s, more than twenty states established bureaus of labor statistics. Many of these bureaus, such as those that emerged in the industrializing states of Ohio, Illinois, Connecticut, Pennsylvania, and Maryland, were initially controlled—either directly or indirectly—by union activists or skilled labor organizations. The Coopers' International Union and the National Association of Mechanical Engineers pushed the Ohio bureau through the state legislature. In Pennsylvania, the Philadelphia Board of Trade complained how the state's bureau was "communistic." The Illinois bureau had strong ties to the Knights of Labor, a relationship that allowed them to disprove Wright's argument that strikes were useless. In revealing, for instance, the benefits of the Haymarket strike, the bureau proved that "out of the 17,029 who work only eight hours, 11,316 have acquired the shorter day as a result of the agitation of May, 1886."[60]

As their preamble makes plain, the Knights of Labor developed a distinct statistical vision that rejected the pricing of progress and strived to make "industrial and moral worth, not wealth, the true standard of individual and national greatness." They also focused far more on inequality and power relations. "The legitimate aim of the Labor Bureau," Powderly noted in the lead-up to his nomination quest, "is to ascertain beyond the shadow of a doubt what the earnings of labor and capital are in order that justice may be done to both, in order that unscrupulous employers will not have it in their power to rob labor of its just dues and take all the profits of the combination of labor and capital for their own aggrandizement." Stressing the importance of open information, Powderly criticized employers for handing over statistics only on the conditions of labor and not on the conditions of capital. The employer, he noted, "was disposed to be generous in the matter of stating what was paid to labor; what labor could live on; how much the workman spent for strong drink; what a fondness the workman had for canned goods; and such other information as could best be given by the workman himself." Clearly criticizing Carroll Wright and Edward Atkinson's cost-of-living figures, Powderly did not let up, slamming the bureaus for turning only laborers into the objects of statistical inquiry while the capitalist's "own affairs were not considered proper subjects for public scrutiny"; "not being obliged to state what his own profits were, or what he spent for strong drink, he made no mention of such insignificant trifles."[61]

The Knights of Labor also broke the gender barrier that had made statistical work an exclusively masculine endeavor. In the early 1880s, Knights of Labor statistician Leonora Barry put an end to the total male domination of social quantification. An Irish immigrant, Barry was widowed in 1881. "I was left, without knowledge of business, without knowledge of work, without knowledge of what the world was, with three fatherless children looking to me for bread," Barry would later note. These miserable conditions likely led to the death of her eldest child. Desperate to find work to keep her other children alive, she got a job at a hosiery mill, where she made 11 cents a day. It was while working at the mill that she joined the Knights of Labor. Barry had a knack for labor organizing and within two years found herself not only the master workman of her own branch but the leader of an entire district assembly of fifty-two locals. She was elected to represent her region at the national general assembly in 1886, where she was one of sixteen women among 660 delegates. While at the national assembly, Barry was made head of the new Department of Women's Work. Her main mission was to traverse the country collecting statistics on women's labor that would reveal "the abuses to which our sex is subjected by unscrupulous employers" and the need for "equal pay for equal work."[62]

By the late 1880s the Knights had an estimated 65,000 female members and Barry had become renowned for the statistical reports she compiled for annual general assemblies. With an arresting depiction of the condition of women's labor in America, Barry's reports combined statistical data with a strong moral critique of industrial capitalism. Her reports focused on both the laborer's wages and the employer's profits, which enabled her to measure the level of exploitation at the American workplace. "The contractor who employed five operatives made 30 cents per unit, or $1.50 a day," she noted in one example, "while each worker received only 30 cents for the entire day's work." "Men's vests are contracted out at 10 cents each," she noted in a second example, "the machine operative receiving 2.5 cents and the finisher 2.5 cents each, making 5 cents a vest for completion." Since twenty vests constituted a day's work, Barry calculated, "a contractor who employed five operatives reaped a dollar a day for doing nothing while his victim has 50 cents for eleven and twelve hours of her life's energies." By the 1890s, however, Barry was once again forced to return to the factory. With no Terence Powderly in the federal government, and with the Knights of Labor all but destroyed, there were no statistical institutions through which Barry could make her voice, and those of countless other women, heard. Nevertheless, in the Progressive Era, statistic-wielding labor activists such as Florence Kelley and Crystal Eastman would follow her trailblazing example.[63]

The Farmers' Alliance, a product of the Populist movement, also embraced bureaus of labor statistics as a political instrument that could bring about social change. The alliance pushed government, at both state and federal levels, to adopt statistical measures that reflected their own values and concerns. The most famous Populist texts of the era often contained statistics designed to educate, enrage, and empower. Sharing the same producerist values as their wage-laboring brethren in the Knights of Labor, Populists also focused on indicators that could measure proprietary independence, asymmetrical power relations, and social inequity. Being farmers, however, their focus naturally gravitated toward a different set of metrics, such as mortgage debt, agricultural tenancy, and unproductive rent.[64]

Thanks to Archibald Russell, agricultural statistics had been collected by the census since 1850. But as befit a member of the American Geographical Statistical Society, such figures focused on output and were mostly used to forecast crop yields or manipulate futures markets. Men such as Russell cared little for such issues as debt, independence, or power, and for the next few decades the agricultural schedule of the census revolved almost entirely around yields, output, and the cash value of farms. The founding of the Department of Agriculture in 1862 changed little, as the department determined early on that circulars should be limited to "two useful objects": prices of farm products and average yields per acre.[65]

Distressed by a wave of foreclosures and energized by Henry George's diatribe against the monopoly on land, the Populist vision succeeded in infiltrating state bureaus of labor statistics in the late 1880s. The first report of the Nebraska Bureau of Labor, for example, examined the percentage of farmers who owned their farms, the interest rate on their mortgages, and whether they were able to save anything above expenses. The Connecticut, Illinois, Michigan, and Ohio bureaus collected similar statistics. The bureaucratic task at hand, however, was an ambitious one, and Populists soon realized they would need the deep pockets of the federal government and a statistical reach that only the U.S. census could provide.[66]

Two pro-George Single Tax activists from St. Louis led the charge, circulating thousands of copies of a petition demanding that the census chief acquiesce to their statistical demands by supplying data on homeownership and debt. Citing a very different set of economic statistics than those of Carroll Wright or the Aldrich Report, the petition declared, "There is a growing feeling that the farmers and other wealth producers do not receive an equitable return for their toil . . . that 95 percent of the wealth is in the hands of less than 30,000 persons; and that the sturdy self-respecting farmer is becoming the American peasant."[67]

The petition took off, and within a few months, the Census Bureau was flooded by hundreds of letters from Farmers' Alliance members, Knights of Labor members, and Single Tax proponents across the country requesting that the demands made by the St. Louis men be met. In a rare moment of statistical success for the producerist coalition, the political pressures paid off and the categories were added to the census—despite the disapproval of both the chair of the Senate Census Committee and Carroll Wright. These figures would play a role in the populist uprising of the 1890s, as commentators used them to show how "monopoly" not only "bleeds the masses" and "concentrates wealth" but also "breeds poverty." William Jennings Bryan's Nebraska newspaper cited these figures to demonstrate that "the census of 1890 showed a general and alarming increase in the proportion of tenants and a corresponding decrease in the proportion of home owners."[68]

Other Populists went in a different direction. Henry George may not have used figures in his best-selling *Progress and Poverty,* but some of his followers who formed Single Tax clubs were anxious to prove his theory of land monopolization with statistics. Matt Roche, head of the West Side Single Tax Club of Chicago, wrote a letter to the U.S. secretary of the interior requesting that the census separate the market value of real estate from the value generated by improvements. Roche was trying to mobilize the government into creating a statistical apparatus that could, by calculating the discrepancy between market prices and improvement values, reveal the "unproductive rent" landlords earned simply by owning space. With such data, George's Single Tax might have gone from theory to reality. But Roche's request was denied.[69]

Barry and Roche have long been forgotten. So has Charles Barzilai Spahr, a Ph.D. student at Columbia University in the early 1880s and a close confidant of muckraker Henry Demarest Lloyd. In his dissertation, later published as *An Essay on the Present Distribution of Wealth in the United States,* Spahr meticulously mined the taxation data at his disposal to make one basic point: as time passed, the distribution of wealth in the United States was becoming more unequal. "Seven-eighths of the families [in America] hold but one-eighth of the national wealth," Spahr concluded, "while one per cent of the families hold more than the remaining ninety-nine." More than a century before Thomas Piketty or Occupy Wall Street, Spahr discovered the "1 percent."[70]

While a few socialists would go on to cite Spahr's book in the first decade of the twentieth century, his findings were mostly ignored. A scathing review written by Columbia professor Richmond Mayo-Smith in the leading academic journal of the era helps explain not just Spahr's historical obscurity but also how mainstream academic economists came to deflect charges that a plutocratic 1 percent was distorting the distribution of wealth. An admirer of Edward Atkinson's writings and an enthusiastic advocate of industrial capitalism, Mayo-Smith had written his own book on economic statistics in 1888, filling it mostly with cost-of-living figures, economic growth metrics, and other market output indicators that made capitalism look good. While Mayo-Smith had been all too keen to price the overall wealth of America in 1880 at $43 billion, he made clear that he did not support statistical investigations of wealth distribution, since "the only share of the product that we can follow out statistically is wages," and "all attempts to get at profits by estimating the total value of the output and comparing with the sum spent on raw materials and on wages are fallacious because they do not take into account risk."[71]

Reluctant to turn his statistical eye toward inequality, Mayo-Smith censured Spahr for collecting such compromising figures. His argument against inequality statistics echoed the consumerist worldview of the Aldrich Report. "Having shown that property and incomes are unequally distributed and that (in his opinion) the inequality is increasing," Mayo-Smith wrote, "Dr. Spahr seems to think that his task is ended. But that is only the beginning. The real question is whether such a concentration of wealth is not a good thing for the whole community." Mayo-Smith then went on to suggest that British economist Sir Robert Giffen's cost-of-living statistics served as a far better benchmark of social progress than wealth distribution, since "the happiness of individuals is measured not according to their ownership of property . . . but according to their command of the enjoyments of life." Downplaying power asymmetries and measuring society solely through the prism of consumer comfort—one would be hard-pressed to find a better articulation of the cultural values that brought about the pricing of progress in Gilded Age America.[72]

EIGHT

The Pricing of Progressivism

"AN EIGHT-POUND BABY is worth, at birth, $362 a pound. That is a child's value as a potential wealth-producer. If he lives out the normal term of years, he can produce $2900 more wealth than it costs to rear him and maintain him as an adult. The figures with regard to earning capacity are given by Irving Fisher, Professor of Political Economy." Thus opens a page-long article in the *New York Times* on January 30, 1910, titled "What the Baby Is Worth as a National Asset: Last Year's Crop Reached a Value Estimated at $6.96 Billion."[1]

While pricing babies by the pound was extreme even for the technocratic Progressive Era, it was common practice in the early twentieth century to hear well-meaning arguments for social reform in which American workers were treated not as empowered democratic citizens but rather as "human harvests." In these analyses, the pricing of everyday life—and everyday Americans—was a frequent occurrence, as market productivity became a consensus benchmark of that widely heralded Progressive dream, "efficiency."[2]

It is also not unusual that the author of this piece got his price data from Yale economist Irving Fisher. Praised by Joseph Schumpeter as "the greatest economist the United States ever produced" and remembered fondly today by both liberal and conservative economists as the founding father of modern-day, mathematical neoclassical economics and monetarist theory, Fisher stood at the heart of the cultural and intellectual development one might call the pricing of progressivism.[3]

While almost completely overlooked by Progressive Era historians— perhaps because he did not fit their preconceived notion of what a Progressive reformer should be—Fisher was a tremendously influential figure in his day. As a *New York Times* contributor, best-selling author, health fanatic, public intellectual, self-proclaimed hygiene expert, social reformer, economic forecaster, statistical wizard, indefatigable politico, and all-around

Progressive pundit, Fisher injected a new form of rigorous market empiricism into the economics departments of American universities and into American civil society more generally. It was Fisher who first brought mathematical models into American economics by offering a neoclassical theory of marginal utility that claimed that market prices reflected subjective value. And it was Fisher, perhaps more than any other American, who formalized, legitimized, and popularized the use of price statistics in Progressive Era political discourse, teaching the American people that if they wanted to argue over the nature of progress or the worthiness of a certain reform, they would have to price it first.[4]

Fisher had compiled the price data cited by the *New York Times* article as part of his lobbying campaign for a National Health Department and the federal regulation of public health. Fisher had convinced President Theodore Roosevelt that his National Conservation Commission should produce a report on "national vitality" that would deal not only with the conservation of natural resources but human resources as well. It was for this report that Fisher methodically capitalized the value of American people at different ages. Implementing the logic of cost-benefit analysis long before it became officially institutionalized by the Army Corps of Engineers in the 1930s, Fisher announced that, taking into account the discounted value of future earnings minus the discounted value of the future cost of care, the American baby was worth saving for he or she was worth $90; by the same type of calculation, a child presently five years old was worth $950, and the average American $2,900. Since even the youngest Americans were worth more than they cost, Fisher argued, government reforms to improve public health were a good economic investment. Aggregating together people of all ages and capitalizing their future income flows into present stocks of wealth, Fisher concluded, "Our population may be valued as assets at more than $250,000,000,000."[5]

Fisher's investmentality found a willing audience in President Roosevelt, an avid supporter of the Progressive Era's efficiency movement. "Our national health is our greatest national asset," Roosevelt wrote to Fisher, also portraying people as human capital. "To prevent any possible deterioration of the American Stock should be a national ambition."[6]

Fisher did not lack in such ambition. He would spend the next thirty years using similar price statistics to prove the viability of his countless reform initiatives, many of which appeared in his best-selling book *How to Live,* which went through ninety printings and sold nearly half a million copies. As president of the Committee on War-Time Prohibition, he argued that outlawing alcohol would "improve economic efficiency" and save American society $2 billion a year. In a groundbreaking cost-benefit analysis of tuberculosis, Fisher estimated that the annual social cost of the disease stood at $1.1 billion. Public health insurance, he argued, would save a whopping $3 billion a year, while treatment of the "insane and the feeble minded" was annually worth $85 million to the American economy.[7]

The last statistic hints at Fisher's interest in eugenics, and it should come as no surprise that Fisher's mission to maximize the market productivity of the American body led him to become the first president of the American Eugenics Society. During his tenure as president, the society used price data as propaganda. At one eugenics "fair," a sign next to a blinking light informed onlookers: "This light flashes every 15 Seconds. Every 15 Seconds $100 of your money goes for the care of persons with bad heredity such as the insane, feeble-minded, criminals and other defectives."[8]

Fisher's almost complete absence from the Progressive canon is striking, but it is not terribly surprising. Embraced by economists as different as the Chicago School's Milton Friedman and the Keynesians Paul Samuelson and Paul Krugman, Fisher defies the conventional historical narrative, still very much present today, that pits pro-government liberals against free-market conservatives. A mathematical economist who once built an actual hydraulic model of a perfectly equilibrating free market, yet also a leading Progressive reformer who fiercely advocated for a government health care plan that would make Obamacare blush, Fisher cannot be pigeonholed into the model of statist liberalism versus laissez-faire conservatism that has remained a historiographic staple since the days of Arthur Schlesinger.[9]

On one hand, Fisher rejected laissez-faire and believed in top-down, expert-guided government reform based on quantitative bureaucratic principles. On the other hand, his reform agenda was nevertheless predicated on a belief that society was nothing more than an income-generating series of market transactions and capital investments. As a result, while Fisher's pricing and capitalizing of everyday life significantly narrowed economic discourse and limited the spectrum of political possibilities, his quantification techniques could nevertheless be implemented in public policies ranging from a strong welfare state to a depoliticized monetary system. The ideological linchpin of his agenda was the notion that society's goal was to maximize the moneymaking productivity of American society and its laboring human capital—an idea that cannot be exclusively labeled as either "liberal" or "conservative."

A product of his time, Fisher stood on the shoulders of other quantifiers who had preceded him. Like so many other Progressive ideas, quantification practices that priced people and progress had made their fair share of Atlantic crossings. Fisher's own footnotes reveal that his techniques for capitalizing the human body had been greatly influenced by British statisticians William Farr, J. S. Nicholson, and Sir Robert Giffen as well as German statistician Ernst Engel, who went so far as to create a mathematical formula to calculate the value of people.[10]

Closer to home were other influences. Citing the cost-benefit calculations of fellow Americans of his era, Fisher became a walking repository of price statistics. Gathering such data was not particularly difficult—there were a great deal of monetized metrics floating around. The Progressive Era is rightly seen as the "twilight of laissez-faire," yet the rejection of free markets and the rise of an administrative state bureaucracy did not bring an end to the pricing of progress—quite the opposite, in fact. In 1911, for instance, the Boston Board of Commerce conducted an inquiry into the corporate cost of the common cold. Surveying 600 employees from "large concerns such as department stores," the government report found that the common cold led to a one-day absence a month (loss of $21 per worker) as well as a 10 percent "loss of energy" and hence "loss of efficiency" (another $3 per worker.) While treating people strictly as moneymakers, this study nevertheless urged that preventative health policies be put into place. Other diseases received price tags as well, usually from government officials such as Dr. Allan McLaughlin, of the United States Public Health Service, or Dr. James Cumming, director of the California State Bureau of Communicable Diseases. For example, typhoid was said to cost American society $271 million per annum, malaria $694 million.[11]

Such calculations became especially popular in the booming life insurance industry, a central site of capital accumulation in the early twentieth century. Hardly a week went by without an article by the likes of E. E. Rittenhouse, of the Equitable Life Assurance Society, declaring that preventable diseases cost American society (and, implicitly, American insurance companies) at least $1.5 billion a year. Other actuarial thinkers went into even deeper analyses. Frederick Hoffman, statistician of the Prudential Insurance Company, priced the American industrial workers' economic value at $300 per year by calculating, in a frank and ironically Marxian fashion, "the value of the product of the labor over and above wages." According to Hoffman, the "total net gain to society" of an industrial laborer who worked for fifty years stood at $15,000. Plugging these figures into his precious actuarial tables, Hoffman then calculated the "economic loss of society" if industrial laborers died young: at age twenty-five, it would equal $13,695; at thirty-five, $10,395; and at fifty, $4,405. The *Wall Street Journal* could not have been more pleased with such findings. "Seldom has statistics done a better service than to call attention to the advantage of preventing waste as a means of increasing the industrial efficiency of the people," it declared. Once again, the pricing of progressivism was calling for "big government" in the form of public health policies that would lengthen American lives. Yet instead of being rooted in the belief that people had the right to live as long as possible, they were driven by an investmentality that claimed the longer people lived, the more money they would produce.[12]

A central site for the pricing of progressivism was Frederick Winslow Taylor's scientific management and the Progressive Era "efficiency movement" it helped spawn. Scientific management was, above all else, an educational campaign that sought to teach workers to maximize their pecuniary opportunities. Behind all the stopwatches, motion studies, and managerial jargon lay a fairly simple system of labor surveillance that sought to incentivize and motivate workers by putting a price tag on their every move through a "differential piece-rate system" of paid bonuses. If a worker labored at a certain pace, he earned a basic rate; if he sped that up, he earned a bonus. Hoping to raise wages yet still lower per-unit labor costs by ramping up labor productivity even more than the bonus was worth, scientific management relied on the fact that laborers would focus on what they could earn rather than what they had actually produced. If Hoffman had used a theory of surplus value to price people, Taylorism was the institutionalization of commodity fetishism.[13]

Yet Progressive Era scientific management, with its pricing of human action, was not limited to the shop floor. Analogies were constantly being made between factory and society as Taylorism, as one historian phrased it, "stepped out of the factory and projected a role for scientific management in the nation at large." Efficiency experts believed that industrial pricing techniques should be applied to everyday life situations and that running a city or a family home was not that different from running a manufacturing or chemical company. For example, feminist reformer and "home economist" Charlotte Perkins Gilman—by no means a devotee of corporate capitalism—nevertheless spoke the language of market efficiency when she made her case for the end of unpaid women's labor in an article titled "The Waste of Private Housekeeping":

> Estimating the present market value of women's labor at charwoman's wages, $1.50 a day, and assuming that we have 15,000,000 working housewives, their labor is worth, per year, $7,500,000,000. One-fifth of them could do the work at a cost of $1,500,000,000, making an annual saving of $6,000,000,000, about $300 per family.[14]

While many Progressives focused on the income-generating capacities of men, women, and children, the natural environment did not escape their propensity to price. "Skunks are an important asset to the country," declared David Lantz of the U.S. Department of Agriculture in 1914, for "they bring to the trappers of the United States $3 million annually." The report was titled "The Economic Value of North American Skunks." In yet another article titled "The Economic Value of Electric Light," Allen Ripley Foote felt the need to drive home his case for well-lit sidewalks by pricing the criminality brought by the dark. Since "the cost of street lighting is about 60 cents per year per population," Foote explained, "ten arc lamps burned every night and all night cost about the same as one policeman." In 1906, a report in the *Baltimore Sun* on hydraulic power calculated that Niagara Falls was worth $122.5 million. Meanwhile on the West Coast, the *Los Angeles Times* was busy explaining to its readers how entomologists had estimated "the annual loss caused in the United States by insects at 700 million."[15]

The Progressive tendency to measure value with price was cropping up in the leading intellectual circles of the day as well. It played a major role even in William James's work on pragmatism. "Grant an idea or belief to be true," James asked in his 1907 *Pragmatism*, "what concrete difference will its being true make in anyone's actual life? How will the truth be realized? What experiences will be different from those that would obtain if the belief were false? What, in short, is the truth's cash-value in experiential terms?" In choosing "cash-value" as his idiom, James equated all "experiences" with market trans-actions. In his eyes, money values were not some airy abstraction but rather the realization of concrete truth. Pragmatism was about gauging the worthi-ness of ideas by their actual impact on people's lives. From this metaphor, it appears that James thought that such practical influences could be evaluated by money.[16]

James's use of the "cash-value" metaphor was no one-time slip of the tongue. It is ubiquitous in his writings and he returned to it repeatedly, de-spite criticism from outsiders. In *The Meaning of Truth* James refers to the above cash-value passage from *Pragmatism* as "the pivotal part of my book." For millennia, Western thinkers had been wary about associating market prices with value. James, on the other hand, made it the epistemological cen-terpiece of truth. When Progressive reformers turned to measure policy out-comes or everyday life in dollars and cents, therefore, they had the implicit backing of perhaps the most respected philosopher in America.[17]

James was not alone. In a series of articles, sociologist Charles Cooley ar-gued that "pecuniary values" had become the base form of value and valua-tion in American society. Unlike economists, sociologists like Cooley thought these monetary values were a man-made institution, born out of "money, banks, markets and its business class." Nevertheless, Cooley too accepted the convergence of social values with pecuniary ones. Claims that the price of a thing "has nothing to do with its higher values, and never can have," argued Cooley, were "bad philosophy." He believed that "pecuniary values are mem-bers of the same general system as the moral and aesthetic values."[18]

There are numerous strands of thought that can be teased out of this pricing of progressivism: the capitalization of the American body, even though slavery with its chattel principle had long since ended; the use of cost-benefit analysis as the central arbiter of social policy and resource allocation; the equating of American progress with the increased growth of market output; the emphasis on society's overall wealth as opposed to its distribution; the notion that money can serve as the basic unit for measuring social value. Yet to under-stand the ideas and assumptions that animated these calculations, we must first take a closer look at the economic, social, and cultural developments that led to their ascendance during the Progressive Era.

Sparked by flows of capital into railroads, real estate, factories, and other channels, the pricing of progress gathered a great deal of steam in the second half of the nineteenth century. By the Progressive Era, it was in full bloom. While alternative social and statistical investigations that did not price everyday life certainly existed in this era—the classic example being the landmark sociological study of urban life known as "The Pittsburgh Survey"—they rarely captured the American imagination in the same manner as price statistics. In fact, historians have shown that such descriptions of social life rarely moved the needle of popular opinion. As a result, monetized indicators such as the Aldrich Report continued their march into the American consciousness in the first two decades of the twentieth century. Even sophisticated, social-oriented activists such as Florence Kelley recognized the power of prices and created intricate neighborhood surveys that mapped the wages of their various inhabitants.[19]

The ascent of price statistics was made possible in these years largely because the local, decentralized proprietary producerism that had been ubiquitous in the earlier part of the nineteenth century—the greatest obstacle to the pricing of progress since the days of Alexander Hamilton—was slowly dissipating, swept away by the bureaucratic and managerial hierarchy of the modern corporation and its two twin institutions: the regulatory administrative state and the private philanthropic foundation. This corporate capitalist revolution (for the change was nothing short of revolutionary) greatly altered the balance of power in America. As distant and hierarchical social relations replaced local and informal ties, as the "visible hand" of the managerial corporation supplanted the competitive marketplace of petty producers, and as elected lawmakers often lost to unelected administrators the capacity to regulate the economy, power that had once resided in the hands of the owners of productive property (and their political representatives) now began to shift into the hands of a nascent class of professional experts (and their bureaucratic bosses and corporate benefactors).[20]

Be they corporate accountants, home economists, business consultants, insurance salespeople, industrial psychologists, government physicians, social workers, academic economists, mechanical engineers, or Carnegie Foundation PR staff, many of these professional experts sought to remake American society as a mechanized "system" that required continuous top-down maintenance, regulation, and social engineering. Preaching the gospel of efficiency, system-making, and rule of experts (unsurprising, since they were the experts), such Progressives rejected the notion that society should be run by individual market choices or democratically determined legal decrees. Rather, they envisioned a society in which professional statistical analysis—not votes or market transactions—would rule. Albeit more bluntly than most, Irving Fisher was articulating the thinking of most middle-class experts when he proclaimed, in an article supporting the abandonment of laissez-faire, that "the world consists of two classes—the educated and the ignorant—and it is essential for progress that the former should be allowed to dominate the latter."[21]

To transform the messiness of the real world into a legible and coherent system that could be governed from above, these Progressives often turned to statistics. As Robert Wiebe has argued, Progressives had a "quantitative ethic" because "it seemed that the age could only be comprehended in bulk." In their view of a properly functioning society, carefully collected data on all aspects of life would go up the bureaucratic hierarchy of a private corporation, government administration, or philanthropic foundation. Objective, efficient decisions made by experts on the basis of these quantification practices would then flow down. Since the corporate consolidation of American society required precisely these novel forms of hierarchical social coordination, pencil-pushing bureaucrats with a penchant for statistical analysis found themselves in positions of power, as centralized accounting practices became a leading method whereby Progressive America not only allocated social resources but articulated social problems.[22]

Whether it's called "corporate liberalism," the "managerial revolution," the "organizational synthesis," or the "iron cage" of instrumental reason, the varying contours of this epochal shift have been well documented. What has often been overlooked, however, is the fact that the dominant unit of statistical measure that came to run this data-driven society was (unlike in similarly bureaucratic Communist Russia) monetary prices. Even things that were never exchanged in the market—babies, Niagara Falls, or typhoid—came to be evaluated in cash. When Progressives spoke of "efficiency," they usually were talking about *pecuniary* efficiency. When they measured "waste," more often than not they did so in dollars and cents, as Elizabeth Perkins Gilman did. When two of the twelve children of Taylorist disciples Frank and Lillian Gilbreth wrote a tongue-in-cheek book about their parents' efficiency craze, they revealingly titled it *Cheaper by the Dozen*. In the Progressive Era, "cheaper" and "better" had become synonymous. By drawing the boundaries of the social around things that could be monetized, perhaps the disenchanted cage of modernity was created not by something as solid as iron but rather by something as immaterial as price.[23]

How to explain the Progressive Era spread of not just statistics but price statistics, not just quantification but market quantification, not just bureaucracy but capitalist bureaucracy? As Oliver Zunz has argued, "big business . . . not government, invented American bureaucracy." Therefore, it makes sense to begin with the corporate crescendo known as the "great merger movement," which shook the very foundations not only of the American economy but American thought and culture. Between 1894 and 1902, thousands of small manufacturers traded in their proprietary autonomy (and gut-wrenching instability) for a pile of stocks in giant corporations they owned but did not control. In 1890, the aggregated amount of capital in publicly traded manufactured companies was a measly $33 million. By 1898, it would be almost $1 billion; five years after that, it would balloon to $5 billion. The fruits of American industry had been securitized, financialized, and divvied up into little bits of dividend-bearing capital. By 1899, two-thirds of all manufactured products were made by corporations, and 65 percent of wage laborers worked for a corporation. By 1919, the end of the Progressive Era, those numbers would rise to 87 and 86 percent, respectively. As Thorstein Veblen noted in 1923, the corporation had become "the master institution of civilized life."[24]

The central goal of private corporations was profit, so it is only natural that their basic unit for measuring performance was price. Whether through internal cost accounting sheets and external shareholder reports, or production schedules and sales estimates, corporations measured success and failure in money. Such cost-conscious, profit-oriented barometers did not, however, remain confined to the private sphere of the corporation. During the Gilded Age, corporate forms of accounting and bureaucracy succeeded in shaping the metrics used by the "statistical state." The great merger movement further solidified this development in the Progressive Era as the massive amount of quantified price information generated by these corporate behemoths made centralized government data collection a far easier enterprise for state bureaucrats. Just as the Aldrich Report leaned on big business for price data regarding its particular sector of the economy, so too did many other government statistical endeavors in the Progressive Era, be it in regard to railroads, utilities, telecommunications, or manufacturing. As the first heads of the Bureau of Labor Statistics in Massachusetts had discovered as early as 1870, it was exceedingly difficult in an industrial, capitalist America to collect decent economic figures if you did not have the aide, and support, of private companies.[25]

As the very existence of large corporations was deemed inevitable in the Progressive Era, and as they funneled great amounts of data to government administrators, the rising regulatory state that accompanied this emergent corporate economy often came to judge these companies on their own terms of priced efficiency. When price statistics traveled out of the corporation and into the world they became highly effective ideology carriers, as many of the corporations' assumptions, worldviews, beliefs, and preferences went with them. As a result of this, the values of nineteenth-century anti-monopolism, which had revolved around producerist questions of corporate power, were largely supplanted by a "pocketbook politics" that centered mostly on comparisons of consumer prices and labor wages. Cost of living became a far more prominent political issue in the Progressive Era (use of the term becomes incredibly more prevalent in the 1910s), as the deflationary Gilded Age came to an end. This led many Progressives—including attorney Louis Brandeis, a future Supreme Court justice and anti-corporate activist—to encourage forms of scientific management in order to reduce waste and thus consumer prices and the cost of living. In fact, it was Brandeis's declaration in 1910 at a public hearing of the Interstate Commerce Commission that increased efficiency could supplant railway rate increases that made Taylorism a household name. Unlike the Pittsburgh Survey's hard-to-summarize analyses, such cost-conscious narratives were devoured by the press since they translated complex political debates into a single price statistic. A day after Brandeis's declaration, for instance, the *New York Times* headline screamed "Roads Could Save $1,000,000 a Day—Brandeis Says Scientific Management Could Do It."[26]

As Brandeis's surprising alliance with Taylor reveals, cost-of-living arguments spanned the political spectrum, meaning different things to different people. While industrialists may have pushed the use of cost-of-living figures in order to lower labor costs, for the left-leaning Catholic priest John A. Ryan and many Progressive laborers and activists, a "living wage" was first and foremost an issue of social justice, not technocratic efficiency.[27]

The voluminous testimonies of the United States Industrial Commission (USIC) on trusts and industrial combinations from 1898 to 1902 demonstrate the state-sanctioned yet corporate-oriented nature of the pricing of progressivism. As the statistical work of USIC expert on corporations Jeremiah Jenks makes plain, reincarnations of the Aldrich Report's cost-of-living figures often became the balancing test through which the federal government distinguished between "good" corporations that reduced costs thanks to efficient economies of scale and "bad" corporations that used their size, market share, and lack of competition to raise prices. The most burning political question was no longer whether corporations were a threat to democracy or freedom, but whether they were economically efficient and consumer friendly.[28]

With price statistics in such a central role, a good deal of corporate regulation and oversight came to be shaped not by legislative statutes—such as the Gilded Age's Granger Laws—but rather by unelected expert statisticians working for independent bodies such as the Federal Trade Commission and the rehabilitated Interstate Commerce Commission. With the Supreme Court lending a hand with such decisions as *Smyth v. Ames,* previously political and moral debates over what a corporation's "fair return" was came to be decided by government bureaucrats with their various corporate-inspired accounting techniques. Even when allocation decisions were being made not by bureaucrats but by judges, price statistics were starting to serve as novel arbiters of policy making. As courts turned away from the unyielding traditionalism of classical legal theory and began to use more-utilitarian tests to balance between property rights and social outcomes, the unit of measure they often turned to was money. It was precisely such developments that led Oliver Wendell Holmes to argue that the "man of the future is the man of statistics and the master of economics."[29]

No one fit the role of Holmes's "man of the future" better than Irving Fisher, and a closer look at his motivations for pricing everyday life serves as a useful lens into the social, ideological, and political forces behind the pricing of progressivism. After Fisher's $90 baby "mystified some people and shocked others," Fisher felt the need to explain himself and his calculations in a letter to the *New York Times*. Standing firmly by his data, Fisher made his case for the pricing of progressivism to the American public:

> Newspapers showed a strong aversion to the harrowing side of the tuberculosis campaign but were always ready to "sit up and take notice" when the cost of tuberculosis in dollars and cents was mentioned. The objection of philanthropists and legislators to contribute funds to tuberculosis sanatorium on the ground of their cost was met by showing that even this money cost was more than repaid to society by saving the lives of breadwinners.

Fisher then went on to say this:

> Human life is much more than a money making machine, but it is only as a moneymaking machine that it has a calculable money value. The figures, which I gave in Boston, were, naturally, not intended to include any sentimental human values in human life. What a baby is worth to its mother could never be calculated; but its value, or rather the value of the average baby as a perspective breadwinner, can be and has been calculated many times.[30]

This is a rather remarkable letter, for it demonstrates how Fisher's pricing of progressivism was, in large part, a product of the corporate capitalist society developing around him. During the Progressive Era, if corporate business groups such as the National Civic Federation could be convinced that worker's compensation minimized risk and rationalized labor costs, that reform had a great chance of becoming law. If, on the other hand, reformers could not persuade big insurance companies that government health insurance would increase their profit margins rather than eat away at their market share, that reform was likely to be shelved. It appears that Fisher, a savvy politician, turned to the pricing of progressivism in part because he understood that the fate of his precious social reforms were often in the hands of budget-conscious lawmakers or managerial elites accustomed to viewing the world as a balance sheet and American "breadwinners" as priced factors of capitalist production. As he made clear in his letter to the editor, Fisher was willing to openly admit that people were, in fact, priceless. Yet he nevertheless chose to package his reformist agenda in a cost-benefit language of priced efficiency, treating people as capital and society as an investment, because such an investmentality was what he believed would resonate with American elites, be they public opinion makers (the "newspapers" he mentions), businessmen (the "philanthropists"), or the state (the "legislators").[31]

Historians of the "organizational synthesis" have rightly recognized the rise of middle management, middle-class reformers, and middling bureaucrats in this era. But they have often done so at the expense of exploring the power of financial elites, corporate directors, and capitalist philanthropists. Fisher knew better than to overlook these elites at the top. As his mentioning of philanthropists suggests, Progressive reformers often found themselves pricing everyday life not only because of some bureaucratic "search for order" but also because wealthy corporate interests frequently served as the gatekeepers of Progressive Era reform. Human life is much more than a moneymaking machine, Fisher seemed to be saying, but *only* by considering it as a moneymaking machine could he produce the kind of market-oriented statistics that would convince America's policymaking elites to actively support federal regulation, social reform, and the nascent welfare state. If you wanted to help people in a corporate capitalist society, you would have to price them and their progress.[32]

The flip side of this argument also appears to be true: in a capitalist society that pushed for social welfare programs in part because they increase market productivity, it may be far more dangerous for inhabitants *not* to be priced. Such was the destiny of Native Americans—a social group that government statistics all but ignored because Americans never bothered to count, let alone price, the social existence of those "Indians not taxed." As a result, their slow extermination and marginalization in the nineteenth and twentieth centuries did not move the proverbial needle on any per-capita wealth statistics or human capital calculations.[33]

———————

The pricing of progressivism was a political, economic, and social development, of course, but it was also an intellectual one. Here too the corporate reconstruction of American capitalism played a central role, as it radically changed the way many upper- and middle-class Americans imagined—and quantified—the world around them. As local businessmen became corporate stockholders, property itself underwent a revolution, and with it the very conception of how it should be valued. Considering property from the point of view of individual petty producers, nineteenth-century Americans equated value with labor and property with tangible *things* that increased or enabled labor productivity. Whether the subject was land, tools, slaves, or machines, the definition of property or wealth was fairly cut-and-dried because it was material. When mid-nineteenth-century Americans sought to price the amount of capital in a given industrial firm or railroad, they believed that the best method for doing so was to estimate the costs of such concrete, productivity-enhancing investments as iron tracks or blast furnaces. If the amount of stock issued by a railroad or firm (already referred to as "capitalization" in this era) seemed to be of greater value than the amount of physical plant and productive property in its possession, nineteenth-century Americans howled about corruption, since they felt that such "watered stock" did not reflect the "real" amount of capital in the firm. The very term "watered stock" reveals the earthly nature of nineteenth-century value theory, as it came from the practice of gorging cattle before they were weighed in the market.[34]

As the great merger movement financialized workshops and factories into a stream of income-yielding corporate bonds and stocks, ideas about how to value property began to change and with them the very notion of what should be considered "real" shifted as well. Slowly but surely, as more middle-class Americans gave up their direct control of productive property for stock dividends and bond yields, property came to be seen not as a tangible thing whose value stemmed from productive labor but rather as an abstract claim whose value stemmed from future revenue flows. By the 1890s, this new approach was being institutionalized by American courts. As John Commons noted in the 1920s, the Minnesota Rate Case of 1890 was one of the first instances in which the Supreme Court argued that "not merely physical things are objects of property but the expected earning power of those things is property."[35]

The financial wizardry of Wall Street mogul Henry Goldman, the man most responsible for turning Goldman Sachs into an investment empire, succinctly demonstrates how ideas about property were changing in light of corporate consolidation. At the turn of the century, three cigar companies merged into the United Cigar (later renamed General Cigar) Company, run by businessman Jacob Wertheim. Wertheim was eager to issue bonds in order to raise long-term capital. Unfortunately, however, the United Cigar

Company—unlike railroads or other heavily mechanized industrial sectors such as steel production—did not have many physical assets that could serve as collateral for such large security issues. Wertheim turned to Goldman for assistance, and the latter did not disappoint. He convinced investors that the United Cigar Company's impressive revenue stream meant it was a safe and profitable investment regardless of what physical assets it had on its books. In so doing, Goldman was shifting the definition of value from something objectively grounded in the physical world to something determined by such subjective notions as future expectations and "goodwill."[36]

The stock market played a similar role in the changing notion of property, wealth, value, and capital. While American capital markets had been growing since the 1850s, the corporate merger movement pushed the stock market to the center of the American economic imagination. Historians have shown that "the economy" did not exist before the twentieth century. What is often overlooked is the fact that "the market" did not exist either. Only after the corporate reconstruction of the United States did Americans begin to think of the stock market as the reified brain of American capitalism. Just as GDP would come to delineate the boundaries of the "the economy," an economic indicator also emerged as the main expression of "the market": the Dow Jones Industrial Average.[37]

Reacting to the consolidation of industrial companies into giant corporations, on May 26, 1896, *Wall Street Journal* editor Charles Dow published a new statistical index in the data-filled pages of his financial newspaper. Tracking the closing stock quotes of twelve newly formed industrial corporations, Dow added up their stock prices and then divided by twelve, thus announcing the birth of the Dow Jones Industrial Average. By the early twentieth century, the industrial average became a piece of information no serious investor ignored. After Dow's death in 1902, the mantle was passed to William Peter Hamilton, his successor as editor of the *Wall Street Journal.* In his book *The Stock Market Barometer,* Hamilton would go on to synthesize Dow's daily editorials into the "Dow theory," arguing that "the market" was not merely an institution for the allocation of resources but also the hive-mind of corporate capitalism. Since rational, well-informed investors reading the corporate analyses produced by Moody's, the Standard Statistics Bureau, Poor's, or the *Wall Street Journal* bought and sold securities according to their future expectations for profit, Hamilton presumed, stock market prices embodied the true value of corporations and the securities they marketed. "The price movements represent the aggregate knowledge of Wall Street and, above all, its aggregate knowledge of coming events," Hamilton claimed. "The market represents everything everybody knows, hopes, believes, anticipates, with all the knowledge sifted down to what Senator Spooner once called, in quoting a *Wall Street Journal* editorial in the United States Senate, the bloodless verdict of the market place."[38]

According to Adam Smith and the classical economists who followed, the wonder of the free market was not that it determined the value of things but rather that it aligned market price with the intrinsic and thus "natural" value of things. Men such as Dow and Hamilton, on the other hand, were suggesting that there was no such thing as intrinsic price; there was only the market. Under this rationale, the very notion of "watered" stock was impossible, since the value of a company, as Henry Goldman argued, was based not on its current physical assets but rather on its future potential in the eyes of investors. The value of a corporation was whatever price investors were willing to pay for its stock. Dow and Hamilton's radical new theory of value would take a few decades to fully catch on. (The ICC in the Progressive Era, for instance, still believed one could measure "fictitious capitalization.") When it did, however, the term "watered stock" began to wane. Today, it is practically nonexistent.[39]

This view of the market and society is radically different from the view that existed in nineteenth-century America, since even things that were not tangible commodities—people's hopes, wants, beliefs, and anticipations—could now supposedly be gleaned from market prices. No longer shackled by the limits of the material, market price was now able to ascend to the epistemic center of American thought. For if prices were merely the representation of subjective desire, *all* valued human experiences could be understood in market terms. If capital was merely future expectations, almost anything could be deemed capital—even babies. As a result, society could be recast as a series of investments in the stock market of everyday life, with American citizens playing the role of corporate securities—and capitalized and valued as such.[40]

Irving Fisher played a major role in this conceptual revolution. What Henry Goldman and businessmen like him had done in practice, Fisher did in theory. In his 1906 *The Nature of Capital and Income*, Fisher offered a novel "stock and flow" definition of capital that became commonplace in modern

THE PRICING OF PROGRESS

economic textbooks. "A stock of wealth existing at a given instant of time is called capital," Fisher explained; "a flow of benefits from wealth through a period of time is called income." Like Goldman, Fisher was turning capital into an abstraction whose value was determined not by tangible things but by future expectations. "If we take the history of prices of stocks and bonds," he argued, "we shall find it chiefly to consist of a record of changing estimates of futurity." This allowed Fisher to vastly expand the definition of what was capital. For instance, he believed that every human being was capital and was "owned," "either by another human being, as in the case of slavery, or by himself, if he is a freeman."[41]

That was not all Fisher capitalized. "Food in the pantry at any instant is capital," he claimed, and "the monthly flow of food through the pantry is income." Incredibly, in Fisher's new theory of value, prices did not even require actual markets. "Articles of wealth which are seldom exchanged, such as public parks, are not commonly thought of as wealth at all, although logically they must be included in this category," he wrote. While this might sound like a pretty serious obstacle to his new theory of capital, Fisher sidestepped it with ease. "In order that there may be a price," he argued, "it is not necessary that the exchange in question shall actually take place. It may only be a contemplated exchange."[42]

Arguing that prices reflected subjective, "contemplated" value was one thing. Getting everyday people to believe so was quite another. The pricing of progressivism may have been on the rise, but it is important to note that it was constantly being contested. The novel approach to valuation taken by Fisher, Dow, Hamilton, and Goldman resonated with the emerging class of corporate stockholders, who saw the value of their stocks rise and fall on the fears and hopes of other investors. But for most Americans, who did not have the privilege of playing the market, it did not make nearly as much sense.

In general, when it came to the pricing of progressivism, only a select few were on board. Monetizing everyday life was mostly an elitist project of upper-middle-class professionals and experts. Everyday working Americans, whether laborers or farmers, were far more skeptical of such calculations, and had their own ideas about this monetizing mania. "Prof. Irving Fisher, says that a baby is worth $90 and adult $4000," noted one daily Philadelphia paper. "That is very clever, no doubt, but figures are notoriously untrustworthy." The paper articulated a far more plebian and cynical view of human capital: "Almost all of us have known babies who were priceless," it quipped, "and many an adult could not get a $4000 loan from a bank if he pledged himself, soul and all." While envisioning people as capital made sense to those who owned capital, such a vision was of little substance to those who did not and were in need of credit.[43]

By the late nineteenth century, moreover, working Americans' faith in the ability of money to represent value had continued the downward spiral that began in the time of the Jacksonian Democrats. In his wildly popular *Looking Backward,* Edward Bellamy reflected the mood of many Americans when it came to the representative powers of cash. In his utopian future, there was no market-based money. "All estimates deal directly with the real things—the fur, iron, wood, wool and labor," explains the futuristic Dr. Leete to our visitor from the past, "of which money and credit were for you the very misleading representative."[44]

Bellamy and the hundreds of socialist-oriented Nationalist Clubs that cropped up in his wake were hardly alone. At its core, agrarian Populism and the Farmers' Alliance were part of a movement that rejected the automatic equating of market prices with value. In their view, money was inherently political, and therefore it should not be allowed to determine value all on its own. On the contrary, populists wanted the issuance of money and credit to be nationalized so that market values could be determined democratically. In "The Philosophy of Prices," Farmers' Alliance leader N. A. Dunning demanded that Congress ensure that the supply of money equal $50 per capita. Many Populists echoed this $50-per-capita policy proposal, including the coalition of farmers' groups who put forth the Ocala Demands and Ignatius Donnelly with his famous 1892 Omaha Platform, which launched the People's Party. Such skepticism regarding money's ability to reflect value were also shared by American socialists, who emerged as an important political force during the Progressive Era. The price of labor, socialists claimed, did not reflect its actual value because of the power asymmetries and exploitation inherent in capitalist relations.[45]

Yet one does not have to look at Populists, Nationalist Clubs, or socialists to see just how much doubt existed regarding the relationship between price and value in America during this time. At the annual banquet of the New York Bankers' Association, two respectable guest speakers challenged the ontological powers of price while J. P. Morgan and other financial dignitaries sat in the audience and listened. Ridiculing the notion that the explosion of credit agencies and market forecasters had rationalized the market so that prices reflected value, the first speaker declared:

> We have weekly reports from Wall Street—special advices . . . giving full information how fortunes are made. But every sensible man not in the rainbow business knows that in financial affairs them who know do not tell, and the men who tell do not know, and that very often a stockbroker is a man who knows the price of everything and the value of nothing.

A second speaker that evening was no less critical about the association of price with value:

> The most profitable business today is that of the man who over-issues stock on anything that will stand still long enough for him to name it. This thing of hiring a lithograph company to manufacture values, and getting some responsible firm to sell it for money and divide the money is the easiest of all. The thing I cannot understand about Wall Street is the rapid change in market values when there is no change in real values.[46]

Clearly, the pricing of progress and progressivism was not yet hegemonic. For it to truly catch on in the long run, proponents would have to come up with a simple, logical, and convincing narrative that equated, to use the terminology of the above speaker, "real values" with "market values." This book opened with a story that tried to do just that. Desperate to equate prices with value, William Petty spun a wonderful yarn about the equal values inherent in growing a bushel of wheat and mining a coin of silver. That story was so convincing in its time that it went on to become the basis of classical economics. Yet with the fall of petty producers and the rise of corporate capitalism, such a labor-based, materialist theory of value would no longer do. In fact, as Marxist socialists made obvious, it was downright dangerous as it could be used to argue for the exploitative nature of capitalism. In an increasingly abstract, financialized, and weightless corporate capitalist world, where economic value had been detached from the tangible things of everyday life and taken a subjective turn, a new, "neoclassical" story was needed that could resonate with the American people and society's changing norms and values. Irving Fisher was just the man to tell it.

———◆———

In the 1870s, in a span of a few years, three separate economists in three separate European countries unknowingly offered up a very similar and rather novel theory of economic value that was based not on an objective labor theory of value but rather on the subjective principle of marginal utility. According to these disparate thinkers, classical economists such as David Ricardo, Karl Marx, and John Stuart Mill had been mistaken: the price of a good was *not* determined by the tangible amount of labor required to produce it. Rather, these neoclassical economists believed value was subjective: the price of any good was set by how much people were willing to pay for it, which, in turn, was determined in large part by the marginal or final increment of utility one derived from consuming it. This principal of diminishing marginal utility opened the door to the first mathematical economic models in history, since these minute changes in utility could only be conceived in mathematic terms as a derivative through the use of differential and integral calculus.[47]

But, like all economic models, the neoclassical theory of marginal utility was not an empirical study of human behavior; rather, it was a constructed narrative of how people act. It was a story. Since Fisher was a wonderful storyteller, capable of turning complex math into digestible and common sense ideas, here is how he explained marginal utility:

> A housewife buys (say) 10 lbs. of sugar at 10 cents per pound. As she closes the bargain she roughly estimates that the last or tenth pound is about worth its price. She did not stop at five pounds for she wanted a sixth more than the 10 cents it cost her.[48]

A rational, calculating housewife—the gendered aspects of Fisher's choice must be pursued further—purchases sugar until the marginal utility she receives from the commodity aligns with its market price. Instantaneously balancing the money cost of sugar with its utilitarian benefit to her family, the housewife fills her shopping cart until equilibrium has been reached between the market price and her own marginal utility. Simple, logical, relatable, and loaded with tacit assumptions regarding human subjectivity, this is vintage Fisher.

Today such ideas are mainstream, but in the late nineteenth century, neoclassical economics was far from an immediate hit. In fact, when a young Irving Fisher turned to mathematical economics in his doctoral dissertation in the early 1890s, it was a nascent discipline in crisis because of one major weakness: utility, the crucial concept that stood at the heart of the marginal revolution, seemed to be utterly immeasurable. Ironically, the very economic thinkers who were pushing for a quantifiable, mathematical economics had developed a concept that, unlike labor time, could not be measured empirically. "But what is the unit of utility?" J. K. Ingram wondered in the *Encyclopaedia Britannica*'s entry "Political Economy." "If we cannot look for something more tangible—not to say more serviceable—than this, there is not much encouragement to pursue such researches, which will in fact never be anything more than academic playthings."[49]

The harsh criticisms hurled at the idea of marginal utility were not lost on the economists who had invented it. British economist Francis Edgeworth came to the conclusion that if mathematical economics was to have a future, utility must become an empirical, measurable unit. In his *Mathematical Psychics*, written in 1881, Edgeworth solved this troubling issue by imagining a "hedonimeter," a machine that would allow one to measure subjective pleasure and pain. "Imagine an ideally perfect instrument, a psychophysical machine, continually registering the height of pleasure experienced by an individual," Edgeworth dreamed, "from moment to moment the hedonimeter varies; the delicate index now flickering with the flutter of passions, now steadied by intellectual activity."[50]

While Edgeworth's "hedonimeter" was clearly an attempt to legitimize the scientific rigor of marginal utility theory, the fact that such a machine was far from becoming a reality ended up only weakening the marginalists' professional standing even more. Likely hinting at Edgeworth's machine, Ingram's *Encyclopaedia Britannica* entry concluded that the "mathematical method" was "necessarily sterile" because "the fundamental conceptions on which the deductions are made to rest are vague, indeed metaphysical, in their character." Edgeworth, it appears, had only made things worse. It was at this moment that a precariously young Irving Fisher entered the debate.[51]

"Mathematical economists," Fisher noted in the preface of his Yale dissertation, "have been taunted with the riddle: What is a unit of pleasure or utility?" For the confident Fisher, however, this was but a rhetorical question. As he explained in the following sentence, he had, in fact, solved the puzzle: "I have always felt that utility must be capable of a definition which shall connect it with its positive or objective commodity relations." Utility, Fisher went on to explain, could be empirically measured, albeit indirectly, through the observation of market transactions. While measuring actual pain and pleasure was impossible, it was also unnecessary: since consumers purchased goods until their marginal utility aligned with price (as we saw in the housewife example), money could serve as the basic unit of value measurement. Like tea leaves of human aspiration, prices could reveal humanity's wants and desires. "The concept of value is made to depend on that of price," Fisher wrote in his 1911 textbook, going on to add in a later chapter that "prices are determined by the actual desires of men."[52]

Fisher had not been the first to think of this idea. In his groundbreaking *Theory of Political Economy*, written in 1871, William Stanley Jevons, one of the three aforementioned marginalist revolutionaries, pretty much made the same point:

> We can no more know nor measure gravity in its own nature than we can measure a feeling; but, just as we measure gravity by its effects in the motion of a pendulum, so we may estimate the equality or inequality of feelings by the decisions of the human mind. The will is our pendulum, and its oscillations are minutely registered in the price lists of the markets.[53]

Such a hedonistic approach to human behavior, however, was challenged throughout the 1870s and 1880s by some of the leading British thinkers of the day, including Henry Sidgwick and Charles Darwin. These men shared the same general objections to such theories of market subjectivity as later American pragmatists: Who said that people make decisions based solely on the pleasure they will derive from their actions? What about other social forces such as custom, habit, or coercion? What determines people's tastes and preferences in the first place? Can one really insulate the individual from the social? With such questions in mind, Fisher offered a solution to this critique by submitting his own ontological "postulate" of human subjectivity:

The plane of contact between psychology and economics is *desire*. It is difficult to see why so many theorists endeavor to obliterate the distinction between pleasure and desire. No one ever denied that economic acts have the invariable antecedent, desire. Whether the necessary antecedent of desire is "pleasure" or whether independently of pleasure it may sometimes be "duty" or "fear" concerns a phenomenon in the second remove from the economic act of choice and is completely within the realm of psychology.

We content ourselves therefore with the following simple psycho-economic postulate: *Each individual acts as he desires.*[54]

This is a radical theory of subjectivity and selfhood. By suggesting that economists need not bother themselves with how preferences are created, shaped, or determined, Fisher had summarily disentangled human subjects from the context of their lives and reimagined them as fully individual, autonomous, atomized, and preexisting beings with a certain set of wants and desires that should simply be taken as a natural given. Fisher's theory did not explore how social class, economic environment, or past cultures shaped and made individuals. In one short paragraph, he managed to erase both history and society from the study of economics. Gone also were all aspects of coercion. In Fisher's model there was no such thing as power, a social relation in which one imposes his or her will on another. *Each individual acts as he desires.* In this very era, William James was suggesting that consciousness was "a kind of external relation." John Dewey was arguing that "individuality is not originally given, but is created under the influences of associated life." Thorstein Veblen was lamenting the fact that economics was not an evolutionary science in which individual agents would be seen as part of a greater historical whole. Irving Fisher was saying precisely the opposite.[55]

But was not Fisher simply articulating the already existing arguments of classical economics? No, he was not. For all the individualizing impulses that existed in classical economics since the time of Adam Smith, their approach to society looked nothing like this. In *The Wealth of Nations,* for example, Smith's theory of value is founded on three principal actors: laborers who earn wages, landlords who earn rent, and capitalists who earn profits. Together, these three income streams make up the price of any object. Say what you will about how Smith may have legitimized certain exploitative social relations, his theory of value was still based on *social relations*. Social position and economic circumstance (for instance, whether one inherited land or owned the means of production) were central to his narrative, as well as those of all other classical economists.[56]

In Fisher's economic theories, however, there is no notion of social relations or class or power or culture. There are only homogeneous and autonomous individuals floating around ahistorical space voluntarily reaching contractual and mutually beneficial agreements of exchange with other autonomous individuals as they rationally calculate how many pounds of sugar they should buy in accordance with their preexisting utility preferences. Where do these utility preferences come from? Why does the housewife have such a sweet tooth? No need to explore that, according to Fisher; it is—to use the parlance of modern-day economists who followed Fisher's lead—"exogenous to the model."

Fisher's approach to human subjectivity became a cornerstone of his economic modeling. The theory appears again, for instance, a few years later when Fisher sought to explain in his undergraduate textbook why some people end up capitalists while other turn out to be wage laborers. According to Fisher, one's social position vis-à-vis the means of production was determined by "human nature" and one's own subjective, inherent, and preexisting time preferences:

> Let us suppose that, through some communistic or socialistic law, the wealth in the United States were divided with substantial equality. It is proposed to show that this equality could not long endure. Differences in thrift alone would reestablish inequality. We cannot suppose that human nature could be so changed and become so uniform that society would not still be divided into "spenders" and savers." . . . If two men have to start with the same income of $1000 a year, but one has a rate of impatience above the market rate of interest and the other has a rate below, the first will continue to get rid of future income for the sake of its equivalent in immediate income, and the other to do exactly the opposite.[57]

Notice how in Fisher's narrative, people and society begin to look a lot like his unit of measure—money. Money is the ultimate homogenizer and leveler. Exchange value flattens all of the hills and valleys of life, transforming them all into commensurable units of measure. The same can be said of the actors in Fisher's model, as there are no laborers, capitalists, or rentiers—just flattened, homogeneous, utility-maximizing consumers with inherent preferences ("savers" vs. "spenders," "rate of impatience") we can observe but not explain, measure but not unpack.[58]

In the above passage we also begin to see the ideological power of neoclassical economics. By erasing the class relations inherent in owning (or not owning) a productive property, Fisher's model painted a meritocratic picture of the United States in which the destiny of each man was determined only by his own choices and preferences. Do not blame social institutions or the inequities of wealth distribution for your economic problems, Fisher argued; blame yourself and your irresponsible rate of impatience above the market rate of interest.[59]

Such a political message suited Fisher, who once referred to socialism as "the red flag of class war" and loathed both labor unions and agrarian Populists. In Fisher's radically abstract and homogeneously classless model of society, where labor could technically hire capital just as easily as capital hired labor, corporate profits stemmed not from monopoly privileges or the exploitation of laborers—common accusations in the politically rambunctious 1890s—but rather from a firm's ability to supply consumers with the products their fully autonomous, utility maximizing minds desired. As Fisher wrote to his brother around the time of his dissertation, the astronomical jump in railroad profits came not from the asymmetrical power relations between capitalist and farmer but rather simply because the railroad's "usefulness to farmers in conveying wheat was immensely increased." By equating market price with subjective value, therefore, Fisher had created a functionalist logic that legitimized the capitalist status quo: if a corporation was raking in the money, it *must* be because it was increasing the utility of society. More than a hundred years later, Harvard economist Gregory Mankiw would make the same argument to legitimize the enormous income inequality in the United States in an article titled "Defending the One Percent."[60]

Fisher's radical theory of market subjectivity was also shaped by his yearning to transform economics into an empirical and quantitative science that would be based on inductive data as well as deductive logic. As Schumpeter eulogized, "Throughout and from the start, Fisher aimed at a theory that would be statistically operative." Fisher took on the thorny problem of utility measurement in his dissertation, therefore, because he recognized that a mathematical, empirical economics would thrive only if there was a quantifiable and observable unit of measure. "In all mathematical sciences," an aging Fisher would later declare, "the first essential is a unit for measurement."[61]

This first essential helped push Fisher to put forth a theory of human subjectivity that would allow him to link utility, value, and price. If price was to become a convincing measure of utility, imbued with real meaning, Fisher *had* to assume that market choices reflected inherent desire. Fisher erased history and society, therefore, in part because ideas of custom or coercion or class or institutional change would have disrupted the notion that people simply purchase what they want. Such a decoupling of utility, desire, price, and value would have been mathematically devastating, as it would have pulled the empirical rug right out from under Fisher's precious price statistics. If the housewife had purchased six pounds of sugar because that was what her mother had always done, or because she had been bombarded by advertisements, or because the neighborhood supermarket no longer carried other natural sweeteners since the rise of the sugar trust, Fisher would have been at pains to align subjective utility with market price. But by ignoring such historical, cultural, or social questions regarding the intentions and motives of people, Fisher was able to shift the analytical spotlight solely onto consumers' observable (and priceable) market decisions.

Fisher did harbor some reservations about his pricing of people, places, and things. Caveats and qualifications regarding this matter can be found not just in his *New York Times* letter but peppered throughout his writings. Yet Fisher clearly believed that maximizing economic efficiency and productivity should be the overarching goal of life. Referring to socialist or left-leaning economic thinkers as a "cult" in the 1940s, he claimed that such theories "start with a false premise, namely that the problem of economic mass welfare is primarily one of distribution whereas, in my opinion it is primarily one of production." Much earlier in life, he wrote to a friend while he was in the midst of working on his dissertation that "the duty of making money seems to me the most direct and imperative of all human obligations, though it be the most natural. This is counter to the views of most college professors; but careful observation has led me to it."[62]

The common denominator of all of Fisher's policy proposals, whether health care, world peace, eugenics, or calendar reform (Fisher believed that for accounting purposes there should be thirteen months with twenty-eight days each so that every month was the same length), was that they would all lead to an increase in market productivity and thus an optimization of human capital. A well-known health fanatic after surviving a bout of tuberculosis, Fisher clearly internalized this capitalization of man, speaking of his own body much the way Carnegie might refer to a blast furnace. "Applying my dearly bought knowledge of hygiene," he wrote with pride in a draft of his autobiography, "to keep my working capacity as close as may be to 100 percent." It is, in fact, in Fisher's penchant for market optimization that one sees the conceptual bridge linking his economic models and Progressive reforms. In his neoclassical model, one balanced the monied costs and benefits of a given commodity in order to optimize individual wellbeing. In his reform proposals, one balanced the monied costs and benefits of a given reform in order to maximize social progress.[63]

In creating the intellectual infrastructure of modern neoclassical economics, Fisher had labored to create a narrative equating value with price that could resonate with the American people while also legitimizing a corporate capitalist society. Yet for money to become, as Fisher desired, the basic unit for measuring not only exchange values but also social, cultural, and political ones, there were two major obstacles that still needed to be overcome: inflation and deflation. If money was going to serve as the new standard of everyday life and the unit of measure through which economic resources and social policy were to be allocated, its value had to remain consistent and stable.

To return to his own example, Fisher argued that the price of sugar was determined by a housewife's own subjective preferences. As a result, if the price of sugar suddenly rose not because she developed more of a hankering for sweets but rather because the amount of money circulating had jumped, Fisher's evaluative link between money and subjective value would be undone. This problem of standardizing and stabilizing the value of money, meanwhile, had not only epistemological ramifications but distributional ones as well: since money was the basic unit in which capital was accumulated, its depreciation in the form of inflation could be devastating to capitalists. As Warren Buffett once put it, "Inflation swindles the equity investor." For capitalism to be sustainable, the value of money *had* to be maintained. In the future-oriented world of corporate capitalism, if money became unstable and unpredictable (or even if there was fear that this might happen), chaos could ensue. "We have standardized every other unit in commerce except the most important and universal unit of all," Fisher expostulated, "the unit of purchasing power. What businessman would consent for a moment to make a contract in terms of yards or cloth or tons of coal, and leave the size of the yard or the ton to chance?"[64]

But how was one to tether the value of money so it did not float away? In the nineteenth century, Americans and Europeans answered this question by turning to the gold standard. The gold standard kept prices from rising by greatly limiting the creation of more money, but it also—as the Populist farmer experienced firsthand—served as a highly effective tool whereby the banking elite could insulate money not only from inflation but also from democratic pressures. The beauty of the gold standard, to the American upper classes, was not in the shimmer of the metal but rather in the fact that its quantity was not determined by legislatures or the state. While the Farmers' Alliance sought to democratize money by passing laws that set the money level, the gold standard depoliticized it.[65]

Irving Fisher was no goldbug. Having helped develop a novel theory of value based on subjective desire, he did not believe that prices should be determined by the total lumps of metal one happened to dig up from the ground in a given year. What is more, Fisher desired a far more elastic mechanism than the gold standard, one in which the amount of money would increase or decline along with the expansion or contraction of the economy. In this regard, Fisher was actually in agreement with the Populists. As a believer in the quantity theory of money, which claims that prices are greatly affected by the amount of money in circulation, he concurred with the Populists that the deflation plaguing them in the Gilded Age was in large part a result of the fact that gold reserves in the United States were not increasing at the same rate as American economic activity. In the early twentieth century, when prices began to rise, Fisher was still not happy, as he blamed inflation on new gold mines that flooded the coffers of banks with too much money.[66]

There is, however, a crucial difference between Fisher and the Populists. In contrast to the Farmers' Alliance, Fisher was horrified by the idea that the government could democratically determine the value of money. Instead, he believed that the government needed to establish a price-stabilizing mechanism that would remain insulated from democratic, populist pressures. At

THE PRICING OF PROGRESS

first Fisher believed that the government could simply create an auto-administrative mechanism to ensure that prices would be pegged to cost-of-living price indices (Fisher was considered the leading expert on such statistical indices). "With the development of index numbers," Fisher declared, "we now have at hand all the materials for scientifically standardizing the dollar." Such indices would standardize the dollar "without putting a dangerous power of discretion in the hands of government officials." Fisher's solution to the abstract vagaries of price was not something as solid as gold but something as intangible as a price index. The solution to the instability of prices was more prices.[67]

Despite some vigorous lobbying on Fisher's part, this plan fell through—although it was much debated by Progressive Era economists. With the founding of the Federal Reserve in 1914, however, Fisher finally had the institution that could ensure the stability of the dollar through the actions not of legislatures but rather index-wielding financial experts. Anticipating Milton Friedman's monetarist theories by a half century, Fisher believed that in addition to serving as a lender of last resort during credit crunches, the Federal Reserve should also "use all of its powers" to stabilize the price level. Fisher and Oklahoma senator Robert Owen tried to get a bill through Congress precisely on this matter, but it failed. Only in the aftermath of the Great Depression and the rise of monetarist policy did Fisher's vision become a reality. Since the 1970s, the Federal Reserve's mandate has been, along with maximum employment, to stabilize the dollar. A quasi-private institution not subjected to the whims of directly elected officials, the Fed's monetary interventions ensure not just the stability of the dollar but the very functioning of American capitalism.[68]

In becoming a master of the price index, Fisher also leveraged his expertise to make himself, and other capitalists, lots of money. In the Roaring Twenties, Fisher formed the Index Number Institute, a forecasting company that supplied investors with tips regarding the stock market. His forecasting model was built on price indices. In his opinion, the ebbs and flow of the "business cycle"—a concept that preoccupied many investors in the 1920s—were largely determined by the increase or decrease in the money supply.[69]

In the end, however, Fisher's belief that prices reflected value helped bring about his own demise. If most Americans have heard of Fisher at all, they know him not for his neoclassical models or pricing of progressivism but rather for declaring, only days before the Wall Street crash of 1929, that the stock market had reached "a permanently high plateau." While most businessmen quickly took their money out of the market after the crash, Irving Fisher could not believe that stock prices could be so detached from reality. He left his money in and ended up losing everything, even his home. Till the end, Fisher believed in equating money and value, and for this he paid a very heavy price.[70]

What are we to make of a Progressive Era in which Irving Fisher is pushed from the margins of the period to the center? To be sure, no single reformer can serve as a stand-in for the movement—Progressivism was far too diverse for that. What is more, Fisher was in many ways a man ahead of his time. Many of his monetarist and neoclassical ideas, especially his erasure of "the social" in favor of his radical notions of market subjectivity, did not become mainstream for decades. While already influential by the 1920s, it was really only in the 1970s and 1980s, as Dan Rodgers has noted in a passage that might well have been summarizing Fisher's dissertation, that "conceptions of human nature that in the post–World War II era had been thick with context, social circumstances, institutions, gave way to conceptions of human nature that stressed choice, agency, performance, and desire."[71]

Nevertheless, Fisher serves as a valuable lens into the era, not least because his equation of social values with monetary ones reflected, despite persistent challengers, the popularity of the pricing of progress in the first two decades of the twentieth century. As William Leach has broadly recognized, this is the era in which "pecuniary values . . . would constitute for many people the base measure of all other values." Acts of pecuniary quantification significantly narrowed the scope of political debate during the Progressive Era by focusing only upon aspects of American life that could be priced, yet they still left a wide spectrum of political wiggle room—much like Fisher's own wide-ranging policy prescriptions. Just as price statistics could be used by Taylorist disciples to deskill labor or neoclassical economists to legitimize corporate profits, so too could monetized metrics assert the need for government investment in public health, environmental conservation, or a higher living wage. The boundaries of twentieth-century economic discourse were being set in these crucial decades of corporate capitalist solidification, and they would go on to include both liberal prime-the-pump Keynesianism and conservative Reagan-era neoliberalism. While there were great differences between these varying economic approaches, they would all go on to treat American society, first and foremost, as an income-generating investment that needed to be priced, managed, and most importantly, grown.[72]

EPILOGUE:
TOWARD GDP

ON JULY 27, 1912, the son of the richest man in the world set off a chain of events that would lead, two decades later, to the crowning moment in our story of the pricing of progress: the state-sanctioned invention of GNP by Simon Kuznets of the National Bureau of Economic Research (NBER) in 1934. From his glamorous New York City offices at 26 Broadway, John D. Rockefeller Jr. wrote a letter that day to Frederick Taylor Gates, his father's most trusted business advisor and one of the central architects in the corporate reconstruction of American capitalism, American medicine, and American philanthropy. In his letter, Rockefeller spoke of a meeting that had been held that spring in Europe between J. P. Morgan, AT&T chief Theodore Vail, and Senator Nelson Aldrich (who just so happened to be the younger Rockefeller's father-in-law). "There was an earnest discussion of the necessity of laying plans," Rockefeller reported to Gates, "towards a systemic education of public sentiment in matters, financial, economic and industrial by the presentation of the facts where untruths are constantly being set forth." Rockefeller then went into more detail:

> The popular opinion which seems to pertain with reference to the great business interests; the radical and ill-digested legislation and thought and speech with reference to economic and financial as well as political questions which is now so rampant; these and other indications of an alarming tendency towards the domination of those things which cause the undermining of law, of property rights, of the very form of government under which this country has been built up, suggested to this group of gentlemen the urgent need for some intelligent, well-conceived, broad, non-political effort to educate public opinion.[1]

Rockefeller was clearly taken with the idea of using "non-political" facts to advance his political goal, namely, the increased popularity of corporate capitalism. When a second meeting with the same cast of characters was held, this time at J. P. Morgan's office on Wall Street, Rockefeller made sure not to miss it. As he tells it, a plan was hatched in that meeting to jointly fund an independent and private research institution that would hire "able men to have charge of the thing." Rockefeller, Morgan, and the financial backers would remain in the background and not be "responsible in any way for the actions of the man in charge, although they would be constantly ready to advise him as to policy and practice."[2]

Of course the institution wouldn't *really* be independent, and everyone in the room that day knew it. In fact, it was the very reason they were there. Like many business-led philanthropic endeavors emerging in the Progressive Era, this was both a form of enlightened paternalism and a sophisticated power play. For men such as Morgan and Rockefeller, the beauty of philanthropy was that while the research bureaus that received their funding could fill their halls with professional experts and claim to be purely objective and independent, the philanthropists themselves could rest easy knowing that with each dollar they donated came the tacit understanding that the institution would probably not do anything to jeopardize their future funding. One does not usually look a capitalist's gift horse in the mouth.[3]

A few weeks later, Rockefeller revised the memo that Theodore Vail had written following the meeting at Morgan's office. It offers a rare inside look into the mind of American capital during the Progressive Era. "Legitimate enterprise and industry have become the objects of unjust suspicion," the memo lamented, as the "force of public opinion has often been brought into opposition with the very forces on which public and private wellbeing and happiness depend." The memo then went on to equate such "wellbeing and happiness" with monetary values. "The prices received by all producers have never been more remunerative or satisfactory. The numbers of consumers and their purchasing power have increased in full proportion to the increase in prices." The implicit message of the memo was clear: if only such price data could reach a larger audience, the public would be far more appreciative of the wealthy businessmen and corporate behemoths responsible for America's economic affluence and "purchasing power."[4]

Now enthralled with the idea of a privately funded research institute, Rockefeller had his top public relations man, Jerome Greene, write up a second memo in the summer of 1912. Greene summarized the goal of the research bureau as the "publication of facts" that would support "the business interests of this country" through "the refutation of misleading and harmful statements."

As only internal memos never intended for outside eyes can do, Greene's document reveals the political imperatives behind the founding of a seemingly nonpolitical research institution. Upset that "the business interests of the country are suffering chiefly from undiscriminating abuse or radical schemes for reform," Greene praised the benefit of having "economists . . . whose connection with the bureau would be to the public a guarantee that investigations and reports issued by authority of the Bureau would be scientifically exact." It is notable that in all of their correspondence, Rockefeller and Greene never thought economists were needed to help businessmen make business decisions. Rather, they thought the main purpose of economists was to serve as a mediator that transformed private "interests" into "exact" facts. At the end of the memo, which both Morgan and Aldrich signed off on, Greene recommended that the head of the bureau be Edwin Gay, the first dean of Harvard Business School and the man who had brought Frederick Winslow Taylor on as a faculty member. Five years later, after some unforeseen obstacles, Gay would become the first president of the National Bureau of Economic Research. Roughly fifteen years after that, the NBER would play a central role in the invention of GNP.[5]

In 1912, Rockefeller had good reason to be enamored with the idea of an independent bureau that would refute "harmful statements." That year, the United Mine Workers had returned to the southern Colorado coal fields owned and operated by Rockefeller's Colorado and Fuel Corporation. Taking over for his father around the turn of the century, the younger Rockefeller had managed to crush the miners' strike in 1904—yet the Colorado labor movement refused to go away. In response, Rockefeller plowed money into paternalist company towns with club rooms and public baths in an attempt to educate his mostly foreign workforce in the American way of life. Rockefeller was clearly no stranger to "education campaigns," and his desire for an economic research bureau that would temper class conflict and legitimize corporate capitalism was consistent with his other tactical moves.[6]

Around when the labor conflict in the Colorado coal mines began to deteriorate once more, Rockefeller's plans for a private research bureau were put into high gear. After being approached by Jerome Greene on Rockefeller's behalf, Edwin Gay agreed to establish a committee of five economists who would advise in the founding of the bureau. Wary that Rockefeller's business interests would destroy the legitimacy of the institution, Gay and the committee noted in their report that the bureau "should not, at the outset, attempt work directly educational in character. Although it is recognized that there is great need of popular education in economics, it is inadvisable that such work of propaganda be undertaken as the first or main task of an institution for scientific research." Gay warned Rockefeller that the bureau should "not only gain the confidence of the scientific world, but it should also be careful to avoid, as far as is consistent with its object, the popular prejudice which might conceivable attend the enterprise generously supported by a great capitalist."[7]

Soon after Greene approached Gay, yet days before the committee met, the situation in Colorado generated such a crisis of corporate legitimacy that Rockefeller no longer merely wanted such a bureau—he desperately needed one. For when the smoke cleared on the Colorado National Guard and Colorado Fuel and Iron's attack on a tent colony of striking coal miners on April 20, 1914, two women and eleven children had been burned to death and Rockefeller's reputation—as well as the reputation of corporate capital in general—was in ashes. "The Ludlow Massacre" was what the country was calling it, a tagline so powerful that even Jerome Greene and Rockefeller's pioneering army of PR men couldn't outspin it.[8]

If Rockefeller dreamed of an expert-run research institution that legitimized corporate capitalism through varying price-based indicators, what he experienced following the Ludlow Massacre was an entirely different factfinding body in the form of the federal government's Commission on Industrial Relations (CIR). Headed by Kansas labor lawyer Frank Walsh, the CIR's public hearings were not a product of the pricing of progressivism but rather one of the last remnants of nineteenth-century free labor and Populism. Reminiscent of the first founders of the Massachusetts Bureau of Labor Statistics in the early 1870s, Walsh, in his questioning of witnesses, focused less on dry price statistics and more on heated moral questions that included exploitative labor practices, industrial democracy, and abysmal working conditions. Such an investigative body spelled disaster for Rockefeller, who was unable to deflect the charges against him with cost-of-living graphs or economic growth statistics. A nation watched as the richest man in the world was forced to listen as Walsh excoriated him for his complicity in the Ludlow Massacre.[9]

Accusations that he killed for coal would only intensify Rockefeller's interest in digging for data. Only now he was more willing to listen to Edwin Gay's advice. In an undated internal memo likely written shortly after Gay's report and the Ludlow Massacre, the foundation continued to note how the bureau was needed because "unrest is widespread"; its "objective" would be "to create a saner attitude on economic and social problems." In the following paragraph, however, under the segment on "obstacles," the memo accepted the fact that they would have "to avoid popular distrust of any institution founded by capitalists. Tact in subjects first undertaken." At the end of the memo, penciled in—perhaps by Rockefeller himself—is the phrase "would need men *outside* of us."[10]

Which "tactful" research project would not conflict with Rockefeller's goal of placating "unrest" while also presenting corporate capitalism in a more positive light? In Gay's committee report, the choice had been easy: the bureau, Gay had advised, should focus on cost-of-living figures and the "collection of data relating to prices, including with the prices of commodities, wages and rents." The Rockefeller Foundation was on board. In the summer of 1914, a second memo by Jerome Greene noted that "the authority" of the research group would depend on its reputation, which "can best be gained by a preliminary study like that of prices."[11]

The Great War, however, broke out soon after Gay had completed his committee report, and the plan for the bureau was temporarily shelved. Gay, meanwhile, would go on to head the War Industries Board, a position that allowed him to gain crucial experience in the bureaucratic collection of enormous amounts of data. Perhaps World War I's greatest impact on the rise of GNP, however, was not Gay's work during the war but rather the installation of a federal income tax. Although Irving Fisher lamented in 1916 that there was no good income data in the United States, by 1920 such data was readily available to economists. As a result, Gay and other NBER leaders quickly turned their attention from more general studies on "prices" to more precise research on income.[12]

Yet while World War I helped bring along national income accounting, it was still private business that was in the statistical driver's seat. Further evidence of corporate capital's crucial role in the formation of the NBER can be found in the fact that the man responsible for reigniting the plan for a bureau after the war was Malcolm Rorty, a top executive at AT&T and a close colleague of CEO Theodore Vail, one of the men who had attended (and perhaps initiated) that first 1912 meeting in which the idea of the bureau had originally been floated. In 1919, Rorty reached out to Max Farrand at the Commonwealth Fund, a philanthropic organization funded mostly by corporate oil, in hopes of getting the ball rolling again on the bureau. Far savvier than Rockefeller, Rorty knew how to speak the language of both corporate power and objective science. He opened his letter by noting that his attempt to organize such a bureau was "largely in connection with efforts being made to set up a campaign of education in opposition to Bolshevism in this country." In the very next line, however, Rorty reassured Farrand that it would be a "wholly independent Bureau of Research . . . established on a truly scientific and independent basis."[13]

Rorty was a farseeing corporate liberal, the kind who believed that stabilizing corporate capitalism and quelling a growing socialist movement required both real social reforms and a general statistical awareness not only of economic growth but also of economic inequality. He also believed that if the bureau was to gain a reputation as an apolitical institution, it would have to bring the labor movement into the fold. Rorty smartly convinced N. I. Stone, a Marx-reading, left-leaning technocrat and onetime statistician of the U.S. Tariff Board, to join his efforts to jump-start the bureau. While driven by different political agendas, both men were interested in uncovering not only the aggregated income of society but also how it was distributed. By the end of the year, thanks in large part to Rorty's talents of persuasion, the National Bureau of Economic Research was founded.[14]

The words "National Bureau" make it sound like a public institution, but it was anything but, as it was privately run and initially funded by the Commonwealth Fund and the Carnegie Foundation. Only a year after its founding, NBER's Oliver Knauth—one of the bureau's leading experts on national income accounting—was already in contact with the Rockefeller Foundation for additional funding. "The NBER called yesterday to say they are getting into an exceedingly tight place financially," reads a memo of the Rockefeller Foundation from 1922. As he lobbied for money, Knauth emphasized to the foundation that the NBER's first report—*Income in the United States*— "will repay those, who have helped the bureau, for their confidence."[15]

Judging by the number of times the bureau (and its future in-house historians) made sure to mention that the board included "every shade of social and political opinion," one might assume that Rorty had dramatically changed the objectives of the bureau since those first Wall Street meetings. But this does not seem to be the case. As one of Rockefeller's assistants pointed out after the formation of the bureau, the contours of the NBER were very much those "developed in connection with an original study made by the [Rockefeller] Foundation under Mr. Greene." That said, the fear of labor uprisings had led to one new and important statistical wrinkle: the NBER's first report would seek to estimate not only the aggregated income of the nation but how it was divided among the American people.[16]

Historians rightly credit NBER's Simon Kuznets with the founding of the GNP metric during the Great Depression. The core principles behind this indicator, however, can already be found in the bureau's first report on national income from 1920. Developing two different ways to estimate national income in order to double-check their work, the bureau concluded that the national income of the United States had grown from $28.8 million in 1909 to $61.0 billion in 1918. In so doing, the economists of the NBER were clearly envisioning the nation more as an income-generating capital investment than as a democratic society of citizens. "The task of putting a figure on the National Income," the report explained, echoing the nineteenth-century developments traced in this book, "is more like the task of valuing a railway system." At the center of the report, meanwhile, appeared the kind of national income figures we now know as GDP. Taking war inflation into account through the use of price indices, the report presented an image of progress to its readers by noting that per capita income had risen from $333 to $372, a figure "much larger in the United States than in any other country."[17]

The report took a genuine interest in economic distribution as well, far more than future, post–World War II NBER reports. Nevertheless, it seemed eager to place a somewhat positive spin on the distribution of wealth, especially in regard to large corporations. For instance, it smartly combined wage laborers and salaried management in its conclusions, a classification that allowed the NBER to claim that employees received around 70 percent of a corporation's income while capital received only 30 percent. Appearing only a year after the United States had experienced an unprecedented wave of strikes following the end of World War I, it appears as if the report sought to defuse class tensions and socialist uprisings by repeating, on numerous occasions, that wages alone did not reflect the "share of labor" since "there is a great deal of work done that is not in the form of agreed-upon wages or salary but rather in the form profits (often referred to by economists as the 'wages of management')." Using an age-old argument by pro-business thinkers to blur the class lines between labor and capital, the report asserted that using income data to measure the "share of labor" was impossible.[18]

While few Americans read the NBER's report, such national income and wealth statistics soon had a cultural impact on Americans' conceptions of themselves and their nation. In a celebratory article from 1925 titled "Uncle Sam Counts His Fabulous Wealth," the *New York Times* cited NBER-backed census figures in order to declare that "Uncle Sam is the nabob of nations." Marking America's "worth" at $320,803,862,000, the article noted that this sum is "undoubtedly the greatest accumulation of material riches in the history of the world" and far more than the value of France, which "was worth 67 billions and Germany, according to her finance minister, but 35." Comparing nation-state values as if they were Model T's or Florida real estate, this mid-1920s article reflected the emerging hegemony of the pricing of progress and the gospel of growth. "No other country has grown rich so fast as the United States, according to statisticians of the National City Bank," the article declared, "a ratio of increase far in excess of that indicated by the generally accepted wealth estimates from other countries." Hovering over the entire article was an image of a smiling Uncle Sam, lying on an endless pile of moneybags.[19]

By the late 1950s, GNP had been born and the NBER had become a prominent fixture in the American political establishment. A *New York Times* piece on the bureau from 1958—a relatively bad year for "the economy"—opened by referring to the corporate-funded NBER as a "non-partisan" and "independent research organization." The article then went on to cite the "official objective" of the bureau, which was "to encourage, in the broadest and most liberal manner, investigation, research and discovery, and the application of knowledge to the well being of mankind." In the following paragraph, the article listed the statistical indicators generated by the bureau so that it could accomplish its aforementioned objective:

> National income, capital formation and its financing, production and productivity, labor problems, prices, business cycles, international economic relations and foreign economies, finance and investment, governmental activity and finances, and economic structures and growth.

With only an amorphous mention of "labor problems," the list makes plain that by the late 1950s the initial political pressure that had led the bureau to focus on economic distribution had waned. "The most liberal" fields of economic investigation into the "well being of mankind" had been narrowed to a series of inquiries into capital formation, economic growth and national income.[20]

Despite framing the bureau as wholly objective, the ideological leanings and policy prescriptions of the NBER's leaders were on display in the *New York Times* description of NBER president and Columbia University economics professor Arthur Burns. "No dogmatist," the article noted, "Dr. Burns nevertheless urges a tax cut of about $5 billion on a full-year basis as the most immediately feasible step in stimulating an upturn. He says that a public works program would have only a delayed effect, coming into play months off, and by then inflation might be the prime problem again." A few years later, Burns—who would go on to become Federal Reserve chairman—got his wish: in the 1960s, Democrats led by President John F. Kennedy pushed through a bill that would significantly lower taxes, especially for the rich, who saw their marginal rate drop by more than 20 percentage points. It was a sign of things to come. In the 1980s, Republicans inspired by Milton Friedman and led by President Ronald Reagan would continue this policy, dropping the top marginal rate 40 percentage points more.[21]

Burns (and his most famous protégé at the bureau, Milton Friedman) preferred tax cuts in part because many of the relevant social considerations that support public works projects—such as class mobility, communal solidarity, racial justice, and the empowerment of the poor through a sense of economic security, dignity, and purpose—were nowhere to be found in the NBER's dollar-denominated databases. As the years passed and the NBER and its economic indicators gained more and more political, social, and cultural traction, the pricing of progress banished such fundamental concerns from American economic policy. Yet the everyday consequences of these crucial, non-pecuniary life issues—and their statistical marginalization—remained all too real. Unlike our annual taxes, we cannot price the social costs of America's pricing of progress. But that does not mean they are not there.[22]

The rise of GDP was a long time coming. Long before the NBER or Simon Kuznets came along, the likes of James Glen, Alexander Hamilton, Samuel Blodget Jr., George Tucker, Hinton Helper, and David Wells—to name but a few of the stars of this book—all tried to develop similar statistical indicators that measured the money-generating capacities of the American people. Much like GDP's national income accounting, these economic indicators treated and quantified American society and its inhabitants not as market commodities or consumer goods but more like factors of production or capital goods whose value could only be gauged by calculating the amount of monetary income or cash flow they annually generated. In this sense, the invention of GDP was the final step not only in the pricing of progress but also the capitalization of American life. Just as investors examined the revenue flows of their real estate, stock dividends, or industrial machines, so too did American macroeconomists come to gauge "economic growth" by measuring the aggregated flow of money produced by the American people with the help of their natural and industrial resources.

That said, there is one important difference between GDP and some of the previous forms of capitalization documented in this book. The likes of William Petty, Thomas Jefferson, and Irving Fisher did not believe it was sufficient to just measure the income-generating productivity flows of the people. Taking things one step further, they sought to discount (or capitalize) this flow of income into a present stock of wealth. This is what allowed Petty to argue not only that the average English laborer creates 7 pence a day, but that he or she is *worth* £138 (or in Fisher's case 250 years later, $2900). The economists who developed GDP and national income accounting, on the other hand, did not take this final step. While GDP measures how much the average American produces (and thus also consumes), it does not examine how much they are theoretically worth as a stock of wealth. Such measures did exist in the mid- to late-twentieth-century, used mostly by government agents in cost-benefit analyses, but they were eventually marginalized in favor of other forms of human monetary valuation.[23]

This, however, does not mean that the notion of human capital disappeared. Far from it. In 1958, the same year the *New York Times* article on the NBER appeared, Jacob Mincer published his epochal article "Investment in Human Capital and Personal Income Distribution." As I have shown, the idea of humans as capital has deep roots in English and American history, reaching back to the enclosure of lands and enslavement of peoples in the seventeenth and eighteenth centuries. Yet it was only in the 1960s, when Mincer joined forces with Gary Becker and began publishing the *Journal of Political Economy,* that the actual term "human capital" exploded onto the scene, becoming the most dominant approach by labor economists for both quantifying people and explaining inequality. Following in the footsteps of their capitalizing forefathers, Mincer and Becker viewed human beings as moneymaking assets. According to them, the difference between the high earnings of the rich and the low earnings of the poor was greatly determined by how much each individual produced. This productivity, in turn, was in large part determined by how much one chose to "invest" in him- or herself, mostly through education and training. To measure the success or failure of one's investment in one's own human capital, economists developed complex econometric measures that relied heavily on personal income earnings surveys supplied and funded by the American government. By 1966, there would be 800 articles published on human capital theory; by 1976, 2,000. Equating—like so many economists before them—individual productivity with individual compensation, the message behind these studies was nearly always the same: if you made a lot of money, it was not only because you yourself (and not, say, the subordinates who worked for you) had generated this cash flow but also because you had invested wisely in yourself. Your net worth was an indicator of your self-worth.[24]

Today, a half century later, human capital has become not just a dominant economic theory but also a hegemonic cultural conception. Investmentality is everywhere. Google the term "invest in yourself," and one of the top results (there are millions) explains how "investing in yourself may be the most profitable investment you ever make. It yields not only future returns, but often a current pay-off as well. The surest way to be successful is to place a priority on investing in both personal and professional growth." Billionaire Warren Buffett advises young people that if "you've maximized your talent, you've got a tremendous asset that can return ten-fold." Numerous self-help sites such as Entrepreneur.com strongly recommend the "3 percent solution for personal development"—just like retaining earnings in a corporation, these gurus recommend investing 3 percent of your annual income in yourself in order to boost your productivity.[25]

Many Americans today see not only themselves as an investment but their nation as well. There is no better evidence of this phenomenon than the unprecedented election of billionaire businessman Donald Trump, whom both CBS News and *U.S. News and World Report* casually referred to as "America's CEO." Trump ran on a platform that equated America with a business, arguing that he would run the country much the way he runs his investments. Trump's treatment of America as an investment was one of the keys to his victory. When a journalist from the *Atlantic* asked Trump voters in 2015 to write in to explain why they supported him, many responded, like Trump, by describing the

United States as a business. "He has successfully led a $20 billion a year family business employing over 20,000 people," wrote one Trump supporter. "He has a proven record of managing money, minimizing debt and maximizing wealth that can be directly transferred to leading our country out of financial ruin." Many of Trump's appointees share this capitalizing vision for America. "I see each individual as human capital, that can be developed to become part of the engine that drives the nation," declared Housing Secretary Ben Carson in 2017 as he sought to explain why he believed poor people should get off welfare.[26] Unlike a majority of Americans, progress-pricing economic indicators embraced the Trump presidency with zeal as investors came to recognize that Trump would run the country with an eye toward corporate profits. The Dow Jones Industrial Average rose 257 points the day after his election and a staggering 14 percent by his one-hundredth day in the White House.

By exploring alternative measures that have fallen by the wayside of history, this book not only historicizes and politicizes the pricing of progress and capitalization of American life but also aims to serve as a "usable past" by offering past forms of social quantification as inspiration for future metrics. Recently, Thomas Piketty and other economists have managed to bring inequality metrics back into the mainstream. This is a significant feat, but there is far more to be done. Placing Americans' well-being, rather than their money-generating capacity, at the center of a national statistical vision might offer opportunities to measure not only the difference between what we earn and what we produce but also countless unpriceable aspects of our lives: loneliness and community, incarceration and addiction, libraries and non-commodities, stress and security, dignity and happiness, solidarity and tolerance, racial justice and gender equality, environmental protection and global sustainability.[27]

That said, a central theme of this book is that the ascent of economic indicators has been closely tied to the rise of American capitalism. It would be naive to suggest that simply replacing one metric with another could have a revolutionary effect on society. American citizens could push their government to institutionalize alternative, non-pecuniary benchmarks such as the gross national happiness measure, used in Bhutan. Yet unless their 401(k) also began maximizing happiness, or their job security became dependent on annual rates of happiness growth, such indicators probably would not carry much economic, social, or political weight. There are no quick fixes. If we are interested in changing the way we measure progress, we need to change not only our metrics but our world.[28]

NOTES
ACKNOWLEDGMENTS
INDEX

NOTES

1. Weld's sermon described in Robert Abzug, *Cosmos Crumbling: American Reform and the Religious Imagination* (New York: Oxford University Press, 1994), 96.

2. New York State Temperance Society, *Circular of the New York State Temperance Society, to the Citizens of the State* (Albany, NY, 1830), 18–19.

3. Michel Foucault, "Governmentality," in *The Foucault Effect: Studies in Governmentality*, ed. G. Burchell, C. Gordon, and P. Miller (Chicago: University of Chicago Press, 1991), 87–105.

4. New York State Temperance Society, *Circular,* 19. One typical definition of human capital is "the productive capacities of human beings as income producing agents": Sherwin Rosen, "Human Capital," in *The New Palgrave Dictionary of Economics,* 2nd ed., ed. Steven N. Durlauf and Lawrence E. Blume (Basingstoke: Palgrave Macmillan, 2008). For the history of the idea of human capital, see B. F. Kiker, "The Historical Roots of the Concept of Human Capital," *Journal of Political Economy* 74, no. 5 (October 1966): 481–499.

5. Irving Fisher, *A Clear Answer to President Taft, the Most Prominent Anti-National Prohibitionist* (Boston: Massachusetts Anti-Saloon League, 1918), 4–5; Richard Hofstadter, *The Age of Reform* (New York: Knopf, 1955).

6. Irving Fisher, "National Vitality: Its Wastes and Conservation," 61st Congress, 2nd Sess., Senate Document No. 419 (Washington, DC: GPO, 1910), 634, 740; Irving Fisher, *The Costs of Tuberculosis in the United States and Their Reduction* (New Haven, CT: Yale University Press, 1909); Irving Fisher and Emily Robbins, *Memorial Relating to the Conservation of Human Life as Contemplated by Bill Providing for a U.S. Public Health Service* (Washington, DC: Government Printing Office, 1912).

7. "Economic Value of Righteousness," *Baltimore Sun,* February 8, 1897; "The Cost of Illiteracy," *Austin Statesman,* July 30, 1917; "More in Asylums than Colleges Says Expert," *New York Tribune,* March 16, 1913.

8. Centers for Disease Control and Prevention, "Excessive Drinking Costs U.S. $223.5 Billion," www.cdc.gov/features/alcoholconsumption, accessed April 8, 2013; Thomas Insel, "Mental Health Awareness Month: By the Numbers," National Institute of Mental Health, May 15, 2015, www.nimh.nih.gov/about/director/2015/mental-health-awareness-month-by-the-numbers.shtml; T. R. Insel, "Assessing the Economic Costs of Serious Mental Illness," *American Journal of*

Psychiatry 165, no. 6 (June 2008): 663–665; Literacy Partners, "Literacy in New York," https://literacypartners.org/literacy-in-america/impact-of-illiteracy, accessed April 8, 2013;

9. For varying arguments on markets, commodification, and the rise of capitalism, see Karl Polanyi, *The Great Transformation* (Boston: Beacon Press, 1944); Joyce Appleby, *The Relentless Revolution: A History of Capitalism* (New York: Norton, 2010); Charles Sellers, *The Market Revolution: Jacksonian America, 1815–1846* (New York: Oxford University Press, 1991); William Cronon, *Nature's Metropolis: Chicago and the Great West* (New York: Norton, 1991); Ellen Meikins Wood, *The Origin of Capitalism* (New York: Monthly Review Press, 1999).

10. For definitions of capitalization, see Martin Giraudeau, "The Business of Continuity," in *Reset Modernity!*, ed. Bruno Latour (Cambridge, MA: MIT Press, 2016), 278–285.

11. Martin Giraudeau, "Towards a History of Capitalization," paper presented at the History of Capitalism seminar, Harvard University, Cambridge, MA, October 2015, Muniesa quoted on 3. See also Fabian Muniesa et al., *Capitalization: A Cultural Guide* (Paris: Presses des Mines, 2017). T. S. Lambert, "The Money or Commercial Value of Man," *Hunt's Merchants Magazine* 35 (July 1856): 34–37.

12. Pope Francis, "Apostolic Exhortation: Evangelii Gaudium," November 23, 2013; James Pethokoukis, "JP Morgan Economist Responds to Pope's Criticism of Capitalism," *Business Insider,* December 2, 2013.

13. Diane Coyle, *GDP: A Brief but Affectionate History* (Princeton, NJ: Princeton University Press, 2014); Joseph Stiglitz, Amartya Sen, and Jean-Paul Fitoussi, *Mismeasuring Our Lives: Why GDP Doesn't Add Up* (New York: New Press, 2010), xviii; Dirk Philipsen, *The Little Big Number: How GDP Came to Rule the World and What to Do about It* (Princeton, NJ: Princeton University Press, 2015); Andrew Yarrow, *Measuring America: How Economic Growth Came to Define American Greatness in the Late Twentieth Century* (Amherst: University of Massachusetts Press, 2011); Ehsan Masood, *The Great Invention: The Story of GDP and the Making and Unmaking of the Modern World* (New York: Pegasus Books, 2016); Phillip Lepenies, *The Power of a Single Number: A Political History of GDP* (New York: Columbia University Press, 2016); Zachary Karabell, *The Leading Indicators: A Short History of the Numbers That Rule the World* (New York: Simon and Schuster, 2014); Dan Hirschman, "Inventing the Economy (or, How we Learned to Stop Worrying and Love the GDP)," Ph.D. diss., University of Michigan, 2016.

14. Philipsen, *Little Big Number,* 1. On the construction of the concepts "developed nation" and "developing nation," see James Ferguson, *The Anti-Politics Machine: "Development," Depoliticization, and Bureaucratic Power in Lesotho* (Cambridge: Cambridge University Press, 1990). On the Chinese government's use of GDP for provincial promotions, see Li Hongbon and Li-An Zhou, "Political Turnover

and Economic Performance: The Incentive Role of Personnel Control in China," *Journal of Public Economics* 89 (September 2005): 1743–1762. For GDP and global warming, see "Stern Review: The Economics of Climate Change," executive summary, www.sternreview.org.uk. For a general overview of GDP, see Jon Gertner, "The Rise and Fall of the G.D.P.," *New York Times,* May 13, 2010.

15. Michael Sandel, *What Money Can't Buy: The Moral Limits of Markets* (New York: Farrar, Straus and Giroux, 2013), 5; Stiglitz, Sen, and Fitoussi, *Mismeasuring Our Lives,* xvii, xix, xx.

16. Along with the aforementioned literature on GDP, see Guy Alchon, *The Invisible Hand of Planning: Capitalism, Social Science and the State in the 1920s* (Princeton, NJ: Princeton University Press, 1985); R. Fogel, E. Fogel, M. Guglielmo, and N. Grotte, *Political Arithmetic: Simon Kuznets and the Empirical Tradition in Economics* (Chicago: University of Chicago Press, 2013; Adam Tooze, *Statistics and the German State 1900–1945: The Making of Modern Economic Knowledge* (Cambridge: Cambridge University Press, 2001); Thomas Stapleford, *The Cost of Living in America: A Political History of Economic Statistics, 1880–2000* (New York: Cambridge University Press, 2009). On the birth of "the economy," see Timothy Mitchell, "Fixing the Economy," *Cultural Studies* 12, no. 1 (1998): 82–101; U. Kalpagam, "Colonial Governmentality and the 'Economy,'" *Economy and Society* 29, no. 3 (2000): 418–438; Daniel Breslau, "Economics Invents the Economy: Mathematics, Statistics, and Models in the Work of Irving Fisher and Wesley Mitchell," *Theory and Society* 32, no. 3 (June 2003): 379–411; Timothy Shenk, "Inventing the American Economy," Ph.D. diss., Columbia University, 2016.

17. Polanyi, *Great Transformation,* 33, 40; Christopher Lasch, *The True and Only Heaven: Progress and Its Critics* (New York: Norton, 1991), 180. See also Ronald Meek, *The Social Science and the Ignoble Savage* (New York: Cambridge University Press, 1976); W. W. Rostow, *Theories of Economic Growth from David Hume to the Present* (New York: Oxford University Press, 1990). On the idea of progress, see Sidney Pollard, *The Idea of Progress: History and Society* (New York: Basic Books, 1969).

18. In seeking to tell the story of economic quantification prior to the twentieth century, I have found the following works invaluable: Patricia Cline Cohen, *A Calculating People: The Spread of Numeracy in Early America* (Chicago: University of Chicago Press, 1982); Judy L. Klein and Mary S. Morgan, eds., *The Age of Economic Measurement* (Durham, NC: Duke University Press, 2001); Paul Studenski, *The Income of Nations, Part One: History* (New York: New York University Press, 1958); Mary O. Furner and Barry Supple, eds., *The State and Economic Knowledge: The American and British Experiences* (Cambridge: Cambridge University Press, 1990); Stapleford, *Cost of Living,* chs. 1–2; Tore Frangsmyr, J. L.

Heilbron, and R. Rider, eds., *The Quantifying Spirit in the Eighteenth Century* (Berkeley: University of California Press, 1991); Judy L. Klein, *Statistical Visions in Time: A History of Time Series Analysis, 1662–1938* (Cambridge: Cambridge University Press, 1997), 23–133; Michael Zakim, *Accounting for Capitalism: The Business Clerk as Social Revolutionary* (Chicago: University of Chicago Press, 2017); Theodore Porter, *Trust in Numbers: The Pursuit of Objectivity in Science and Public Life* (Princeton, NJ: Princeton University Press, 1997); Margo Anderson, *The American Census: A Social History* (New Haven, CT: Yale University Press, 1988).

19. See Ian Hacking, *The Taming of Chance* (Cambridge: Cambridge University Press, 1900); Theodore Porter, *The Rise of Statistical Thinking 1820–1900* (Princeton, NJ: Princeton University Press, 1986); Stephen M. Stigler, *The History of Statistics: The Measurement of Uncertainty before 1900* (Cambridge, MA: Harvard University Press, 1986); B. S. Yamey, "Scientific Bookkeeping and the Rise of Capitalism," *Economic History Review* 1 (1949): 99–113; Jonathan Levy, "Accounting for Profit and the History of Capital," *Critical Historical Studies* 1, no. 2 (Fall 2014): 171–214; Bruce G. Carruthers and Wendy Nelson Espeland, "Accounting for Rationality: Double-Entry Bookkeeping and the Rhetoric of Economic Rationality," *American Journal of Sociology* 97, no. 1 (1991): 31–69.

20. Michael Zakim and Gary Kornblith, "Introduction," in *Capitalism Takes Command: The Social Transformation of Nineteenth Century America* (Chicago: University of Chicago Press, 2011), 1.

21. On numeracy of American women, see Ellen Hartigan-O'Conner, *The Ties That Buy: Women and Commerce in Revolutionary America* (Philadelphia: University of Pennsylvania Press, 2009). For slaves, see Tom Wickman, "Arithmetic and Afro-Atlantic Pastoral Protest: The Place of (In)numeracy in Gronniosaw and Equiano," *Atlantic Studies* 8 (2011): 189–212.

22. Today, in other words, economic indicators are culturally hegemonic. See Jackson Lears, "The Concept of Cultural Hegemony: Problems and Possibilities," *American Historical Review* 90 (June 1985): 567–593.

23. James Henry Hammond, *Selection from the Letters and Speeches of James H. Hammond* (New York, 1866), 315.

24. J. Pease Norton, "The Economic Advisability of Inaugurating a National Department of Health," *Albany Law Journal,* November 1906, 338.

25. Jeffrey Sklansky, "Labor, Money and the Financial Turn in the History of Capitalism," *Labor: Studies in Working-Class History of the Americas* 11, no. 1 (2014): 35; Sven Beckert, "History of American Capitalism," in *American History Now,* ed. Eric Foner and Lisa McGirr (Philadelphia: Temple University Press, 2011), 314–335.

26. Paul Starr and William Alonso, eds., *The Politics of Numbers* (New York: Russell Sage Foundation, 1986); Wendy Nelson Espeland and Michael Sauder, "Rank-

ings and Reactivity: How Public Measures Shape Social Worlds," *American Journal of Sociology* 113, no. 1 (July 2007): 1–40.

27. On things that cannot be priced, see Sandel, *What Money Can't Buy*; Vivianna Zelizer, *Pricing the Priceless Child: The Changing Social Value of Children* (Princeton, NJ: Princeton University Press, 1994); Lisa Heinzerling and Frank Ackerman, *Priceless: On Knowing the Price of Everything and the Value of Nothing* (New York: Norton, 2004); Steven Kelman, "Cost-Benefit Analysis: An Ethical Critique," *Regulation* 5, no. 1 (1981): 33–40.

28. Frederick Winslow Taylor, *The Principles of Scientific Management* (New York: Harper, 1911), 7.

29. For economic growth's role in improving American lives, see Robert J. Gordon, *The Rise and Fall of American Growth: The U.S. Standard of Living since the Civil War* (Princeton, NJ: Princeton University Press, 2016).

1. THE POLITICAL ARITHMETIC OF PRICE

1. Joan Thirsk, "Enclosing and Engrossing, 1500–1640," in *Agricultural Change: Policy and Practice: Chapters from the Agrarian History of England and Wales*, vol. 3, *1500–1750*, ed. Joan Thirsk (Cambridge: Cambridge University, 1990), 54–125; Robert Brenner, "Agrarian Class Structure and Economic Development in Pre-industrial Europe," *Past and Present* 70 (1976): 30–75; Robert Allen, *Enclosure and the Yeoman* (Oxford: Clarendon Press, 1992); Mark Overton, *Agricultural Revolution in England: The Transformation of the Agrarian Economy 1500–1850* (Cambridge: Cambridge University Press, 1996).

2. Stephen Primatt, *The City and Country Purchaser and Builder* (London, 1680), 15. For changing notions of property, see C. B. McPherson, "Capitalism and the Changing Concept of Property," in *Feudalism, Capitalism and Beyond*, ed. Eugene Kamenka and R. S. Nealde (London: Hodder and Stoughton, 1975), 105–124.

3. On the percentage of landlords, see Eric Kerridge, *The Agricultural Revolution* (London: Routledge, 1967), 24; G. E. Mingay, *English Landed Society in the Eighteenth Century* (London: Routledge, 1963), 24; G. E. Mingay, *The Gentry: The Rise and Fall of a Ruling Class* (New York: Longman, 1976), 57–60. On the income flow of freehold peasants, see F. M. L. Thompson, "The Social Distribution of Landed Property in England since the Sixteenth Century," *Economic History Review* 19, no. 3 (1966): 505–517; J. R. Wordie, "The Chronology of English Enclosure, 1500–1914," *Economic History Review* 36, no. 4 (Nov. 1983): 486, 494.

4. Primatt, *City and Country*, 15; Lawrence Stone, *The Crisis of the Aristocracy, 1558–1641* (Oxford: Oxford University Press, 1965), 153–159; Brenner, "Agrarian Class Structure," 59–63. On higher rents after enclosure, see Allen, *Enclosure and the*

Yeoman, 16–17. On increases in productivity, see E. L. Jones, "Agriculture and Economic Growth in England, 1660–1750: Agricultural Change," *Journal of Economic History* 25 (1965): 1–18. On the Enlightenment and the cultural origins of improvement and productivity increases, see Joel Mokyr, *A Culture of Growth: The Origins of the Modern Economy* (Princeton, NJ: Princeton University Press, 2016); Paul Slack, *The Invention of Improvement: Information and Material Progress in Seventeenth Century England* (Oxford: Oxford University Press, 2014).

5. For the abstraction of labor and land, see Joyce Appleby, *Economic Thought and Ideology in Seventeenth-Century England* (Princeton, NJ: Princeton University Press, 1978), 20; Karl Polanyi, *The Great Transformation* (Boston: Beacon Press, 1944). For the etymology of "rent," see *Oxford English Dictionary,* 3rd ed., 2009 update, s.v. "rent, n.¹" "rent, n.²"

6. For the economics of feudal societies, see Witold Kula, *An Economic Theory of the Feudal System: Towards a Model of the Polish Economy, 1500–1800* (London: New Left Books, 1976), 29–39. For the marginal role of money as measure of value in feudal life, see Witold Kula, *Measures and Men,* trans. R. Szreter (Princeton, NJ: Princeton University Press, 1986), 194–195; Emmanuel Le Roy Ladurie, *The Peasants of Languedoc,* trans. John Day (Urbana: University of Illinois Press, 1974); Michael Postan, *The Medieval Economy and Society* (Harmondsworth: Penguin, 1974).

7. For the monastic survey, see Peter J. Bowden, "Agricultural Prices, Farm Profits and Rents, 1500–1640," in Joan Thirsk and Peter J. Bowden, ed., *Chapters from the Agrarian History of England and Wales: Volume 1* (Cambridge: Cambridge University Press, 1990), 107. On the relationship between rent rates and market values, see Kula, *Feudal System,* 29, 67; Keith Tribe, *Land, Labour and Economic Discourse* (London: Routledge, 1978), 27–32.

8. Brenner, "Agrarian Class Structure," 45; Robert Brenner, "The Agrarian Roots of European Capitalism," *Past and Present* 97 (1982): 29, 34–35. On the sweeping away of feudal obligation, see J. R. T. Hughes, *Social Control in the Colonial Economy* (Charlottesville: University of Virginia Press, 1976), 29, 41–44. For the changing conception of rent, see Tribe, *Land, Labour and Economic Discourse,* 25–27; Stone, *Crisis of the Aristocracy,* 303–332, esp. 309; Kerridge, *Agriculture Revolution,* 332.

9. Robert Loder, *Robert Loder's Farm Accounts, 1610–1620,* ed. G. E. Fussell (London: Royal Historical Society, 1936), xxiii–xxvii, 92–105. For Loder as nascent capitalist, see R. A. Bryer, "The Genesis of the Capitalist Farmer: Towards a Marxist Accounting History of the Origins of the English Agricultural Revolution," *Critical Perspectives on Accounting* 17, no. 4 (May 2006): 367–397.

10. Henry Best, *Rural Economy in Yorkshire in 1641,* ed. George Andrews (London, 1857), 38, 130. For the Royal Society survey, see R. Lennard, "English Agriculture under Charles II: The Evidence of the Royal Society's Enquiries," *Economic*

History Review 4 (1932): 39–41; Joyce Bankes and Eric Kerridge, eds., *The Early Records of Bankes Family at Winstanley* (Manchester: Manchester University Press, 1973), 19. For other productivity measures, see Bowden, *Economic Change*, 71–79; Craig Muldrew, *Food, Energy and the Creation of Industriousness: Work and Material Culture in Agrarian England, 1550–1780* (Cambridge: Cambridge University Press, 2011), 260–298.

11. Quoted in Barry Coward, *The Stanleys, Lord Stanley and the Earls of Debry: The Origins, Wealth and Power of a Landowning Family* (Manchester: Manchester University Press, 1983), 94; Claire E. Cross, *The Puritan Earl: The Life of Henry Hastings, Third Earl of Huntington 1536–1595* (New York: Palgrave McMillan, 1966), 105.

12. On "years of purchase" and the pricing of present values by future flows, see William Deringer, *Calculated Values: Finance, Politics, and the Quantitative Age, 1688–1776* (Cambridge, MA: Harvard University Press, forthcoming); Primatt, *City and Country Purchaser*, 4–5, 15–17.

13. Henry Phillips, *The Purchasers Pattern: Shewing the True Value of Any Purchase of Land or Houses, by Lease or Otherwise* (London, 1653), 4; William C. Baer, "The Institution of Residential Investment in Seventeenth-Century London," *Business History Review* 76, no. 3 (Autumn 2002): 541–542. See also H. J. Habakkuk, "The Long-Term Rate of Interest and the Price of Land in the Seventeenth Century," *Economic History Review* 1 (1952): 26–45.

14. See Isaac Newton, *Tables of Renewing and Purchasing of the Leases of Cathedral Churches and Colleges* (Cambridge, 1686), 22. See also Primatt, *City and Country Purchaser*, 4; William Leybourn, *Panarithmologia* (London, 1693), D4; Deringer, *Calculated Values*.

15. Gervase Markham, *A Way to Get Wealth* (London, 1660), 113; Walter Blith, *The English Improver Improved* (London, 1653), 3, 120. Similar works of the era include John Smith, *England's Improvement Reviv'd* (London, 1670), and Sir Richard Weston, *Discourse on Husbandry of Brabant and Flanders* (London, 1645).

16. W. G. Hoskins, "Harvest Fluctuations and English Economic History 1620–1759," *Agricultural History Review* 16, no. 1 (1968): 15–31; Willian Petyt, *Britannia Languens* (London, 1680), 238. For this new conception of labor, see Edgar Furniss, *The Position of the Laborer in a System of Nationalism: A Study in the Labor Theories of the Later Mercantilists* (New York: Houghton Mifflin, 1920); Ted McCormick, "Population: Modes of Seventeenth Century Demographic Thought," in *Political Economy in Early Modern Britain and Its Empire,* ed. Phillip J. Stern and Carl Wennerlind (New York: Oxford University Press), 25–46.

17. *A Discourse of the Common Weal of this Realm of England* (London, 1581), 64. Hugh Oldcastle, *A Brief Instruction and Maner How to Keepe Bookes of Accompts* (London, 1543); Charles Wilson, *Mercantilism* (London: Routledge and Paul,

1963), 10. On double-entry accounting, see Jane Gleeson-White, *Double Entry: How the Merchants of Venice Created Modern Finance* (New York: Norton, 2013); Jacob Soll, *The Reckoning: Financial Accountability and the Rise and Fall of Nations* (New York: Basic Books, 2014). See also Fernand Braudel, *The Wheels of Commerce* (Berkeley: University of California Press, 1982), 204.

18. Samuel Fortrey, *English Interest and Improvement* (London, 1663), 29, but also 3, 12, 27, 36-37; Charles Davenant, *An Essay upon the Probable Methods of Making a People Gainers in the Balance of Trade* (London, 1699), 24, 13, 53; Petyt, *Britannia Languens*, 238.

19. Sir Francis Brewster, *Essays of Trade and Navigations in Five Parts* (London, 1695), 117-118; Furniss, *Position of the Laborer*; McCormick, "Population."

20. William Petty, *Political Arithmetick* (London, 1690), preface. For Bacon and Petty, see Ted McCormick, *William Petty and the Ambitions of Political Arithmetic* (Oxford: Oxford University Press, 2009); Mary Poovey, *A History of the Modern Fact: Problems of Knowledge in the Sciences of Wealth and Society* (Chicago: University of Chicago Press, 1998), 94-116.

21. Charles Davenant, "Of the Use of Political Arithmetic in All Considerations about Trade and Revenue," in *The Political and Commercial Works of That Celebrated Writer, Charles D'Avenant*, ed. Charles Whitworth (London, 1771), 146-147; Karl Marx, *Theories of Surplus Value, Part I*, trans. Emile Burns (Moscow: Progress Publishers, 1967), 1. On Petty as the father of national income accounting, see Paul Studenski, *The Income of Nations* (New York: New York University Press, 1961), 1:11-15; Richard Stone, *Some British Empiricists in the Social Sciences, 1650-1900* (New York: Cambridge University Press, 1997), 3-48. For Petty's place in the pre-Smith history of economic thought, see E. A. Johnson, *Predecessors of Adam Smith: The Growth of British Economic Thought* (New York: Prentice Hall, 1937), 93-117.

22. David McNally, *Political Economy and the Rise of Capitalism* (Berkeley: University of California Press, 1990), 46-51; Poovey, *Modern Fact*, 120-138; McCormick, *William Petty*, 84-119.

23. For Petty's life, see Hull's introduction in Sir William Petty, *The Economic Writings of Sir William Petty*, ed. Charles Henry Hull (London, 1899), 1:xiii-xxxiii; McCormick, *William Petty*, 14-84; Thomas E. Jordan, *A Copper Farthing: Sir William Petty and His Times 1623-1687* (Sunderland: University of Sunderland Press, 2007).

24. On Ireland as experiment, see Hull, "Introduction," in Petty, *Economic Writings*, lxv-lxvi; Petty, "Political Anatomy of Ireland," in *Economic Writings*, 1:129.

25. Samuel Hartlib, *A Discoverie for Division or Setting out of Land* . . . (London, 1653). For the Hartlib Circle, see McCormick, *William Petty*, 41-44, 56-57; Carl Winnerland, "Hartlibian Political Economy and the New Culture of Credit," in *Mercantilism Reimagined*, ed. Phillip J. Stern and Carl Wennerlind (New York: Oxford University Press, 2014), 74-97; Toby C. Barnard, "The Hartlib Circle and

the Cult and Culture of Improvement in Ireland," in *Samuel Hartlib and the Universal Reformation: Studies in Intellectual Communication,* ed. Mark Greengrass, Michael Leslie, and Tim Raylor (Cambridge: Cambridge University Press, 1994), 281–329.

26. For the Down Survey maps and charts, see the Down Survey of Ireland website, Trinity College, Dublin, http://downsurvey.tcd.ie.

27. William Blackstone, *Commentaries on the Laws of England* (London, 1765); G. E. Aylmer, "The Meaning and Definition of 'Property' in Seventeenth-Century England," *Past and Present* 86 (1980): 87–97.

28. On Petty's theory of value, see Poovey, *Modern Fact,* 72–76, 128–138; Ronald Meek, *Studies in the Labor Theory of Value* (New York: Monthly Review Press, 1956), 32–44; Tony Aspromourgos, "The Invention of the Concept of Social Surplus: Petty in the Hartlib Circle," *European Journal of the History of Economic Thought* 12, no. 1 (2005): 1–24.

29. William Petty, *The Petty Papers: Some Unpublished Writings of Sir William Petty,* ed. Marquis of Lansdowne (London, 1927), 1:77; William Petty, "Treatise of Taxes and Contributions," in *Economic Writings,* 49–51.

30. Petty, "Treatise of Taxes," 43.

31. Ronald Meek recognizes Petty's use of labor time as the birth of a labor theory of value. But Petty, unlike Marx, believed it is nature that creates surplus value, not labor. Meek, *Studies in the Labor Theory of Value,* 32–40.

32. Petty, "Treatise of Taxes," 44. On such mixing of the inductive and deductive, see Poovey, *Modern Fact,* 13, 132.

33. Petty, "The Political Anatomy of Ireland," in *Economic Writings,* 181–182; Petty, "Treatise of Taxes," 45. For Petty's ongoing mission to find a commensurable unit of value other than money, see Appleby, *Economic Thought and Ideology,* 82; Phil Mirowski, *More Heat than Light* (Cambridge: Cambridge University Press, 1989), 150–153.

34. Thomas Hobbes, *Leviathan* (London, 1651), 54; C. B. Macpherson, *The Political Theory of Possessive Individualism: Hobbes to Locke* (Oxford: Oxford University Press, 1962), 37–46, 53–68. In Petty's papers, there is a reading list of philosophical works that Petty made out for his sons. The only English books on the list were by Hobbes. See Petty, *Petty Papers,* 2:5. On Hobbes's impact on Petty, see Quentin Skinner, "Thomas Hobbes and His Disciples in England and France," *Comparative Studies in Society and History* 8 (1965–1966): 153–167.

35. Petty, "Verbum Sapienti," in *Economic Writings,* 105–106.

36. Studenski, *Income of Nations,* 11–15; Stone, *Some Empiricists,* 26–31.

37. Petty, "Verbum Sapienti," in *Economic Writings,* 105–108.

38. Ibid., 108–111. Petty capitalizes people again a few years later in "Political Arithmetick," *Economic Writings,* 257. See also B. F. Kiker, "The Historical Roots of

the Concept of Human Capital," *Journal of Political Economy* 74, no. 5 (October 1966): 481–482.

39. On commodity fetishism, see Karl Marx, *Capital: A Critique of Political Economy,* vol. 1, ch. 1, sec. 4, www.marxists.org; Gyorgy Lukacs, *History and Class Consciousness: Studies in Marxist Dialectics* (Cambridge, MA: MIT Press, 1971).

40. T. C. Bernard, "Sir William Petty, Irish Landowner," in *History and Imagination: Essays in Honor of H. R. Trevor Roper,* ed. Hugh Lloyd-Jones, Valerie Pearl, and Blair Worden (London: Duckworth, 1981), 201–217; McCormick, *William Petty,* 84–117.

41. T. C. Bernard, "Sir William Petty," 201; Poovey, *Modern Fact,* 121–126.

42. Petty, *Petty Papers,* 1:90.

43. Petty, "Verbum Sapienti," 109–110; Petty, "Political Anatomy of Ireland," 147.

44. Petty, "Treatise of Taxes," 26; Petty, "Verbum Sapienti," 108.

45. Charles Tilly, *Coercion, Capital and European States, 990–1990* (Cambridge: Blackwell, 1990), 70–91, 151–161; Michael Braddick, *State Formation in Early Modern England* (Cambridge: Cambridge University Press, 2000), 11–47, 180–281; Douglass North and Barry Weingast, "Constitutions and Commitment: The Evolution of Institutions Governing Public Choice in Seventeenth Century England," *Journal of Economic History* 49, no. 4 (December 1989): 803–832. On the novel use of the word *state,* see John Guy, *Tudor England* (Oxford: Oxford University Press, 1988), 350–352.

46. Figures cited in Michael Braddick, *Parliamentary Taxation in Seventeenth Century England* (London: Boydell and Brewer, 1995), 3; For the synergy between Crown and market-oriented landholders see Stone, *Crisis of the Aristocracy,* ch. 5; Tilly, *Coercion,* 87–91, 153–159; Barrington Moore, *Social Origins of Dictatorship and Democracy* (Boston: Beacon Books, 1966), 3–40. On the shift in state policy regarding market expansion, see Carla Gardina Pestana, *The English Atlantic in the Age of Revolution 1640–1661* (Cambridge, MA: Harvard University Press, 2007).

47. On Petty and taxation, see McCormick, *William Petty,* 135–147, 156–160; Michael Braddick, *The Nerves of State: Taxation and Financing of the English State, 1558–1714* (Manchester: Manchester University Press, 1996), 114–116, 150.

48. Petty, "Treatise of Taxes," 71.

49. Petty, "Verbum Sapienti," 119; Petty, "Treatise of Taxes," 70. On the importance of legitimacy, see Braddick, *State Formation,* 1–24, 68.

50. Braddick, *State Formation,* 233–234. For state spending, see C. D. Chandaman, *The English Public Revenue* (Oxford: Clarendon Press, 1975). On the power dynamic between King and Parliament, see North and Weingast, "Constitutions and Commitment," 815–817; F. W. Maitland, *The Constitutional History of England* (Cambridge: Cambridge University Press, 1919), 280–305.

51. On liberalism, see Pierre Manent and Jerrold Seigel, *An Intellectual History of Liberalism* (Princeton, NJ: Princeton University Press, 1996). On the shift from arbitrary whims to rational policy, see North and Weingast, "Constitutions and Commitments."

52. Edward Misselden, *The Circle of Commerce* (London, 1623), 17; J. G. A. Pocock, *The Machiavellian Moment: Florentine Political Thought and the Atlantic Republic Tradition* (Princeton, NJ: Princeton University Press, 1975).

53. Yuval Noah Harrari, *Sapiens: A Brief History of Human Kind* (New York: Vintage, 2011), 136–138; Hans J. Nissen, Peter Damerow, and Robert K. Englund, *Archaic Bookkeeping: Writing and Techniques of Economic Administration in the Ancient Near East* (Chicago: University of Chicago Press, 1993), 36.

54. *Anglo-Saxon Chronicle*, trans. and ed. M. J. Swanton (New York: Routledge, 1998), entry cited is from 1085 C.E.; Ann Williams and G. H. Martin, eds., *Domesday Book* (London: Penguin, 2002), 183–185. See also David Roffe, *Decoding Domesday* (London: Boydell and Brewer, 2015); Sally Harvey, *Domesday: Book of Judgment* (Oxford: Oxford University Press, 2014).

55. Rosamund Faith, "Hide," in *The Blackwell Encyclopedia of Anglo-Saxon England*, ed. Michael Lapige (London: Blackwell, 2001); Harvey, *Domesday*, 210–220; Roffe, *Decoding Domesday*, 190–198, 217–219, 226; Kula, *Measures and Men*, 29–42. For the hierarchy of feudalism, see Marc Bloch, *Feudal Society*, trans. L. A. Manyon (Chicago: University of Chicago Press, 1961); David Crouch, *The Birth of Nobility: Constructing Aristocracy in England and France 900–1300* (London: Routledge, 2005)

56. Jean Christophe-Agnew, *Worlds Apart: The Market and the Theater in Anglo-American Thought, 1550–1750* (New York: Cambridge University Press, 1988), 17–57; Herodotus quoted on 21. For Aristotle's economic writings, see Arthur Eli Monroe, *Early Economic Thought: Selections from Economic Literature Prior to Adam Smith* (Cambridge, MA: Harvard University Press, 1945), 1–31, quoted on 18, 20. For Aristotle's economic theory, see Finley, "Aristotle and Economic Analysis," *Past and Present* 47 (1970): 3–25; Thomas J. Lewis, "Acquisition and Anxiety: Aristotle's Case against the Market," *Canadian Journal of Economics* 11 (February 1978): 69–90.

57. Merav Haklai, "Money in the Roman Empire: Institutional Diversity at Work" (forthcoming book manuscript); Nathan Matthews, "The Valuation of Property in the Roman Law," *Harvard Law Review* 34 (1920–1921): 229–251; Aquinas's *Summa Theologica*, question LXXVII, cited in Monroe, *Early Economic Thought*, 53. On the "just price" as well as skepticism of market values, see E. P. Thompson, "The Moral Economy of the English Crowd," *Past and Present* 50 (February 1971); Raymond de Roover, "The Concept of the Just Price: Theory and Economic Policy," *Journal of Economic History* 18, no. 4 (December 1958):

418–434; David Friedman, "In Defense of Thomas Aquinas and the Just Price," *History of Political Economy* 4 (Summer 1980): 234–242.

58. Agnew, *Worlds Apart,* 18–40; Alan Everitt, "The Marketing of Agricultural Produce," in *Agricultural Change,* 467–495. See also Fernand Braudel, *Afterthoughts on Material Civilization and Capitalism* (Baltimore: Johns Hopkins University Press, 1977).

59. Inquisition cited in Hubert Hall, ed., *A Formula Book of English Official Historical Documents* (Cambridge: Cambridge University Press, 1909), 181. See also *The Domesday of Inclosures,* ed. I. S. Leadam (London, 1897); Edwin Gay and I. S. Leadam, "The Inquisition of Depopulation in 1517 and the 'Domesday of Inclosure,'" *Transactions of the Royal Historical Society* 44 (1900): 231–303.

60. Leadam, *Domesday of Inclosures,* 1:38–40

61. Adam Smith, *An Inquiry into the Nature and Causes of the Wealth of Nations,* ed. Edwin Cannan (London: Methuen, 1904), book IV, ch. 5; book I, ch. 7. For Petty's popularity in 1690s, see Appleby, *Economic Thought,* 138. For the decline, see Walter Houghton Jr., "The English Virtuoso in the 17th Century," *Journal of Historical Ideas* 3 (1942): 211–219. For lack of state support, see Karen Johannisson, "Society in Numbers: The Debate over Quantification in 18th Century Political Economy," in *The Quantifying Spirit in the 18th Century,* ed. J. L. Heilbron, Tore Frangsmyr, and Robin Rider (Berkeley: University of California Press, 1990), 348–350; Peter Buck, "People Who Counted: Political Arithmetic in the Eighteenth Century," *Isis* 73, no. 1 (March 1982): 28–45.

62. On "fictitious commodities," see Polanyi, *Great Transformation.* On how the eighteenth century was no market society, see Tribe, *Land, Labor and Economic Discourse*; Malachy Postlethwayt, "Political Arithmetic," in *The Universal Dictionary of Trade and Commerce* (London, 1744).

63. Jonathan Swift, *A Modest Proposal for Preventing the Children of Poor People from Being a Burden on Their Parents or Country and Making Them Beneficial to the Publick* (London, 1729).

2. SEEING LIKE A CAPITALIST

1. "Alexander Hamilton's Final Version of the Report on the Subject of Manufacturers," December 5, 1791, *Founders Online,* National Archives, last modified March 30, 2017; original source: *The Papers of Alexander Hamilton* (henceforth *PAH*), ed. Harold C. Syrett, assoc. ed. Jacob E. Cooke (New York: Columbia University Press, 1961–1987), 10:230–340. For Hamilton's statistical plans, see Alexander Hamilton, *Industrial and Commercial Correspondence of Alexander Hamilton,* ed. Arthur H. Cole (New York: Kelley, 1968), xv–xxvii; Jacob Cooke, "Tench Coxe, Alexander Hamilton, and the Encouragement of American Manufacturers," *William and Mary Quarterly* 32 (1975): 370–392.

2. "Treasury Dept Circular to the Supervisors of the Revenue," June 22, 1791, in *PAH*, 8:497–498. This was in fact the second time that Hamilton had sought out economic data on American manufacturing. On January 25, 1790, he sent a similar request to Benjamin Lincoln. *PAH*, 6:208.

3. "Treasury Department Circular," August 13, 1791, *PAH*, 9:35–36.

4. Condict's letter enclosed in Dunham to Hamilton, September 9, 1791, *PAH*, 9:193; Peter Colt to John Chester, July 12, 1791, *PAH*, 9:319–324; Nathaniel Gorham to Hamilton, October 13, 1791, *PAH*, 9:371–372. For more disappointing returns in Connecticut, see Benjamin Huntington to John Chester, August 24, 1791, *PAH*, 9:329–330; William Hillhouse to John Chester, September 6, 1791, *PAH*, 332–334; Amasa Learned to John Chester, September 14, 1791, *PAH*, 9:338–339; James Davenport to John Chester, September 16, 1791, *PAH*, 9:340–341; William Williams to John Chester, September 29, 1791, *PAH*, 9:353–355.

5. George Cabot to Hamilton, September 6, 1791, *PAH*, 9:177–180; O. Burr & Company to John Chester, September 12, 1791, *PAH*, 9:336–338; Chauncey Whittlesey to John Chester, September 27, 1791, *PAH*, 9:342–343; Jonathan Palmer Jr. to John Chester, September 15, 1791, *PAH*, 9:339–340.

6. Henry Wynkoop to Hamilton, August 29, 1791, *PAH*, 9:123–124; John Neville to Hamilton, October 27, 1791, *PAH*, 9:419–420; John Beale Bordley to Hamilton, November 11, 1791, *PAH*, 9:490–492.

7. Timothy Pickering to Hamilton, October 13, 1791, *PAH*, 9:375–377.

8. Richard Peters to Hamilton, August 27, 1791, *PAH*, 9:114–116.

9. Walker letter enclosed in Daniel Stevens to Hamilton, September 3, 1791, *PAH*, 9:170; Thomas Newton to Edward Carrington, November 28, 1791, *PAH*, 278–279. For the detailed surveys see Drury Ragsdale to Edward Carrington, September 29, 1791, *PAH*, 9:280–282; Edward Stevens to Edward Carrington, October 6, 1791, *PAH*, 9:300–302; For Carrington's role in these surveys see Carrington to Hamilton, October 4 and October 8, 1791, *PAH*, 9:275–279, 299–300.

10. Newton to Carrington, September 28, 1791; Edward Carrington to Hamilton, October 8, 1791, *PAH*, 9:273; Anselm Bailey to Thomas Newton, August 23, 1791, *PAH*, 9:280.

11. For the Whiskey Rebellion and its aftermath, see Thomas Slaughter, *The Whiskey Rebellion: Frontier Epilogue to the American Revolution* (New York: Oxford University Press, 1986).

12. Douglas A. Irwin, "The Aftermath of Hamilton's Report on Manufactures," *Journal of Economic History* 64 (September 2004): 800–821; Stuart Bruchey, "Economy and Society in an Earlier America," *Journal of American History* 47 (1987): 299–319; Ron Chernow, *Alexander Hamilton* (New York: Penguin Books, 2005), 362–289; Stanley Elkins and Eric McKitrick, *The Age of Federalism: The*

Early American Republic, 1788–1800 (New York: Oxford University Press, 1995), 258–263.

13. Hamilton, *Selected Writings,* 284.

14. Ibid., 281; Adam Smith, *Wealth of Nations,* book IV, ch. 2, para. 9; book II, ch. 3, para 2. For Hamilton's paraphrasing of Smith, see Harold C. Syrett's footnotes in *PAH,* 10:230–304, as well as Edward Bourne, "Alexander Hamilton and Adam Smith," *Quarterly Journal of Economics* 8, no. 3 (April 1894): 328–344. For works that portray Hamilton as an anti-Smithian "mercantilist" thinker, see Elkins and McKitrick, *Age of Federalism,* 774 n. 64.

15. For Smith's place in the longer history of economic thought, see Johnson, *Predecessors of Adam Smith*; Terence Hutchinson, *Before Adam Smith: Emergence of Political Economy, 1662–1776* (London: Blackwell, 1988).

16. "Pay Book of the State Company of Artillery Commanded by Alexander Hamilton [1777]," *PAH,* 1:373–412.

17. Chernow, *Hamilton,* 104.

18. Christopher Leslie Brown, "Empire without America," in *Abolitionism and Imperialism in Britain, Africa and the Atlantic,* ed. Derek R. Petersen (Columbus: Ohio University Press, 2010), 88–89. For Postlethwayt's assistance to Walpole and the Royal African Company, see Robert J. Bennet, "Malachy Postlethwayt, 1707–1767: Genealogy and Influence of an Early Economist and 'Spin-Doctor,'" *Genealogists Magazine* 1 (2006): 1–8; Eric Williams, *Capitalism and Slavery* (Chapel Hill: University of North Carolina Press, 1944), 49–54.

19. Malachy Postlethwayt, *The National and Private Advantage of the African Trade Considered* (London, 1746), 1–2; *The African Trade, the Great Pillar and Support of the British Plantation Trade in America* (London, 1745), 15.

20. Malachy Postlethwayt, *The Universal Dictionary of Trade and Commerce, Volume 2* (London, 1751).

21. See relevant entries in ibid.

22. Hamilton, "The Continentalist No. VI," *PAH,* 3:99–106. For Hamilton's reliance on Postlethwayt, see Chernow, *Hamilton,* 105, 150, 290, 341; Hamilton, "Pay Book."

23. Hamilton, "Pay Book"; Postlethwayt, *Universal Dictionary,* "Land."

24. On Hamilton's desire to shape America in the image of England, see Lawrence S. Kaplan, *Alexander Hamilton: Ambivalent Anglophile* (Wilmington, DE: Scholarly Resources, 2002), 79–99.

25. Bernard Bailyn, *The Ideological Origins of the American Revolution* (Cambridge, MA: Belknap Press of Harvard University Press, 1992); see also J. G. A. Pocock, *The Machiavellian Moment:Florentine Political Thought and the Atlantic Republic Tradition* (Princeton, NJ: Princeton University Press, 1975).

26. In 1770, there were 18,884 slaves and 1515 whites on St. Croix. N. A. T. Hall, *Slave Society in the Danish West Indies: St. Thomas, St. John and St Croix* (Mona, Jamaica: University of the West Indies Press, 1992), 5.

27. For slavery and quantification, see David Graeber, *Debt: The First 5000 Years* (Brooklyn, NY: Melville House, 2012), 163–211.

28. For young Hamilton's desire to get off the island, see Hamilton to Edward Stevens, November 11, 1769, *PAH,* 1:4–5. For the English flavor of St. Croix, see Hall, *Slave Society,* 13. For the importance of the Caribbean to the industrial revolution, see Williams, *Capitalism and Slavery*; Sidney Mintz, *Sweetness and Power: The Place of Sugar in Modern History* (New York: Penguin, 1986). For the rise of British capitalism and Western slavery, see Robin Blackburn, *The Making of New World Slavery* (New York: Verso, 1998), 217–277, 509–581; Kenneth Morgan, *Slavery, Atlantic Trade and the British Economy, 1660–1800* (Cambridge: Cambridge University Press, 2000); Immanuel Wallerstein, *The Modern World-System: Mercantilism and the Consolidation of the European World-Economy, 1600–1750,* vol. 2 (New York: Academic Press, 1980).

29. Arthur Stinchcombe, *Sugar Island Slavery in the Age of Enlightenment* (Princeton, NJ: Princeton University Press, 1996), 49, 89–95, 118; Hall, *Slave Society,* 29, 40, 73–74; Richard Dunn, *Sugar and Slaves: The Rise of the Planter Class in the English West Indies* (Chapel Hill: University of North Carolina Press, 1972), 188–263; Richard Sheridan, *Sugar and Slavery: An Economic History of the British West Indies, 1623–1775* (Kingston, Jamaica: Canoe Press, 1974). Capital investment figures from B. L. Solow, "Caribbean Slavery and British Growth: The Eric Williams Hypothesis," *Journal of Development Economics* 17 (1985): 99–115.

30. On the failure of Caribbean islands to develop into full-fledged settler societies, see Trevor Bernard, "A Failed Settler Society: Marriage and Demographic Failure in Early Jamaica," *Journal of Social History* 28 (1994): 63–82.

31. Robert E. Wright and David J. Cowen, *Financial Fathers: The Men Who Made America Rich* (Chicago: University of Chicago Press, 2006); Thomas McCraw, *The Founders and Finance: How Hamilton, Gallatin and Other Immigrants Forged a New Economy* (Cambridge, MA: Harvard University Press, 2012). The section on Hamilton and the Caribbean is titled "St. Croix and Trauma."

32. Alexander Hamilton to Nicholas Cruger, October 31, 1771, November 4, 1771, November 12, 1771, Hamilton to William Newton, November 16, 1771, *PAH,* 1:9–14.

33. On the extreme monoculture of the Caribbean, see Robert William Fogel, *Without Consent or Contract: The Rise and Fall of American Slavery* (New York: Norton, 1994), 21–26.

34. Nicholas Cruger to Henry Cruger, June 5, 1772, June 6, 1772; Nicholas Cruger to John H. Cruger, March 19, 1772; while these letters can be found at the Library of

Congress, they are not part of Syrett's compilation. See Broadus Mitchell, *Alexander Hamilton: Youth to Maturity, 1755–1788* (New York: Macmillan, 1957), 1:485 n. 71; Robert Hendrickson, *The Rise and Fall of Alexander Hamilton* (New York: Dodd, Mead, 1981), 29; James Oliver Horton, "Alexander Hamilton: Slavery and Race in a Revolutionary Generation," *New York Journal of American History* 55 (Spring 2004): 16–24. For the slave auctions, see *Royal Danish American Gazette,* January 26, 1771. For the figures on the Christiansted slave trade, see William Cissel, "Alexander Hamilton: The West Indian 'Founding Father,'" Christiansted National Historical Site, National Park Service, July 2004. For a vivid depiction of the St. Croix slave auctions, see Paul Erdmann Isert, *Letters on West Africa and the Slave Trade,* trans. and ed. Selena Axelrod Winsnes (Oxford: Oxford University Press, 1992).

35. For Hamilton's vague and oft-exaggerated anti-slavery views, see James Flexner, *The Young Hamilton: A Biography* (New York: Fordham University Press, 1997), 38–39. In his papers, it is clear that Hamilton continued to buy and sell slaves for either himself or his in-laws. See "Account with John Baker Church," June 15, 1797, *PAH,* 21:109–122, which mentions $90 "paid price of Negro Woman," as well as "Cash Book 1782–1791," *PAH,* 3:6–67, which mentions "negro wench Peggy."

36. Thomas Tryon, *Tryon's Letters, Domestick and Foreign* (London, 1700), 202; Mintz, *Sweetness and Power,* 47; Dunn, *Sugar and Slaves,* 191, 195.

37. Hamilton to *Royal Danish American Gazette,* September 6, 1772, *PAH,* 1:34–38; Hall, *Slave Society,* 95; Richard Sheridan, "The Plantation Revolution and the Industrial Revolution, 1625–1775," *Caribbean Studies* 9 (1969): 5–25.

38. Hamilton, *Selected Writings,* 283. For the assumption that Hamilton was thinking of England, see Syrett's footnotes in "Alexander Hamilton's Final Version of the Report," esp. n. 140, *PAH,* 10:230–340.

39. Peter Coclanis, *The Shadow of a Dream: Economic Life and Death in the South Carolina Low Country, 1670–1920* (New York: Oxford University Press, 1989); Peter Wood, *Black Majority* (New York: Norton, 1975); John McCusker and Russell Menard, *The Economy of British America, 1607–1789* (Chapel Hill: University of North Carolina Press, 1991), 181. For South Carolina planters' devotion to economic development and British notions of progress, see Joyce Chaplin, *Anxious Pursuit: Agricultural Innovation and Modernity in the Lower South, 1730–1815* (Chapel Hill: University of North Carolina Press, 1996).

40. Thomas Nairne, A *Letter from South Carolina: Giving an Account of the Soil, Air, Product, Trade, Government, Laws . . . Together with the Manner and Necessary Charges of Settling a Plantation There, and the Annual Profit It Will Produce* (London, 1710), 48.

41. Ibid., 48–49.

42. Ibid., 54.

43. John Norris, *Profitable Advice for Rich and Poor . . . With Propositions for the Advantageous Settlement of People, in General, but Especially the Laborious Poor, in That Fruitful, Pleasant and Profitable Country, for Its Inhabitants* (London, 1712), 58–59. For other examples of such pricing of progress in South Carolina, see Walter Edgar, *South Carolina: A History* (Charleston: University of South Carolina Press, 1998), 150–151; Chaplin, *Anxious Pursuit,* 9. As early as 1645, Barbados planters were calculating that a slave would repay his cost in a year and a half. See Nuala Zahedieh, "Economy," in *The British Atlantic World, 1500–1800,* ed. David Armitage and Michael J. Braddick (New York: Palgrave Macmillan, 2002), 57. See also Justin Roberts, *Slavery and Enlightenment in the British Atlantic* (New York: Cambridge University Press, 2013).

44. "Queries Relating to the Province of South Carolina Propounded by the Lords of Trade and Plantations," August 23, 1720, and "Endorsed Draught of instructions to James Glen, England Governor of South Carolina," September 7, 1739, both in Great Britain Board of Trade Records, Box 2, Library of Congress, Washington, DC.

45. *Colonial South Carolina: Two Contemporary Descriptions,* ed. Chapman Milling (Columbia: University of South Carolina Press, 1951), 41–42; James Glen, "An Attempt Towards an Estimate of the Value of South Carolina for the Right and Honorable the Lords Commissioners for Trade and Plantations, 1751," in *The Colonial South Carolina Scene: Contemporary Views, 1697–1774,* ed. H. Roy Merrens (Columbia: University of South Carolina Press, 1977), 184.

46. John Drayton to James Glen, July 3, 1769, and "Rice Account," 1761–1766, folder 5, James Glen Papers (henceforth JGP), Thomas Cooper Library, University of South Carolina, Columbia.

47. Untitled itemized statement of Glen's annual income since his return from South Carolina, folder 7, [1773], JGP.

48. James Glen to John Drayton, August 24, 1774, JGP, folder 7. For further evidence that Glen charged his brother 6 percent interest, see draft of "Letter to William Drayton," apparently from 1776, JGP, folder 8.

49. For Hamilton's financial wizardry, see E. James Ferguson, *The Power of the Purse: A History of American Public Finance* (Chapel Hill: University of North Carolina Press 1961); Robert Wright, *Hamilton Unbound: Finance and the Creation of the American Republic* (Westport, CT: Greenwood Press, 2002); Bray Hammond, *Banks and Politics in America from the Revolution to the Civil War* (Princeton, NJ: Princeton University Press, 1991), 89–172; Chernow, *Hamilton,* 344–362.

50. Ferguson, *Power of the Purse,* 3–24; Hammond, *Banks and Politics,* 3–40; Theodore Thayer, "The Land-Bank System in the American Colonies," *Journal of Economic History* 13 (1953): 145–159; Dror Goldberg, "The Massachusetts Paper Money of 1690," *Journal of Economic History* 69, no. 4 (December 2009): 1092–1105.

NOTES TO PAGES 62–66

51. Hammond, *Banks and Politics,* 32. Christine Desan, "From Blood to Profit: The Transformation of Value in the American Constitutional Tradition," *Journal of Policy History* 26 (2008): 26–46.

52. Alexander Hamilton, "Report on a National Bank," December 13, 1790, in *Reports of the Secretary of Treasury* (Washington, DC, 1828), 1:55–56, 64.

53. Ibid., 70. On Hamilton the banker, see Hammond, *Banks and Politics,* 114–141.

54. Hamilton, "Report on a National Bank," 64

55. Hamilton, *Selected Writings,* 281, 284.

56. Lowery to Hamilton, October 14, 1791, *PAH,* 9:379–2382. The best summary of the SUM remains Joseph S. Davis, *Essays in the Earlier History of American Corporations* (Cambridge, MA: Harvard University Press, 1917), 1:347–522.

57. Cabot to Hamilton, September 6, 1791, *PAH,* 9:177–180.

58. Coxe to Tennant and Ress Co. (?), November 4, 1778, and Coxe to Robert Barclays, February 25, 1784, Coxe Family Papers (henceforth CFP), reel 1, Historical Society of Pennsylvania, Philadelphia, PA. See also CFP, box 289, for eighteenth-century British trade statistics, and CFP, vol. 249, box 1, for estimates of Philadelphia exports in 1789. On Coxe, see Jacob E. Cooke, *Tench Coxe and the Early Republic* (Chapel Hill: University of North Carolina Press, 1978). For Philadelphia merchants in this era, see Thomas Doerflinger, *A Vigorous Spirit of Enterprise: Merchants and Economic Development in Revolutionary Philadelphia* (Chapel Hill: University of North Carolina, 2001). For the mercantile press of the era, see David P. Forsyth, *The Business Press in America* (Philadelphia: Chilton, 1965)

59. For Coxe's wide-ranging speculation in land, and prophetic views on cotton and coal, see Cooke, *Coxe,* 100–108, 311–332; Coxe to unnamed, April 7, 1802, CFP, box 63, folder 11; Land Papers, CFP, box 117, folder 9, 1810; "Proposals for Settling Lands in Pennsylvania," vol. 317, CFP; "Account of the Quality Situation of Tench Coxe's Lands in Oswego Township," vol. 266, box 1, CFP.

60. Tench Coxe, A *View of the United States of America* (Philadelphia, 1794), 51, 78–80, 104, 261; William Cooper to Coxe, April 9, 1793, CFP. For the Virginia survey, see Stevens to Carrington, October 6, 1791, *PAH.* For the fundamental difference between merchants who buy commodities and capitalists who buy "nature and man," see Polanyi, *Great Transformation,* 42. For Coxe's data collecting as well as his work on the 1810 census, see Cooke, "Encouragement of American Manufacturers"; Cooke, *Tench Coxe,* 497–502.

61. Coxe, *View of the United States,* 386–400.

62. For the machinations and controversy surrounding Hamilton's moves, see Ferguson, *Power of the Purse,* 289–326; Hammond, *Banks and Politics,* 89–114; Elkins and McKitrick, *Age of Federalism,* 77–163; Richard Sylla, "Hamilton and the Federalist Financial Revolution, 1789–1794," *New York Journal of American History* 55 (Spring 2004). For the financial revolution in England, see Chris Desan,

Making Money: Coin, Currency and the Coming of Capitalism (Oxford: Oxford University Press, 2014).

63. For Hamilton's many calculations on the national debt, see first and second drafts of his Report on Public Credit. On capitalizing taxing power, see Elkins and McKitrick, *Age of Federalism,* 116. For Hamilton's fiscal revolution, see Max Edling and Mark Kaplanoff, "Alexander Hamilton's Fiscal Reform: Transforming the Structure of Taxation in the Early Republic," *William and Mary Quarterly* 61, no. 4 (2004): 713–744.

64. Hamilton, *Selected Writings,* 287–288; Elkins and McKitrick, *Age of Federalism,* 118; Hammond, *Banks and Politics,* 62–64, 122–125; R. Sylla, R. Wright, and D. Cowen, "Alexander Hamilton, Central Banker: Crisis Management during the U.S. Financial Panic of 1792," *Business History Review* 83, no. 1 (2009): 61–86.

65. On Blodget's business affairs, see Marquis James, *Biography of a Business, 1792–1942: Insurance Company of North America* (Indianapolis, IN: Bobbs-Merrill, 1942), 11–17; W. B. Bryan, *A History of the National Capital from Its Foundation through the Period of the Adoption of the Organic Act* (New York: Macmillan, 1914), 187–226.

66. Samuel Blodget, *Thoughts on Increasing Wealth and National Economy of the United States* (Washington, DC, 1801), iii; Timothy Mitchell, "Fixing the Economy," *Cultural Studies* 12, no. 1 (1998): 82–101.

67. Blodget, *Thoughts on Increasing Wealth,* 4.

68. Ibid., 11, 19.

69. Samuel Blodget, *Economica: A Statistical Manual for the United States of America* (Washington, DC, 1806), 8, 57–62.

70. Ibid., 80.

71. Ibid., 89. On Blodget as father of GDP, see Paul Rohde and Richard Sutch, "Estimates of National Product before 1929," *Historical Statistics of the United States: Millennial Edition Online,* hsus.cambridge.org.

72. For the dearth of capital in early America, see Douglass North, *The Economic Growth of the United States 1790–1860* (New York: Prentice Hall, 1966).

73. Tench Coxe, *A Brief Examination of Lord Sheffield's Observations on the Commerce of the United States* (London, 1792); Coxe, *A Statement of the Arts and Manufacturers . . . 1810* (Philadelphia, 1814).

74. Hamilton, "Report on Manufactures," *Selected Writings,* 309; United States Congress, Committee on Ways and Means, *Report of the Committee of Ways and Means on the Memorial of the Manufacturers of the City of New York* (Washington, DC, 1814); Philadelphia Society for the Promotion of American Manufacturers, *The Committee Appointed on the Part . . . to Report a Plan in Aid of the Internal Industry* (Philadelphia, 1817).

75. Tench Coxe, *A Statement of the Arts and Manufacturers of the United States* (Philadelphia, 1814), 36; state-by-state tables appear on unnumbered pages in second half of book. *Fourth Census of the United States* (Washington, DC, 1821), 25.
76. Coxe, *View of the United States*, 62, 104, 201.
77. Kenneth Hafertepe, "Samuel Blodget," in *American National Biography Online*, http://www.anb.org. On the failure of the SUM, see Elkins and McKitrick, *Age of Federalism*, 271, 274, 279–280.

3. THE SPIRIT OF NON-CAPITALISM

1. Inventory of Benjamin Tower, Business Instruments Collection (henceforth BIC), 1600–1969: Series I, Inventories, box 4, folder 12, Baker Library, Harvard Business School, Boston. Inventory of Daniel McNeil, box 4, folder 13, BIC. See Zacharia Penn's from 1802, folder 14, BIC, for probate pricing of a half-dozen slaves. On the early American embrace of commerce, see Richard Lyman Bushman, "Markets and Composite Farms in Early America," *William and Mary Quarterly* 55 (1998): 351–357; T. H. Breen, *The Marketplace of Revolution: How Consumer Politics Shaped American Independence* (New York: Oxford University Press, 2005); Jan De Vries, *The Industrious Revolution: Consumer Behavior and the Household Economy, 1650 to the Present* (New York: Cambridge University Press, 2008), 95–96.
2. Russell Sackett account book, Manuscripts and Archives Division, New York Public Library; Matthew Patten, *The Diary of Matthew Patten* (Concord, NH: Rumford, 1903), 354; Martha Ballard, *The Diary of Martha Ballard, 1785–1812*, ed. Robert and Cynthia McCausland (Camden, ME: Picton Press, 1992), 274, 296, 322; House Carpenters of the Borough of Pittsburgh, *The Book of Prices Adopted by the House Carpenters of the Borough of Pittsburgh* (Pittsburgh, PA: S. Engels, 1813). For "book credit," see Christopher Clark, *The Roots of Rural Capitalism: Western Massachusetts, 1780–1860* (Ithaca, NY: Cornell University Press, 1990), 32–35. For exchange of money for labor (which is not the same as wage labor), see Jeanne Boydston, *Home and Work: Housework, Wages, and the Ideology of Labor in the Early Republic* (Oxford: Oxford University Press, 1990), 30–56.
3. On the alienability of land, see Claire Priest, "Creating an American Property Law: Alienability and Its Limits in American History," *Harvard Law Review* 120 (December 2006); Elizabeth Blackmar, "Inheriting Property and Debt," in *Capitalism Takes Command: The Social Transformation of Nineteenth-Century America*, ed. Michael Zakim and Gary John Kornblith (Chicago: University of Chicago Press, 2012), 93–119; David B. Ryden and Russell B. Menard, "South Carolina's Colonial Land Market: An Analysis of Rural Property Sales, 1720–1775," *Social Science History* 29, no. 4 (Winter 2005): 600; Malcolm

Rohrbough, *The Land Office Business: The Settlement and Administration of American Public Lands, 1789–1837* (New York: Oxford University Press, 1968). On American property rights being more absolutist than those in England, see Christopher Tomlins, *Freedom Bound: Law, Labor and Civic Identity in Colonizing English America, 1580–1865* (New York: Cambridge University Press, 2010), 160 n. 86.

4. *Annals of Congress,* January 1820, 16th Congress, 1st Session, House of Representatives, 1:922. I found five newspapers that covered the manufacturing census: *New York National Advocate,* January 18, 1814; *Boston Repertory,* January 24, 1814; *Boston Daily Advertiser,* January 25, 1814; *Maryland Republican Star,* February 8, 1814; and the *American Advocate* in Hallowell, Maine, February 12, 1814.

5. Carl Degler, *Out of Our Past* (New York: Harper, 1983), 2. For capitalism being present at America's birth, see also Louis Hartz, *The Liberal Tradition in America* (New York: Harvest, 1955).

6. Richard Hakluyt, *Discourse Concerning Western Planting* (London, 1584), ch. 13; David W. Galenson, "The Settlement and Growth of the Colonies: Population, Labor and Economic Development," in *The Cambridge Economic History of the United States,* ed. Stanley Engerman and Robert Gallman (Cambridge: Cambridge University Press, 1999), 135–207; Tomlins, *Freedom Bound,* 159–190. For early English visions of America as an investment, see Jack Greene, *The Intellectual Construction of America: Exceptionalism and Identity from 1492 to 1800* (Chapel Hill: University of North Carolina Press, 1997), 36–46.

7. Richard S. Dunn, "Penny Wise and Pound Foolish: Penn as a Businessman," in *The World of William Penn,* ed. Richard S. Dunn and Mary Maples Dunn (Philadelphia: University of Pennsylvania Press, 1986), 37–54. For Penn's experiences managing his father's estates in Ireland as well as the rent rates he received, see William Penn, *My Irish Journal, 1669–1670,* ed. Isabel Grubb, introduction by Hiram Morgan (Cork: University College, 1952), 16.

8. Susan Myra Kingsbury, ed., *Records of the Virginia Company* (Washington, DC: GPO, 1906–1935), 3:21. For the orderly nature of the company's plans, see James Horn, *A Land as God Made It: Jamestown and the Birth of America* (New York: Basic Books, 2008), 180–183. For such requests to the Massachusetts Pilgrims by London financier Thomas Weston, see Willard Stone, "Accounting Woes, Pilgrim Style," *Massachusetts CPA Review,* 1960, 7–8. See also Andrew Fitzmaurice, "The Commercial Ideology of Colonization in Jacobean England: Robert Johnston, Giovanni Botero and the Pursuit of Greatness," *William and Mary Quarterly* 64, no. 4 (October 2007): 791–820.

9. Edward Dufferd Neill, *History of the Virginia Company of London: With Letters to the First Colony* (London, 1860), 180. On the fall of the Virginia Company, see Wesley Frank Craven, *Dissolution of the Virginia Company: The Failure of a*

Colonial Experiment (Oxford: Oxford University Press, 1932); Edmund Morgan, *American Slavery, American Freedom: The Ordeal of Colonial Virginia* (New York: Norton, 1975), 101–102.

10. Galenson, "Settlement and Growth of the Colonies," 144; Dunn, "Penny Wise and Pound Foolish," 38, 48–52. On the lord proprietors' failure to collect even quit-rents, see Alvin Rabushka, *Taxation in Colonial America* (Princeton, NJ: Princeton University Press, 2010), 52–64.

11. Mira Wilkins, *The History of Foreign Investment in the United States* (Cambridge, MA: Harvard University Press, 1989), 27; Alice Hanson Jones, *Wealth of a Nation to Be: The American Colonies on the Eve of the Revolution* (New York: Columbia University Press, 1980), 225.

12. John Bateman, *The Great Landowners of Great Britain and Ireland* (London, 1883). The study was known as the "Modern Domesday Book." For earlier estimates of English landownership, see G. E. Mingay, *The Gentry: The Rise and Fall of a Ruling Class* (New York: Longman, 1976), 55–59. On American tenantry, see Alan Kulikoff, *From British Peasants to Colonial American Farmers* (Chapel Hill: University of North Carolina Press, 2000), 116–117, 127, Van Rensselaer quoted on 116. For the rare instance in which tenant farming did succeed, see Sung Bok Kim, *Landlord and Tenant in Colonial New York: Manorial Society, 1664–1775* (Chapel Hill: University of North Carolina Press), 1978.

13. Hector St. John de Crèvecoeur, *Letters from an American Farmer* (Belfast, 1783), 48.

14. Norris, "Profitable Advice for Rich and Poor," 16. Land tax entries in Caroline County (VA) Land Tax Book, 1802, University of Virginia Library, Charlottesville. For 70–30 tenant/owner ratio, see Hermann Wellenreuther, "A View of Socio-Economic Structures of England and the British Colonies on the Eve of the American Revolution," in *New Wine in Old Skins: A Comparative View of Socio-Political Structures and Values Affecting the American Revolution,* ed. Erich Angermann, Marie-Luise Frings, and Herman Wellenreuther (Stuttgart: Klett, 1976), 14–40. See also James Henretta, *The Origins of American Capitalism: Collected Essays* (Boston: Northeastern University Press, 1991), 189; On land/labor ratio, see Charles Sellers, *The Market Revolution: Jacksonian America, 1815–1846* (New York: Oxford University Press, 1991), 4.

15. 1703 quitrent accounts, page 17, Proprietor of Pennsylvania Accounts, 1701–1704, Library Company of Philadelphia, Philadelphia.

16. John Winthrop, *The Journal of John Winthrop, 1630–1649,* ed. Richard S. Dunn and Laetitia Yeandle (Cambridge, MA: Harvard University Press, 1996), 273; Sharon Salinger, "Artisans, Journeymen and the Transformation of Labor in Late Eighteenth-Century Philadelphia," *William and Mary Quarterly* 40, no. 1 (January 1983): 67. On indentured servitude, see Christopher Tomlins, *Law, Labor and Ideology in the Early American Republic* (Cambridge: Cambridge University

Press, 1993); Tomlins, *Freedom Bound*, 35–44, 60–61, 78–92; Edmund Morgan, "Slavery and Freedom: The American Paradox," *Journal of American History* 59 (June 1972): 5–29. On the need for unfree labor in a land-abundant and labor-scarce society, see Evsey Domar, "The Causes of Slavery and Serfdom: A Hypothesis," *Journal of Economic History* 30, no. 1 (1970): 18–22; Heywood Fleisig, "Slavery, and the Supply of Agricultural Labor, and the Industrialization of the South," *Journal of Economic History* 36, no. 3 (1976): 572–597. On reliance on family labor due to a lack of wage laborers, see Gavin Wright, *The Political Economy of the Cotton South: Household, Markets and Wealth in the Nineteenth Century* (New York: Norton, 1978).

17. Adam Smith, *Wealth of Nations*, book 1, ch. 6, para. 17; Maurice Dobb, *Theories of Value and Distribution since Adam Smith* (Cambridge: Cambridge University Press, 1975), 38–65; David McNally, *Political Economy and the Rise of Capitalism* (Berkeley: University of California Press, 1990), 209–258.

18. Smith, *Wealth of Nations*, book 1, ch. 6, para. 23.

19. Benjamin Franklin, "The Nature and Necessity of a Paper Currency (1729)," in *Franklin: The Autobiography and Other Writings* (New York: Cambridge University Press, 2004), 151.

20. On Franklin's tendency to adapt English ideas to American reality, see Gordon Wood, *The Americanization of Benjamin Franklin* (New York: Penguin, 2005). On Franklin and political arithmetic, see Joyce Chaplin, *The First Scientific American: Benjamin Franklin and the Pursuit of Genius* (New York: Basic Books, 2007), 79–82, 141–143, 279–280. On Franklin's importance to the development of the labor theory of value, see Ronald Meek, *Studies in the Labor Theory of Value* (New York: Monthly Review Press, 1956), 40–41. On the labor theory of value in America, see James L. Huston, *Securing the Fruits of Our Labor: The American Concept of Wealth Distribution 1765–1900* (Baton Rouge: Louisiana State University Press, 1998).

21. On the relationship between capitalism and the ownership of scarce resources, see John E. Roemer, *Free to Lose: An Introduction to Marxist Economic Philosophy* (Cambridge, MA: Harvard University Press, 1988); Elizabeth Blackmar, *Manhattan for Rent, 1785–1850* (Ithaca, NY: Cornell University Press, 1991).

22. On how much produce did not reach the market, see Clark, *Roots of Rural Capitalism*, 28; Wright, *Political Economy of the Cotton South*, chs. 2–3; Carole Shammas, "How Self-Sufficient Was Early America?" *Journal of Interdisciplinary History* 13, no. 2 (Autumn 1982): 247–272. For the politics of "homespun," see Michael Zakim, *Ready-Made Democracy: A History of Men's Dress in the American Republic, 1760–1860* (Chicago: University of Chicago Press, 2006), 11–36; Laurel Thatcher Ulrich, *The Age of Homespun: Objects and Stories in the Creation of an American Myth* (New York: Knopf, 2001).

23. According to Thomas Cochran, there existed an "American habit of talking in terms of capital values rather than income." Thomas Cochran, *Business in American Life: A History* (New York: McGraw-Hill, 1974), 44. On the shifting ways Americans valued land, see Blackmar, "Inherited Property and Debt"; Morton Horwitz, *The Transformation of American Law, 1780–1860* (Cambridge, MA: Harvard University Press, 1979), 56; James Willard Hurst, *Law and the Conditions of Freedom in the Nineteenth Century United States* (Madison: University of Wisconsin Press, 1956), 33–71.

24. Jones, *Wealth of a Nation to Be,* xxvii; Articles of Confederation, article VIII. For the failed 1783 amendment, see Carrol Wright, *The History and Growth of the U.S. Census* (Washington, DC: GPO, 1900), 12; For evidence of how market prices played almost no role in early American tax assessments, see Albemarle Sheriff's Ledger, 1782–1783, Special Collections Department, University of Virginia Library, Charlottesville. The sheriff assesses taxes without ever asking the price of anything.

25. Paul David, "New Light on a Statistical Dark Age: U.S. Real Product Growth before 1840," *American Economic Review* 57, no. 2 (May 1967): 294–306; John J. McCusker and Russell R. Menard, *The Economy of British America 1607–1789* (Chapel Hill: University of North Carolina Press, 1985), 68.

26. See Sackett Russell Account Book and Ervin Account Book, Manuscripts and Archives Division, New York Public Library; Daniel Coffin Account Book, BIC. On the worldview behind these balancing acts, see Bruce H. Mann, "Rationality, Legal Change and Community in Connecticut, 1690–1740," *Law and Society Review* 14 (1980): 196–198.

27. Puritan merchant cited in *The Apologia of Robert Keyne, 1653: The Self Portrait of a Puritan Merchant,* ed. Bernard Bailyn (New York: Harper and Row, 1964), 68. For the notion that profit in this era was the measure of income and outgo, see Jonathan Levy, "Accounting for Profit and the History of Capital," *Critical Historical Studies* 1, no. 2 (Fall 2014): 171–214. For the claim that early American merchants, industrialists, and farmers were similar since neither calculated return on capital, see Naomi Lamoreaux, "Rethinking the Transition to Capitalism in the Early American Northeast," *Journal of American History* 90 (2003): 437–461. For colonial mercantile accounting, see Gary John Previts and Barbara Dubis Merino, *A History of Accounting in America: An Historical Interpretation of the Cultural Significance of Accounting* (New York: Wiley, 1979), 5–7, 10–12, 24, 30; Rob Bryer, "Americanism and Financial Accounting Theory, Part 1: Was America Born Capitalist?" *Critical Perspectives on Accounting* 23 (2012): 511–555.

28. Winifred Rothenberg, "Farm Account Books: Problems and Possibilities," *Agricultural History* 58, no. 2 (April 1984): 106–112. On disinterest in yields, see Patricia Cline Cohen, *A Calculating People: The Spread of Numeracy in Early America*

(New York: Routledge, 1999), 82; E. P. Thompson, "The Moral Economy of the English Crowd," *Past and Present* 50 (February 1971): 78. For a critique of cliometrics' anachronisms, see Francesco Boldizzoni, *The Poverty of Clio: Resurrecting Economic History* (Princeton, NJ: Princeton University Press, 2011).

29. David Szathmary, *Shays' Rebellion: The Making of an Agrarian Insurrection* (Amherst: University of Massachusetts Press, 1980); James P. Whittenburg, "Planters, Merchants and Lawyers: Social Change and the Origins of the North Carolina Regulation," *William and Mary Quarterly* 34 (1977): 215–238.

30. Thomas Jefferson, *Notes on the State of Virginia* (Paris, 1782), 303. For American dread not of markets but of market dependence, see Daniel Vickers, "Competence and Competition: Economic Culture in Early America," *William and Mary Quarterly* 47, no. 1 (January 1990): 3–29; James Henretta, "Families and Farms: *Mentalité* in Pre-Industrial America," *William and Mary Quarterly* 35 (1978), 3–32; Bushman, "Markets and Composite Farming"; Winifred B. Rothenberg, "The Market and Massachusetts Farmers, 1750–1855," *Journal of Economic History* 41 (1981): 283–314; John Taylor, *Arator, Being a Series of Agricultural Essays, Practical and Political* (Petersburg, VA, 1818), 22. For the subsistence nature of early American farming and farmers' disregard for income maximization, see also McCusker and Menard, *Economy of British America,* 300.

31. On the lack of an "absentee mentality," see Peter Kolchin, *American Slavery, 1619–1877* (New York: Hill and Wang, 2003), 29–33; Blackmar, "Inheriting Property and Debt," 95; Trevor Bernard, "A Failed Settler Society: Marriage and Demographic Failure in Early Jamaica," *Journal of Social History* 28 (1994): 63–82.

32. Patten, *Diary,* 326. Alfred Chandler recognized the lack of internal accounts on the early American slave plantation; Alfred Chandler, *The Visible Hand: The Managerial Revolution in American Business* (Cambridge, MA: Harvard University Press, 1977), 66.

33. Lincoln County, North Carolina, 1820, Census returns, microfilm, National Archives, Worcester, MA; Coxe, *Statement of the Arts and Manufacturers,* vi.

34. Instructions of 1820 census cited from Wright, *History and Growth of the United States Census,* 133–135; Zakim, "Inventing Industrial Statistics."

35. Hamilton, "Report on Manufacturers," 129; Coxe, *View of the United States,* 55. For Coxe's erasure of women, see Boydston, *Home and Work,* 30–56.

36. Arthur Young to George Washington, January 18, 1792, *Papers of George Washington* (henceforth *PGW*), University of Virginia Press, Digital Edition, http://rotunda.upress.virginia.edu/founders/GEWN. For a typical tour of England, see Arthur Young, *A Six Month Tour through the North of England* (London, 1770). On Young, see John Gazley, *The Life of Arthur Young 1741–1820* (Philadelphia: American Philosophical Society, 1973).

37. George Washington to Arthur Young, August 15, 1791, December 5, 1791, *PGW*. For the list of questions, see the circular sent out by George Washington to a number of farmers on August 25, 1791, *PGW*.

38. George Washington to Arthur Young, June 18, 1791, *PGW*.

39. On Jefferson as quantifier, see Garry Wills, *Inventing America: Jefferson's Declaration of Independence* (New York: Doubleday, 1978), 93–164; Cohen, *Calculating People*, 109–115. For Jefferson's library catalog, see *Thomas Jefferson's Library: A Catalog with Entries in His Own Order,* ed. James Gilreath and Douglas L. Wilson (Washington, DC: Library of Congress, 1989).

40. Arthur Young to George Washington, January 17, 1793, *PGW*.

41. Thomas Jefferson to George Washington, June 28, 1793, Papers of Thomas Jefferson, Founders Online, https://founders.archives.gov/about/Jefferson; Washington to Richard Peters, May 16, 1793, *PGW*. Peters's response to Young is enclosed in Richard Peters to George Washington, June 20, 1793, *PGW*.

42. Peters to Washington, June 20, 1793, *PGW*. For similar American critiques of English aristocracy see Hutson, *Securing the Fruits,* 29–58.

43. Peters to Washington, June 20, 1793, *PGW*.

44. Ibid.

45. John Ball, *Autobiography* (Grand Rapids, MI, 1925), 8. For the statistical gazetteer, see Cohen, *Calculating People,* 152–165.

46. Jedidiah Morse, *American Geography* (London, 1792), 284–286.

47. Benjamin Franklin, "Observations Concerning the Increase of Mankind," in *The Papers of Benjamin Franklin,* ed. Leonard Labaree (New Haven, CT: Yale University Press, 1961), 4:225–234.

48. Smith, *Wealth of Nations,* book 1, ch. 8; William Horsley, *The Universal Merchant* (London, 1753), xv. For mercantilists' love of population growth, see Edgar Furniss, *The Position of the Laborer in a System of Nationalism: A Study in the Labor Theories of the Later Mercantilists* (New York: Houghton Mifflin, 1920).

49. Jeremy Belknap, *The History of New Hampshire* (Philadelphia, 1784), 178; David Ramsay, *Selections from His Writings* (Philadelphia: American Philosophical Society, 1965), 185. On early America's main goal being reproduction of republican citizens, see Richard White, *Railroaded: The Transcontinentals and the Making of Modern America* (New York: Norton, 2012), 293.

50. Franklin, "Interest of Great Britain Considered," *Papers of Benjamin Franklin,* 9:73–74; Jefferson, *Notes on the State of Virginia,* 89. See James Cassedy, *Demography in Early America: Beginnings of the Statistical Mind, 1600–1800* (Cambridge, MA: Harvard University Press, 1969), ch. 9; Drew McCoy, *The Elusive Republic: Political Economy in Jeffersonian America* (Chapel Hill: University of North Carolina Press, 1996), 50–51, 114–119, 126–129; Jefferson's letter to Madison quoted on page 127.

51. Most books interested in slavery and capitalism focus on the antebellum cotton South. See Walter Johnson, *River of Dark Dreams: Slavery and Empire in the Cotton Kingdom* (Cambridge, MA: Belknap Press of Harvard University Press, 2013); Ed Baptist, *The Half Has Never Been Told: Slavery and the Making of American Capitalism* (New York: Basic Books, 2014). For the notion that cotton slavery was different from what had come before, see Anthony Kaye, "The Second Slavery: Modernity in the Nineteenth Century South and the Atlantic World," *Journal of Southern History* 75 (2009): 627–650.

52. For differences between American and Caribbean slavery, see Richard Dunn, *A Tale of Two Plantations: Slave Life and Labor in Jamaica and Virginia* (Cambridge, MA: Harvard University Press, 2014); David W. Galeson, "The Settlement and Growth of the Colonies: Population, Labor, and Economic Development," in *The Cambridge Economic History of the United States,* ed. Robert Gallman and Stanley Engerman (New York: Cambridge University Press, 1996), 175; On tobacco slavery, see Justin Roberts, *Slavery and Enlightenment in the British Atlantic* (New York: Cambridge University Press, 2013), 18; Phillip Morgan, *Slave Counterpoint: Black Culture in the Eighteenth Century Chesapeake and Low Country* (Chapel Hill: University of North Carolina Press, 1998), 100–101.

53. Smith, *Wealth of Nations,* book 1, ch. XI. On the absentee mentality, see Kolchin, *American Slavery,* 34–36; Galeson, "Settlement and Growth of Colonies," 164. On Chesapeake planters' disinterest in maximizing revenues or aggregating income, see Lorena Walsh, *Motives of Honor, Pleasure and Profit: Plantation Management in the Colonial Chesapeake, 1607–1673* (Chapel Hill: University of North Carolina Press, 2010), 12.

54. George Washington to Arthur Young, *PGW,* November 1, 1787. For Atlantic slave traders' treatment of slaves as commodities, see Gregory O'Malley, *Final Passages: The Intercolonial Slave Trade of British America* (Chapel Hill: University of North Carolina Press, 2016).

55. Robin Einhorn, *American Taxation, America Slavery* (Chicago: University of Chicago Press, 2008), 29, 49; James Glen, "An Attempt Towards an Estimate of the Value of South Carolina for the Right and Honorable the Lords Commissioners for Trade and Plantations, 1751," in *The Colonial South Carolina Scene: Contemporary Views, 1697–1774,* ed. H. Roy Merrens (Columbia: University of South Carolina Press, 1977), 185; British Board of Trade visitor quoted in Blodget, *Economica,* 80.

56. Advertisement dated November 6, 1827, in Slavery Documents, 1796–1864, reel 1, University of Virginia Library, Charlottesville.

57. W. E. B. Dubois, *The Suppression of the African Slave Trade to the United States of America, 1638–1870* (Baton Rouge, LA, 1896), 235–238; Adam Rothman, *Slave Country: American Expansion and the Origins of the Deep South* (Cambridge, MA:

Harvard University Press, 2007), 21; Steven Deyle, "The Irony of Liberty: Origins of the Domestic Slave Trade," *Journal of the Early Republic* 12 (Spring 1992).

58. *Boston-News Letter,* no. 112, June 10, 1706; *Weekly Magazine* 1, no. 2 (February 10, 1798): 62; Chaplin, *First Scientific American,* 82; Franklin, "Observations Concerning the Increase," 52.

59. Notes on Arthur Young's letter to George Washington, June 18, 1792, Papers of Thomas Jefferson.

60. Ibid.

61. Jefferson quoted in Joyce Appleby, *Thomas Jefferson: The American President Series* (New York: Times Books, 2003), 77. See also Ned and Constance Sublette, *American Slave Coast: A History of Slave-Breeding Industry* (Chicago: Monthly Review Press, 2015); Winthrop Jordan, *White over Black: American Attitudes towards the Negro, 1550–1812* (Chapel Hill: University of North Carolina Press, 1968), 430.

62. For reprint, see *Farmer's Register* 5, no. 6 (October 1, 1837): 338–339.

4. THE AGE OF MORAL STATISTICS

1. *Appendix to the Congressional Globe,* Senate, 28th Congress, 1st Session, February 1844, 708.

2. Calhoun's letter to Pakenham can be found in "Proceedings of the Senate and Documents Relative to Texas," 28th Congress, 2nd Session, 1844, Senate Document 341, 52.

3. For the leading studies on "moral statistics" in Europe, see Society for the Education of the Poor, *Moral Statistics of the Highlands and Islands of Scotland* (Inverness, 1826); André-Michel Guerry, *Essai sur la Statistique Morale de la France* (Paris, 1833); Joseph Fletcher, "Moral and Educational Statistics of England and Wales," *Journal of the Statistical Society of London* 10 (1847): 193–221 and 12 (1849): 151–176. For use of the term in the United States, see *American Tract Society Annual Reports,* 1845, 73; Nahum Capen and Jesse Chickering, *Letters Addressed to the Hon. John Davis, Concerning the Census of 1849* (Washington, DC: T. Ritchie, 1849); *Minutes of the General Assembly of the Presbyterian Church* (Philadelphia, 1840), 4. For moral statistics, see Frank Hamilton Hankins, *Adolphe Quetelet as Statistician* (New York: AMS Press, 1908), ch. IV; Michael J. Cullen, *The Statistical Movement in Early Victorian Britain: The Foundations of Empirical Social Research* (New York: Barnes and Noble, 1975).

4. Patricia Cline Cohen, *A Calculating People: The Spread of Numeracy in Early America* (Chicago: University of Chicago Press, 1982), 175–205

5. *Anti-Slavery Bugle,* March 2, 1850. For anti-slavery almanacs, see Teresa Goddu, "The Antislavery Almanac and the Discourse of Numeracy," *Book History* 12 (2009): 129–155.

6. For the social changes under way in this era, see Paul Johnson, *A Shopkeeper's Millennium: Society and Revivals in Rochester, New York, 1815–1837* (New York: Hill and Wang, 1979); Michael Zakim, *Ready-Made Democracy: A History of Men's Dress in the American Republic, 1760–1860* (Chicago: Chicago University Press, 2003); Mary Ryan, *Cradle of the Middle Class: The Family in Oneida County, New York, 1790–1865* (New York: Cambridge University Press, 1983); Seth Rockman, *Scraping By: Wage Labor, Slavery and Survival in Early Baltimore* (Baltimore: Johns Hopkins University Press, 2009).

7. For paternalist justifications of slavery in the South, see Lacy K. Ford, *Deliver Us from Evil: The Slavery Question in the Old South* (New York: Oxford University Press, 2009); Jeffrey Young, *Domesticating Slavery: The Master Class in Georgia and South Carolina, 1670–1837* (Chapel Hill: University of North Carolina Press, 1999); Stephen Stowe, *Intimacy and Power in the Old South: Ritual in the Lives of the Planters* (Baltimore: Johns Hopkins University Press, 1990); Eugene Genovese, *The World the Slaveholders Made: Two Essays in Interpretation* (New York: Vintage, 1974), 195–235.

8. Michel Foucault, *Discipline and Punish: The Birth of the Prison* (New York: Vintage, 1995); Michel Foucault, "Governmentality," in *The Foucault Effect: Studies in Governmentality,* trans. R. Braidotti, ed. G. Burchell, C. Gordon, and P. Miller (Chicago: University of Chicago Press, 1991).

9. On money, see Jeffrey Sklansky, *Sovereign of the Market: The Money Question in Early America* (Chicago: Chicago University Press, 2017); Stephen Mihm, *A Nation of Counterfeiters: Capitalists, Con Men, and the Making of the United States* (Cambridge, MA: Harvard University Press, 2009); Bray Hammond, *Banks and Politics in America from the Revolution to the Civil War* (Princeton, NJ: Princeton University Press, 1991), 326–369; Peter Temin, *The Jacksonian Economy* (New York: Norton, 1969);

10. Joseph Worcester, *The American Almanac of Useful Knowledge* (Boston: Bowen, 1838), 189; *American Almanac* (Boston, 1836), 87.

11. For the rise of moral statistics in Europe, see Cullen, *Statistical Movement*; Felix Driver, *Power and Pauperism: The Workhouse System, 1834–1884* (New York: Cambridge University Press, 2004), 10–11; Nikolas Rose, "Calculable Minds and Manageable Individuals," *History of Human Sciences* 1 (October 1988): 179–200; F. Mort, *Dangerous Sexualities: Medico-Moral Politics in England since 1830* (London: Routledge, 1987), 11–47; Ian Hacking, "Biopower and the Avalanche of Printed Numbers," *Humanities in Society* 5 (1982): 279–295; Libby Schweber, *Disciplining Statistics: Demography and Vital Statistics in France and England, 1830–1885* (Durham, NC: Duke University Press, 2006).

12. For liberalism and statistics, see Schweber, *Disciplining Statistics*, 1–7; Ted Porter, *Trust in Numbers: The Pursuit of Objectivity in Science and Public Life* (Princeton,

NJ: Princeton University Press, 1996). For statistics and "population," see Michel Foucault, *Security, Territory, Population: Lectures at the Collège de France, 1977–1978* (New York: Palgrave Macmillan, 2009); Michel Foucault, *The Birth of Biopolitics: Lectures at the Collège de France, 1978–1979* (New York: Palgrave Macmillan, 2009); Bruce Curtis, *The Politics of Population* (Toronto: University of Toronto Press, 2001). On the rise of statistics, see Ian Hacking, *The Taming of Chance* (Cambridge: Cambridge University Press, 1990); Ted Porter, *The Rise of Statistical Thinking, 1820–1900* (Princeton, NJ: Princeton University Press, 1986), 41–55; Cullen, *Statistical Movement*, 78–89.

13. Cullen, *Statistical Movement*, 20–42. On Farr, see John Eyler, *Victorian Social Medicine: The Ideas and Methods of William Farr* (Baltimore: Johns Hopkins University Press, 1979). For Chadwick, see Richard Lewis, *Edwin Chadwick and the Public Health Movement, 1832–1854* (London: Longmans Green, 1952).

14. On the Manchester Statistical Society, see Cullen, *Statistical Movement*, 105–119; James Phillips Kay, *The Moral and Physical Condition of the Working Classes in the Cotton Manufacture in Manchester* (London, 1832), 61. For the industrial revolution in Manchester, see Sven Beckert, *Empire of Cotton: A Global History* (New York: Knopf, 2015), 56–82.

15. Kay, *Moral and Physical Condition*, 63; Cullen, *Statistical Movement*, 105–112, 143. On the Gregs, see Michael James, *From Smuggling to Cotton Kings: The Greg Story* (Cirencester, UK: Memoirs, 2010).

16. Cullen, *Statistical Movement*, 108; *Report of a Committee of the Manchester Statistical Society on the Condition of the Working Classes in an Extensive Manufacturing District* (London, 1838).

17. William Farr, *First Annual Report of the Register-General of Birth, Deaths and Marriages in England* (London, 1839), 89.

18. *Mechanics Magazine and Register of Inventions and Improvements* 4, no. 1 (1834): 14; Francis Lieber, "The Approaching Census," *United States Magazine and Democratic Review* 5 (1839): 79. Lemuel Shattuck to J. H. Lister, Register General of England, February 20, 1839; Shattuck to Thomas Rowe Edmonds, June 29, 1839; Shattuck to Dr. Rothenberg, April 21, 1849, March 14, 1850; Shattuck to Adolphe Quetelet, August 27, 1849; all in Lemuel Shattuck Papers, Massachusetts Historical Society, Boston (henceforth LSP). On Shattuck and the ASA, see Walter F. Wilcox, "Lemuel Shattuck, Statist, Founder of the American Statistical Association," *Journal of the American Statistical Association* 35 (1940): 224–235; Paul Fitzpatrick, "Leading American Statisticians in the Nineteenth Century," *Journal of the American Statistical Association* 52 (1957): 301–321; ASA circular dated April 4, 1840, LSP.

19. *Green-Mountain Freeman*, January 1, 1846. For the rise of European-like social relations in America, see Jonathan Glickstein, *American Exceptionalism, Amer-*

ican Anxiety: Wages, Competition and Degraded Labor in the Antebellum United States (Charlottesville: University of Virginia Press, 2002).

20. Walter Licht, *Industrializing America: The Nineteenth Century* (Baltimore: Johns Hopkins University Press, 1995), 21–45; Sean Wilentz, *Chants Democratic: New York City and the Rise of the American Working Class, 1788–1850* (New York: Oxford University Press, 2004), 23–107; Bruce Laurie, *Artisans into Workers: Labor in Nineteenth-Century America* (New York: Hill and Wang, 1989).

21. Licht, *Industrializing America*, 34–44; Wilentz, *Chants Democratic*, 107–145; Jonathan Prude, *The Coming of Industrial Order: Town and Factory in Rural Massachusetts, 1810–1860* (Amherst: University of Massachusetts Press, 1983); Alan Dawley, *Class and Community: The Industrial Revolution in Lynn* (Cambridge, MA: Harvard University Press, 1976); Amy Dru Stanley, *From Bondage to Contract: Wage Labor, Marriage and the Market in the Age of Slave Emancipation* (New York: Cambridge University Press, 1999).

22. For industrial discipline, see Prude, *Industrial Order*, 28, 111; Thomas Dublin, *Women at Work: The Transformation of Work and Community in Lowell, Massachusetts, 1826–1860* (New York: Columbia University Press, 1981), 59–61. On transiency rates and the spatial segregation of classes, see Stephen Thenstrom, *Poverty and Progress: Social Mobility in a Nineteenth Century City* (Cambridge, MA: Harvard University Press, 1980). For the changing politics of the era, see Samuel P. Hays, "The Changing Political Structure of the City in Industrial America," *Journal of Urban History* 1 (November 1974): 6–37.

23. On Lowell and the Boston Associates as reluctant revolutionaries, see Robert Dalzell, *Enterprising Elite: The Boston Associates and the World They Made* (Cambridge, MA: Harvard University Press, 1987), Appleton quote on 12.

24. Joseph Sturge, *A Visit to the United States in 1841* (London, 1842), 143–145. Moral statistics also cropped up in the local newspaper. See, for instance, *Lowell Offering*, December 1843, 47; Rev. Henry A. Miles, *Lowell, As It Was, and As It Is* (Lowell, 1845), 128, 131.

25. Ryan, *Cradle of the Middle Class*, 105–107, quote from 116.

26. *Twentieth Annual Report of the American Tract Society* (New York, 1845), 73. On religious changes under way, see Johnson, *Shopkeeper's Millennium*; Daniel Walker Howe, *What Hath God Wrought: The Transformation of America, 1815–1848* (New York: Oxford University Press, 2009), 164–202. For statistics in sermons, see Robert Abzug, *Cosmos Crumbling: American Reform and the Religious Imagination* (New York: Oxford University Press, 1994), 90–99.

27. "Lemuel Shattuck Diary," LSP; "The University of Michigania's Primary School," *Michigan Alumni Quarterly Review* 55 (1948): 41.

28. Lemuel Shattuck, *Report to the Committee of the City Council Appointed to Obtain the Census of Boston for the Year 1845* (Boston, 1846), iv; prospectus of "The Philanthropist" in LSP, box 1.

29. *Minutes of the General Assembly of the Presbyterian Church* (Philadelphia, 1840), 4; American Temperance Society cited in *The Farmer's Cabinet and American Herd-Book* 5, no. 10 (1841): 326–327; *Annual Report of the New York Magdalen Society*, 1830; Ryan, *Cradle of the Middle Class*, 61, 109.

30. Ryan, *Cradle of the Middle Class*, 125; New York, Oswego County, *R. G. Dun & Co. Credit Report Volumes*, vol. 512, 69, Baker Library, Harvard Business School, Boston. For the Mercantile Credit Agency, see Scott Sandage, *Born Losers: A History of Failure in America* (Cambridge, MA: Harvard University Press, 2006).

31. Josiah Quincy, *Massachusetts, General Court, Committee on Pauper Laws* (Boston, 1821); Blanche Coll, *Perspectives in Public Welfare: A History* (Washington, DC: U.S. Social and Rehabilitation Service, 1969), 25. On state prisons, see Edward Ayers, *Vengeance and Justice: Crime and Punishment in the 19th Century American South* (New York: Oxford University Press, 1985); Adam Hirsch, *The Rise of the Penitentiary: Prisons and Punishment in Early America* (New Haven, CT: Yale University Press, 1980). On the rise of the asylum, see David Rothman, *Discovery of the Asylum: Social Order and Disorder in the New Republic* (Boston: Little, Brown, 1971).

32. Quoted in Rothman, *Discovery of the Asylum*, 84.

33. For colonial times, see "Schedule of Expenditures for the Maintenance of the Poor of New-Castle County, from Jan. 1802 to Jan. 1803 by the Trustees of the Poor," *Early American Imprints*, Series 2, no. 50380; *An Account of the Philadelphia Dispensary Instituted for the Medical Relief of the Poor, April 12, 1786* (Philadelphia, 1803), 17; New York Secretary of State report cited in *Yazoo City Whig*, May 23, 1845.

34. Shattuck, *Census of Boston*, 107, 125–126; Capen and Chickering, *Letters*, 9.

35. *Congressional Globe*, 25th Congress, 3rd Session, February 1839, 209; *The Man*, November 27, 1834; Sklansky, "William Leggett and the Melodrama of the Market."

36. Humphrey quoted in Abzug, *Cosmos Crumbling*, 90–99.

37. Isaac Richmond Barbour, *A Statistical Table Showing the Influence of Intemperance on the Churches* (Boston, 1831). For Walker's figures, see *The Voice of Freedom*, November 30, 1839. On temperance and industrialization, see Johnson, *Shopkeeper's Millennium*, 79–93.

38. *McDowall's Journal*, February–May 1834; *Annual Report of the New York Magdalen Society*, 1830. For prostitution censuses, see "Report by the New York Female Reform Society," in Butt Ender, *Prostitution Exposed, or, A Moral Reform Directory* (New York, 1839); *Licentiousness, Its Effects and Causes* (Boston, 1846). For Cincinnati's "census of prostitutes," see *Cincinnati Daily Gazette*, December 13

and December 15, 1858. See also Timothy J. Gilfoyle, *City of Eros: New York City, Prostitution, and the Commercialization of Sex, 1790–1920* (New York: Norton, 1994), 57–59; *Encyclopedia of Prostitution and Sex Work,* ed. Melissa Hope Ditmore (Westport, CT: Greenwood Press, 2006), 293.

39. George Templeton Strong, quoted in Lawrence Friedman, *Crime and Punishment in America* (New York: Basic Books, 1993), 367; *The Sun* and Foster in Gilfoyle, *City of Eros,* 59.

40. William Sanger, *History of Prostitution* (New York, 1858), 458.

41. "The Slave Power—Morally," *The Liberty Almanac* (New York, 1849), 40.

42. Horace Mann, *Third Annual Report of the Board of Education* (Boston, 1840), 50–56, 74–78; Mann, *Sixth Annual Report of the Board of Education* (Boston, 1843), 55. For Mann, see Michael Katz, *The Irony of Early School Reform* (Cambridge, MA: Harvard University Press, 1968).

43. Katz, *Irony of Early School Reform,* 28–29, 43; Horace Mann, *Twelfth Annual Report of the Board of Education* (Boston, 1849), 60.

44. William Woodbridge, *American Annals of Education* (Boston, 1834), 255; *American Republican and Baltimore Daily Clipper,* December 11, 1845; *Niles National Register,* March 9, 1841; *New York Tribune,* March 14, 1844.

45. Shattuck, *Census of Boston,* 119.

46. *The Spirit of Democracy* (Woodsfield, OH), February 5, 1848; *Carrollton* (OH) *Free Press,* July 2, 1847; *Antislavery Bugle,* July 6, 1850. For government reports, see Oz Frankel, *States of Inquiry: Social Investigations and Print Culture in Nineteenth Century Britain and the United States* (Baltimore: Johns Hopkins University Press, 2006).

47. Edward Jarvis, "Statistics of Insanity in the United States," *Boston Medical and Surgical Journal* 27, no. 7 (September 21, 1842). For the scandal surrounding insanity statistics, see Cohen, *Calculating People,* 175–205. For Jarvis, see Gerald Grob, *Edward Jarvis and the Medical World of the Nineteenth Century* (Knoxville: University of Tennessee Press, 1978).

48. Edward Jarvis, "Statistics of Insanity," *Boston Medical and Surgical Journal* 27, no. 17 (November 30, 1842).

49. *Hunt's Merchants Magazine* 8 (1843): 290; "Reflections on the Census of 1840," *Southern Literary Messenger* 9 (June 1843): 340–342, 350.

50. Cohen, *Calculating People,* ch. 6.

51. Samuel Woodward, *Tenth Annual Report of the Trustees of the State Lunatic Asylum at Worcester, Massachusetts* (Boston, 1842); *Phrenological Journal and Magazine of Moral Science* 17 (1843): 318.

52. Jarvis quoted in Rothman, *Discovery of the Asylum,* 115–116.

53. "Reflections on the Census of 1840."

54. "Errors in the Sixth Census," 28th Congress, 2nd Session, 1845, House Document 116.

55. *The Examiner* (Louisville, KY), June 23, 1849; Theodore Parker, "Letter on Slavery," *Collected Works of Theodore Parker*, vol. 5, *Discourses on Slavery* (London, 1863), 51.

56. "American Almanac," *Southern Literary Messenger* 2 (1835): 68; "Popular Knowledge the Necessity of Popular Government," *Southern Literary Messenger* 19 (1843): 298. Lieber's memorial can be found in his "Approaching Census," 79.

57. James Oakes, *Slavery and Freedom: An Interpretation of the Old South* (New York: Norton, 1990), 41. For social control on the plantation, see Caitlin Rosenthal, "Slavery's Scientific Management: Masters and Managers," in *Slavery's Capitalism,* ed. Sven Beckert and Seth Rockman (Philadelphia: University of Pennsylvania Press, 2016), 62–87; Drew Faust, *James Henry Hammond and the Old South: A Design for Mastery* (Baton Rouge: Louisiana State University Press, 1985). On the notion that plantations were prisons, see Walter Johnson, *River of Dark Dreams: Slavery and Empire in the Cotton Kingdom* (Cambridge, MA: Harvard University Press, 2013), 209–244.

58. Josiah Nott, "Life Insurance," *De Bow's Review* 3 (May 1847); Reginald Horsman, *Josiah Nott of Mobile: Southerner, Physician and Racial Theorist* (Baton Rouge: Louisiana State University Press, 1987); Nott to Shattuck, October 20, 1846, LSP; Josiah Nott, "Statistics of Southern Slave Population," *De Bow's Review* 4 (November, 1847): 275–277; Calhoun quoted in William Dexter Williams, *A Discourse on Slavery* (Concord, 1839).

59. Michael Tadman, *Speculators and Slaves: Masters, Traders and Slaves in the Old South* (Madison: University of Wisconsin Press, 1989), 12. For the internal slave trade, see Walter Johnson, *Soul by Soul: Life inside the Antebellum Slave Market* (Cambridge, MA: Harvard University Press, 1999); Walter Johnson, ed., *The Chattel Principle: Internal Slave Trades in the Americas* (New Haven, CT: Yale University Press, 2004).

60. Corpus of Historical American English, corpus.byu.edu/coha/; Google Ngram, Newsbank's American Historical Newspapers.

61. *The Madisonian,* September 8, 1838; *Illinois Free Trader and LaSalle County Commercial Advertiser,* June 24, 1842; *Rutland Herald,* June 13, 1837, and April 19, 1842; *American Sentinel,* February 10, 1830, *Carroll Free Press,* August 5, 1836; *The Emancipator,* November 15, 1838, July 19, 1838, and March 29, 1838; *Philadelphia Inquirer,* May 5, 1830; *Southern Argus,* November 14, 1837.

62. William Gouge, *History of Paper Money and Banking* (New York, 1835), 97; Vale quoted in Joseph Leon Blau, *Social Theories of Jacksonian Democracy: Representative Writings* (New York: Hafner, 1974), 237.

63. Adams quoted in Gordon Wood, *The Radicalism of the American Revolution* (New York: Vintage, 1991), 318; Byllesby quoted in Joseph Dorfman, *The Economic Mind in American Civilization* (New York, 1946), 1:638. For American conceptions of labor exploitation, see James L. Huston, *Securing the Fruits of Our Labor: The American Concept of Wealth Distribution 1765–1900* (Baton Rouge: Louisiana State University Press, 1998), part II; Wilentz, *Chants Democratic*, 145–255. On money and the crisis of representation in this era, see Sklansky, *Sovereign of the Market*, part II. For inflation and its political backlash, see Temin, *Jacksonian Economy*, 59–91; Hammond, *Banks and Politics*, 115–144. For the impact that the Second Great Awakening had on feelings toward money, see Mark Noll, *God and Mammon: Protestants, Money and the Market, 1790–1860* (New York: Oxford University Press, 2001).

64. Josiah Warren's poem quoted in Dorfman, *Economic Mind*, 1:671, Josiah Warren, *Equitable Commerce: A New Development of Principles* (New York, 1852); Darryl Jones and Donald Pitzer, *New Harmony Then and Now* (Bloomington: Indiana University Press, 2011), 74. For equitable labor exchange, see Robert Owen's letter to the *London Times*, October 5, 1832. The idea of time banks has not gone away; see Edgar Cahn, "Time Banking: An Idea Whose Time Has Come?" *Yes Magazine*, April 7, 2013.

65. Mann, *Twelfth Report*, 54; Shattuck, *Census of Boston*, 137–138.

66. Nott to Shattuck, October 20, 1846, LSP. For Nott's failed attempts to use statistics to prove his racist theories, see Nott to Samuel George Morton, October 15, 1844, July 20, 1845, and July 15, 1845, Samuel Morton Papers, Library Company of Philadelphia, Philadelphia; Nott, "Statistics of Southern Slave Population." On Nott, the census, and mulatto statistics, see Margo Anderson, *The American Census: A Social History* (New Haven, CT: Yale University Press, 1988), 37–40; Jennifer Hochschild, "Racial Reorganization and the United States Census 1850–1930: Mulattoes, Half-Breeds, Mixed Parentage, Hindoos, and the Mexican Race," *Studies in American Political Development* 22 (2008): 59–96.

67. Nott, "Statistics of Southern Slave Population." On the rise of slave life insurance, see Sharon Murphy, *Investing in Life: Insurance in Antebellum America* (Baltimore: Johns Hopkins University Press, 2010).

68. Washington Irving, "The Creole Village," *Knickerbocker Magazine,* November 12, 1836. See Google Ngram for the explosion of the term in the 1850s.

5. THE HUNT FOR GROWTH

1. *Post-Dispatch* quoted in Jeanette C. Lauer and Robert H. Lauer, "St. Louis and the 1880 Census: The Shock of Collective Failure," *Missouri Historical Review* 76 (1982): 152; *St. Louis Globe-Democrat*, June 19, 1880; *Illinois State Register* quoted in *St. Louis Globe-Democrat*, June 22, 1880.

2. *St. Louis Globe-Democrat,* June 19, 1880; *Post-Dispatch* quoted in Lauer and Lauer, "St. Louis and the 1880 Census," 154; *St. Louis Globe-Democrat,* June 20, 1880.

3. *St. Louis Globe-Democrat,* June 19 and June 24, 1880; Lauer and Lauer, "St. Louis and the 1880 Census," 153–154.

4. *St. Louis Globe-Democrat,* June 22, 1880; Lauer and Lauer, "St. Louis and the 1880 Census." For census recounts, see Margo Anderson, *The American Census: A Social History* (New Haven, CT: Yale University Press, 1988), 78; Robert G. Borrows, "The Ninth Federal Census of Indianapolis: A Case Study in Civic Chauvinism," *Indiana Magazine of History* 73, no. 1 (March 1977): 1–16.

5. Little has been written on the magazine. See Richard Hofstadter, *Anti-Intellectualism in American Life* (New York: Vintage, 1966), 245–254; Frank Luther Mott, *History of American Magazines,* vol. 1, *1741–1850* (Cambridge, MA: Harvard University Press, 1930), 696–697.

6. Freeman Hunt, *Lives of American Merchants* (New York, 1856), 1:iv. For the ties between business elites and urban growth, see Harvey Molotch, "The City as a Growth Machine: Toward a Political Economy of Place," *American Journal of Sociology* 82, no. 2 (September 1976): 309–322. For a more celebratory approach to this culture of growth, see Daniel Boorstin, *The Americans: The National Experience* (New York: Random House, 1965), 113–161.

7. For growth in the twentieth century, see Robert M. Collins, *More: The Politics of Economic Growth in Postwar America* (New York: Oxford University Press, 2000); Andrew Yarrow, *Measuring America: How Economic Growth Came to Define American Greatness in the Late Twentieth Century* (Amherst: University of Massachusetts Press, 2011).

8. Hunt's letters were so popular he published them in book form. See Freeman Hunt, *Letters about the Hudson River and Its Vicinity* (New York, 1836), 1, 12, 13–14; Gideon Miner Davison, *The Fashionable Tour in 1825: An Excursion to the Springs, Niagara, Quebec and Boston* (Saratoga Springs, NY, 1825), 40.

9. Hunt, *Letters about the Hudson,* 19. On the fashionable tour literature of the era, see Richard H. Gassan, *The Birth of American Tourism: New York, the Hudson Valley, and American Culture, 1790–1830* (Amherst: University of Massachusetts Press, 2008), 73–77.

10. Hunt, *Letters about the Hudson,* 15. Hunt left behind few papers. For Hunt's career, see Burton R. Pollin, "Poe, Freeman Hunt, and Four Unrecorded Reviews of Poe's Work," *Texas Studies in Literature and Language* 16, no. 2 (Summer 1974): 306; Henrietta Larson, "Plutarch's Lives of Trade: The First Series of American Business Biographies," *Bulletin of the Business Historical Society* 20 (February 1946): 28–32; Jerome Thomases, "Freeman Hunt's America," *Mississippi*

Valley Historical Review 30 (1943): 395–407; "Freeman Hunt on the Science of Business," *Business History Review* 18 (1944): 9–10.

11. For Hunt's obituary, see *New York Times,* March 4, 1858.

12. Bray Hammond, *Banks and Politics in America from the Revolution to the Civil War* (Princeton, NJ: Princeton University Press, 1991), chs. 6–7; John Denis Haeger, *The Investment Frontier: New York Businessmen and the Economic Development of the Old Northwest* (Albany: State University of New York Press, 1981), 8–12; Alfred Chandler, *The Visible Hand: The Managerial Revolution in American* (Cambridge, MA: Harvard University Press, 1977), 15–47.

13. Lance E. Davis and Robert J. Cull, *International Capital Markets and American Economic Growth, 1820–1914* (New York: Cambridge University Press, 2002), 1, 4–10.

14. Mira Wilkins, *The History of Foreign Investment in the United States, 1914–1945* (Cambridge, MA: Harvard University Press, 1989), 55–62; Myers, *Financial History,* 106–113; William Roy, *Socializing Capital: The Rise of the Large Industrial Corporation in America* (Princeton, NJ: Princeton University Press, 1997), 57–77; George Taylor, *The Transportation Revolution, 1815–1860* (New York: Routledge, 1977); Carter Goodrich, *Canals and American Economic Development* (New York: Columbia University Press, 1961).

15. Davis and Cull, *International Capital,* 6.

16. Wilkins, *History of Foreign Investment,* 55–67; Myers, *Financial History,* 143–147.

17. Paul Gates, "Frontier Land Business in Wisconsin," *Wisconsin Magazine of History* 52, no. 4 (Summer 1969): 306; "The Role of the Land Speculator in Western Development," *Pennsylvania Magazine of History and Biography* 66, no. 3 (July 1942): 314–333. On canals and city investment, see also William Cronon, *Nature's Metropolis: Chicago and the Great West* (Chicago: Chicago University Press, 1991), ch. 1; Patrick McLear, "Speculation, Promotion and the Panic of 1837 in Chicago," *Journal of the Illinois State Historical Society* 62 (Summer 1969): 135–146.

18. Elizabeth Blackmar, *Manhattan for Rent, 1785–1850* (Ithaca, NY: Cornell University Press, 1991), 184–189. For the significance of urban real estate see Thomas C. Cochran, "The Entrepreneur in American Capital Formation," in *Capital Formation and Economic Growth* (Princeton, NJ: Princeton University Press, 1955), 337–394.

19. John Haeger, *John Jacob Astor: Business and Finance in the Early Republic* (Detroit: Wayne State University Press, 1991). For a sense of Astor's real estate investments, see John Jacob Astor Business Records, 1784–1892, box 5, volumes 36–38, Baker Library, Harvard Business School, Boston; "Kittredge and Maynard Account Book, 1831–1837," Records Relating to Estate, Real Estate and Private

Investment Management, 1765–1914, series II, Baker Library, Harvard Business School, Boston.

20. Contract between Henry Betts and Samuel Ruggles, Samuel Ruggles Papers (henceforth SRP), Manuscripts and Archives Division, New York Public Library, box 1, folder 21. For Ruggles, see also Daniel Thompson, *Ruggles of New York: A Life of Samuel E. Ruggles* (New York: Columbia University Press, 1946).

21. On the cities as capitalized investments, see David Harvey, *The Urban Experience* (Baltimore: Johns Hopkins University Press, 1986), 17–59, 90–109; Molotch, "City as a Growth Machine."

22. Goodrich, *Canals and American Economic Development*, 224–232; Jeffrey Williamson, "Antebellum Urbanization in the American Northeast," *Journal of Economic History* 25, no. 4 (December 1965): 592–608.

23. Samuel Ruggles, *Tabular Statements from 1840 to 1870, of the Agricultural Products of the States and Territories of the United States of America* (New York, 1874). For the statistical conference and the preparation of his report, see Department of State invitation from May 14, 1869, Ruggles to Bureau of Statistics, July 9, 1869, documents dated February 8 and December 26, 1869, box 1, folder 16, SRP; for "bushels to head," see circular dated June 19, 1869, box 1, folder 16, SRP. See also material in box 1, folder 27, SRP.

24. Benjamin Tallmadge to Samuel Ruggles, December 18, 1831, and Ruggles to Tallmadge, January 23, 1832, box 1, folder 15, SRP.

25. Ruggles to Tallmadge, January 23, 1832, box 1, folder 15, SRP. For his paid commissions, see October 17, 1833, box 1, folder 21; box 2, folder 19, SRP.

26. On plats, see Jon Petersen, *The Birth of City Planning in the United States* (Baltimore: Johns Hopkins University Press, 2003), 1–22; John Reps, *The Making of Urban America: A History of City Planning in the United States* (Princeton, NJ: Princeton University Press, 1965). For cities and canals, see Harry Scheiber, *Ohio Canal Era: A Case Study of Government and the Economy, 1820–1861* (Athens: Ohio University Press, 1968).

27. Thomas Ford, *A History of Illinois: From Its Commencement as a State in 1818 to 1847* (Chicago, 1854), 123. On land values in Chicago, see Homer Hoyt, *One Hundred Years of Land Values in Chicago: The Relationship of the Growth of Chicago to the Rise of Its Land Values, 1830–1933* (Chicago: University of Chicago Press, 1933), 36–38. For land speculation, see also Robert Swierenga, *Pioneers and Profits: Land Speculation on the Iowa Frontier* (Ames: Iowa State University Press, 1968); McLear, "Speculation, Promotion, and the Panic."

28. Michael J. Doucet, "Urban Land Development in Nineteenth Century North America," *Journal of Urban History* 8, no. 3 (May 1982): 317–318.

29. "Proposals for Publishing a Monthly Periodical, to Be Called the Merchants' Magazine and Commercial Review," *American Broadsides and Ephemera,* series 1,

no. 5313 (1838); *Hunt's Merchants' Magazine and Commercial Review* (henceforth *HMM*) 1 (1839): 192.

30. George White to Arthur Bronson, September 21, 1833, November 13, 1833, April 1, 1834, June 26, 1834, Bronson Family Papers, box 18, Manuscripts and Archives Division, New York Public Library.

31. See Butler's diary of his and Bronson's 1833 trip in Charles Butler Papers, Library of Congress, Washington, DC. For capitalists' desire for economic knowledge in this era, see Michael Zakim, "Producing Capitalism," in *Capitalism Takes Command: The Social Transformation of Nineteenth-Century America*, ed. Michael Zakim and Gary John Kornblith (Chicago: University of Chicago Press, 2012).

32. *HMM* 1 (1839): 1.

33. Hunt cited in "Freeman Hunt on the Science of Business," 9–10. On the Panic of 1837, see Jessica Lepler, *The Many Panics of 1837: People, Politics and the Creation of a Transatlantic Financial Crisis* (New York: Cambridge University Press, 2013); Scott Nelson, *A Nation of Deadbeats: An Uncommon History of America's Financial Disasters* (New York: Vintage, 2013), 48–95.

34. *HMM* 21 (1849): 143; Freeman Hunt, "The Moral End of Business," *HMM* 1 (1839): 390; Freeman Hunt, *Worth and Wealth: A Collection of Maxims, Morals, and Miscellanies for Merchants and Men of Business* (New York, 1856), 106. See Richard Weiss, *The American Myth of Success: From Horatio Alger to Norman Vincent Peale* (New York: Basic Books, 1969), 37–47.

35. The ever-changing list of organizations that sponsored and praised the magazine appeared on the back cover of each edition. For the history of the business press before Hunt's, see David Forsyth, *The Business Press in America* (Philadelphia: Chilton Books, 1964).

36. "Letter from the Hon. Henry Clay," *HMM* 21 (1849): 368; letter from Abbot Lawrence to Freeman Hunt printed in *Daily National Intelligencer*, July 15, 1854; *HMM* 31 (1854): 262; *HMM* 24 (1851), back cover.

37. Edgar Allan Poe, "The Literati of New York," *Godey's Magazine and Lady's Book* 32 (1846), 269–270. For Minard's maps, see Arthur H. Robinson, "The Thematic Maps of Charles Joseph Minard," *Imago Mundi* 21 (1967): 95–108.

38. Data are based only on the statistical section of each issue and do not include whatever statistics appeared in the middle of articles.

39. A random sampling of fifty issues of the *New-York Commercial Advertiser* from 1800 until 1825 revealed that more than 80 percent of the articles on the census were related to congressional representation and not economic issues. See also Timothy Pitkin, *A Statistical View of the Commerce of the United States* (New York, 1817).

40. Chickering to Hunt, July 17, 1847, Jesse Chickering Papers, David M. Rubenstein Rare Book and Manuscript Library, Duke University, Durham, NC, box 2.

41. Jesup Wakeman to Jesup Scott, 1833(?), Jesup Scott Papers (henceforth JSP), Toledo Public Library, Toledo, OH, box 1, folder 1; Federal Writers' Project, *Ohio: The Ohio Guide* (Columbus, 1940), 326; Scott quoted in Charles Glaab, "Jesup W. Scott and a West of Cities," *Ohio History* 73 (1964): 3–12. For Scott's initial desire to move to the area for business reasons, see Jesup Scott to John E. Hunt, July 1828, box 1, folder 1, JSP. For Toledo speculation, see real estate map collection at the Toledo Public Library, which contains numerous plats that detail who owned each part of the city. See also Harry N. Scheiber, "Entrepreneurship and Western Development: The Case of Micajah T. Williams," *Business History Review* (1963): 345–368; H. E. Davis, "Elisha Whittlesey and Maumee Land Speculation," *Northwest Ohio Quarterly* 15 (1943): 139–158. For Scott, see Cronon, *Nature's Metropolis*, 35–46; Henry Nash Smith, *Virgin Land: The American West as Myth and Symbol* (Cambridge, MA: Harvard University Press, 1971), 155–164.

42. See map in JSP that reveals exactly where he owned land in Toledo. Jesup Scott, "Note in Reply to an Attack on JW Scott in the Maumee River Times," 1844, box 1, folder 1, JSP.

43. For Scott's life on the frontier, see his son Frank's unpublished autobiography, "Autobiography—Frank J. Scott," box 1, folder 8, JSP; Jesup Scott, *Miami of the Lake*, December 11, 1833.

44. For a representative sample of these arguments, see Jesup Scott, "The Progress of the West," *HMM* 14 (1846): 163–165; Jesup Scott, "Commercial Cities and the Towns of the United States," *HMM* 19 (1848): 385; Jesup Scott, "The Growth of Towns in the United States," *HMM* 25 (1851): 559–565; Jesup Scott, "Our American Lake Cities," *HMM* 31 (1854): 403–413. A list of all of Scott's contributions to *HMM* can be found in box 1, folder 12, JSP.

45. J. W. Scott, "The Internal Trade of the United States," *HMM* 8 (1843): 32. Scott was quoting a British member of Parliament.

46. Ibid.

47. Scott, "Our American Lake Cities," 404, 410–411; Scott, "Growth of Towns," 562; Scott, "Internal Trade," 35; Cronon, *Nature's Metropolis*, 398 n. 68.

48. Scott, "Internal Trade," 35.

49. Jesup Scott, *Ohio and Michigan Emigrant Guide* 1 (1833): 2, 25, in box 1, folder 12, JSP; Jesup Scott's lecture before the Maumee City Lyceum, November 29, 1842, box 1, folder 3, JSP.

50. Ely quoted in Tipton Snavely, *George Tucker as Political Economist* (Charlottesville: University of Virginia Press, 1964), 14. For the book version of the serialized works, see George Tucker, *The Laws of Wages, Profits and Rent* (New York, 1837). See also George Tucker, *Progress of the United States in Population and Wealth for Fifty Years* (New York: Hunt's Merchants' Magazine Press, 1843). For Tucker's economic thought, see Joseph Dorfman, *The Economic Mind in American*

Civilization, 1606–1865 (New York: Viking Press, 1949), 2:538–551, 881–889; Paul Keith Conkin, *Prophets of Prosperity: America's First Political Economists* (Bloomington: Indiana University Press, 1980), 152–166.

51. For the study of political economy in early America, see Dorfman, *Economic Mind,* 2:503–512, 695–713.

52. For the Tuckers in Bermuda, see Julia C. Mercer, "Genealogical Notes from Bermuda," in *Tyler's Quarterly Historical and Geographical Magazine,* various issues from 1942 to 1947. On slave surnames and slave trading, see Virginia Berhnard, *Slaves and Slaveholders in Bermuda, 1616–1782* (Columbia: University of Missouri Press, 1999), 74, 231.

53. George Tucker to J. Meredith, May 2, 1837, George Tucker Papers, University of Virginia Library, Charlottesville. For Tucker's eclectic writings, see Robert C. McLean, *George Tucker: Moral Philosopher and Man of Letters* (Chapel Hill: University of North Carolina Press, 1961).

54. George Tucker, *Letters from Virginia Translated from the French* (Baltimore, 1816); George Tucker, *The Valley of the Shenandoah* (New York, 1824); Christopher Michael Curtis, *Jefferson's Freeholders and the Politics of Ownership in the Old Dominion* (New York: Cambridge University Press, 2012), 90–93; George Tucker, *Voyage to the Moon* (New York, 1827), 82.

55. For Malthusian thought, see Robert L. Heilbroner, *The Worldly Philosophers: The Lives, Times and Ideas of the Great Economic Thinkers* (New York: Touchstone, 1953), 75–105; Snavely, *Tucker,* 57. For Malthusianism in America, see Joseph J. Splenger, "Population Theory in the Antebellum South," *Journal of Southern History* 2 (August 1936): 360–389; Joseph J. Splenger, "Population Prediction in Nineteenth Century America," *American Sociological Review* 1, no. 6 (December 1936): 905–921.

56. George Tucker, "Theory of Profits," *HMM* 2 (1840): 91.

57. George Tucker, "Progress of Population and Wealth," *HMM* 8 (1843): 429.

58. Tucker, *Progress of the United States,* 58, 101–118, 127–143.

59. Ibid., 195.

60. Ibid., 195, 200–201.

61. Ibid., 201–211.

62. George Tucker, *The Life and Philosophy of George Tucker* (Bristol: Thoemmes Continuum, 2004), 84; Edwin Troxell Freedley, *A Practical Treatise on Business* (Philadelphia, 1853), 275; John Macgregor, *The Progress of America from the Discovery by Columbus to 1847* (London, 1847), 747–754.

63. *Daily Ohio Statesman* (Columbus), January 18, 1851; *Boston Daily Advertiser,* September 26, 1870. Ohio newspapers put perhaps the greatest emphasis on population statistics, with Cincinnati leading the way. The statistical charts of Charles Cist, editor of the Cincinnati *Daily Gazette,* and Edward Mansfield, editor of the

Cincinnati Chronicle, appeared in papers across the country. Cist also published numerous statistical gazetteers and was employed by the census. Mansfield later became the first commissioner of statistics in Ohio.

64. *Ohio State Journal* (Columbus), July 23, 1850.

65. De Bow's letters to Hunt are lost, but one can get a sense of what he wrote from Hunt's responses. See Hunt to De Bow, July 23, 1850, De Bow Papers, Rubenstein Library, Duke University, Durham, NC. For De Bow, see Ottis Clark Skipper, *J. D. B. De Bow: Magazinist of the Old South* (Athens: University of Geogia Press, 1958). For Debow's imperialist plans, see Walter Johnson, *River of Dark Dreams: Slavery and Empire in the Cotton Kingdom* (Cambridge, MA: Harvard University Press, 2013), 312–339.

66. James De Bow, "A Professorship of Commerce," *De Bow's Review* 6 (August, 1848):111.

67. "Public Lands of Texas," *De Bow's Review* 13 (July 1852): 53.

68. For evidence that declines in fertility were linked to fear of landless labor, see Michael Haines and J. David Hacker, "The Puzzle of Antebellum Fertility Decline in the United States: New Evidence and Reconsideration," National Bureau of Economic Research Working Paper No. 12571, October 2006. For female contraceptives in this era, see Janet Brodie, *Contraception and Abortion in Nineteenth Century America* (Ithaca, NY: Cornell University Press, 1987).

69. *The Crisis! An Appeal to Our Countrymen, on the Subject of Foreign Influence in the United States* (New York, 1844), 23. The anti-growth ideology was apparent in New York City by the 1820s. See William Jackson's letter to the *Working Man's Advocate* against the city's population growth. Jackson's letter was reprinted in the *Free Enquirer* (New York), June 12, 1830. For working-class consciousness and racism, see David Roediger, *The Wages of Whiteness: Race and the Making of American Working Class* (New York: Verso, 1999), 43–94.

70. Horace Mann, *Twelfth Annual Report of the Board of Education* (Boston, 1849), 56; Lemuel Shattuck, *Report to the Committee of the City Council Appointed to Obtain the Census of Boston for the Year 1845* (Boston, 1846), 11, 31.

71. Jesse Chickering, *Immigration into the United States* (Boston, 1846), 48–49

72. Buchanan to Chickering, July 9, 1847, Jesse Chickering Papers.

73. *St. Louis Globe-Democrat,* June 20, 1880.

74. For a link between the frontier thesis and the census maps, see Gerald Nash, "The Census of 1890 and the Closing of the Frontier," *Pacific Northwest Quarterly* 71 (July 1980): 98–100; Francis Amasa Walker, *Statistical Atlas of the United States* (Washington, DC, 1874), 1, 4. For Walker's work on the census, see Matthew G. Hannah, *Governmentality and the Mastery of Territory in Nineteenth-Century America* (New York: Cambridge University Press, 2000).

6. THE CORONATION OF KING CAPITAL

1. On Helper and his book, see David Brown, *Southern Outcast: Hinton Rowan Helper and the Impending Crisis of the South* (Baton Rouge: Louisiana State University Press, 2006); George Fredrickson, *The Arrogance of Race: Historical Perspectives on Slavery, Racism and Social Inequality* (Middletown, CT: Wesleyan University Press, 1988), 28–54; David Potter, *The Impending Crisis, 1848–1861* (New York: Harper and Row, 1976), 386. On the inaccuracies of Helper's account, see Robert Fogel and Stanley Engerman, *Time on the Cross: The Economics of American Slavery* (New York: Norton, 1974), 158–191. For a contemporary critique of his figures, see Samuel Wolfe, *Helper's Impending Crisis Dissected* (Philadelphia, 1860).

2. Fredrickson, *Arrogance of Race*, 28; Hinton Rowan Helper, *The Impending Crisis in the South: How to Meet It* (New York, 1857), v.

3. Helper, *Impending Crisis*, 35, 39, 54, 64–66, 71, 283, 286.

4. Ibid., 107–108.

5. Eric Foner, *Free Soil, Free Labor, Free Men: The Ideology of the Republican Party before the Civil War* (New York: Oxford University Press, 1970), 42, 43, 50, 62; Robert Fogel, *Without Consent or Contract: The Rise and Fall of American Slavery* (New York: Norton, 1989), 310–388.

6. *Congressional Globe*, 30th Congress, 2nd Session, February 26, 1849, 318; Elwood Fisher, *Lecture on the North and South Delivered before the Young Men's Mercantile Library Association of Cincinnati, Ohio* (Cincinnati, 1849), 20.

7. Fisher, *Lecture on the North and South*, 6–9. Fisher's lecture was published in numerous places. See *Southern Quarterly Review*, July 1849, 273–311; *De Bow's Review* 7 (1849): 134–145; *De Bow's Review* 15 (1857): 304–316; *Southern Literary Messenger* 25 (1859): 81. In a letter to Calhoun, Fisher claimed he sold 200,000 copies. See Elwood Fisher to Calhoun, John C. Calhoun Papers, October 29, 1849, Library of Congress, Washington, DC.

8. David Christy, "Cotton Is King or Economic Relations of Slavery," in *Cotton Is King and Pro-Slavery Arguments,* ed. E. N. Elliot (Augusta, GA, 1860), 221; Samuel A. Cartwright, "The Education, Labor and Wealth of the South," in *Cotton Is King and Pro-Slavery Arguments,* ed. E. N. Elliot (Augusta, GA, 1860), 879.

9. See Louis McLane, *Documents Relative to the Manufacturers in the United States,* 2 vols. (New York, 1869). For the report's content, see Naomi Lamoreaux, "Rethinking the Transition to American Capitalism," *Journal of American History* 90 (2003): 444–445.

10. Helper, *Impending Crisis*, v.

11. R. G. Dun & Company Credit Report Volumes, Oswego County, New York, 1847, vol. 512, Baker Library, Harvard Business School, Boston. On Dun & Co. and

the changing nature of credit companies, see Rowena Olegario, *A Culture of Credit: Embedding Trust and Transparency in American Business* (Cambridge, MA: Harvard University Press, 2006). For the pricing of people's worth, see also Scott Sandage, *Born Losers: A History of Failure in America* (Cambridge, MA: Harvard University Press, 2006).

12. Fogel, *Without Consent*, 326 n. 3. On the rise of the Republican Party and Abraham Lincoln's presidency, see Eric Foner, *A Fiery Trial: Abraham Lincoln and American Slavery* (New York: Norton, 2011). On the relationship between anti-slavery and capitalism, see Amy Dru Stanley, *From Bondage to Contract: Wage Labor, Marriage and the Market in the Age of Slave Emancipation* (New York: Cambridge University Press, 1998); Thomas Bender, ed., *The Antislavery Debate: Capitalism and Abolitionism as a Problem of Historical Interpretation* (Berkeley: University of California Press, 1992).

13. Foner, *Free Soil,* 44.

14. For ideological differences between North and South, see Foner, *Free Soil;* James Oakes, *Slavery and Freedom: An Interpretation of the Old South* (New York: Knopf, 1990); David Brion Davis, *The Problem of Slavery in the Age of Revolution, 1770-1823* (Ithaca, NY: Cornell University Press, 1975); Eugene Genovese, *The Political Economy of Slavery: Studies in the Economy and Society of the Slave South* (New York: Pantheon, 1965). For the capitalist sides of slavery, see Sven Beckert and Seth Rockman, eds., *Slavery's Capitalism: A New History of American Economic Development,* (Philadelphia: University of Pennsylvania, 2016).

15. "An Act to Lay and Collect a Direct Tax within the United States," July 14, 1798, in *The Public Statutes at Large of the United States of America,* ed. Richard Peters (Boston, 1845), xxxvi; Robert Carter Letter and Day Book, Robert Carter Papers, Rubenstein Library, Duke University, Durham, NC.

16. Robert Fogel, "American Slavery: A Flexible, Highly Developed Form of Capitalism," in *Society and Culture in the Slave South,* ed. J. William Harris (New York: Routledge, 1992), 83. For specific slave rentals, see American Slavery Documents Collection (henceforth ASDC), 1757-1867, Rubenstein Library, Duke University, Durham, NC, box 1, folder 83; box 1, folder 90; box 2, folder 12. For specific slave insurance policies, see "Life Insurance Policies for Two Slaves," June 7, 1859, ASDC, box 2, folder 29.

17. *De Bow's Review,* quoted in Frederic Bancroft, *Slave Trading in the Old South* (Columbia: University of South Carolina Press, 1931), 342; James Henry Hammond, *Selection from the Letters and Speeches of James H. Hammond* (New York, 1866), 345. On slave mortgages, see Bonnie Martin, "Slavery's Invisible Engine: Mortgaging Human Property," *Journal of Southern History* 76 (2010): 817-866. On their highly liquid nature, see Richard Holcombe Kilbourne Jr., *Debt, Investment, Slaves: Credit Relations in East Feliciana Parish, Louisiana,*

1825–1885 (Tuscaloosa: University of Alabama Press, 1995). For finance and slavery, see articles by Daina Ramey Berry and Kathryn Boodry in *Slavery's Capitalism*, 146–178; Ed Baptist, *The Half Has Never Been Told: Slavery and the Making of American Capitalism* (New York: Basic Books, 2014), chs. 7–8.

18. Frederick Douglass, "American Slavery, American Religion, and the Free Church of Scotland: An Address Delivered in London, England, on May 22, 1846," in *American Slavery: Report of a Public Meeting* (London, 1846); Fogel and Engerman, *Time on the Cross*, 60–78.

19. Solomon Northup, *Twelve Years a Slave* (New York, 1853), 165. On "hands," see Caitlin Rosenthal, "Slavery's Scientific Management: Master and Managers," in *Slavery's Capitalism*, 62–86. For weighing cotton, see John Wesley Monett's "The Cotton Crop" in Joseph Holt Ingraham, *The Southwest by a Yankee* (New York, 1835), 2:281–291.

20. William Chambers, *Things as They Are in America* (Philadelphia, 1854), 270–280; "List and Inventory of the Negroes on the Plantation of Messrs Bruce, Seddon and Williams," November 22, 1849, box 11, Bruce Family Papers, University of Virginia Library, Charlottesville.

21. New Orleans market observer quoted in "Auction Notes and Prizes," March 14, 1851, New Orleans, ASDC, box 2, folder 7. For Betts and Gregory, see "Documents Detailing the Prices of Betts and Gregory Slave Market," 1860–1861, ASDC, box 2, folder 36. For the casual correspondence regarding slave prices, see "Letter on Relative Prices of Men, Women, and Children," January 4, 1860, ASDC, box 2, folder 32; "Auctioneer's Letter," January 15, 1860, ASDC, box 2, folder 101; "Slave Pricing Sheets," ASDC, box 2, folder 94; "Amounts Acquired from Sales of Slaves," ASDC, box 2 folder 97; "Letter Detailing the Dropping and Unsustainable Price of Slaves," ASDC, box 2, folder 38.

22. Hammond Diary, November 5, 1841, box 34, reel 17, James Henry Hammond Papers, microfiche, Library of Congress, Washington, DC; Drew Gilpin Faust, *James Henry Hammond and the Old South: A Design for Mastery* (Baton Rouge: Louisiana State University Press, 1982), 111; Hammond, *Speeches and Letters*, 312–315. See Hammond's article "Report of the Committee of the Barnwell Agricultural Society," *Farmers Register* 9 (October 31, 1841) for more productivity figures.

23. James De Bow, *The Industrial Resources of the Southern and Western States* (New Orleans, 1852), 234. For moral statistics, see De Bow, "Physical and Moral Condition of the Blacks," *De Bow's Review* 4 (1847): 290–291; De Bow, "Productive Energies and Spirit of Massachusetts," *De Bow's Review* 4 (1847): 459–474. For similar capitalizing calculations, see "Agriculture of the South and West," *De Bow's Review* 2 (1846): 340–345; "Southern Agriculture," *De Bow's Review* 4 (1847): 442–445, 579–585; "Sea Island Cotton in Florida," *De Bow's Review* 4 (1847): 250–256.

24. James De Bow, "Professorship of Public Economy, Commerce, Statistics in the University of Louisiana," *De Bow's Review* 4 (1847): 414. On the Louisiana Bureau of Statistics, see Ottis Clark Skipper, *J. D. B. De Bow: Magazinist of the Old South* (Athens: University of Georgia Press, 1958), 83, and *De Bow's Review* 6 (1848): 79; 8 (1849): 32, 422; 9 (1850): 286.

25. A partial ledger remains in the De Bow papers that gives a sense of an increase in subscriptions but never the total number. See Ledger 1, part 1, De Bow Papers, David M. Rubenstein Rare Book and Manuscript Library, Duke University, Durham, NC.

26. James De Bow, "Future of the South," *De Bow's Review* 10 (February 1851): 132–146.

27. Christy, "Cotton Is King," 21, 27; see also productivity chart on 125.

28. Quote from Matthew Hale Smith, *Twenty Years among the Bulls and Bears of Wall Street* (New York, 1896), 523. Almost nothing has been written on Kettell. See Alfred Chandler, *Henry Varnum Poor: Business Editor, Analyst and Reformer* (Cambridge, MA: Harvard University Press, 1956), 335; an obituary can be found in *Daily Alta California*, October 23, 1878. On Bennett and the rise of the penny press, see Dan Schiller, *Objectivity and the News: The Public and the Rise of Commercial Journalism* (Philadelphia: University of Pennsylvania Press, 1981). For examples of Kettell's financial journalism, see "Progressive Wealth and Commerce of Boston," *Hunt's Merchants' Magazine* 15 (1846): 34; "The Commercial Growth and Greatness of New York," *Hunt's Merchants' Magazine* 5 (1841): 30–44; "Influence of Railroads," *De Bow's Review* 12 (June 1852): 671–673; "Progress of American Commerce, Agriculture and Manufacture," *De Bow's Review* 4 (September 1847): 85–95.

29. Thomas Prentice Kettell, *Southern Wealth and Northern Profits* (New York, 1860), 3–4.

30. On Poor's editorials, see Alfred Chandler Papers, box 10, folder 5, Baker Library, Harvard Business School, Boston. Poor's pieces were reprinted as a book titled *Secession: Its Effect upon the Commercial Relations between the North and South, and upon Each Section* (London, 1861). For Poor as the epitome of finance capital in this age, see Noam Maggor, *Brahmin Capitalism: Frontiers of Wealth and Populism in America's First Gilded Age* (Cambridge, MA: Harvard University Press, 2017).

31. For Poor's interest in moral statistics, see Chandler Papers, box 11, folders 2–4.

32. Poor, *Secession*, 16. On Poor's friendship with De Bow, see *American Railroad Journal* 23 (1850): 693.

33. Ellis Sylvester Chesbrough, *Tabular Representation of the Present Condition of Boston, in Relation to Railroad Facilities, Foreign Commerce, Population, Wealth, Manufactures* (Boston, 1851), 16. On Boston as a railroad financial center, see Ar-

NOTES TO PAGES 174-177

thur Johnson and Barry Supple, *Boston Capitalists and Western Railroads: A Study in the Nineteenth Century Railroad Investment Process* (Cambridge, MA: Harvard University Press, 1967); Maggor, *Brahmin Capitalism,* ch. 3; Richard White, *Railroaded: The Transcontinentals and the Making of Modern America* (New York: Norton, 2012), 42, 141, 146.

34. See Alfred Chandler, *The Railroads: The Nation's First Big Business* (New York: Harcourt, 1965); Dorothy Adler, *British Investment in American Railroads* (Charlottesville: University of Virginia Press, 1970); Thomas Cochran, *Railroad Leaders, 1845–1890: The Business Mind in Action* (Cambridge, MA: Harvard University Press, 1953); Nick Salvatore, *Eugene V. Debs: Citizen and Socialist* (Urbana: University of Illinois Press, 2007).

35. Cronon, *Nature's Metropolis,* 81.

36. Alfred Chandler, *The Visible Hand: The Managerial Revolution in American Business* (Cambridge, MA: Belknap Press, 1977), 89; U.S. Department of Commerce, *Historical Statistics of the United States, Colonial Times to 1970* (Washington, DC: GPO, 1975), series Q 329–345; William Roy, *Socializing Capital: The Rise of the Large Industrial Corporation* (Princeton, NJ: Princeton University Press, 1997), 88–99.

37. Margaret Myers, *A Financial History of the United States* (New York: Columbia University Press, 1970), 120; U.S. Department of Commerce, *Historical Statistics,* series Q 346–355.

38. Henry Grew Account Book, 1851–1862, Records Relating to Estate, Real Estate and Private Investment Management, 1765–1945, Baker Library, Harvard Business School, Boston, vol. 1; Samuel Finley Vinton Estate Accounts, vol. 1, 29–34, Manuscripts and Archives Division, New York Public Library.

39. Charles Caldwell, "Thoughts on the Moral and Other Indirect Influences of Railroads," *New-England Magazine* 2 (April 1832): 288, 292, 298; Pennsylvania House of Representative quoted in John Lauritz Larson, *Internal Improvement: National Public Works and the Promise of Popular Government in the Early United States* (Chapel Hill: University of North Carolina Press, 2002), 235; "Report of the Committee on Railroads," *Documents of the State Senate of New York,* Senate No. 38, February 14, 1839, 8.

40. Poor and previous editor quoted in James A. Ward, *Railroads and the Character of America 1820–1887* (Knoxville: University of Tennessee Press, 1986), 70, 129. On the changing view of corporations, see Oscar and Mary Handlin, "Origins of the American Business Corporation," *Journal of Economic History* 1 (1945): 22–23; Pauline Maier, "The Revolutionary Origins of the American Corporation," *William and Mary Quarterly* 50 (January 1993); 51–84.

41. For Fillmore, see Lyle Emerson Nelson, *American Presidents Year by Year* (New York: Routledge, 2015), 252; Jesup Scott, "Railroads of the Great Valley," *HMM*

27 (July 1852): 44–51; J. E. Bloomfield, "Our Canals and Our Railways," *HMM* 41 (November 1859): 547–553; Kettell, "Influence of Railroads," 673.

42. The railroad prospectus was not an American invention, and many were printed in London in the 1830s. See *Prospectus of the Great Leinster and Munster Railway* (London, 1836). For investment prospectuses in general, an overlooked genre, see Baring Archives online collection, www.baringarchive.org.uk.

43. *Report of Committee upon the Statistics of Business and of the Engineer upon the Survey of the Several Routes for the Contemplated New York and Hartford Railroad via Danbury* (Hartford, CT, 1845), 4; *Facts and Estimates Relative to the Business on the Route of the Contemplated Providence and Worcester Railroad* (Providence, RI, 1844). On the importance of potential traffic, see Chandler, *Henry Varnum Poor*, 48–49, 107. See also *American Railroad Journal* 33 (1860): 404.

44. *Facts and Estimates Relative to . . . Providence and Worcester Railroad*, 7, 23–26.

45. *Report of the Directors of the Boston and Maine Railroad to the Stockholders at Their Annual Meeting* (Boston, 1849), 5; *Report of the Boston and Maine* (Boston, 1850), 10; *Report of the Boston and Maine* (Boston, 1851), 6, 12, 13; *Report of the Boston and Maine* (Boston, 1852), 14; *Report of the Boston and Maine* (Boston, 1853), 11–12. All citations from published reports found at the National Archives 2, College Park, MD.

46. For a sampling of the tables prepared by Poor, see *American Railroad Journal* 25 (1852): 232, 410–411, 506–507, 552, 561–562, 600, 776, 689–690. For an early circular, see "Photostat of 1854 Questionnaire," August 21, 1854, Chandler Papers, box 10, folder 11. To see how this questionnaire developed over time, see "Statistical Returns" form filled out by the Kansas Pacific, December 31, 1878, Chandler Papers, box 10, folder 16. For Poor's success, see Chandler, *Henry Varnum Poor*, 34, 47.

47. *Report of the Chicago, Burlington and Quincy Railroad Company* (Chicago, 1855), 31.

48. Poor, *American Railroad Journal* 25 (1852): 506; Chandler, *Henry Varnum Poor*, 218.

49. Hinton Helper, *Noonday Exigencies in America* (New York: Bible Brothers, 1871), 162.

50. For the census compendium, see J. D. B. De Bow, *Statistical View of the United States* (Washington, DC, 1854); Margo Anderson, *The American Census: A Social History* (New Haven, CT: Yale University Press, 1988), 53.

51. Thomas Kettell to Samuel Tilden, January 7, 1845, Samuel Tilden Papers, box 4, Manuscripts and Archives Division, New York Public Library.

52. *Boston Courier*, June 27, 1827.

53. Nathan Hale, *Report of the Board of Directors of Internal Improvements . . . on the Practicability and Expediency of a Railroad from Boston to the Hudson River* (Boston, 1829), 30. Hale clearly internalized this "new arithmetic." See his endless income/freight calculations in Hale Family Papers, box 5, folders 5–8, Sophia Smith Collection, Smith College, Northampton, MA.

54. John Hammond, *Tabular Statement of the Cost, Revenue and Expenditures of the Several Finished Lines of the Canals and Railroads of the Commonwealth* (Harrisburg, PA, 1841), iii; Israel Andrews, *Trade and Commerce of the British American Colonies and upon the Great Lakes and Rivers,* 32nd Congress, 1st Session, Senate Doc. 112 (Washington, DC, 1853), 4.

55. Archibald Russell, *Principles of Statistical Inquiry* (New York, 1839), iv. For Russell, see Anderson, *American Census,* 36–37; U.S. Dept. of Agriculture, Statistical Reporting Service, *The Story of U.S. Agricultural Estimates* (Washington, DC, 1969), 7.

56. Russell, *Principles,* 5; Michael Zakim, "Inventing Industrial Statistics," *Theoretical Inquiries in Law* 11 (2010): 290–294.

57. Russell, *Principles,* 64–65.

58. Ibid., 115–117. For patent office statistics, see U.S. Senate, Document No. 105, 25th Congress, 2nd Session (1837) U.S. Congress, House of Representatives, Document No. 109, 27th Congress, 3rd Session (1842), 4–5.

59. Compare Carroll Wright, *History and Growth of the United States Census* (Washington, DC: GPO, 1900), 234, with Russell, *Principles,* 100; Ezra Seaman, *Essays on the Progress of Nations* (New York, 1846), 127, 302–305. On the 1840 census, see Patricia Cline Cohen, *A Calculating People: The Spread of Numeracy in Early America* (Chicago: University of Chicago Press, 1982), ch. 6.

60. Wright, *History and Growth,* 235, 312. On the scientific nature of the 1850 census, see Carroll Wright, "Address," *Journal of the American Statistical Association* 1 (1908): 7; Anderson, *American Census,* 53.

61. John K. Wright, "The American Geographical Society, 1852–1952," *Scientific Monthly* 74, no. 3 (March 1952): 121–131; Paul J. Fitzpatrick, "Statistical Societies in the United States in the Nineteenth Century," *American Statistician* 11 (1957): 13–21; "American Geographical Society," *Hunt's Merchants' Magazine* 25 (1851): 648–649; John Disturnell, *A Gazetteer of the State of New York* (New York, 1840); *The Western Traveller: Embracing the Canal and Railroad Routes from Albany* (New York, 1844); *New York as It Is* (New York, 1837).

62. "Origin of the Society," *Bulletin of the American Geographical and Statistical Society* 1, no. 1 (August 1852): 3–14; updated member lists appear in each bulletin. Mansfield was editor of the *Cincinnati Chronicle, Cincinnati Gazette,* and *Railroad Record.* He wrote a great deal for the *New York Times* under the pen name "Veteran Observer." For *New York Times* editor Henry Raymond's emphasis on business statistics, see Henry Raymond to George Jones, March 11, 1846, folder 17, Henry Raymond Papers, Manuscript and Archives Division, New York Public Library.

63. For relevant papers, see "Transactions of the Society," *Bulletin of the American Geographical and Statistical Society* 1, no. 1 (August 1852): 13, 61, 105; "Transac-

tions of the Society," *Bulletin of the American Geographical and Statistical Society* 11 (January 1857): 23, 33, 39, 47.

64. E. C. Strazinsky, *Catalogue of the Library of the American Geographical and Statistical Society* (New York, 1857); "Transactions of the Society," *Bulletin of the American Geographical and Statistical Society* 11 (January 1857): 6–11; "Memorial," *Bulletin of the American Geographical and Statistical Society* 11 (January 1857): 16–18. For lobbying efforts, see *Report of the Joint Special Committee of the Chamber of Commerce and American Geographical Statistical Society on the Extension of the Decimal System to Weights and Measures of the United States* (New York, 1857); John Jay, A *Statistical View of American Agriculture . . . with Suggestions for the Schedules of the Federal Census in 1860* (New York, 1859). For typical railroad boosterism, see Henry V. Poor, "Railroad to the Pacific," *Bulletin of the American Geographical and Statistical Society* 1, no. 1 (August 1852): 83–100.

65. Chicago Daily Tribune, *Chicago in 1864: Annual Review of the Trade, Business and Growth of Chicago and the Northwest* (Chicago, 1865); J. R. Dodge, *West Virginia: Its Farms and Forests, Mines and Oil Wells* (Philadelphia, 1865); Minnesota Bureau of Statistics, *Minnesota: Its Progress and Capabilities* (St. Paul, 1862); Boston Board of Trade, *Statistics of Cotton Manufacture* (Boston, 1861); Lorin Blodget, *The Commercial and Financial Strength of the United States* (New York, 1864).

66. For Civil War debt, see Robert Wright, *The US National Debt, 1787–1900*, vol. 4 (London: Pickering and Chatto, 2005).

67. On the economic costs and financing of the Civil War, see Heather Cox Richardson, *The Greatest Nation of the Earth: Republican Economic Policies during the Civil War* (Cambridge, MA: Harvard University Press, 1997); Henrietta Larson, *Jay Cooke, Private Banker* (Cambridge, MA: Harvard University Press, 1936). For David Wells, see Herbert Ferleger, "David A. Wells and the American Revenue System," Ph.D. diss., Columbia University, 1942; Nancy Cohen, *The Reconstruction of American Liberalism, 1865–1914* (Chapel Hill: University of North Carolina Press, 2002), 86–95, 151–157, 179–186.

68. David A. Wells, *Our Burden and Our Strength: A Comprehensive and Popular Examination of the Debts and Resources of Our Country* (Boston, 1864), 1–2, 10.

69. John Murray Forbes to Edward Atkinson, August 26, 1864, box 12, folder 13, Edward Atkinson Papers, Massachusetts Historical Society, Boston. For numerous examples of letters praising his pamphlet, see the incoming letters from the fall of 1864 in David Wells Papers, Library of Congress, Washington, DC, box 1, reel 1. The list includes some of the most influential men in America: William Seward, William Cullen Bryant, Edward Everett, and Henry Carey. Godkin quoted in Ferleger, "David A. Wells," 10.

70. Little has been written on the Treasury Department's Bureau of Statistics. See *Report on the Commission on the Bureau of Statistics of the Treasury Department* (Washington DC, 1877). On the role of the Civil War in the increase of American state capacities, see Richard Bensel, *Yankee Leviathan: The Origins of Central State Authority in America, 1859–1877* (Cambridge: Cambridge University Press, 1991). For Civil War statistics, see New York Bureau of Military Statistics, *Annual Report* (Albany, 1864); E. B. Elliot, *On the Military Statistics of the United States* (Berlin, 1863).

71. David Ames Wells, *Report of the Special Commissioner of the Revenue upon the Industry, Trade, Commerce, Etc.* (Washington, DC: GPO, 1869), 10–22, 28.

72. Abraham Lincoln, "Speech in United States House of Representative on Internal Improvements," *Collected Works of Abraham Lincoln*, ed. Roy Basler (New Brunswick, NJ: Rutgers University Press, 1953), 1:489. For the emancipation of slaves in the District of Columbia, see Foner, *Fiery Trial*, 199–200; Daniel Reaves Goodloe, *Inquiry into the Causes Which Have Retarded the Accumulation of Wealth and Increase of Population in the Southern States: In Which the Question of Slavery Is Considered in a Politico-Economic Point of View* (Washington, DC, 1846)

73. "The President's Message," *New York Times*, December 2, 1862; the article included statistical charts. For the rare mention of Lincoln's love of quantification, see Anderson, *American Census*, 67.

7. STATE OF STATISTICAL WAR

1. U.S. Senate Committee on Finance, *Wholesale Prices, Wages, and Transportation: Report by Mr. Aldrich from the Committee on Finance, Part I* (Washington, DC, 1893); for an earlier version, which included only a two-year time series, see U.S. Senate Committee on Finance, *Retail Prices and Wages: Report by Mr. Aldrich from the Committee on Finance* (Washington, DC, 1892). For the politics behind the Aldrich report, see Thomas Stapleford, *The Cost of Living in America: A Political History of Economic Statistics* (New York: Cambridge University Press, 2009), 41–50.

2. Finance Committee, *Wholesale Prices*, 27–184.

3. On the American state in the late nineteenth century, see Stephen Skowronek, *Building a New American State: The Expansion of National Administrative Capacities 1877–1920* (New York: Cambridge University Press, 1982); Richard Bensel, *Yankee Leviathan: The Origins of Central State Authority in America, 1859–1877* (Cambridge: Cambridge University Press, 1991); Morton Keller, *Affairs of State: Public Life in Late Nineteenth Century America* (Cambridge, MA: Belknap Press of Harvard University Press, 1977).

4. Finance Committee, *Wholesale Prices*, 6–7. On Carroll Wright's career as a labor statistician, see James Leiby, *Carroll Wright and Labor Reform: The Origins of Labor Statistics* (Cambridge, MA: Harvard University Press, 1960); Mary O. Furner, "Knowing Capitalism: Public Investigation and the Labor Question in the Long Progressive Era," in *The State and Economic Knowledge: The American and British Experiences,* ed. Barry Supple and Mary Furner (New York: Cambridge University Press, 1990), 241–286. On the consolidation of the American bourgeoisie, see Sven Beckert, *Monied Metropolis: New York City and the Consolidation of the American Bourgeoisie, 1850–1896* (New York: Cambridge University Press, 2003).

5. William Kelley, *Speeches, Addresses, and Letters* (New York: Greenwood, 1969), 273, 289; Committee on Finance, *Retail Prices and Wages*, 1. On tariffs, see Joanne Reitano, *The Tariff Question in the Gilded Age: The Great Debate of 1888* (University Park: Pennsylvania State University Press, 1994).

6. Finance Committee, *Wholesale Prices*, 5.

7. Ibid., 8–12, 60–61, quote on 11; Stapleford, *Cost of Living*, 41–56.

8. On free labor producerism see Eric Foner, *Free Soil, Free Labor, Free Men: The Ideology of the Republican Party before the Civil War* (New York: Oxford University Press, 1970); Christopher Lasch, *The True and Only Heaven: Progress and Its Critics* (New York: Norton, 1991). On the consumerist turn and the labor question, see Lawrence Glickman, *A Living Wage: American Workers and the Making of a Consumer Society* (Ithaca, NY: Cornell University Press, 1997); Roseanne Currarino, *The Labor Question in America: Economic Democracy in the Gilded Age* (Urbana-Champaign: University of Illinois Press, 2011); Jackson Lears, *Fables of Abundance: A Cultural History of Advertising in America* (New York: Basic Books, 1995). On the improvement in material well-being in this era, see Robert Gordon, *The Rise and Fall of American Growth: The U.S. Standard of Living since the Civil War* (Princeton, NJ: Princeton University Press, 2016).

9. Joseph Kennedy, *Eighth Census of the United States* (Washington, DC, 1864), 512.

10. Frederick Winslow Taylor, *The Principles of Scientific Management* (New York: Harper and Brothers, 1911), 20; David Montgomery, *Workers' Control in America: Studies in the History of Work, Technology and Labor Struggles* (Cambridge: Cambridge University Press, 1979).

11. Jeff Sklansky, *The Soul's Economy: Market Society and Selfhood in American Thought, 1820–1920* (Chapel Hill: University of North Carolina Press, 2002), 171–190; Ronald L. Meek, *Studies in the Labor Theory of Value* (New York: Monthly Review Press, 1953), 22–70 Mark Blaug, *Economic Theory in Retrospect* (New York: Cambridge University Press, 1978), 37–52; Eli Cook, "The Neoclassical Club: Irving Fisher and the Progressive Origins of Neoliberalism," *Journal of the Gilded Age and Progressive Era* 15 (July 2016): 246–262.

12. Andrew Carnegie to W. L. Abbott, October 28, 1888, and Carnegie to Abbott, on July 4, 1888, Andrew Carnegie Papers, box 10, Library of Congress, Washington, DC. On Carnegie's obsession with costs, see Harold Livesay, *Andrew Carnegie and the Rise of Big Business* (Boston: Little, Brown, 1975), 41. For rise of managerial capitalism and cost accounting see, Alfred Chandler, *The Visible Hand: The Managerial Revolution in American Business* (Cambridge, MA: Belknap Press, 1977), 109–120, 268–279; Paul Garner, *Evolution of Cost Accounting to 1925* (Tuscaloosa: University of Alabama Press, 1954); Gary John Previts and Barbara Dubis Merino, *A History of Accounting in America: An Historical Interpretation of the Cultural Significance of Accounting* (New York: Wiley, 1979), 116–119. For a contemporary work on cost accounting, see Henry Metcalf, *The Cost of Manufacturers and the Administration of Workshops, Public and Private* (New York, 1885).

13. On humans as machines, see Anson Rabinbach, *The Human Motor: Energy, Fatigue and the Origins of Modernity* (Berkeley: University of California Press, 1992).

14. Grover Cleveland, "Fourth Annual Message," December 7, 1896, www.presidency.ucsb.edu/ws/?pid=29537. For Jarvis's correspondence, see folder on Select Committee on the Ninth Census in Records of the Select Committee of the House of Representatives, ch. 22.58, docket number 41A-F28.4, National Archives I, Washington, DC; Edward Jarvis, *Ninth Census of the United States* (Washington, DC: GPO, 1869), 8.

15. James Livingston, *Origins of the Federal Reserve System: Money, Class and Corporate Capitalism, 1890–1913* (Ithaca, NY: Cornell University Press, 1989); Martin Sklar, *The Corporate Reconstruction of American Capitalism, 1890–1916: The Market, the Law, and Politics* (New York: Cambridge University Press, 1988). On how Americans "read the market" in this era see Peter Knight, *Reading the Market: Genres of Finance Capitalism in Gilded Age America* (Baltimore: Johns Hopkins University Press, 2016).

16. "Miscellaneous Schedules, Petitions, Statements, Statistics, Reports Memoranda, Resolutions and Fragments Relating to the Tariff," Nelson Aldrich Papers, reel 53, Library of Congress, Washington, DC.

17. On the indexes in the Aldrich Report, see Stapleford, *Cost of Living*, 41–47.

18. Wesley Mitchell, *A History of Greenbacks* (Chicago: University of Chicago Press, 1903). On the "storm-tossed" world of capitalism and risk see Jon Levy, *Freaks of Fortune: The Emerging World of Capitalism and Risk in America* (Cambridge, MA: Harvard University Press, 2012).

19. On this free labor coalition, see David Montgomery, *Beyond Equality: Labor and the Radical Republicans, 1862–1872* (Urbana: University of Illinois Press, 1981); Leon Fink, *Workingmen's Democracy: The Knights of Labor and American Populists* (Urbana: University of Illinois Press, 1985); Nick Salvatore, *Eugene V. Debs: Citizen and Socialist* (Urbana: University of Illinois Press, 2007). On laissez-faire in this era, see

NOTES TO PAGES 200-204

Sidney Fine, *Laissez Faire and the General-Welfare State: A Study of Conflict in American Thought, 1865-1901* (Ann Arbor: University of Michigan Press, 1956).

20. For the Massachusetts bureau, see Charles F. Pidgin, *History of the Bureau of Statistics of Labor of Massachusetts and of Labor Legislation in the State* (Boston: Wright and Potter, 1876), 23; Leiby, *Carroll Wright*, 39-76; Lauren Coyle, "The Birth of the Bureau: Surveillance, Pacification, and the Statistical Objectivity Metanarrative," *Rethinking Marxism* 22, no. 4 (2010): 544-568.

21. *Daily Evening Voice,* November 3, 1865. For Steward, see Montgomery, *Beyond Equality,* 249-260. On Oliver, see Jesse H. Jones, "Henry Kemble Oliver, a Memorial," Massachusetts Bureau of Labor Statistics (MBLS), *Seventeenth Annual Report* (Boston, 1886): 14-24. On McNeill, see George McNeill, *The Labor Movement: The Problem of Today* (Boston, 1887).

22. Mary Poovey, *A History of the Modern Fact: Problems of Knowledge in the Sciences of Wealth and Society* (Chicago: University of Chicago Press, 1998), xv-xvii; MBLS, *First Annual Report* (Boston, 1869 / 1870), 8, 23, 38, 131.

23. MBLS, *First Annual Report,* 18-23, 25-31, 134.

24. Ibid., 134; Karl Marx, "On the First International," *The Karl Marx Library,* vol. 3, trans. and ed. S. K. Padover (New York: McGraw-Hill, 1973), 516. On the Eight Hour Day movement, see Roy Rosenzweig, *Eight Hours for What We Will: Workers and Leisure in an Industrial City, 1870-1920* (New York: Cambridge University Press, 1985).

25. MBLS, *First Annual Report,* 7-13, 18-19. The term "unequal distribution of wealth" is used three times in this first report; see 38, 185, 187.

26. *Lowell Daily Citizen,* June 2, 1871; *Chicago Tribune,* May 28, 1871. For *Free Trader* and many other quotes praising the bureau, see MBLS, *Fourth Annual Report* (Boston, 1872 / 1873), 18-26. For attempts to abolish, see "Abolishment of Bureau of Labor Statistics," April 23, 1872, Bills Rejected 1872, House Unpassed Legislation (SC1 Series 230), Massachusetts State Archives, Boston.

27. *Cincinnati Gazette,* June 16, 1871; *Atlanta Constitution,* June 13, 1871; "The Labor Question in Massachusetts," *Nation,* June 8, 1871.

28. Abraham Lincoln, *Speeches and Letters of Abraham Lincoln, 1832-1865* (New York: Dutton, 1907), 26.

29. Report of Commission on the Hours of Labor, House Document 98 (February 1866), 29, 35, 49. See also Nancy Cohen, *Reconstruction of American Liberalism, 1865-1914* (Chapel Hill: University of North Carolina Press, 2002), 34-38

30. Edward Atkinson, "The Condition of Labor in Massachusetts," *Nation,* June 22, 1871.

31. MBLS, *Third Annual Report* (Boston, 1871 / 1872), 293-335; MBLS, *Fourth Annual Report,* 172, 228. As opposed to regular property taxes, the rate of taxation on savings banks deposits was less than 1 percent.

32. "Resolve in Relation to the Bureau of Statistics of Labor," Bills Rejected 1873, House Unpassed Legislation (SC1 Series 230), Massachusetts State Archives, Boston; MBLS, *Fourth Annual Report,* 10–12; *Boston Daily Advertiser,* April 29 and May 4, 1872. The *Boston Daily Advertiser* covered the bureau somewhat obsessively; see also May 5, 1871, and April 29 and May 12, 1873.
33. Springfield *Republican,* April 26, 1872; *Boston Commonwealth,* quoted in MBLS, *Fourth Annual Report,* 27–29.
34. Charles Francis Adams Jr., "Critical Notices: Third Annual Report of the Bureau of Statistics of Labor," *North American Review* 115 (1872): 210–220; John Sproat, *The Best Men: Liberal Reformers in the Gilded Age* (New York: Oxford University Press, 1968); Henry Villard, "Introductory Note," *Journal of Social Science* 1 (1869): 5; E. L. Godkin, "Legislation and Social Science," *Journal of Social Science* 3 (1870): 115; Edward Atkinson, "The Inefficiency of Economic Legislation," *Journal of Social Science* 4 (1871): 114. For ASSA, see Thomas Haskell, *The Emergence of Professional Social Science: The American Social Science Association and the Nineteenth-Century Crisis of Authority* (Baltimore: Johns Hopkins University Press, 2000).
35. On the success of Gilded Age reform "experts" in depoliticizing economic debate, see Cohen, *Reconstruction of American Liberalism;* Leiby, *Carroll Wright,* 29.
36. Leiby, *Carroll Wright,* 76–142, 163–171. For the marginalization of the original bureau heads, see Charles Francis Gettemy, *The Massachusetts Bureau of Statistics, 1868–1915* (Boston: Wright and Potter, 1915).
37. MBLS, *Fifth Annual Report* (Boston, 1874), 334; MBLS, *Sixth Annual Report* (Boston, 1875), 447; Pidgin, *History of the Bureau of Statistics of Labor of Massachusetts,* 78, 86, 89.
38. Wright quoted in MBLS, *Thirteenth Annual Report* (Boston, 1882), 419. For Wright's use of moral statistics, see MBLS, *Fifth Annual Report,* ch. 3; MBLS, *Sixth Annual Report,* chs. 1, 2, 5; MBLS, *Eighth Annual Report* (Boston, 1877), chs. 2, 4, 5; MBLS, *Ninth Annual Report* (Boston, 1878), chs. 2, 5. For Wright's cost of living, see MBLS, *Fifteenth Annual Report* (Boston, 1884), 438; MBLS, *Eighth Annual Report,* 87. For the MBLS founders' cost-of-living calculations, see MBLS, *Third Annual Report,* 251–257, 468–529.
39. Gompers and Gunton quoted in Glickman, *Living Wage,* 2–3.
40. Furner, "Knowing Capitalism," 249–261.
41. "Town of Pullman—Revenue from Dwellings, 1894," Pullman Company Archives, Office of the President, George M. Pullman Files, 1867–1897, Business Papers, box 7, folder 101, Newberry Library, Chicago.
42. For Wright's favorable report on Pullman town, see MBLS, *Sixteenth Annual Report* (Boston, 1885), 3–26; Leiby, *Carroll Wright,* 160. Doty's wife wrote the classic account of Pullman town. See Mrs. Duane Doty, *The Town of Pullman:*

Its Growth with Brief Accounts of Its Industries (Pullman, IL, 1893). See also Richard Schneirov, Shelton Stormquist, and Nick Salvatore, eds., *The Pullman Strike and the Crisis of the 1890s: Essays on Labor and Politics* (Urbana: University of Illinois Press, 1999).

43. *Report of the Special Commissioner of the Revenue for 1866,* First Annual Report (Washington, DC, 1867), 21–22.

44. Ibid., 22.

45. Wells, *Report of the Special Commissioner of the Revenue,* Third Annual Report (Washington, DC, 1869), 16, 31.

46. Atkinson to Wells, October 12, 1875, Edward Atkinson Papers (henceforth EAP), carton 15, vol. 7, Massachusetts Historical Society, Boston. For a sample of Atkinson's work as a treasurer, see Atkinson to E. C. Hutchins, September 5, 1857; Atkinson to C. M. Jenkins, September 21, 1857, EAP, vol. 1. For examples of his attention to costs, see Atkinson to James Brown, February 17 and February 22, 1858, EAP, vol. 1. For examples of his penchant for profit maximization, see Atkinson to Benjamin Saunders, November 20, 1858, EAP, vol. 1. For his interest in lowering labor costs, see, for example, Atkinson to Thomas Clegg, April 20, 1858, EAP, vol. 1, in which he hatches a plan to put fugitive slaves to work in his factories. On his argument against slavery, see his *Cheap Cotton and Free Labor* (Boston, 1861).

47. H. Thomas Johnson, "Early Cost Accounting for Internal Management Control: Lyman Mills in the 1850s," *Business History Review* 46 (Winter 1972); Chandler, *Visible Hand,* 528 n. 64.

48. Livingston, *Origins of the Federal Reserve,* 37.

49. Atkinson to Wells, April 11, 1866, EAP, vol. 2; Atkinson to Wells, November 21, 1865, EAP, vol. 2. For the masterful way in which Atkinson "turned" Wells, see letters to Wells on November 21, 1866, January 9, 1867, and February 6, 1867, EAP, vol. 2. For the argument that Atkinson was responsible for Wells's intellectual shift, see also Daniel Horowitz, "Genteel Observers: New England Economic Writers and Industrialization," *New England Quarterly* 48 (March 1975): 65–83.

50. Atkinson to Wells, n.d. [1875], EAP, vol. 6. Atkinson's talk was later published; see his *The Distribution of Products* (Boston, 1885), 59.

51. Atkinson to William E. Hooper and Sons, June 18, 1885, EAP, carton 17, vol. 18.

52. Atkinson to Wright, December 13, 1884, EAP, carton 17, vol. 18; Atkinson to Putnam, June 13, 1885 and Atkinson to Atwater, May 23, 1885, EAP, carton 17, vol. 18.

53. Atkinson to Atwater, April 23, 1885, EAP, carton 16, vol. 17. For Atwater's approval of Atkinson's plans, see Atwater to Atkinson, May 8, 1885, carton 16, vol. 17, and June 23, 1885, carton 17, vol. 18, EAP; MBLS, *Seventeenth Annual Report* (Boston,

NOTES TO PAGES 215-218

1886), 249; Atkinson, "The Food Question in American and Europe," *Century* 33 (December 1886), 242.

54. Andrew Carnegie to Atkinson, 1896, EAP, carton 7; Edward Atkinson, *The Science of Nutrition* (Boston, 1886), 30. On the Aladdin oven, see Edward Kirkland, "Scientific Eating: New Englanders Prepare and Promote a Reform," *Proceedings of the Massachusetts Historical Society* 86 (1974): 28–52; Harvey Levenstein, "The New England Kitchen and the Origins of Modern American Eating Habits," *American Quarterly* 32 (1980): 369–386.

55. On Atwater's calorimeter, see Nick Cullather, "The Foreign Policy of the Calorie," *American Historical Review* 112 (2007): 337–364; Harvey Levenstein, *Revolution at the Table: The Transformation of the American Diet* (Berkeley: University of California Press, 2003), 73.

56. *Philadelphia Inquirer* quoted in Naomi Aronson, "Nutrition as a Social Problem," *Social Problems* 29, no. 5 (June, 1982): 481; Debs to Atkinson, May 4, 1892, carton 5, EAP; E. M. Chamberlin, "Reply to Edward Atkinson," in Atkinson, *The Margins of Profits* (Boston, 1887), 58.

57. Aronson, "Nutrition as a Social Problem," 481.

58. "Preamble to the Constitution of the Knights of Labor, 1881," *Constitution of the General Assembly, District Assemblies, and Local Assemblies of the Order of the Knights of Labor in America* (Marblehead, MA, 1883). On the Knights of Labor and labor statistics, see Jonathan Grossman and Judson Maclaury, "The Creation of the Bureau of Labor Statistics," *Monthly Labor Review* 98 (February 1975): 27–30; Stapleford, *Cost of Living,* 27–28. On Powderly's desire to be head of the labor bureau, see Craig Phelan, *Grand Master Workman: Terence Powderly and the Knights of Labor* (Westport, CT: Greenwood Press, 2000), 48. MBLS, *Seventh Annual Report* (Boston, 1877), xv.

59. Terence Powderly, *Thirty Years of Labor* (Columbus, OH, 1889), 315.

60. William Brock, *Investigation and Responsibility: Public Responsibility in the United States, 1865–1900* (Cambridge: Cambridge University Press, 1984), 158, 168; Department of Commerce and Labor, *Bulletin of the Bureau of Labor* 54 (September 1904); Stapleford, *Cost of Living,* 10–14; Bureau of Labor Statistics of Illinois, *Fourth Biennial Report* (Springfield, 1886), 170.

61. Powderly, *Thirty Years of Labor,* 160.

62. Barry quoted in National Woman Suffrage Association, *Report of the Industrial Council of Women* (Washington, DC, 1888), 155; Knights of Labor, *Proceedings of the General Assembly,* 1886 report (Minneapolis, 1887), 952. For Barry, see Eleanor Flexner, *Century of Struggle: The Woman's Rights Movement in the United States* (Cambridge, MA: Harvard University Press, 1959), 177, 190–193; Philip S. Foner, *Women and the American Labor Movement: From the First Trade Unions to the Present* (New York: Free Press, 1979), 205–206.

63. Knights of Labor, *Proceedings of General Assembly,* 1888 report (Philadelphia, 1889), 9-10; Knights of Labor, *Proceedings of the General Assembly,* 1887 report (Minneapolis, MN, 1888), 1581.

64. George K. Holmes, "Mortgage Statistics," *Publications of the American Statistical Association* 2, no. 9 (March, 1890): 1-21; George K. Holmes, "Tenancy in the United States," *Quarterly Journal of Economics* 10, no. 1 (October 1895): 34-53. For the Farmers' Alliance, see Lawrence Goodwyn, *The Populist Moment: A Short History of the Agrarian Revolt in Americ*a (New York: Oxford University Press, 1978); Charles Postel, *The Populist Vision* (New York: Oxford University Press, 2009).

65. U.S. Department of Agriculture, *The Story of U.S. Agricultural Estimates* (Washington, DC, 1969), 7.On agricultural statistics in forecasting, see Jamie Pietruska, *Looking Forward: Prediction and Uncertainty in Modern America* (Chicago: University of Chicago Press, 2017). On manipulation of futures, see Bruce Baker and Barbara Hahn, *The Cotton Kings: Capitalism and Corruption in Turn-of-the-Century New York and New Orleans* (New York: Oxford University Press, 2016).

66. John Jenkins, *First Biennial Report of the Bureau of Labor and Industrial Statistics of Nebraska* (Omaha, NE, 1886); Samuel Hotchkiss, *Fourth Annual Report of the Connecticut Bureau of Labor Statistics* (Hartford, CT, 1888); *Fifth Annual Report of the Bureau of Labor and Industrial Statistics of Michigan* (Lansing, MI, 1888), 91-355. On Henry George, see John L. Thomas, *Alternative America: Henry George, Edward Bellamy, Henry Demarest Lloyd and the Adversary Tradition* (Cambridge, MA: Harvard University Press, 1983), ch. 5; Postel, *Populist Vision,* 229-232.

67. The demands appeared in dozens of newspapers. See, for instance, "A Demand to Have the Next U.S. Census Show the Mortgage Indebtedness," *Aberdeen* (SD) *Daily News,* November 27, 1889; *Indiana State Sentinel,* November 20, 1889. See also Levy, *Freaks of Fortune,* 186-187.

68. For the census report, see George K. Holmes and John S. Lord, "Report of Farms and Homes: Proprietorship and Indebtedness in the United States," *Eleventh Census of the United States* (Washington, DC, 1896). For the political struggle over debt and tenancy figures, see Holmes, "Mortgage Statistics." For the Farmers' Alliance support of the resolution, see N. A. Dunning, *Farmers' Alliance History and Agricultural Digest* (Washington, DC, 1891), 121. For the use of Holmes's figures to rail against monopoly and elites see *The Dawn* (Ellensburg, WA), April 3, 1897; *Anaconda* (MT) *Standard,* January 18, 1897; *Commoner* (Lincoln, NE), October 2, 1901; *Evening Bulletin* (KY) February 26, 1895.

69. Matt Roche to Secretary Bliss, January 26, 1898, Letters Received, Compiled 1894-1904, Record Group 48: Records of the Office of the Secretary of the Interior, National Archives 2, College Park, MD.

70. Charles Spahr, *An Essay on the Present Distribution of Wealth in the United States* (Boston, 1896), 69. For the little we know of Spahr's life, see the pamphlet *In Memory of Charles B. Spahr* (New York: Social Reform Club, 1905).

71. Richmond Mayo-Smith, *Statistics and Economics* (Baltimore, 1888), 97–101. For evidence that Mayo-Smith lived in a large estate on the Upper East Side and had a butler, see "Columbia Professor Killed by Fall," *New York Times,* November 12, 1901.

72. Richmond Mayo-Smith, "Review," *Political Science Quarterly* 12 (1897): 346–348.

8. THE PRICING OF PROGRESSIVISM

1. "What the Baby Is Worth as a National Asset," *New York Times,* January 30, 1910.

2. David Starr Jordan, *The Human Harvest: A Study of the Decay of Races through the Survival of the Unfit* (Boston: Beacon Press, 1907). For the Progressive Era efficiency movement, see Samuel Haber, *Efficiency and Uplift: Scientific Management in the Progressive Era 1890–1920* (Chicago: University of Chicago Press); William Atkin, *Technocracy and the American Dream: The Technocrat Movement, 1900–1941* (Berkeley: University of California Press, 1977), 1–27; David Noble, *America by Design: Science, Technology, and the Rise of Corporate Capitalism* (Oxford: Oxford University Press, 1979).

3. Joseph Schumpeter, *Ten Great Economists from Marx to Keynes* (New York: Oxford University Press, 1951), 223; James Tobin, "Neoclassical Theory in America: J. B. Clark and Fisher," *American Economic Review* 75 (December 1985): 28–38; "Irving Fisher (1867–1947)," *American Journal of Economics and Sociology* 64 (January 2005): 19–42; Daniel Breslau, "Economics Invents the Economy: Mathematics, Statistics and Models in the Work of Irving Fisher and Wesley Mitchell," *Theory and Society* 32 (June 2003): 379–411.

4. For a sampling of Fisher's *New York Times* articles, which range from banking reform, Prohibition, labor strikes, and eugenics to health insurance, school hygiene, tariff policy, and electoral politics, see "Gold Inflation Makes Living High," July 1, 1917; "Wartime Prohibition," May 27, 1917; "Prof. Fisher's Advice," August 30, 1916; "Novel Suggestion to Curb the High Cost of Living," January 7, 1912; "Empty Cradles Worst War Horror," July 25, 1915; "War Is Teaching Us Not to Waste Human Life," August 20, 1916; "Roosevelt Failed to Get Radical Democratic Vote," January 5, 1918; "Some Probable Economic Effects of the War," August 30, 1914; "Fisher Assails Protection," November 6, 1916. For his economic forecasting, see Walter Friedman, *Fortune Tellers: The Story of America's First Economic Forecasters* (Princeton, NJ: Princeton University Press, 2013), 51–86. For his "pricing of progressivism," see "School Hygiene as Profitable Investment," *New York Times,* June 22, 1913; "The Money Value of Human Beings," *New York Times,* March 19, 1916.

5. Irving Fisher, "National Vitality: Its Wastes and Conservation," 61st Congress, 2nd Session, Senate Document 419 (Washington, DC, 1910), 739. Fisher devoted chapter 12 in his report to measuring "the money value of increased vitality." For *New York Times* coverage, see "Measuring the Nation's Vitality in Dollars and Cents," October 31, 1909; "Can Easily Add Fifteen Years to Our Average Life," March 5, 1911.

6. Theodore Roosevelt to Irving Fisher, May 8, 1907, box 2, Irving Fisher Papers, Yale University, New Haven, CT.

7. Irving Fisher, *A Clear Answer to President Taft, the Most Prominent Anti-National Prohibitionist* (Boston: Massachusetts Anti-Saloon League, 1918), 4–5; Fisher, "National Vitality," 623, 742; Irving Fisher, *The Costs of Tuberculosis in the United States and Their Reduction* (New Haven, 1909); Irving Fisher and Eugene Lyman Fisk, *How to Live: Rules for Healthful Living, Based on Modern Science* (New York: Funk and Wagnalls, 1916). On Fisher and Prohibition, see Irving Fisher to William Elliot, December 8, 1915; March 3, 1916, box 3, Fisher Papers.

8. The quote appears in an exhibit of the American Eugenics Society at the Sesqui-centennial Exposition in Philadelphia in 1926. For images of the exhibit, see the Fitter Families Collection, American Philosophical Society, Philadelphia, image no. 1565. For Fisher's thoughts on eugenics see Irving Fisher, "Impending Problems of Eugenics," *Scientific Monthly* 13, no. 3 (September 1921): 214–231. For the intersection of eugenics and economics in the Progressive Era, see Thomas C. Leonard, "Eugenics and Economics in the Progressive Era," *Journal of Economic Perspectives* 19, no. 4 (Fall 2005): 207–224.

9. Eli Cook, "Gabriel Kolko's Unfinished Revolution," *Jacobin*, June 25, 2014.

10. See J. S. Nicholson, "The Living Capital of the United Kingdom," *Economic Journal* 1 (March 1891); 95–107; William Farr, *Vital Statistics: Memorial Volume of Selections from the Reports and Writings of William Farr* (London: Sanitary Institute, 1885), esp. 536; Ernst Engel, *Der Werth des Menschen* (Berlin: Leonhard Simon, 1883); Robert Giffen, *Essays in Finance* (London, 1880). On the European influence on Progressive reform, see Daniel Rodgers, *Atlantic Crossings: Social Politics in a Progressive Age* (Cambridge, MA: Belknap Press of Harvard University Press, 2000).

11. Thomas Reilly, "Head Colds from the Standpoint of the Internist," *American Journal of the Medical Sciences* 153, no. 5 (May 1917); *Boston Daily Globe,* February 27, 1911; "America's First Duty," *Wall Street Journal,* July 22, 1916; "Economic Loss by Typhoid Fever," *Hartford Courant,* December 6, 1912; "Malaria Is Cause of Economic Loss," *San Francisco Chronicle,* March 3, 1916; Fisher, "National Vitality," 742. On the "twilight of laissez-faire," see Rodgers, *Atlantic Crossings,* 76–111.

12. "The Cost of Destroying Life," *Austin Statesman*, January 10, 1913; "Social Value of a Man's Work," *Wall Street Journal*, July 13, 1906. For the insurance industry and the valuation of people, see Dan Bouk, *How Our Days Became Numbered: Risk and the Rise of the Statistical Individual* (Chicago: University of Chicago Press, 2015), ch. 6. For connections between insurance and "human capital," see also Jon Levy, *Freaks of Fortune: The Emerging World of Capitalism and Risk in America* (Cambridge, MA: Harvard University Press, 2012), 61. For insurance companies and social reform see Olivier Zunz, *Making America Corporate 1870–1920* (Chicago: University of Chicago Press, 1990), 39, 92–95.

13. For Taylorism, see Haber, *Efficiency and Uplift*; Daniel Nelson, *Frederick W. Taylor and the Rise of Scientific Management* (Madison: University of Wisconsin Press, 1980).

14. Haber, *Efficiency and Uplift*, ix, 29; Charlotte Perkins Gilman, "The Waste of Private Housekeeping," *Annals of the American Academy of Political and Social Science* 48 (July 1913): 92. For similar arguments, see Mary Pattison, *The Business of Home Management* (New York, 1915). On the history of home economics, see Carolyn Goldstein, *Creating Consumers: Home Economists in Twentieth Century America* (Chapel Hill: University of North Carolina Press, 2012). For the society-as-factory worldview, see Robert Weibe, *Search for Order, 1877–1920* (New York: Farrar, Straus and Giroux, 1967), 146.

15. Allan Ripley Foote, *Economic Value of Electric Light and Power* (Cincinnati, 1889), 36; David Lantz, "Economic Value of North American Skunks," U.S. Department of Agriculture bulletin no. 587, Washington, DC, 1914; "Birds' Economic Value," *Los Angeles Times*, September 29, 1916; "The Aesthetic versus the Economic Value of Niagara Falls," *Scientific American* 62 (1906): 2506.

16. William James, *Pragmatism and Other Writings* (New York: Penguin, 2000), 88; George Cotkin, "William James and the Cash-Value Metaphor," *ETC: A Review of General Semantics* 42, no. 1 (Spring 1985): 37–46.

17. James, *Pragmatism and Other Writings*, 135.

18. Charles Cooley, *Social Process* (New York: Scribner's, 1918), 333; Charles Cooley, "The Sphere of Pecuniary Valuation," *American Journal of Sociology* 19 (September 1913): 203. See also Charles Cooley, "The Progress of Pecuniary Valuation," *Quarterly Journal of Economics* 30 (November 1915): 1–21.

19. On the Pittsburgh Survey and its general failure to catch on, see Maurine Greenwald and Margo Andersen, eds., *Pittsburgh Surveyed: Social Science and Social Reform in the Early Twentieth Century* (Pittsburgh: University of Pittsburgh Press, 1996), 9. For Kelley's wage maps, see *Hull-House Maps and Papers: A Presentation of Nationalities and Wages in a Congested District of Chicago* (New York, 1895).

20. For the corporate capitalist revolution see Alfred Chandler, *The Visible Hand: The Managerial Revolution in American Business* (Cambridge, MA: Belknap Press, 1977); James Livingston, *Pragmatism and the Political Economy of Cultural Evolution* (Chapel Hill: University of North Carolina Press, 1997); Wiebe, *Search for Order*; Levy, *Freaks of Fortune*, esp. ch. 8; William Appleman Williams, *The Contours of American History* (New York: World, 1961); James Weinstein, *The Corporate Ideal in the Liberal State* (New York: Farrar, Straus and Giroux, 1971); Alan Trachtenberg, *The Incorporation of America: Culture and Society in the Gilded Age* (New York: Hill and Wang, 1982). While weakened, the proprietary, petit-bourgeois middle class remained a thorn in corporate capitalism's side. See Robert Johnston, *The Radical Middle Class: Populist Democracy and the Question of Capitalism in Progressive Era Portland, Oregon* (Princeton, NJ: Princeton University Press, 2002).

21. Irving Fisher, "Why Has the Doctrine of Laissez Faire Been Abandoned?" *Science* 25 (January 4, 1907): 20. Not all self-proclaimed Progressives were middle-class professionals. See Daniel Rodgers, "In Search of Progressivism," *Reviews in American History* 10, no. 4 (December 1982): 113–132; Elizabeth Sanders, *Roots of Reform: Farmers, Workers and the American State 1877–1917* (Chicago: University of Chicago Press, 1999). On the worldview of these middle-class professionals, see Richard Hofstadter, *Age of Reform* (New York: Vintage, 1960), 131–257.

22. On this quantitative ethic, see Wiebe, *Search for Order*, 40–43, 147–154; Theodore M. Porter, *Trust in Numbers: The Pursuit of Objectivity in Science and Public Life* (Princeton, NJ: Princeton University Press, 1997). For "system," see Joanne Yates, *Control through Communication: The Rise of System in American Management* (Baltimore: Johns Hopkins University Press, 1993).

23. For the cultural power of money in this era, see Jackson Lears, *Rebirth of a Nation: The Making of Modern America* (New York: Harper, 2010), 51–92. On corporate liberalism, see Jeffrey Lustig, *Corporate Liberalism: The Origins of Modern American Political Theory* (Berkeley: University of California Press, 1986). For the organizational synthesis, see Louis Galambos, "The Emerging Synthesis in Modern American History," *Business History Review* 44, no. 3 (Autumn 1970): 279–290. On the "Iron Cage" (or, to be more accurate, the "shell as hard as steel"), see Peter Baehr, "The 'Iron Cage' and the 'Shell as Hard as Steel': Parsons, Weber, and the *Stahlhartes Gehäuse* Metaphor in the Protestant Ethic and the Spirit of Capitalism," *History and Theory* 40, no. 2 (May 2001): 153–169; Frank Gilbreth Jr. and Ernestine Gilbreth Carey, *Cheaper by the Dozen* (New York: Harper, 1948).

24. Zunz, *Making America Corporate*, 39; Thorstein Veblen, *Absentee Ownership and Business Enterprise in Recent Times: The Case of America* (New York: Huebsch,

1923), 86. For corporate percentages see *Thirteenth Census* (Washington, DC, 1910), 8:135; *Fourteenth Census of the United States* (Washington, DC, 1920) 8:14; Roy, *Socializing Capital*, 6; Naomi Lamoreaux, *The Great Merger Movement in American Business, 1895–1904* (New York: Cambridge University Press, 1988); Adolf Berle and Gardiner Means, *The Modern Corporation and Private Property* (New York: Transaction, 1932), esp. 14–15.

25. Daniel Hirchman, "Inventing the Economy, or: How We Learned to Stop Worrying and Love the GDP," Ph.D. diss., University of Michigan, 2016, 64–65. For the various forms of corporate bureaucracy see Zunz, *Making America Corporate*.

26. *New York Times* headline cited in Lears, *Rebirth of a Nation*, 261. For typical cost-of-living statistics see Bureau of Labor Statistics, *Bulletin* 39 (1902); 45 (1903); and 51–54 (1904), as well as the bureau's eighteenth and nineteenth annual reports; Thomas Stapleford, *The Cost of Living in America: A Political History of Economic Statistics* (New York: Cambridge University Press, 2009), 50–77; Meg Jacobs, *Pocketbook Politics: Economic Citizenship in Twentieth Century America* (Princeton, NJ: Princeton University Press, 2005), 15–52; Mary O. Furner, "Knowing Capitalism: Public Investigation and the Labor Question in the Long Progressive Era," in *The State and Economic Knowledge: The American and British Experiences*, ed. Barry Supple and Mary Furner (New York: Cambridge University Press, 1990), 260–286. On the inevitability of the modern corporation in Progressive thought, see Lustig, *Corporate Liberalism*. On Brandeis's support for Taylorism, see Oscar Kraines, "Brandeis' Philosophy of Scientific Management," *Western Political Quarterly* 13, no. 1 (March 1960): 191–201. A Google Ngram of the term "cost-of-living" shows a skyrocketing usage around 1910.

27. On living wage, see John A. Ryan, *A Living Wage: Its Ethical and Economic Aspects* (New York: Macmillan, 1906).

28. Jeremiah Jenks, "Industrial Combinations and Prices," in USIC, *Report of the Industrial Commission* (Washington, DC, 1900), 1:39–57; Jeremiah Jenks, "The Economic Outlook," *Dial* 10 (1890): 252. See also USIC, *Report of the Industrial Commission*, 7:16; James Livingston, *Origins of the Federal Reserve System: Money, Class and Corporate Capitalism, 1890–1913* (Ithaca, NY: Cornell University Press, 1986), 35–41.

29. Thomas McCraw, *Prophets of Regulation: Charles Francis Adams, Louis D. Brandeis, James M. Landis, Alfred E Kahn* (Cambridge, MA: Belknap Press, 1984), 59–60, 80–142; Stephen Skowronek, *Building a New American State: The Expansion of National Administrative Capacities, 1877–1920* (New York: Cambridge University Press, 1982), 248–284. For Granger Laws and the Populist desire for statutory regulation that continued well into the Progressive Era, see Elizabeth Sanders, *Roots of Reform: Farmers, Workers, and the American State, 1877–1917* (Chicago: University of Chicago Press, 1999). For the rehabilitation of

the ICC and the changing form of railroad accounting in the wake of *Smyth v. Ames,* see Gerald Berk, *Alternative Tracks: The Constitution of American Industrial Order, 1865–1917* (Baltimore: Johns Hopkins University, 1997), 153–162; Oliver Wendell Holmes, "The Path of the Law," *Harvard Law Review* 457 (1897).

30. Fisher, "Money Value of Human Beings."

31. For the politics of Progressive Era reform, see Rodgers, *Atlantic Crossings,* 235–267; Michael McGerr, *The Rise and Fall of the Progressive Movement in America, 1870–1920* (New York: Oxford University Press, 2005). For the National Civic Federation, see Weinstein, *Corporate Ideal.*

32. For Fisher's lobbying of the Carnegie Foundation, see Fisher to Elliot, January 16, 1908, Fisher Papers. For his use of price statistics as a lobbying point see Fisher to Elliot, December 9, 1909, box 3, Fisher Papers. For the collision between class interests and elite reformism, see David Huyssen, *Progressive Inequality: Rich and Poor in New York, 1890–1920* (Cambridge, MA: Harvard University Press, 2014).

33. For the census's treatment of Native Americans, see Matthew Hannah, *Governmentality and the Mastery of Territory* (New York: Cambridge University Press, 2000), 208–218.

34. On watered stock, see Roy, *Socializing Capital,* 249; William Cook, *The Corporation Problem: The Public Phases of Corporations, Their Uses, Abuses* (New York: Putnam's, 1891).

35. John Commons, *Legal Foundations of Capitalism* (New York: Macmillan, 1924), 11–46, quote on 16; Herbert Hovenkamp, *The Opening of American Law: Neoclassical Thought, 1870–1970* (New York: Oxford University Press, 2014), 163–164; Morton Horwitz, *The Transformation of American Law, 1870–1960: The Crisis of Legal Orthodoxy* (New York: Oxford University Press, 1992), 162.

36. Walter Sachs, "The Reminiscences of Walter E. Sachs," Oral History Collection of Columbia University, Butler Library, New York, vol. 1, 87; Charles D. Ellis, *The Partnership: The Making of Goldman Sachs* (New York: Penguin, 2009), 4–10.

37. A Google Ngram on the term "the market" reveals that it did not take off until the turn of the twentieth century (and did not explode, revealingly, until the 1980s). On Wall Street power in this era, see Steve Fraser, *Every Man a Speculator: A History of Wall Street in American Life* (New York: HarperCollins, 2005), 155–193. On how Wall Street changed everyday American social conceptions in this era, see Julia Ott, *When Wall Street Met Main Street: The Quest for an Investors' Democracy* (Cambridge, MA: Harvard University Press, 2012), 9–55.

38. William Peter Hamilton, *The Stock Market Barometer: A Study of Its Forecast Value Based on Charles H. Dow's Theory of the Price Movement* (New York: Harper, 1922), 8. For Charles Dow, his theory, and the Dow Jones Industrial Average, see Justin Fox, *The Myth of the Rational Market* (New York: Harper, 2011), 15–18; Robert Rhea, *The Dow Theory* (New York: Barron's, 1932); Lloyd Wendt, *The*

Wall Street Journal: The Story of Dow Jones and the Nation's Business Newspaper (New York: Rand McNally, 1982). The best source of Dow's editorials is S. A. Nelson, *The ABC of Speculation* (New York: Nelson's, 1904).

39. For a similar argument linking corporate capitalism to the "will theory" of contract, see Roy Kreitner, *Calculating Promises: The Emergence of Modern American Contract Doctrine* (Palo Alto, CA: Stanford University Press, 2006), 227–239. On the relation between "market" and "natural" price in classical economics, see Adam Smith, *An Inquiry into the Nature and Causes of the Wealth of Nations,* ed. Edwin Cannan (London: Methuen, 1904), book 1, ch. 7.

40. For the tendency of neoclassical economics to price all human experience, see Duncan Kennedy, "The Role of Law in Economic Thought: Essays on the Fetishism of Commodities," *American University Law Review* 34 (1985): 939–1001.

41. Irving Fisher, *Elementary Principles of Economics* (New York: Macmillan, 1911), 3, 38; Iriving Fisher, *The Nature of Capital and Income* (New York: Macmillan, 1906), 205.

42. Fisher, *Elementary Principles,* 15.

43. *Evening Public Ledger,* March 3, 1916.

44. Edward Bellamy, *Looking Backward* (New York: Dover, 1996), 151; John L. Thomas, *Alternative America: Henry George, Edward Bellamy, Henry Demarest Lloyd, and the Adversary Tradition* (Cambridge, MA: Belknap Press, 1983), 237–262.

45. N. A. Dunning, *The Philosophy of Money and Its Relation to Domestic Currency* (Washington, DC, 1890), 189. For the Ocala Demands, see *Proceedings of the Supreme Council of the National Farmers' Alliance and Industrial Union* (1890), 32–33; for the Omaha Platform, see Ignatius Donnelly, "National People's Party Platform," *World Almanac, 1893* (New York, 1893), 83–85. For the Populist view on money and finance, see Charles Postel, *The Populist Vision* (New York: Oxford University Press, 2007), 137–173; for socialism in the Progressive Era, see James Weinstein, *The Decline of Socialism in America: 1912–1925* (New Brunswick, NJ: Rutgers University Press, 1984).

46. "Bankers Hear Figures, but Only of Speech," *New York Times,* December 21, 1904.

47. On the marginalist revolution see, Mark Blaug, "Was There a Marginal Revolution?" *History of Political Economy* 4, no. 2 (1972): 269–280; Margaret Schabas, *A World Ruled by Number: William Stanley Jevons and the Rise of Mathematical Economics* (Princeton, NJ: Princeton University Press, 1990); Dorothy Ross, *The Origins of American Social Science* (New York: Cambridge University Press, 1991), 172–219.

48. Irving Fisher, *Mathematical Investigations in the Theory of Value and Prices* (New York: Kelley, 1892), 19.

49. *Encyclopaedia Britannica,* 9th ed., vol. 19, s.v. "Political Economy." Ingram was not alone in his critique. See John Cairnes, *The Character and Logical Method of*

Political Economy (London, 1875), vi. For a neoclassical view of the problem of utility measurement, see George Stigler, "The Development of Utility Theory," which appeared in two parts in the *Journal of Political Economy:* 58, no. 4 (August 1950): 307–327; and 58, no. 5 (October 1950): 373–396. For more on the problem of measuring utility, see Dorfman, *Economic Mind,* 3:243–252.

50. Francis Y. Edgeworth, *Mathematical Psychics: An Essay on the Application of Mathematics to the Moral Sciences* (London, 1881), 101. See also David Colander, "Retrospectives: Edgeworth's Hedonimeter and the Quest to Measure Utility," *Journal of Economic Perspectives* 21, no. 2 (Spring 2007): 215–226.

51. *Encyclopaedia Britannica,* s.v. "Political Economy."

52. Fisher, *Mathematical Investigations,* 5; Fisher, *Elementary Principles,* 13, 534.

53. William Stanley Jevons, *The Theory of Political Economy* (London: Macmillan, 1879), 12. On Jevons and the rise of mathematical economics, see Schabas, *A World Ruled by Number.*

54. Charles Darwin, *The Descent of Man* (London, 1871), 76–77; Henry Sidgwick, *The Methods of Ethics* (London, 1874), 29–42; Jacob Viner, "The Utility Theory and Its Critics," *Journal of Political Economy* 33 (1925): 369–387; Fisher, *Mathematical Investigations,* 11.

55. James quoted in Livingston, *Pragmatism,* 142; John Dewey, "Reconstruction in Philosophy," *The Middle Works of John Dewey 1899–1924,* ed. Jo Ann Boydston (Carbondale: Southern Illinois University Press), 11:193; Thorstein Veblen, "Why Isn't Economics an Evolutionary Science?" *Quarterly Journal of Economics* 12, no. 4 (1898): 373–397.

56. Dobb, *Theories of Value,* 38–65. For a similar treatment of classical versus neoclassical economics see Ross, *Origins of American Social Science,* 122.

57. Fisher, *Elementary Principles,* 478.

58. For the homogenizing powers of neoclassical economies, see Breslau, "Economics Invents the Economy."

59. For Fisher's criticism of labor unions, see *New York Times,* September 1, 1916. Fisher was also against Populist monetary reforms. See Roy Kreitner, "Money in the 1890s: The Circulation of Politics, Economics and Law," *UC Irvine Law Review* 1, no. 3 (2011): 975–1013.

60. Irving Fisher, "Economists in Public Service: Annual Address of the President," *American Economic Review* 9, no. 1 (March 1919): 10; Irving Fisher to Bert Fisher, August 17, 1890, box 1, Fisher Papers. On the classless nature of neoclassical economics, see Stephen Marglin, "What Do Bosses Do? The Origins and Functions of Hierarchy in Capitalist Production, Part I," *Review of Radical Political Economics* 6, no. 2 (1974): 60–112; Gregory Mankiw, "Defending the One Percent," *Journal of Economic Perspectives* 27, no. 3 (2013): 21–34.

61. Schumpeter, *Ten Great Economists*, 223; Irving Fisher, "An Address on the Irving Fisher Foundation," September 11, 1946, in *Works of Irving Fisher,* ed. William Barber (London: Pickering and Chatoo, 1997), 1:29.

62. Fisher, "Address on the Irving Fisher Foundation," 1:29; Fisher to Graham, Summer 1889, box 1, Fisher Papers.

63. "Extracts from Biography," box 6, Fisher Papers. Fisher's health fanaticism led him not to drink alcohol, coffee, or tea, nor did he eat chocolate, pepper, refined sugar, or bleached white flour.

64. For the distributional repercussions of inflation, see Thomas Piketty, *Capital in the Twenty First Century,* trans. Arthur Goldhammer (Cambridge, MA: Harvard University Press, 2014), 103–113; Warren Buffet, "Inflation Swindles the Equity Investor," *Fortune,* May 1977; Irving Fisher, "A Remedy of the Cost of Living: Standardizing the Dollar," *American Economic Review* 3, no. 1 (March, 1913): 27.

65. For the politics of the gold standard, see Gretchen Ritter, *Goldbugs and Greenbacks: The Antimonopoly Tradition and the Politics of Finance in America* (New York: Cambridge University Press, 1999).

66. Kreitner, "Money in the 1890s."

67. Fisher, "Standardizing the Dollar," 23; Irving Fisher, "A Compensated Dollar," *Quarterly Journal of Economics* 27, no. 2 (February 1913): 213–235; Irving Fisher, *The Purchasing Power of Money: Its Determination and Relation to Credit, Interest and Crises* (New York: Macmillan, 1926); Irving Fisher, *The Money Illusion* (New York: Adelphi, 1928). On Fisher's writings on stable money, see also reel 2:5, Fisher Papers.

68. For a roundtable of seven economists on Fisher's plans, see "Standardizing the Dollar—Discussion," *American Economic Review* 3, no. 1 (March 1913): 29–51. For Fisher and the Fed, see Thomas Cargill, "Irving Fisher Comments on Benjamin Strong and the Federal Reserve," *Journal of Political Economy* 100, no. 6 (December 1992): 1273–1277, Fisher quoted on 1274; Milton Friedman and Anna Schwarz, *The Great Contraction, 1929–1933* (Princeton, NJ: Princeton University Press, 1965); Michael Bordo and Hugh Rockoff, "The Influence of Irving Fisher on Milton Friedman's Monetary Economics," National Bureau of Economic Research Working Paper no. 17267, August 2011.

69. Friedman, *Fortune Tellers*, 51–85.

70. Robert Loring Allen, *Irving Fisher: A Biography* (Cambridge, MA: Blackwell Publishers, 1993), 269; Friedman, *Fortune Tellers,* 80–83.

71. Daniel Rodgers, *Age of Fracture* (Cambridge, MA: Belknap Press of Harvard University Press, 2011), 3. On the diversity of the Progressive Era, see Rodgers, "In Search of Progressivism." On "the social," see Rodgers, *Atlantic Crossings,* 20–32.

72. William Leach, *Land of Desire: Merchants, Power and the Rise of a New American Culture* (New York: Vintage Books, 1994), 7.

EPILOGUE: TOWARD GDP

1. John D. Rockefeller Jr. to Frederick Taylor Gates, July 27, 1912, Rockefeller Family Papers (henceforth RFP), Record Group 2, Series F—Economic Reform, box 18, folder 143, Rockefeller Archive Center, Sleepy Hollow, NY. For Gates, see Richard E. Brown, *Rockefeller Medicine Men: Medicine and Capitalism in America* (Berkeley: University of California Press, 1979); John Baick, "Cracks in the Foundation: Frederick T. Gates, the Rockefeller Foundation, and the China Medical Board," *Journal of the Gilded Age and Progressive Era* 3, no. 1 (2004): 59–89.

2. Rockefeller to Gates, July 27, 1912, RFP, box 18, folder 143. See also Rockefeller to Nelson Aldrich, August 26, 1912, RFP, box 18, folder 143.

3. For philanthropy and capitalism, see Peter Dobkin Hall, *Inventing the Non-Profit Sector and Other Essays on Philanthropy, Voluntarism, and Nonprofit Organizations* (Baltimore: Johns Hopkins University Press, 1992). On corporate paternalism, see Andrea Tone, *The Business of Benevolence: Industrial Paternalism in the Progressive Era* (Ithaca, NY: Cornell University Press, 1997); David Huyssen, *Progressive Inequality: Rich and Poor in New York, 1890–1920* (Cambridge, MA: Harvard University Press, 2014).

4. "Bureau of Economic Research Memo Originally Drawn by Theo. Vail and Here Revised by John D. Rockefeller and JDG," August 21, 1912, RFP, box 18, folder 143. JDG is Jerome Greene.

5. Jerome Greene memo, August 22, 1912, box 18, folder 143; For the House of Morgan's seal of approval, see H. V. Davison to Rockefeller, August 28, 1912, RFP, box 18, folder 143; Solomon Fabricant, "Toward a Firmer Basis of Economic Policy: The Founding of the National Bureau of Economic Research," NBER Working Paper, 1984. On Gay, see Herbert Heaton, *A Scholar in Action, Edwin F. Gay* (Cambridge, MA: Harvard University Press, 1952); on Gay's support of Taylorism, see Jeffrey Cruickshank, *The Harvard Business School, 1908–1945: A Delicate Experiment* (Boston: Harvard Business School Press, 1987), 55–60.

6. Thomas Andrews, *Killing for Coal: America's Deadliest Labor War* (Cambridge, MA: Harvard University Press, 2010), 207–230, 234–240. For welfare capitalism in this era, see David Brody, *Workers in Industrial America: Essays on the Twentieth Century Struggle* (New York: Oxford University Press, 1980).

7. Edwin Gay, "Report of Committee to the Rockefeller Foundation," August 4, 1914, RFP, box 18, folder 143. The committee met on April 30, 1914, ten days after the Ludlow Massacre.

8. For Rockefeller's public relations, see Rockefeller to Gates, April 18, 1914; Jerome Greene to Rockefeller, July 6, 1914, and May 6, 1914; RFP, box 18, folder 143.

9. For the Ludlow Massacre and Walsh's harsh questioning of Rockefeller, see *Industrial Relations: Final Report and Testimony* (Washington, DC: GPO, 1916), 1:269, 9:8298–8304; Mary O. Furner, "Knowing Capitalism: Public Investigation and the Labor Question in the Long Progressive Era," in *The State and Economic Knowledge: The American and British Experiences*, ed. Barry Supple and Mary Furner (New York: Cambridge University Press, 1990), 274–285; Graham Adams, *The Age of Industrial Violence, 1910–1915: The Activities and Findings of the U.S. Commission on Industrial Relations* (New York: Columbia University Press, 1966), 165–166.

10. Undated memo of the Rockefeller Foundation, RFP, box 18, folder 143.

11. Jerome Greene Memo, August 27, 1914, RFP, box 18, folder 143.

12. For the impact of World War I on the forming of the NBER, see Timothy Shenk, "Inventing the American Economy," Ph.D. diss., Columbia University, 2016, ch. 1. For the War Industries Board, see Guy Alchon, *The Invisible Hand of Planning: Capitalism, Social Science, and the State in the 1920s* (Princeton, NJ: Princeton University Press, 1985), ch. 3. For the importance of the income tax, see Hirschman, "Inventing the Economy," 67–68.

13. Malcolm Rorty to Max Farrand, Commonwealth Fund Papers (henceforth CWFP), series 1, box 223, August 9, 1919, Rockefeller Archive Center, Sleepy Hollow, NY. For Rorty's plans, see also N. I. Stone to John Frey, August 19, 1919, CWFP, series 1, box 223.

14. Fabricant, "Toward a Firmer Basis," 3–8; undated memo, "The Annual Value Product of American Industry," CWFP, series 1, box 223.

15. Memo, Oliver Knauth to Mr. Fosdick, April 18, 1922, RFP, box 18, folder 143. See also Knauth to Fosdick, March 21, 1922, RFP, box 18, folder 143.

16. Lathrop Brown to Starr J. Murphy, February 7, 1921, RFP, box 18, folder 143; Fabricant, "Toward a Firmer Basis," 8; Richardson to Rockefeller, June 30, 1921, RFP, box 18, folder 143.

17. National Bureau of Economic Research (NBER), *Income in the United States, Its Amount and Distribution 1909–1919* (New York: NBER, 1921), 6, 141–150. For the treatment of national income like an investment, see also undated memo, "The Annual Value Product of American Industry," CWFP, series 1, box 223.

18. NBER, *Income in the United States*, 90. On the emergence of national income and the decline in interest in distribution, see Dan Hirschman, "Inventing the Economy, or: How We Learned to Stop Worrying and Love the GDP," Ph.D. diss., University of Michigan, 2016, 71–75, 173.

19. "Uncle Sam Counts His Fabulous Wealth," *New York Times*, January 25, 1925.

20. Richard Rutter, "Economic Weather Bureau Adds to Data and Their Interpretation," *New York Times*, April 20, 1958.

21. Rutter, "Economic Weather Bureau." On Burns, an important yet overlooked economist, see Saul Engelbourg, "The Council of Economic Advisors and the Recession of 1953–1954," *Business History Review* 54, no. 2 (1980): 192–214; Wells Wyatt, *Economist in an Uncertain World: Arthur Burns and the Federal Reserve, 1970–1978* (New York: Columbia University Press, 1994).

22. Friedman wrote dozens of NBER working papers and a number of books. See www.nber.org/authors/milton_friedman. For Friedman and the rise of neoliberalism, see Angus Burgin, *The Great Persuasion: Reinventing Free Markets since the Depression* (Cambridge, MA: Harvard University Press, 2012)

23. For an excellent overview of the changing ways in which the American government has priced the value of a human life, see Binyamin Appelbaum, "As U.S. Agencies Put More Value on a Life, Businesses Fret," *New York Times*, February 16, 2011.

24. Jacob Mincer, "Investment in Human Capital and Personal Income Distribution," *Journal of Political Economy* 66, no. 4 (August 1958): 281–302; Hirschman, "Inventing the Economy," 174–180.

25. Royale Scuderi, "3 Valuable Ways to Invest in Yourself," Lifehack, www.lifehack.org/articles/lifestyle/3-valuable-ways-to-invest-in-yourself.html, accessed April 6, 2017; Eddy Ricci, "The 3 Percent Solution for Personal Development," Entrepreneur.com, July 10, 2014.

26. Associated Press, "Donald Trump Says He'll Run America like His Business," *Fortune*, October 27, 2016; David Brodwin, "America's CEO," *U.S. News and World Report*, January 20, 2017; Conor Friedersdorf, "What Do Donald Trump Voters Really Want?" *Atlantic*, August 17, 2015; Arthur Delaney and Zach Carter, "Ben Carson Thinks the Government Warehouses People," *Huffington Post*, January 12, 2017.

27. For Piketty, see Eli Cook, "The Progress and Poverty of Thomas Piketty," *Raritan Quarterly Review* 35, no. 2 (Fall 2015): 1–19.

28. For gross national happiness, see Alejandro Adler, "Gross National Happiness in Bhutan: A Living Example of an Alternative Approach to Progress," *Social Impact Research Experience Journal* 1 (2009): 1–137.

ACKNOWLEDGMENTS

Stepping out of an undergraduate microeconomics class at Tel Aviv University—my head whirring with derivative-finding calculus techniques with which I had been instructed to maximize any production function I came across—I entered into an American history class and discovered my calling. Instead of being force-fed iron-clad equations, I was confronted with an awe-inspiring set of open-ended questions not only about the rise of American capitalism, but about the very nature of the human experience in modern times. That American history class was taught by Michael Zakim, and I thank him for opening this world up to me and graciously supporting me ever since.

At Harvard a few years later, Sven Beckert immediately took a disheveled Israeli-American under his wing, just as his Program on the Study of Capitalism was taking off. He has lent an enthusiastic helping hand ever since, teaching me the tiniest intricacies of global economic history while passionately pushing me to ask big questions. I never would have dared to write a book that covers a span of nearly three hundred years without his mentorship and vision. Also at Harvard, Lizabeth Cohen provided endless wisdom and guidance, constantly encouraging and challenging me to refine, rewrite, and rethink the nitty-gritty contours of this project. When a new chapter wasn't to her liking, she would not only let me know it, but would supply me with a detailed list of reasons why. When my daughters were born, she gave me the keys to her office so I could get some work done. Big thanks are also in order to Chris Desan, who taught me how central banks work and was willing to slog through a summer of neoclassical economics. Morton Horwitz served as the elder statesman of this project, and his intellectual fingerprints are all over this book. John Stauffer's infinite knowledge helped shape the earliest versions of this project. Arthur Patton-Hock's office and mind were always open. I never would have been able to juggle my work and newborn twins without his never-ending patience and support.

At the Rutgers Center for Historical Analysis, where I completed a post-doctoral fellowship, I received even more support as I was writing the final chapter on the Progressive Era. As friend, editor, teacher, and all-around mensch, Jackson Lears had a great impact on this project and served as an intellectual model. Toby Jones, in particular, was a big asset to the project, especially when we argued. James Delbourgo, Julia Fein, and Courtney Fullilove were there to rein me in and make me feel at home. Charlie Riggs and I spent hours talking history and theory in New Brunswick bars, and I cherish those moments.

The warm welcome I received from Eran Shalev, Gur Alroey, Nira Pancer, Ori Amitay, Zur Shalev, Stefan Ihrig, Dotan Leshem, Roei Davidson, Ilan Talmud, Ely Aaronson, Zeev Shulman, Tomer Ben Horin, and the General History Department at the University of Haifa upon my return to Israel has been unbelievable. Ifat Mizrachi has made my arrival in Haifa so much smoother, easier, and more pleasurable. The intellectual energy at the University of Haifa, the comraderie among the faculty, and the diversity of the students and their passion for justice and equality gave me much inspiration during those difficult last months of endless revising.

Along the way, many have read versions of this book and given crucial feedback. Jamie Pietruska, Eran Shalev, Jeff Skalnsky, and anonymous-yet-awesome reader #2 were kind enough to read the manuscript and supply invaluable comments and recommendations for changes. Jon Levy commented early on at a conference of the Organization of American Historians and helped set the tone for the rest of the project. Tom Stapleford's spot-on critique of an early version of Chapter 7 was badly needed. Members of Lizabeth Cohen's reading group supplied the best peer reviews one could ask for. The intellectual firepower at the Harvard history of capitalism reading group helped me get my theoretical ducks in a row. Back in Israel, a political economy reading group kept me sharp while improving the chapter on Irving Fisher. Thanks go to Roy Kreitner, Noam Yuran, and Anat Rosenberg.

There are so many debts to so many others. I don't know where I would be without Noam Maggor, who first showed me the ropes at Harvard. Brian Hochman, David Kim, Nick Donofrio, Brian McCammack, Pete L'Official, Jack Hamilton, Tim McGrath, George Blaustein, and Derek Etkin let an undrafted, foreign walk-on join the ACBL. Adam Shinar, Rudi Batzell, Maggie Gram, Andrew Pope, Caitlin Rosenthal, Holger Droessler, Balraj Gill, Nadav Orian-Peer, David Singerman, Brian Goldstein, Anna Lvovsky, Joshua Specht, Eitan Kensky, Charles Petersen, Summer Shafer, Marisa Egerstrom,

Katherine Stephens, Shaun Nichols, and Jeremy Zallen all helped to make this book much better.

Generous funding supplied the precious time and needed resources to make the archival research behind this book possible. At Harvard, the Thomas Cochran Fellowship in Business and Economic History was key, as were grants from the Charles Warren Center, the Tobin Project, and Harvard Law School's Institute for Global Law and Policy. In my final year at Harvard, I was lucky enough to be a graduate fellow at the Radcliffe Institute for Advanced Study, where I had the privilege to absorb the daily brilliance of the Radcliffe fellows. An Andrew W. Mellon Foundation Postdoctoral Fellowship in the history department at Rutgers University let me delve into more archives with minimal teaching obligations. A Fulbright Postdoctoral Scholar Fellowship gave me the precious time I needed to complete the book manuscript. Countless archivists made my life so much easier. I'd especially like to thank the librarians at the Baker Library of Harvard Business School, the New York Public Library Manuscripts and Archives Division, the Library of Congress, the National Archives (I and II), Massachusetts Historical Society, Duke University's David M. Rubenstein Rare Book and Manuscript Library, the Rockefeller Archive Center, the University of Virginia Library, the Newberry Library in Chicago, the Women's History Archives at Smith College, and the Massachusetts State Archives.

I also wish to thank Harvard University Press for seeing this book through. Joyce Seltzer was everything I could have asked for in an editor. At the earliest of stages, she recognized the bigger picture behind this project and helped me bring that vision to life. Stephanie Vyce gave terrific advice. Debbie Masi of Westchester Publishing Services did an incredible production-editing job.

Some elements of Chapter 1 are informed by my article "The Pricing of Everyday Life," *Raritan Quarterly Review* 32.3 (Winter 2013): 109–121, and portions of Chapter 8 first appeared in "The Neoclassical Club: Irving Fisher and the Progressive Origins of Neoliberalism," *Journal of the Gilded Age and Progressive Era* 15.3 (July 2016): 246–262.

From an early age, my parents inspired me to be an intellectual. Dad, it is far from a coincidence that I followed in your footsteps. Be it 2 AM sessions on the porch about gender history or help reading letters from eighteenth-century planters, my mother has been a big part of this project. Sarah and Leeshai were a big help both babysitting and uncovering the inner politics behind Chinese GDP figures. Benjy is the IT man for this project and, more importantly, the best brother ever. David and Maxine Cook were indispensable, offering much-needed assistance. I also would like to thank my in-laws, Rani and Aviva, who have been like a second set of parents with their long-standing and never-ending devotion.

Most importantly, I'd like to thank Tali. Dragging you from our warm Tel Aviv home to those freezing Cambridge winters, I don't think I've ever actually told you something I've always known: I never could have done any of this without you. You are my biggest supporter, my most thoughtful (and beautiful) critic, my favorite person, my dearest friend, and the love of my life. I am so lucky to know that whatever the next steps on our journey might be, I will be taking them with you. But not just you. Mika, Ella, and Rona will be there too. And for those truly amazing gifts, Tali, I will be forever grateful.

INDEX

Adams, Charles Francis, Jr., 202, 205
Adams, John, 125
Adams, John Quincy, 120
African Americans. *See* blacks
agriculture, 83; in colonial America, 77,
    84–86; decline in population engaged in,
    146; in early modern England, 17–21, 25; in
    early U.S., 89–91; of family farms, 134;
    Hamilton's attempt to collect data on,
    45–47; statistics collected on, 183, 184
alcohol consumption, nineteenth-century
    statistics on, 1–4
Aldrich, Nelson, 191, 193, 198, 255, 257
Aldrich Report, 191–199, 230, 232–234
American Eugenics Society, 225
American Federation of Labor (AFL),
    207–208
American Geographical and Statistical
    Society (AGSS), 184–186
American Railroad Journal, 171, 176, 179
American Republican Party, 156
American Social Science Association, 205
American Statistical Association (ASA),
    107, 120
American Temperance Society, 112
American Tract Society, 111, 112
Appleton, Nathan, 109–110
Aquinas, Thomas (saint), 39
Arbuthnot, John, 51
Aristotle, 39
Arthur, Chester A., 216
Astor, John Jacob, 136
Atkinson, Edward, 204, 210–215
Atkinson, James, 79
Atwater, Wilbur Olin, 214–215

Bacon, Sir Francis, 24–26
balance of trade, 22–23
Ball, John, 91–92
Ballard, Martha, 74

Baltimore, Lord, 76, 77
Bankes, James, 20
Bank of New York, 61
Banks, Nathaniel, 161
banks and banking: in early U.S., 60–63;
    Massachusetts savings banks, 204–207;
    Wall Street, 237–239, 242, 251
Barry, Leonora, 11, 218
Becker, Gary, 264–265
Beekman, David, 54–55
Bellamy, Edward, 241
Bennett, James, 170
Best, Henry, 20
Betts, Henry, 137
Blackmar, Elizabeth, 87, 136
blacks, 10–11, 15; Calhoun on, 100–101;
    insanity among, 119–121; literacy statistics
    for, 117; Nott on life insurance for, 126–127;
    statistics on, 101–103, 123
Blackwell, 26
Blodget, Samuel, Jr., 68–70, 72, 73, 86
Boston (Massachusetts), 173, 174
Boston Tontine Association, 68
Brandeis, Louis, 233
Bronson, Arthur, 140–141
Bruce, James Coles, 167
Bryan, William Jennings, 220
Buchanan, James, 114, 157
Buffett, Warren, 250, 265
Bureau of Statistics (U.S.), 188
Burns, Arthur, 263
Burt, Armistead, 100
Butler, Charles, 141
Byllesby, Langdon, 125

Cabot, George, 45, 64
Caldwell, Charles, 176
Calhoun, John C., 100–102, 120, 123
caloric energy, 29, 197–199
calorimeters, 215

Degler, Carl, 76
Dewey, John, 246
Disturnell, John, 185
Domesday Book, 38
"Domesday of Inclosures," 40
Donnelly, Ignatius, 241
Doty, Duane, 208
Douglass, Frederick, 166
Dow, Charles, 238, 239
Dow Jones Industrial Average, 7, 238
Down Survey, 25–27, 32
Drayton, John, 59
Dun, R. G., 163
Dun and Co., 163
Dunning, N. A., 241

Eastman, Crystal, 219
economic growth: anti-growth ideology on, 310n69; Blodget on, 69; GDP as measure of, 8; Hamilton on, 67
economic indicators, 15–16; Aldrich Report leading to, 192; alternative, 11–12; balance of trade as first, 22–23; history of, 9–10; moral statistics leading to, 103
economics: mathematical models used in, 224; neoclassical, 250–254
economy: on "the," 9, 16, 134, 230, 233, 271n16; Blodget's use of word, 68; stock market in, 238
Edgeworth, Francis, 244
Edmonds, Thomas Rowe, 107
education: crime and, 117–118; moral statistics on, 116–117
efficiency, 223, 231–232
Eight Hour League, 200
Einhorn, Robin, 96
electric lighting, 228
Ely, Richard, 149
enclosure movement: in England, 17–18, 40, 91; in Ireland, 26
Engel, Ernst, 226
England: American colonies of, 59–60, 76–78; balance of trade of, 22–23; becomes a nation-state, 34; and capitalism, 30–35, 75–83, 87–90, 114; enclosure movement in, 17–18, 40; first census in, 41; history of economic measurement in, 37–38; Ireland

conquered by, 24–27; land ownership in, 78–79; and moral statistics, 105–107; political arithmetic and taxation in, 35–37
English Civil War, 36
Erie Canal, 133–135, 137
eugenics, 225
Europe: Hunt's coverage of, 144; moral statistics in, 104, 107–108
Evans, George H., 114

Falkner, Roland, 192
Farmers' Alliance, 219, 241, 251
Farr, William, 105, 107, 226
Farrand, Max, 259–260
Federal Reserve, 252
Federal Trade Commission (FTC), 234
feminism, 88
feudalism, 17–19, 36–41, 105
Fillmore, Millard, 143, 177
Fisher, Elwood, 161–162
Fisher, Irving, 223–226, 259, 264; on capitalization, 5–6; criticisms of, 240–241; on marginal utility, 243–246; neoclassical economic theories of, 246–253; on pricing of progressivism, 223–226, 231–239; Prohibition advocated by, 3; on rule by experts, 231; stock defined by, 239–240
Fitoussi, Jean-Paul, 9
Fogel, Robert, 163, 166
food: as capital, Fisher on, 240; consumption of, 213–216; as fuel, 197
Foote, Allen Ripley, 228
Forbes, John Murray, 187–188
Fortrey, Samuel, 23
Foster, George G., 116
Foucault, Michel, 2
France, 262
Francis (pope), 7–8
Franklin, Benjamin, 81–82, 92–94, 213; on value of slaves, 98
Fredrickson, George, 159
Friedman, Milton, 252, 263
Frost, Morgan, 163

Garfield, James, 197
Gates, Frederick Taylor, 255
Gates, Sir Thomas, 77

to, 109–110; in U.S. of early nineteenth
century, 108–109
industrial revolution, 105–106, 108, 197
inflation, 250–251
Ingram, J. K., 244
insane asylums, 113, 119–121
Insurance Company of North America, 68
interest rates, rents tied to, 21
Interstate Commerce Commission (ICC), 234
investmentality, 164, 172, 188; definition of, 2;
in England, 20, 26, 41, 50, 88–91; and Fisher,
224–227; and Hamilton, 53–57; lack of in
Early America, 97; and pricing of progress,
6, 14–15; in South Carolina, 58–59
Ireland, 24–27, 32–34
Irving, Washington, 127

Jacksonian Era, 101–103, 109–114, 117,
123–125, 133, 176, 181, 241
James, William, 228–229, 246
Jarvis, Edward, 119–121, 197
Jefferson, Thomas, 264; economic policies
of, 68; on population, 94; on proprietary
independence, 86; on value of slaves,
98–99; whiskey tax repealed under, 47;
Young and, 90
Jenks, Jeremiah, 234
Jevons, William Stanley, 245

Kay, James Phillips, 106
Kelley, Florence, 219, 230
Kelley, William "Pig Iron," 192
Kennedy, John F., 263
Kennedy, Joseph, 181, 186
Kettell, Thomas, 170–172, 177, 181
King, Gregory, 41, 70
Kittredge and Maynard (firm), 136
Knauth, Oliver, 260
Knights of Labor, 216–218
Kornblith, Gary, 10
Kuznets, Simon, 8, 255, 261

labor: in agricultural England, 18–22; in
Aldrich Report, 195–196; as commodity,
189; costs of, 12, 91, 96, 98, 150–153,
209–215; Petty on value of, 30–34;
productivity vs. compensation, 123, 188;

slavery and, 163–168; woman and erasure
of, 88–90
labor movement: beginnings of, 125; and
conflict, 258–259; Knights of Labor in,
216–218; Wright and, 209. *See also* unions
Labor Reform Party (Massachusetts), 200
labor statistics bureaus: Farmers' Alliance
support for, 219; in Massachusetts, 200–209,
213–215; in states, 216–217; U.S., 216
labor theory of value, 213, 241–242; Franklin
on, 82
land: George on taxation of, 220; ownership
of, 78–80; Petty on value of, 27–32; rental
of, 17–19; speculation in, 65, 132–136,
141–145, 157; valuation of, 20–21, 83
Lantz, David, 228
Lasch, Christopher, 9
Lawrence, Abbot, 143, 160
Leach, William, 253
Leggett, William, 114
liberalism, 9–10, 23, 36–37, 49, 104–105, 164,
223; corporate, 231
Lieber, Francis, 107, 122
life insurance, 126–127, 226–227
Lincoln, Abraham, 163, 188–190, 203, 212
literacy statistics, 117
Livingston, James, 212
living wage, 194, 207, 234, 254
Loder, Robert, 19–20
London Statistical Society, 105, 107
Looking Backward (Bellamy), 241
Lowell (Massachusetts), textile mills in,
109–110
Lowery, Thomas, 63–64
Ludlow Massacre, 258–259

machines, treating people as, 197, 213, 235–237
Malthus, Thomas, 151
Manchester Society, 106–107
Mankiw, Gregory, 248
Mann, Horace, 117, 125, 156–157, 161
Mansfield, Edward, 186, 309–310n63
manufacturing: censuses of (1810 and 1820),
65, 71, 88; Franklin on, 94; Hamilton's
data on, 43–49, 86; mergers in, 232; in
U.S. of early nineteenth century, 108–110
marginal utility, 243–246